Nineteenth-Century British Music Studies
Volume 1

Nineteenth-Century British Music Studies

Volume 1

Edited by
BENNETT ZON

Ashgate

Aldershot • Brookfie d USA • Singapore • Sydney

Published by
Ashgate Publishing Limited
Gower House
Croft Road
Aldershot
Hants GU11 3HR
England

Ashgate Publishing Company
Old Post Road
Brookfield
Vermont 05036–9704
USA

British Library Cataloguing in Publication Data

Nineteenth-Century British Music Studies, Vol. 1
    (Music in Nineteenth-Century Britain)
    1. Music—Great Britain—19th century.
    I. Zon, Bennett.
    780.9'034'0941

Library of Congress Cataloguing-in-Publication Data

Nineteenth-century British music studies/edited by Bennett Zon.
    (Music in Nineteenth-Century Britain)
    Papers deriving from the inaugural conference of the Society for the Study of Music in Nineteenth-Century Britain, held at the University of Hull, July 1997.
    Includes index.
    ISBN 1-84014-259-6 (hc.)
    1. Music—Great Britain—19th century—History and criticism.
    I. Zon, Bennett.   II. Society for the Study of Music in Nineteenth-Century Britain.   III. Series.
    ML285.5.N56   1999
    780'.941'09034—dc21   98–54371
                                                                CIP
                                                                MN

ISBN 1 84014 259 6

This book is printed on acid free paper

Typeset in Sabon by Manton Typesetters, 5–7 Eastfield Road, Louth, Lincs, LN11 7AJ

Printed and bound in Great Britain by MPG Books Ltd, Bodmin, Cornwall

Contents

General Editor's Preface

It was while listening to Joseph Kerman's keynote speech at the 1995 Maynooth International Musicological Conference that I was first struck with the idea of a conference dedicated to the study of music in nineteenth-century Britain. It was in response to what seemed to be Joseph Kerman's suggestion that the advent of the 'New Musicology' arose in part out of some vague and general feeling that good musical sources were drying up. His printed version of the text does not bear out this sentiment to any great extent, although there remains in his writing a certain trace of scepticism about the future of some categories of source study. Needless to say I do not share in this concern, because, as I listened to him, I began to think of an area of musicology rich in sources, but which lay virtually untouched, in relative terms, by modern scholars. This was music in nineteenth-century Britain, and it was this topic which was to form the basis of the very first Music in Nineteenth-century Britain conference, held at the University of Hull in July 1997.

The essays included in this, the first, volume of *Nineteenth-Century British Music Studies*, comprise a selection of papers given at that conference. The Hull conference, as Nicholas Temperley indicates in his preface to this volume, was predicated on debunking, and to some rationalizing the origins of, the 'Land ohne Musik' reputation. The present collection of essays follows on from this work, each providing a window of discussion for future research. From Temperley's 'Xenophilia in British Musical History' to Richard Kitson's reevaluation of James William Davison, the breadth of research indicates a study in its own advent. From historiographical issues to instruments and performing ensembles; from the Wesley family to local history; and from repertoire, genre and concert life to analysis and criticism: the richness of the study becomes immediately apparent in the reading of these wide-ranging explorations of the period. Not only do we have collected here research which covers new ground with new sources, we also have the beginnings of a revision of attitude – an attitude engendered admittedly as much by nineteenth-century musicians and writers as by more modern musicologists. This set of essays, however, marks a transition in its own right. It describes precisely what Joseph Kerman, in his keynote speech at Maynooth, hesitantly calls 'Musicology in Transition'. With this volume, and with the second biennial conference already arranged for Durham, 1999, we have the clearest indication possible of musicology in transition.

It remains for me to thank various individuals who helped inaugurate the Music in Nineteenth-Century Britain conferences, as well as those involved in the preparation of this volume. Special thanks go to Nicholas Temperley, not only for providing the conference with the inaugural keynote speech, but also for his ongoing endorsement of my efforts with regard to nineteenth-century British music studies. In terms of administration, Philip Olleson, Leanne Langley, Rosemary Williamson, and I formed the first working committee of the biennial conference, and although my thanks to them have been expressed many times before, I wish to acknowledge formally their great help and commitment. Philip Olleson, in addition to assisting with the organization of the conference, also provided extensive and invaluable editorial advice for the preparation of the present volume, and for this I am especially grateful. I would also like to express my deepest thanks to Rachel Lynch, commissioning editor at Ashgate, who has shown nothing but the strongest support for the endeavours represented in this book. It was to Rachel that I first took the idea of a series of books called Music in Nineteenth-Century Britain, and it is to Rachel that *Nineteenth-Century British Music Studies* owes its existence. Finally, I would like to thank my wife Clare, who was administrator of the Hull conference. Without her help the Hull conference, as well as the present collection of essays, would have never got off the ground.

Bennett Zon
Hull, 1999

List of Plates and Figures

Plates

Figures

List of Tables and Music Examples

Notes on Contributors

Allan W. Atlas is Distinguished Professor of Music at the Graduate School of The City University of New York, where he heads the Doctoral Program in Music and the Center for the Study of Free-Reed Instruments. He has recently published *Renaissance Music* in W. W. Norton's Introduction to Music History series.

Stuart Campbell is Lecturer in Music at the University of Glasgow. Russian music of the nineteenth and twentieth centuries is his central interest. Cambridge University Press published his anthology in translation, *Russians on Russian Music, 1830–1880*, in 1994 and will shortly bring out a sequel for 1880 to 1917.

Catherine Dale is a Senior Lecturer in Music at the University of Hull. She has published extensively on analysis and twentieth-century music. She is the author of two books on Schoenberg and is currently writing a book on analysis in nineteenth-century Britain for Ashgate Publishing.

Jeremy Dibble, born in Essex in 1958, read Music at Trinity College, Cambridge and the University of Southampton before being appointed Lecturer in Music at University College, Cork, in 1987. While at Cork he published his first major book on the life and music of Sir Hubert Parry with Oxford University Press. In 1993 he joined the staff at the University of Durham where he is now Reader in Music and Head of Department. He has written widely on British and Irish music of the Victorian, Edwardian and Georgian eras, has written articles for numerous periodicals, journals and dictionaries and has acted as editorial consultant on the music of Parry and Stanford for various recording companies. Recent publications include essays for *Vaughan Williams in Perspective* (1998) and *To Talent Alone: The Royal Irish Academy 1848–1998* (1998). He is now finishing a volume of Parry's violin sonatas for *Musica Britannica* and a major study of the life and work of Sir Charles Villiers Stanford for OUP.

David J. Golby is completing a doctoral thesis on the violin in England during the eighteenth and nineteenth centuries at St Hugh's College, Oxford. He is an active and experienced teacher and freelance performer on the violin and viola. A book for Ashgate on instrumental teaching in nineteenth-century Britain is planned for 2001.

Trevor Herbert is Professor of Music and Arts Staff Tutor for Wales at the Open University. He has written extensively on the history of brass instruments and their repertoire. An extended version of his 1991 book *Bands* will be published by Oxford University Press in 1999.

Peter Horton is Acting Reference Librarian and Research Co-ordinator at the Royal College of Music. He has edited the complete anthems of Samuel Sebastian Wesley for *Musica Britannica* and is working on a study of the composer's life and music, to be published by Oxford University Press.

Richard Kitson is Associate Director of the Center for Studies in Nineteenth-Century Music at the University of Maryland College Park, for which he has contributed, as author or editor, 35 volumes dealing with the musical life of Britain and the United States.

Simon McVeigh is Professor and Head of Music at Goldsmiths College, University of London. He completed his doctoral studies at Oxford and moved to Goldsmiths after several years as a lecturer at Aberdeen University. Publications include articles on violin music and on historical performance practice, such as those dealing with ornamentation in the *New Oxford Companion to Music*. He has also researched widely in the area of music and society: a book entitled *Concert Life in London from Mozart to Haydn* was published by Cambridge University Press in 1993, and he has contributed numerous articles to the *Oxford Companion to British Culture, 1776–1832*. Current work includes research on the late Baroque violin concerto and on music in nineteenth-century London. He was editor of the Royal Musical Association's *Research Chronicle* from 1991 to 1994. In addition he is a violinist and baroque violinist, and has been involved in numerous first performances of string quartets in the Purcell Room and elsewhere.

Barbara Mohn gained her MA in musicology, English literature and medieval and modern history at the University of Bonn. After a period as a visiting student at the University of Exeter, and post-graduate researcher in London, she is completing her PhD thesis on English oratorio in the nineteenth century. She is currently an editor at Carus-Verlag, Stuttgart and her publications include works on oratorio and Mendelssohn.

Philip Olleson is Senior Lecturer in Music in the School of Continuing Education of the University of Nottingham. He has written extensively on Samuel Wesley and on aspects of music in early nineteenth-century Britain. He is the editor of *The Letters of Samuel Wesley: Professional Correspondence, 1797–1837* (Oxford, Clarendon Press, forthcoming) and the co-editor (with Michael Kassler) of *A Samuel Wesley Sourcebook* (Ashgate Publishing, forthcoming).

Nicholas Temperley was born in England in 1932 and educated at Cambridge, where he received a PhD in 1959 for a dissertation on 'Instrumental Music in England, 1800–1850'. He was on the music faculty at Cambridge from 1961 to 1966, and since 1967 has taught musicology at the University of Illinois at Urbana-Champaign. He has devoted much of his career to the study and revival of nineteenth-century British music. He wrote *The Music of the English Parish Church* (Cambridge, 1979) and edited Volume 5 of The Athlone (later Blackwell) History of Music in Britain series, *The Romantic Age, 1800–1914*, and *The Lost Chord: Essays on Victorian Music* (Bloomington, Indiana, 1989). He has published editions of works by Crotch, Loder, Pierson, Pinto, Sterndale Bennett and S. Wesley, as well as a volume of English songs from 1800 to 1860 (*Musica Britannica*, 43, with Geoffrey Bush) and *The London Pianoforte School, 1766–1860* (20 vols, 1984–87).

Susan Wollenberg was Clara Sophie Deneke music scholar at Lady Margaret Hall, Oxford, studying with Egon Wellesz and Bernard Rose. She took her D.Phil. (under the supervision first of Egon Wellesz, and later Frederick Sternfeld), with a thesis on Baroque keyboard music. Since 1972 she has been a University Lecturer on the Faculty of Music, at the University of Oxford, teaching at Lady Margaret Hall and (since 1986) Brasenose College. Among her published work and papers given to international conferences on a variety of subjects, she has been invited to contribute chapters on music and musicians to the eighteenth- and nineteenth-century volumes of the *History of the University of Oxford*. She is preparing a book on music at Oxford in those centuries.

Caroline Wood is Lecturer in Music at the University of Hull. Her main research interest is French opera of the seventeenth and eighteenth centuries, but a recent invitation to look at the music collection at Burton Constable has led to the present study.

Bennett Zon is Lecturer in Music at the University of Hull, where he divides his teaching between musicology and composition. As a musicologist he is general editor of the Music in Nineteenth-Century Britain series (Ashgate), and editor of *Nineteenth-Century British Music Studies*. He is also part owner of the nineteenth-century mailbase on the web. He is author of *The English Plainchant Revival* (Oxford University Press, 1999) and is currently working towards completion of *Historicizing Music: The Evolution of Musicology in Nineteenth-Century Britain*. As a composer he has held numerous international commissions, ranging from St John's College, Cambridge, to the Concerto Soloists of Philadelphia, and has had performances throughout America and Europe. He is currently writing his first symphony, commissioned by the Hull Philharmonic to celebrate the millennium.

Foreword

I first became interested in nineteenth-century British music when I was at school and heard Sydney Watson making some sweeping judgements about Victorian hymn tunes – how they were treacly, oily, sentimental and so on. But I loved these tunes, and could not quite understand what was supposed to be wrong with them. As I was showing interest in church music it was arranged for me to go to tea with Dr Fellowes at Windsor Castle, where he was a minor canon of St George's Chapel. Perhaps it was hoped that he would talk me out of my hang-up. At first he talked entirely about cricket. While his wife was making the tea he told me he had attended every Eton-Winchester match since 1882 (this was about 1949), and began getting into the details. I had to feign interest for a while. At last, with some help from Mrs Fellowes, I finally got him around to music, and I asked him what he thought of Barnby and Stainer. This was a slightly mischievous question, because I knew he had devoted most of his energy to the music of the Golden Age, and I expected some choice epithets like those that Watson had used. But he put up a spirited defence of Barnby, and said he was an excellent musician who had done a lot for the Bach revival. Then he told me how he had chatted with Stainer shortly before 1900, and how Stainer had confessed that he regretted having written so many anthems too easily, saying that people had told him they were 'just the thing they wanted'.

When the time came for me to choose a topic for my PhD work at Cambridge, I said I wanted to specialize in English music of the early nineteenth century. I met with a lot of opposition. The college organists and church musicians who dominated the Cambridge musical world in those days were still dazzled by Elizabethan and Jacobean music, so recently recovered. They were still trying to root out their instinctively Romantic musical thinking, and they probably felt that any emphasis on the nineteenth century was counter-revolutionary. The principal musicologist on the faculty, Thurston Dart, thought I was mad. More moderate advisers thought I was indulging in a gesture of rebellion, which would cost me my career. Everyone was sure the nineteenth century was a dark age of music and no good could come of messing about in it.

When it was clear that I was going to do it, I did get sympathy and support from my supervisors, first Philip Radcliffe and then Charles Cudworth. I had the satisfaction of exploring virtually unknown territory. But for a long time I felt I was on a lonely path. I had an eerie feeling that I was facing the same prejudice that had confronted the Victorian composers themselves.

So I felt greatly honoured to be invited to address the inaugural conference for Music in Nineteenth-Century Britain, which was held in Hull in July 1997. The event was a milestone in the field of scholarship in which I have worked all my life. True, it was not quite the first conference devoted to nineteenth-century British music; there have been Victorian Studies conferences taking music as their theme, such as the one at Leicester University in 1979. But this was the first one organized by a music department, and that, I believe, was a new and significant step for which Bennett Zon deserves much of the credit. Moreover, I was astonished when I saw that 36 papers were to be given at Hull, and to hear that there were still more that could not be accommodated. I would be interested to know whether students are still steered away from this period by their advisers.

I doubt if the prejudice is dead yet. But it has been overtaken by more general changes. Professional musicology barely existed in Britain in the 1950s (in fact Dart would not accept the label 'musicologist' for himself, insisting that he was just a musician). Now, musicology is very firmly established here. The older, German-based musicology was about early music, about all the Renaissance period; and the opening up of the nineteenth century, even for German music, has come only in the last few decades. Strictly speaking, musicology assumes that any music is a worthy subject of study in its historical and cultural context, regardless of intrinsic value. Popular music has been opened up to scholarship, and it is a most promising area in nineteenth-century Britain, hardly visible in this volume. The 'new musicology' also plays down the importance of individual composers in cultural history.

Few of the chapters in this volume deal directly with the artistic value of the music they talk about. Some establish the factual and technical information on which future histories and evaluations will be built. Some, of course, do not talk about British compositions at all, but about musical life in Britain, or the reception of music of other nations. All this makes for a totally different climate from the one I knew as a student. But the old prejudice long guarded the musical life of nineteenth-century Britain against aggressive snooping, and kept it intact for the present generation.

Scholars who are attracted to the music of nineteenth-century Britain have the advantage of exploring a landscape that is still largely unfamiliar. They have an abundance of sources, because the period is only a century old, and because the Victorians had a lucky obsession with documentation and statistics. They have a fascinating age to deal with, the summit of Britain's greatness in many fields and also a time of profound changes in society and ideology. They have a period that excites enormous interest in the scholarly world, but for which other scholars lack the expertise to deal with music. This volume helps to show where music fits into the picture.

Nicholas Temperley

PART ONE
Introduction

CHAPTER ONE

Xenophilia in British Musical History

Nicholas Temperley

This chapter addresses the 'Land ohne Musik' idea. I know it is a stale topic, but at the same time it has to be *the* topic for any introduction to the area of nineteenth-century British music. Now that we are getting serious about the history of British music in the nineteenth century, it is time to review the historiography. I'm sure there are few scholars who still think that Britain is, or ever was, a land without music. But I am equally sure that those who work in this field are aware of the ghostly presence of this idea, and have had to deal with it in one way or another. I would like to take this opportunity to bring the question to some sort of resolution.

Another old chestnut is 'The Dark Age of British Music'.[1] I suggest that it is essentially the same idea as 'Das Land ohne Musik', since both cover a period that generally includes all or part of the nineteenth century. A 'dark age' implies a 'light age' to follow, and the term came into use at about the same time as the 'English Musical Renaissance' idea, that is, about the turn of the century.[2] When historians began to talk about a rebirth or a renaissance, they could highlight the dawn by emphasizing the darkness that had come before it. But the Victorians themselves could not see any approaching dawn, and believing that there was something wrong with them, they kept saying 'The English are not a musical people'. This was translated as 'Das Land ohne Musik'. But all these formulations are rooted in the same belief: that nineteenth-century Britain was an unmusical place.

I would like to look at three nineteenth-century statements of this belief, one British and two foreign. Among many British examples, one

---

[1] Some writers use 'English' when they mean 'British', as can be seen by a glance at the 'Select bibliography'. I am using it in the strict sense, to refer to England alone – except, of course, when I quote other writers who have used it more loosely. 'British' includes Scotland and Wales, but not Ireland: the United Kingdom in the nineteenth century was 'of Great Britain and Ireland'.

[2] A possible source for this phrase was a short-lived French journal called *La Renaissance Musicale*, first published on 6 March 1881. It supported the Wagnerian avant-garde and French nationalism.

of the most significant is found in *The Musical World*, which spoke of
'the old-fashioned and still fashionable twaddle in high quarters – that
the English cannot be a musical people'.[3] Notice especially the word
'old-fashioned' implying that the idea was far from new in 1841,[4] and
the words 'fashionable' and 'high quarters', to which I will return later.

The Belgian historian and critic François Fétis addressed the subject
in his 'Letters on the State of Music in London', published in the *Revue
musicale* and translated as a special treat for readers of *The Harmonicon*.[5]
Fétis wrote that 'An English composer beholds neither glory nor profit
in the effects of his labour; who, then, shall induce him to write? ... We
need not wonder if in London we find only arrangers, who esteem their
labours no more than the public'. The important thing to notice here is
that Fétis was not himself delivering an unfavourable judgement of
contemporary British composers. (He praised several of them quite
warmly later on in his *Biographie universelle des musiciens*, more especially John Field and William Sterndale Bennett.) Rather he was reporting
on the low opinion that the English had of their own composers.

So it was with Robert Schumann. In 1837 he was at pains to repudi-
ate the saying 'Englischer Komponist, kein Komponist'.[6] 'Old prejudices
have been weakened by the names of Field, Onslow, Potter, Bishop,
etc.', he wrote, but above all he drew his readers' attention to the
creative power of Bennett.[7] Schumann's stand in support of Bennett had
no chance of being popular with his readers. It is a testimony to his
courage and honesty.

In an age of growing musical nationalism, only the English played
down the value of their own music. As Warren D. Allen put it in his
valuable survey of music histories, 'The opposite of chauvinism appears
in English histories of music during the Victorian era'.[8] Nationalists of
other countries, certainly including many Germans, were only too happy
to take them at their word. It gave them a cast-iron justification for
doing what they wanted to do anyway – to eliminate Britain as a
possible competitor for musical prestige. F. J. Crowest wrote in 1881:

[3] *The Musical World*, 15 (1841), 155.

[4] Much earlier instances are cited in P. M. Young, *A History of British Music*, London,
1967, p. 281.

[5] F. Fétis, 'Letters on the State of Music in London', *The Harmonicon*, 7 (1829), 276.
Fétis's facts were challenged in detail by the editor, William Ayrton, but his general point
hit the bull's eye.

[6] R. Schumann, 'An English composer is no composer', *Neue Zeitschrift für Musik*, 24
February 1837.

[7] Ibid., 3 January 1837.

[8] W. D. Allen, *Philosophies of Music History. A Study of General Histories of Music
1600–1960*, revd edn, New York, 1962, p. 124.

'We have the continental reputation of being the Great Unmusical Power of Europe – strong enough in commerce and steam, but devoid of musical talent, invention, and discrimination'. German music histories of this period tend to ignore British music altogether, or to give perfunctory mention to a few composers. Emil Naumann's five-volume history of music (completed in 1885) was so deficient that Sir Frederick Ouseley, when editing a translation, had to add special chapters on British music.[9]

A subset of this idea was the illusion that the English (as opposed to the Scots, Irish and Welsh) had no 'national' music or folk song. William Chappell in 1859 blamed this on Burney's *History* and Crotch's *Specimens*.[10] George Alexander Macfarren had to publish an article to refute the belief,[11] but the idea was too deep-seated to be so easily eradicated. 'Das Land ohne Musik' had become dogma.

The idea spread not only in space, but in time. Just as nineteenth-century European critics took the Victorians at their own valuation, so did twentieth-century historians. Alfred Einstein, in his *Music in the Romantic Era*, gives space only to Sullivan, and even then strictly as a satirist. Carl Dahlhaus, in his book *Nineteenth-Century Music*, follows suit, declining to evaluate or discuss Sullivan's music as such. Leon Plantinga's is the only non-British general history of nineteenth-century music that gives serious consideration to a number of British composers. It is the same with general histories, where music itself is often slighted. The classic *Portrait of an Age: Victorian England* by G. M. Young makes no mention of music at all, not even when discussing the accomplishments of young ladies for the marriage market. Here he goes beyond negative judgement of English composition to the ludicrous extreme of pretending that music played no significant part in Victorian life. From judgements like these the 'Land ohne Musik' idea was reformulated as the 'Dark Age of Music'.

The British arrived late in the arena of musical nationalism, perhaps because they had felt unchallenged in most other contests. A few intellectuals such as Ayrton, George Hogarth, Chappell and Macfarren asserted British claims to musicality; but musical nationalism did not become a movement until late in the century.[12] That was when the

---

[9] F. A. G. Ouseley, chs 31, 46, in E. Naumann, *History of Music*, 5 vols, London, [1886].

[10] William Chappell, *Popular Music of the Olden Time*, London, 1855–59, vol. I, pp. vi–vii.

[11] G. A. Macfarren, 'The English are not a Musical People', *Cornhill Magazine*, 18 (1868), 344–63.

[12] I have discussed Macfarren's early efforts in 'Musical Nationalism in English Romantic Opera', in N. Temperley (ed., *The Lost Chord*, Bloomington, IN, 1989, pp. 143–57. See also Jean Marie Hoover, 'Construction of National Identities: Opera and Nationalism in the British Isles', PhD dissertation, Indiana University, 1999.

Musical Renaissance idea was adumbrated, then proclaimed. Rural English folk music was discovered, the Golden Age and Henry Purcell were elevated, Henry Davey announced that the art of composition had been an English invention. But the belief that Britain in recent times had been an unmusical nation was still unchallenged. The terminology was changed to represent a temporary rather than a permanent state. Darkness was now followed by light, or death by rebirth.

This has turned out to be a durable concept. Was it a verdict based on a consensus of independent aesthetic judgements? Or was it a historical construct derived from factors outside music?

Table 1.1 points to the correct answer to this question. It shows the time limits of the 'dark age' and the 'renaissance' as assessed by a series of writers, arranged in chronological order. I have tried to include all authors who have offered a serious assessment of nineteenth-century British musical composition, and who have made a clear statement about a dark, lean or low period followed by a rebirth or improvement. Some authors, such as Gerald Abraham, Cyril Ehrlich, Eric Mackerness, Percy Young and myself, are missing, because we did not subscribe to any judgement of that kind.

Nobody has put the beginning of the 'dark age' earlier than 1695, the year of Purcell's death. Some have put it as late as 1800, or left it undefined. There is an even more striking lack of agreement about the end of the 'dark age' and the starting-point of the 'renaissance'. This critical change of direction is marked by the upward-pointing arrow. The result of these two uncertainties is that there is stark divergence in the evaluation of the nineteenth century itself. For some writers, it is the dark age; for others, it is the dawn. Colles saw a 'precipitous ascent' just where Blom saw a 'nadir'.

The upward-pointing arrow tends to move farther and farther to the right as you go down the page and the date of the source gets later. This cannot altogether be explained by the tendency to downgrade the immediately previous age and to boost one's own era. Both Davey in 1895 and Howes in 1966 perceived a rebirth in about 1880; on the other hand both Ouseley in 1885 and Hadow in 1931 saw a revival beginning in about 1800. The 1830s marked a downturn in the view of two historians but an upturn in the eyes of four others. Fellowes, discussing only cathedral music, saw two revivals, one about 1837 and another, following a mid-Victorian trough, in about 1885.

So it is the *idea* of darkness followed by rebirth that commands agreement among historians. Opinions about *which* music is dark and which is reborn vary too widely to amount to a consensus of aesthetic judgements.

There is further variation. In two branches of British music to which I have given close attention, namely piano music and parochial church

Table 1.1 Chronologies of the 'dark age' and 'renaissance'

Source	1700	1714	1760	1800	1837	1850	1880	1900
Ouseley, 1886	↗	'lowest ebb'			'good music of every kind'			
Hueffer, 1889		↗				'great improvement of the "Spirit of Music"'		
Davey, 1895				'disrepute'			↗ 'awakening'	
Fuller Maitland, 1902						'low point'; 'unfruitful' ↗	↗ 'Renaissance'	– –
Walker, 1907		↗	'dark stretch'	↗ 'nadir of composition'		↗ [dark stretch continues?] ↗ 'Renaissance'		– –
Bumpus, 1908			↗ cathedral music 'stood still'					
Forsyth, 1916		↗		energies devoted to imperial expansion			↗ 'national awakening'	– –
Hadow, 1931		↗	'dark age'	↗		'dawn and progress of the English Renascence'		– –
Colles, 1934							'precipitous ascent'	– –
Fellowes, 1941	↗			'poverty' of cathedral music, 'lean period'		'great revival' ↗	'sentimentalism', ↗ 'revival'	
Blom, 1942			↗ 'decline'	?→		↗ 'nadir'	↗ 'Renascence'	– –
Mellers, 1946			↗	'dark ages'		'nadir'	'Renascence'	– –
Howes, 1966							↗ 'Renaissance'	
Long, 1971	↗			church music in 'decline'				↗ 'awakening'
Pirie, 1979			↗		'darkest hour'			↗ 'Renaissance'
Banfield, 1985					↗ songs: 'overall impression of worthlessness'			
Beedell, 1992				↗	'decline'			↗
Stradling & Hughes, 1993							↗ 'Renaissance'	– –

music, I found patterns that were quite different, both from each other and from the preponderant modern view of a renaissance just before 1900. In piano music there was a summit of achievement in the 1790s, followed by a slow decline that lasted well into the twentieth century.[13] In Anglican parish church music, there are two distinct chronologies, one of urban, the other of rural church music. For urban church music the high point seemed to come in the 1860s, followed by a slight decline and then a second rise after 1900, and an apparently terminal decline after 1950. For rural church music, now often called West Gallery Music, the apogee was about 1800 or 1810, followed by a slow decline towards extinction at the end of the century.[14] In all these cases I am speaking not of musical activity or quantity, but of the quality of original music, measured by my own judgement and by the staying power of compositions. Another example is cathedral music, where William Gatens arrived at a considered judgement that the High Victorian period was a summit of achievement; this is the very period for which Fellowes constructed a special valley between early and late Victorian revivals. In opera, Eric Walter White sees a rebirth in 1834 followed by an eclipse after the failure of the Pyne-Harrison company in 1869.

The change of terminology ('Land ohne Musik' to dark age followed by renaissance) came with the rise of English or British nationalism in the late Victorian era.[15] This, it now seems clear, had little to do with music, but was motivated by the emergence of Germany, and to some extent the United States, as economic, political and potentially military rivals. So long as Britain was clearly the world leader among nations, we welcomed foreign imports, including music. But an era of protectionism was coming. In this new climate, British-born composers suddenly found that they were admired and encouraged by their compatriots. New sources of income were forthcoming; works were commissioned; critics were friendly. The 'inducement' to compose ambitiously, which Fétis had found lacking in 1829, was now there. Composers responded to it, and were in turn rewarded. At last, a cumulative momentum could be built up and the rebirth was on its way. I am not in any way denying that it took place.

---

[13] See N. Temperley (ed.), *The London Pianoforte School 1766–1860*, 20 vols, New York and London, 1984–87, vol. 1, Introduction.

[14] See N. Temperley, *The Music of the English Parish Church*, 2 vols, Cambridge, 1979.

[15] Scottish, Welsh, and Irish nationalism, reacting against domination by England, are another story altogether, and will not be discussed here.

If my interpretation is right, the negative factor in the nineteenth century was not an absence of musical talent or inventiveness, but a failure of confidence. This has two consequences that I think are important for future research: we can focus on the belief itself and try to explain it; and we should rid ourselves of the belief when studying and evaluating British music of the nineteenth century.

Explaining the 'unmusical Victorians' idea

Clearly, the Victorians and their predecessors were not generally inclined to kowtow to foreigners. It was a time of self-confidence, bordering on truculence, not only in military, naval and political affairs, but in such matters as science, technology, manufactures, currency, sport, dress, language, domestic manners and habits, and all kinds of other things. Even in the visual arts there was not much sense of inferiority. We have to find the reason for an inferiority complex that pertained specifically to music. Here are some of the explanations that have been put forward.

One, favoured by some of the earlier writers, might be called the luck of the draw: that after the early death of Purcell, Britain simply did not get lucky enough to draw a first-rate composer until, let us say, Elgar. This theory is difficult to take seriously today. It adopts the view that musical geniuses arrive fully packaged from heaven, Mozart being the supreme example. Nowadays we find it easier to believe that even the most gifted people need a conducive environment to develop greatness. Mozart certainly had one. The lack of one in Britain is exactly what we are trying to explain.

Some writers have tried to connect unmusicality with phlegm, which is the humour most often associated with the British. Fétis wrote that 'their habitual calm renders them less disposed to the cultivation of music'.[16] This explanation, also, is difficult to take seriously. For one thing, music can express calm just as well as excitement; for another, we had abundant energy for fighting, sport, money-making and literature.

Another old theory points to Handel as the root cause of the trouble. Ernest Walker (1907) considered that British composers' inventiveness was crushed by pressure to imitate Handel, even 100 years after his death, and then by the similar domination of Mendelssohn. The passage was retained by Jack Westrup when he revised Walker's book in 1952.[17]

---

[16] Fétis, 'Letters on the State of Music', p. 276.

[17] E. Walker, *A History of Music in England*, Oxford, 1907, pp. 235–6, 261; 3rd edn, pp. 271, 294–5. See also Naumann, *History*, vol. 4, p. 912.

I did my best to squash it as long ago as 1960,[18] but it is still alive and kicking. Even if it were true, it would surely be a manifestation of the sense of inferiority, not a cause of it. The living Handel may have taken active steps to crush his rivals, but after his death there was only his music to carry on the job. We still need to explain why British composers felt unable to develop independently of Handel's music.

Henry Davey, who in 1895 published the first history of British music based on original research, was inclined to put it all down to the over-centralization of power and wealth in London after 1700, which deprived British composers of the multiple opportunities open to musicians in countries like Germany and Italy.[19] Henry Hadow agreed.[20] This theory may account for any deficiency of musical life in the provinces. But in London foreign composers enjoyed enormous success. Why could not native composers do the same? Again, this is not really an explanation.

Some writers have blamed the Puritans. They are a tempting target, and one can not even be accused of any unacceptable prejudice if one attacks them. Now there were certainly groups of people in the nineteenth century who still retained much of the Puritan ethic. And although the Puritans never disapproved of music as such, they did frown on several of the main opportunities for music, including the theatre, dancing, Sunday recreation, and organs and choirs in worship. But again, their strictures would have fallen just as hard on foreign music as on the native product. And it is now generally agreed that Britain was exceptionally hospitable to foreign music in the nineteenth century.

Hadow offered a second and more convincing reason (his first being over-centralization): 'the almost formal exclusion of music from a liberal education'. He published an essay called 'The Place of Music in Humane Letters', based on a set of lectures delivered at the Rice Institute at Houston, Texas, in 1926[21] (and it is worth remembering that the Americans adopted and even augmented British negative attitudes in their thinking about their own music). It is indisputable that music did not hold in Britain the high intellectual status that it enjoyed in Germany or France. But that does not in itself explain why the British welcomed foreign music and assumed it was superior to their own.

Ann Beedell, in her interesting book *The Decline of the English Musician 1788–1888*, even suggests that the abrupt emigration of the hero of her book, William Castell, in 1826 was due to the 'failure of English

[18] N. Temperley, 'Handel's Influence on English Music', *Monthly Musical Record*, 90 (1960), 163–74.

[19] H. Davey, *History of English Music*, London, 1895, revd 1921, pp. 336–7, 443–4.

[20] W. H. Hadow, *English Music*, London, 1931, p. 105.

[21] W. H. Hadow, *Collected Essays*, London, 1928, pp. 272–89.

musical culture', which she puts down to the refusal of leaders of opinion such as Locke, Johnson, Chesterfield or even Burney to admit music to full status as an art and an intellectual pursuit.[22] But this again runs up against the awkward fact that music of all kinds was enormously popular in Britain throughout this period; Beedell herself describes the 'craze' for music in the later eighteenth century and the success of organizations like the Philharmonic Society in the nineteenth. Castell was a mediocre violinist in the London theatres. Clearly, his living did not depend on whether the music he played was highly regarded by the intelligentsia. It only had to find an audience. It is abundantly clear from Beedell's own account that he left because he was not a very good musician, had messed up his finances and wanted to get away from his wife.

But certainly, Britain differed radically from the other great European powers in its attitude to its own music. I believe we must look for an explanation in some unique characteristic of British society. Surely the most striking difference between Britain and most other countries at this time was its liberalism: its greater political, economic and social freedom. Another European country provides a parallel case. The Netherlands suffered an even steeper musical decline, if measured by the production of famous composers; it began earlier, with the death of Sweelinck in 1621. And The Netherlands, like Britain, was notable for a relatively liberal social system. In both nations, liberalism nourished explosive growth in economic and political power. Is there some way in which it could also have caused a decline in musical self-confidence?

Already in the eighteenth century, Britain was known for upward social mobility of a kind that was hardly possible in France, Spain, Italy or the Holy Roman Empire. Social-climbing was resisted by those already at the top. One way in which the truly blue-blooded could separate themselves from the ambitious parvenu was by cultivating *foreign* art, literature and music, which were still beyond the climber's grasp. Italian opera was well suited to this purpose, and so it was cultivated, for the most part, as a snobbish entertainment, not as a serious intellectual pursuit. It was desirable not for its intrinsic qualities, but simply because it was exclusive.

But, it will be argued, by the nineteenth century royal and aristocratic patronage had lost their monopoly in Britain; the nobility could no longer control musical taste. In Dent's view this fact was itself the reason for what he called 'the English attitude towards music'.[23] By

---

[22] A. Beedell, *The Decline of the English Musician 1788–1888*, Oxford, 1992, pp. xiii, 38–49.

[23] E. Dent, 'Early Victorian Music', in G. M. Young (ed.), *Early Victorian England*, Oxford, 1934, p. 252.

1830, he wrote, 'the magnificence of the aristocracy had become more restrained, while the middle classes, whose rise to power was perhaps the most significant factor in Victoria's reign, had not yet attained artistic culture'. I think Dent missed the point here. The middle classes had been rising in power for centuries, and had been the chief consumers or promoters of the madrigal, the consort song, the Restoration semiopera and much else of the greatest English music. Although they did not yet control politics in the nineteenth century, they were a formidable economic, social and cultural force. Institutions like the Philharmonic Society were run by professional musicians, not noblemen. This was surely a heaven-sent opportunity to overthrow the philistinism and xenophilia of the nobility, and to assert musical values that were rooted in middle-class taste.

I have argued this myself in the past, but I no longer believe it. True, middle-class life in Britain was self-supporting; but it was always coloured by the hope of rising in the social scale, and this amounted to a strong inducement to ape aristocratic tastes. The temptation was much weaker in countries like Austria where the class boundaries were fixed and impenetrable. Fétis was struck by this in 1829, when he wrote that in England 'the taste of the aristocracy is a law to which all must bow'.[24] And *The Musical World*, in a passage already quoted, dismissed the idea that the English were unmusical as 'fashionable twaddle' emanating from 'high quarters'.

In the freely capitalistic climate of Britain, success involved becoming a gentleman or lady. Middle-class music-lovers were under great pressure to adopt the preference of their betters: for Italian opera, French ballet and so on. Performers and composers were obliged to cater to these preferences.

An outward sign was the effort of musicians to seem as foreign as possible by the use of titles like Signor and Madame. This hardly changed until the 1880s, the time when Covent Garden stopped translating German, Russian and English operas into Italian. Fuller Maitland wrote in 1902:

> It is to be observed that among the better classes of English female singers are an increasing number who boldly call themselves 'Mrs.', and who do not appear to have suffered any pecuniary inconvenience from the abandonment of 'Mme.', which was *de rigueur* for married musical ladies not so long ago.'[25]

---

[24] Fétis, 'Letters on the State of Music', p. 276.

[25] J. A. Fuller Maitland, *English Music in the XIXth Century*, London, 1902, pp. 281–2. Ironically, Fuller Maitland himself used a foreign term, 'renaissance', to christen the new movement itself. This was well before the word had begun to be widely used, in English-language writing, for an earlier period of musical history. See also note 2 above.

In the nineteenth century the preference for foreign musicians was gradually extended to Germans, then, in the 1890s, to Russians and other Slavic peoples, though their languages never enjoyed the same cachet as French or Italian. But a more deadly aspect of British aristocratic taste than xenophilia was the one identified by Hadow and Beedell – the rejection of music as a serious intellectual pursuit. Here the British nobility were emphatically at odds with their continental peers. John Hullah declared that in England, unlike the Continent, the upper classes were ignorant of and indifferent to music. And now the upwardly mobile had to imitate this, too!

In Britain, a musician had no chance of becoming a gentleman by practising his craft. Burney's great ambition was to be accepted as a man of letters, and only when he did so was the door opened to gentlemanly society. Cyril Ehrlich, in his seminal book on the musical profession, has written: 'Success, whether achieved within the profession or by marrying money, required more than musical talents: sensitivity to niceties of social behaviour and confidence to brazen out solecisms, an eye for the main chance, and careful bookkeeping.'[26] He is thinking here mainly of financial success. But he also cites a mid-nineteenth-century guidebook on the choice of a profession (by a lawyer named Byerly Thomson) as saying that whereas the professions of law, medicine and the church assign 'a certain position in the social scale', a musician may be 'an itinerant fiddler, and of the lowest grade of society; or a man of the highest attainments, moving in the most exclusive circles, and occupying an exalted position in the literary world'.[27] The key word here is 'literary'. Making music in itself led to neither financial reward nor social acceptance, because gentlemen did not make music. Musicians were thus divided into those with a liberal education who had access to polite society, and those who did not. Ehrlich sees a 'widening social gap between the two breeds'.

In the Victorian world, social standing – respectability and gentlemanliness – was everything. It was not only the route to wealth. Still more importantly, perhaps, it was the key to less measurable sources of happiness such as friendship, self-respect, confidence, esteem. It was pursued with a desperately competitive intensity, by all except those who already had it and those who had no hope of attaining it: in other words, by our friends the middle classes. Social standing could not be

---

[26] C. Ehrlich, *The Music Profession in Britain Since the Eighteenth Century: A Social History*, Oxford, 1985, p. 32.

[27] H. B. Thomson, *The Choice of a Profession: A Concise Account and Comparative Review of the English Professions*, London, 1857; cited in Ehrlich, *Music Profession*, p. 43.

won by serious composition, because the arbiters of taste continued to confer their favours on continental music. Therefore composers who were not born to the purple were driven by almost irresistible pressure to give up their hopes of greatness, and to follow rather than lead. Percy Young put it bluntly, in an aside to his discussion of Stanford: 'To get by in the social round, the British composer needed to resemble his betters. At the end of the road of musico-social respectability was the lure of a knighthood: for most composers knighthood was the kiss of death. It was a token of achievement in anything but creative activity.'[28] He quotes the well-known comparison of Brahms and Sullivan by Dr Paperitz, a teacher in Leipzig:

> Of the two I think Sullivan had the greater natural musical talent; but Brahms will not write a note he doesn't think worthy of his gift … As for Sullivan, he settles in London, and writes and publishes things quite unworthy of genius. He is petted by royalty, mixes in aristocratic circles, acquires expensive tastes which oblige him to prostitute his talents for money-making works. As a consequence, his modes of expression deteriorate, and England and the world are robbed of the fruit of his God-given gifts.[29]

If Paperitz was thinking of the Savoy operas when he spoke of prostitution, I am sure nobody here would accept his judgement for a moment. But his general point has all too much truth in it.

And why did Brahms not have to mix in aristocratic circles (though, incidentally, Liszt and Wagner did so)? Because in Germany, creative musical achievement in itself conferred eminence and high status.

Social emulation of the upper classes was the spur that energized the middle classes to the great achievements of the Victorian age. It was highly desirable, no doubt, in the army, and navy, the civil and colonial services, the law, medicine and business. It did no damage in the arts of the word: fiction, poetry, drama, oratory, where the English language naturally reigned. In music, emulation of the upper classes was disastrous, because they had long since downplayed its value and adopted foreignness as their shibboleth. That is the point of my argument.

Some Victorians were well aware of this, and they saw that the only kind of musician who could escape was one who was born a gentleman. (Ladies were excluded because of a different set of prejudices.) There were few enough gentleman musicians, for as Ehrlich points out, 'the vast majority of gentlemen … were born and bred away from music'.[30]

---

[28] Young, *History of British Music*, p. 517.

[29] Samuel Midgley, *My 70 Years' Musical Memories*, London: Novello, 1930, pp. 21–2; cited in Young, *History of British Music*, p. 509.

[30] Ehrlich, *Music Profession*, p. 72.

In Dent's view, 'That a gentleman should become a real professional musician remained utterly unthinkable until almost the end of the Queen's reign'.[31] Not quite utterly: there were a few exceptions, but when a gentleman did try to take up music seriously, it was in the teeth of opposition from his family and mentors. Henry Hugo Pierson quarrelled with his father, a canon and fellow of an Oxford college, but was chosen for the Edinburgh professorship in 1844, in preference to Wesley and Sterndale Bennett, the two most promising composers of the time, because his social standing brought honour to the chair. It was a similar story when Ouseley, the son of a baronet, applied for the Oxford B.Mus. He too met with opposition; but he was later the obvious choice for professor because he was the social equal of the dons and could make music respectable. The 1865 Committee to enquire into the state of musical education, set up by the Society for the Encouragement of the Arts, Manufactures and Commerce, is discussed by Ehrlich.[32] Several witnesses stressed the importance of appointing a gentleman amateur as principal of the Royal Academy of Music, and the policy was later carried out for the Royal College, when Sir George Grove was selected. This was not petty snobbery. These earnest Victorians had a clear vision that the only way to raise the general esteem and self-confidence of British musicians was to raise their social standing.

Francis Hueffer saw a great improvement in 1889, for, he said, 'musicians are no longer separated from the rest of society by the barrier which of old took the shape of a cord'.[33] Elsewhere he pointed out that other countries could 'look back upon generations of intelligent amateurs', but 'With us the general culture of the art as a national growth is of comparatively recent origin'.[34]

Fuller Maitland, who came from the gentry himself, also saw this when he discussed the future prospects of the musical renaissance. He identified the leaders as Mackenzie, Parry, Thomas, Cowen and Stanford, and added: 'It is not insignificant that the majority of these leaders came

---

[31] Dent, 'Early Victorian Music', p. 253.

[32] Society for the Encouragement of Arts, Manufactures and Commerce, *First Report of the Committee Appointed to Inquire into and Report on the State of Musical Education at Home and Abroad*, London, 1866; Ehrlich, *Music Profession*, pp. 88–98.

[33] F. Hueffer, *Half a Century of Music in England 1837–1887: Essays Towards a History*, London, 1889, p. 3. The 'cord' is illuminated in another source, speaking of conditions early in the life of Michael William Balfe (1808–70): 'When [a musician] was suffered to appear in the saloons of the great and mighty, a silken rope was drawn across a portion of the room in which he was to perform, to mark the boundary of his situation, and the estimation in which he was held personally' (William A. Barrett, *Balfe: His Life and Work*, London, 1882, p. 3).

[34] Hueffer, 22.

from a class that had before their time been too seldom represented in the musical profession.'[35] The fact that there was now a group of leading composers who were fairly confident of their social position was, perhaps, the turning-point in the whole process. They could afford to take a relatively independent course, and cultivate art for art's sake in the way that every self-respecting Romantic composer had done. The disappointments of some earlier British composers, such as Bennett or Loder, and of some institutions, such as the Philharmonic Society, can be seen as casualties in a struggle to maintain high artistic standards of British composition when the times did not reward such attitudes.

Hardly had a group of British composers won a measure of artistic independence than they were rebuked for exercising it. Davey in 1895 actually chided composers for writing music for which there was no immediate demand:

> The great geniuses of the past ... were practical men, writing for particular performances by particular resources, while a modern composer, both in England and Germany, thinks only of his inner consciousness and his artistic conscientiousness, and has his works published before they have been heard. As Ruskin's and William Morris's views of art extend, they may some day reach our best composers, and cause them to give their attention to works which are practically useful and actually needed. Then we shall perhaps have original art-works.[36]

British composers had really arrived if they were liable to be accused of being too idealistic. Davey added a footnote in 1921: 'This paragraph now fortunately requires considerable qualification.'

My conclusion on this very complex question is that the fundamental problem for British composers in the nineteenth century was the general belief that they were inferior. I attribute this mainly to the xenophilia and philistinism of the aristocracy, established long before as a way of emphasizing their exclusive status, but maintained in the nineteenth century by the middle classes in their all-consuming need to join the ranks of the gentry.

Re-evaluation of art music

If we now accept that it was the belief in British composers' inferiority, rather than their actual inferiority, that stunted their growth, we can

---

[35] Fuller Maitland, *English Music*, p. 187.
[36] Davey, *History of English Music*, 451. In his 1921 revision Davey added a footnote admitting that this situation had improved.

surely suspend that belief and take a fresh and unbiased look at the music. In many cases, of course, the lack of confidence forced on composers by the attitudes of society may have actually prevented them from creating any worthwhile music. But it is always possible that some of them succeeded in producing compositions of high quality, which never had the chance to establish themselves in the face of prejudice, but which can be given that chance now.

The situation is parallel, in some ways, to the case of women's music, or women's achievements in other fields. Until recent times it was taken for granted that women were generally incapable of equalling men in creative power and originality, or in the logical application of principles. Now, this view is more or less exploded. But when the view was generally held, it may have actually prevented potentially creative women from realizing their potential. There is nothing to be done about that now; the artefacts they might have created do not exist. The best one can do is to look at what remains, searching more vigorously and more impartially than earlier investigators, and try to give it a new and more honest appraisal.

For this kind of search, music presents a special difficulty that does not exist with (say) poetry or painting. If you discover a poem or a watercolour that you think deserves to be better known, all you have to do is publish it. But with music, there is the intermediate hurdle of performance. First, you have to look at the scores, whether printed or manuscript, and pick out ones that seem to have merit. This is a skill that only a few people possess – and certainly, not all musicologists: the ability to hear music in the mind when looking at a score. The next stage is to persuade someone to perform it. This demands other skills that musicologists like me do not necessarily have, such as charm and eloquence, and it also requires money. If the performance is to influence critics and public, it has to be by a well-known and highly competent performer. A single hearing is not enough; a broadcast and a recording will be needed, followed by an edition, and one is still at the mercy of reviewers, who may very well hold fast to the belief that nineteenth-century British composers were worthless by definition.

It can be done. In the late 1950s I discovered the sonatas and songs of an unknown genius, George Frederick Pinto, and his merits were eventually recognized by non-British scholars such as Alexander Ringer and William S. Newman;[37] then some of his music was performed by Ian Hobson and there have been several recordings, one by Emma Kirkby.

---

[37] Alexander L. Ringer, 'Beethoven and the London Pianoforte School', *Musical Quarterly*, 56 (1971), 754–7; William S. Newman, *The Sonata Since Beethoven*, Chapel Hill, NC, 1969, pp. 567–71.

Then there was Edward Loder's *Raymond and Agnes*. With the financial support of my college and some local businesses, I got it on the stage for a week at the Arts Theatre, Cambridge, in 1966. The critics admitted to some astonishment that an unknown Victorian composer could have produced a work like that. Andrew Porter wrote that by comparison with Bellini as represented by *Il pirata*, 'Edward Loder is a genius, his *Raymond and Agnes* a mine of richly inventive music'; Stanley Sadie spoke of 'ensembles which would not disgrace middle-period Verdi' and choruses of 'tremendous vitality'.[38] The BBC broadcast a shortened version, which was recently re-aired. I could not persuade Musica Britannica to publish the score, though they have recently given due space to more established nineteenth-century masters such as Field, Sterndale Bennett, the Wesleys, Parry and Stanford.

Some contributors to this volume discuss lost treasures of this kind. It is very likely that there are more to be found – if only because prejudice has steered most investigators to other hunting grounds. I urge readers to search out and promote them.

Select bibliography

Abraham, G. E. R., *A Hundred Years of Music*, London, 1938; revd 1949, 1979.

Allen, W. D., *Philosophies of Music History. A Study of General Histories of Music 1600–1960*, revd edn, New York, 1962.

Banfield, S., *Sensibility and English Song*, Cambridge, 1985.

Beedell, A. V., *The Decline of the English Musician 1788–1888*, Oxford, 1992.

Blom, E., *Music in England*, London, 1942.

Bumpus, J. S., *A History of English Cathedral Music, 1549–1889*, London, 1908.

Colles, H. C., *The Oxford History of Music*, Vol. 7, *Symphony and Drama 1850–1900*, London, 1934.

———. *Voice and Verse: A Study in English Song*, London, 1928.

Dahlhaus, C., *Die Musik des 19. Jahrhunderts*, Wiesbaden, 1980; tr J. Bradford Robinson, Berkeley, 1989.

Davey, H., *History of English Music*, London, 1895; revd 1921.

Dent, E. J., 'Early Victorian Music', in G. M. Young (ed.), *Early Victorian England*, Oxford, 1934.

---

[38] Andrew Porter in the *Financial Times*, 19 May 1966; Stanley Sadie in *The Times*, 3 May 1966.

Ehrlich, C., *The Music Profession in Britain Since the Eighteenth Century: A Social History*, Oxford, 1985.

Einstein, A., *Music in the Romantic Era*, London, 1947.

Fellowes, E. H., *English Cathedral Music from Edward VI to Edward VII*, London, 1941.

————. *English Cathedral Music*, 5th edn, revd J. A. Westrup, London, 1969.

F[orsyth], C., 'Nationalism. Modern Schools', ch. 16 in C. V. Stanford and C. Forsyth (eds), *A History of Music*, London, 1916.

Fuller Maitland, J. A., *English Music in the XIXth Century*, London, 1902.

Gatens, W. J., *Victorian Cathedral Music in Theory and Practice*, Cambridge, 1986.

Hadow, W. H., *English Music*, London, 1931.

Howes, F., *The English Musical Renaissance*, London, 1966.

Hueffer, F., *Half a Century of Music in England 1837–1887: Essays Towards a History*, London, 1889.

Knepler, G., *Musikgeschichte des 19. Jahrhunderts*, Berlin, 1961.

Long, K. R., *The Music of the English Church*, London, 1971.

Mackerness, E. D., *A Social History of English Music*, London, 1964.

Mellers, W., *Music and Society: England and the European Tradition*, London, 1946.

Ouseley, F. A. G., ch. 31, 'On the State of Music in England after the Death of Purcell'; ch. 46, 'Modern English Music', in E. Naumann (eds), *The History of Music*, 5 vols, trans. F. Prager, London, [1886], vol. 4, pp. 912–26; vol. 5, pp. 1274–1314.

Parry, C. H. H., *Summary of the History and Development of Mediæval and Modern European Music*, London, 1905.

Pirie, P. J., *The English Musical Renaissance*, London, 1979.

Plantinga, L., *Romantic Music: A History of Musical Style in Nineteenth-Century Europe*, London, 1984.

Stradling, R. and Hughes, M., *The English Musical Renaissance 1860–1940: Construction and Deconstruction*, London, 1993.

Walker, E., *A History of Music in England*, Oxford, 1907; 3rd edn, revd J. A. Westrup, London, 1952.

White, E. W., *The Rise of English Opera*, London, 1951.

Young, G. M., *Portrait of an Age: Victorian England*, London, 1936.

Young, P. M., *A History of British Music*, London, 1967.

PART TWO
Historiography

CHAPTER TWO

History, Historicism, and the Sublime Analogy

Bennett Zon

In English writing of the middle to later part of the nineteenth century there are effectively three means of, or rather foils for, interpreting the history of music, each of which is essentially analogic in critical substance. The first is through direct analogy with other arts. This is marked by the appropriation of art-criticism terminology and the paralleling of music aesthetics and writings on the visual and literary arts. The second is through theologized contextualization, in which music history is placed largely within the language of a Christological framework, though one often amplified by reference to the visual arts. The third category of definition can for convenience be called progressional and/or evolutionary historicism, mostly based hermeneutically on Darwin though frequently discursive in this regard. In reference to the artistic and theological analogies, which form the basis of this chapter, it is the contiguousness between notions of historicity and aesthetic conventions of the sublime which magnify their definitions. In the third category it is the appropriation of scientifically approved modes of perception which ostensibly lend credibility to the analogy. In any one of the three cases, however, the dominant structural feature in their definition is the extra-musical analogy, and the writing examined in this chapter evinces this trait consistently.

Art-music history

Amongst the earliest nineteenth-century writings on music history to draw analogy from the visual and literary arts is William Crotch's *Substance of Several Courses of Lectures on Music*. It is in the second chapter of Crotch's lectures that the then prominent composer and writer on music enumerates his three well-known styles of music, namely the sublime, the beautiful and the ornamental, and it is at the very outset, in his introduction, that he pays homage to the artist Joshua Reynolds. In this latter respect Crotch defines music broadly as a painterly analogy and places it within the context of the imagination. Quoting from Reynolds he writes: 'To enlarge the boundaries of the art, as well as to fix its principles, it is necessary that that art and those principles should be considered in their correspondence with the principles of other arts, which, like this, address themselves primarily and principally to the imagination.'[1] In describing the three constituent elements of music Crotch retains much of the terminology and aesthetic import of Reynolds, as well as that of Uvedale Price, author of *An Essay on the Picturesque* (1794). As for the sublime he defines this as based on principles of vastness and incomprehensibility, with its most obvious realization being that of sacred music (including oratorio). The sublime also mitigates against the inclusion of levity as inadmissible in contrast to the 'awful and striking' *images* of the sublime. As so often happens throughout his lectures, Crotch also identifies the sublime musical object with concomitants of infinity: 'Infinity, and, what is next to it, immensity, are among the most efficient causes of this quality'.[2] Two remaining elements which can contribute to (but are not necessarily prerequisites for) the sublime are uniformity and simplicity. Crotch describes uniformity as often the cause of the sublime and defines it in terms of naturalistic imagery: the '*equal* [current author's italics] gloom which is spread over all nature before a storm'; a '*blaze* [current author's italics] of light unmixed with shade'.[3] Simplicity, on the other hand, is said to have its opposite in intricacy. Raphael's cartoons are said to be simply sublime; the large portico of the Grecian Parthenon or the long arcade of a Roman aqueduct, simple grandeur; a Gothic cathedral intricately sublime. It is in these conceptions of the sublime that Crotch finds musical translation:

> In music, the great compass of notes employed in a full orchestra conveys an idea of *vastness* [current author's italics] undefined. A *uniform* succession of major chords, the most agreeable of all sounds, resembles a blaze of light; while the unintelligible combination of extraneous discords conveys a feeling like that caused by darkness. The clearness [*simplicity*] of harmony in the madrigal of many voices, or in the full anthem, and the deep science of the organ fugue [*intricacy*] produce sublimity from seemingly opposite causes; as also a passage performed by many voices or instruments in unisons or octaves [*simplicity*], and one in full and florid counterpoint [*intricacy*].[4]

Not surprisingly perhaps is Crotch's acceptance of the synthetic nature of his terminology, and the fact that those features which enunciate

---

[1] William Crotch, *Substance of Several Courses of Lectures on Music*, London, 1831, p. 26.
[2] Ibid., p. 32.
[3] Ibid., p. 33.
[4] Ibid., pp. 34–5.

a delimitation do so by necessity. Crotch says as much when he claims that the three styles are seldom found to be distinct – in fact he does not give a credible example of their standing alone. Nevertheless the three styles are presented by him as separate, albeit diverse of a given unity. The sublime and the beautiful combine (perhaps not equally) when 'the melody is simple and slow, the harmony full and plain, and the expression chaste and solemn',[5] as imagerically related to the 'wisdom of Minerva's countenance' or 'the majesty of Juno's'. The sublime and the ornamental combine in the landscapes of Rubens and Gaspar, and in music they are illustrated 'by those choruses in which the voices are dignified and the accompaniments varied and playful'.[6] Beauty and ornament also blend in music 'wherever there is flowing and elegant melody, with playful and ingenious accompaniment'.[7] Nevertheless, the blending of styles inherently undermines their quality, and it is the sublime (or the 'pure sublime' as Crotch calls it) which is distinguished as the greatest music. Crotch further presents the sublime as the most enduring, and hence traditional, of the three styles. He writes of the sublime, beautiful and ornamental styles paralleling those of the Doric, Ionian and Corinthian orders. And again, referring to Christian architecture of the twelfth, thirteenth and following centuries he speaks hierarchically of the 'massive columns and impenetrable walls of the Norman fabrics' (the sublime), the 'lighter shafts and aspiring arches of the early pointed style' (the beautiful), and the 'superabundance of ornament in the perpendicular style' (ornamental)[8] which he deports as an indication of decline. In terms of music 'It is sublime if it inspires veneration, beautiful if it pleases, ornamental if it amuses'.[9] In chronological terms the sublime is the earliest, the ornamental the latest. Referring to the former Crotch differentiates between music of the ancients, i.e. Greek and Roman, and ancient music, meaning that of the sixteenth, seventeenth and early part of the eighteenth centuries. What music of the ancients Crotch knows of he calls simple and sublime and not unlike then current sacred music.

Similarly, national music is 'supposed to be the remains, or at least a close imitation, of the music of the ancients'.[10] Numerous references to music of the ancients and national music are given, from Jewish cantillation to Chinese and Greek tunes, but at no time does Crotch

---

[5] Ibid., p. 36.
[6] Ibid., p. 37.
[7] Ibid.
[8] Ibid., p. 42.
[9] Ibid., p. 43.
[10] Ibid., p. 68.

suggest that their sublimity will increase by virtue of their age (and ageing) alone. Indeed their ancientness is by no means to be confused with inherent qualities of sublimity. Dance music, for instance, can be ancient but is not sublime. The sublime in an ancient music is, moreover, governed by a calculus of its inherent, perceived and chronologically received qualities, rather than in an abstract concentration of sublimity. Guidonian chants were, for example, originally Gregorian or Ambrosian, having themselves been derived from earlier (perhaps heathen or Jewish) music traditions. The sublimity of Guidonian chant, therefore, arises not necessarily in its origination alone but in its continued and continuous prosecution of perceivable qualities. It is in this way that material accretions to the chant can affect its character and sublimity, irrespective of any transformations. Crotch calls it a common error 'to suppose that antiquity alone creates the veneration we feel for church music',[11] and at the same time he opines that 'The rust of antiquity will never constitute sublimity'. Again he derides the notion that every age improves upon the preceding one, citing the decline from perfection of pure sublime (sacred) music from the middle of the seventeenth century. Modern church music, although advanced in some areas, has not advanced in respect of the sublime, characteristics of which are immutable and differentially opposed to prevailing contrivances. As sublimity is 'the highest walk of our art as of every other'[12] according to Crotch, our art (music) is on the decline. In other words, sublimity is not something which can be acquired through scientific advancement or through ecclesiastical contextualization. Its attributes function independently and are to some extent immutable, though variable.

Other forms of music, such as madrigals, potentially as sublime as church music, were gradually tainted by excesses of beauty, having begun as generically sublime, and glees even more so, especially given their proclivity for stylistic gloss without substance. By the eighteenth century, owing to various genre-related declines, the sublime had siphoned into the organ fugue (or instrumental contrapuntal genres), whilst oratorio and opera (vocal harmony, or melody and accompaniment) had become the repository of the beautiful. Instrumental styles, therefore, inclined to become greatly advanced, whilst vocal music progressed very little. Nevertheless, because vocal music is superior to instrumental music (and the sublime to the beautiful), 'as it includes it as an accompaniment in every thing except glees',[13] sacred music did not improve, whereas secular music did. The ornamental became the

---

[11] Ibid., p. 71.
[12] Ibid., p. 73.
[13] Ibid., p. 77.

most cultivated and the sublime 'the most neglected'.[14] The remedy to this situation was for composers to study vocal polyphony of the sixteenth and seventeenth centuries.

The music of the sublime, according to Crotch's aesthetics, is premised on the internal effectiveness, or perhaps affectiveness, of the object. Rejecting the notion that 'whatever does not produce effect cannot be worthy of our admiration', he says of the sublime that of all styles it may be the 'least attractive at first'.[15] The same reasons which cause him to posit this also cause him to defend the sublime as the most deserving in this regard. Rather than dazzling or amusing, the sublime 'elevates and expands the mind, filling it with awe and wonder'.[16] It also increases in effect with more study, and ultimately it is (and is to be) adored. Not surprisingly, therefore, the musical basis of the sublime for Crotch is clearly Gregorian chant, though more for chant's capacity to be adapted than for it in its own right. It is almost too pure in an 'original' form to be perceived as sublime. In this sense the sublime becomes to some extent a refractory projection upon chant's historicity, eliding with history only through chronological permutations. The antiquity of chant, therefore, becomes an ancillary value dispensed within the context of an advancing linearity of time. Gregorian chants enhance the affective compositional balance of those composers who so choose to use them. The chants in themselves are, moreover, somehow valueless and invaluable. The fact that Crotch defines the sublime through chant's historical applications, rather than through its historical placements, makes chant's origins less significant in terms of its sublimity. Its sublimity is in fact not innate but earned through a continuously traditionalizing history. In other words, the sublime is not an all-encompassing value but an accretative function within history. Gregorian chants, in Crotch's terms, are consequently referred to via Guido, Byrd, Mozart, Josquin and Tallis, to name but a few. Of Guido he writes that

> The Gregorian chant, used in the seventh century, is quoted by Leo in his Dixit Dominus, in C. The notes to which Guido proposed a pedale or holding note in the bass, together with that pedale, form a passage remarkable for its high antiquity; for the pedal note, though called his invention, he must have heard on the bagpipe, and in all national pastoral music; this passage has been used as half and full close by almost every composer of sacred music, down to the Requiem of Mozart, his last production.[17]

---

[14] Ibid.
[15] Ibid., p. 79.
[16] Ibid., p. 80.
[17] Ibid., p. 81.

Again, for Crotch the delimiting element in chant is that its sublimity is derivative of its perpetuity, not its elemental qualities. The very fact that Mozart could be mentioned as deriving his music from chant speaks volumes of the historicist contrivance: Crotch is determined to perceive antiquity as a vehicle, not a vessel. He refers to Tallis's Litany in the same light, claiming that the chants he used were not his own, but older, and still used in most cathedrals. In other words the sublimity of Tallis lies in his polarization of antiquity and modernity, with the binding dynamic being the sublime. Sublimity, again, is an achievement through time, rather than an a priori component of it. At the University of Oxford Aldrich supplied chants, and these constitute 'a perfect specimen of pure sublimity, totally unlike the music of the present day'.[18] Yet again modernity and antiquity form a dialectical objectification of the sublime, and in this case Crotch goes so far as to describe them as pure as well, and 'totally unlike the sounds of singing, harping, piping, marching, and dancing, which their inventors had heard in national music'.[19] As Crotch goes on to say, however, chant-related tunes such as Aldrich's, are suited to sacred subjects 'and remind the hearer of no other style'. They are in this sense antonymously modern, enduing the sublime with religiosity, to the extent that religion is historical rather than relevantly current. Even the tunes used by the Reformers project the sublime through their simple and harmonious style. In contrast, the foundling hymns, with psalms made out of glees and songs, are to be utterly abolished and denounced. It is, consequently, possible to admit of new church music, but as Crotch says, 'no new style'. In other words, sacred music is stylistically self-contained and non-reflexive, despite being built and developed upon the immutable foundation of chant.

Chant, then, is an untransfixible confluence, charging music with sublimity. It is defined by later analogic applications. Tye and Tallis, di Lasso and Palestrina must therefore not be deemed barbarous and antiquated, especially as their share in the sublime is sempiternal, rather than dated. Though 'something rich and strange' their music retains its relevance through the power of its sublimity. Even hybrid forms, such as the madrigal, retain sublimity, despite being primarily beautiful. They do so because of their provision of sacredness in which they find their origin, and the context in which their applications were realized. Monteverde [sic], Converso [sic], Marenzio and dal Calaliero, amongst the Italians; Byrd, Morley, Dowland, Weelkes, Wilbye and Este, amongst the English, are all mentioned. Nevertheless their adaptation for church use in England bears no comparison to the music

---

[18] Ibid., p. 82.
[19] Ibid.

of Byrd written expressly for the purpose and for which the composer used Ambrosian chant, 'treated with consummate skill'.[20] The chant used in Allegri's mass for Good Friday likewise is also Ambrosian and causes the words 'Jerusalem is wasted quite' and 'Desolate and void' to resonate with historicity as well as voluble sentiment. The latter, Crotch says, reminds the listener 'slightly of the first subject' with which the anthem commenced and now concludes. The whole is a unique example of 'fine writing, and of the pure, sublime, and sacred style'.[21] From the period of vocal polyphony emerged opera and oratorio, both principally differing from the former in their choice of secular words. The effect of secularity is essentially to deprive music of its sublimity, although from this point onwards Crotch associates elements of sublimity with scientific counterpoint. Indeed, from this point in Crotch's lectures he finds difficulty in conferring sublimity upon any later music. Sublimity within the modern becomes something gained through contrapuntal proximities to the old sublime. Carissimi, for example, is held out as 'full of ingenuity and solemn effect', but his music is not sublime.

Theologizing the sublime musical past

There are in the writings of Formby and Pugin obvious parallels with Crotch, especially in regard to notions of the sublime. In Formby and Pugin, however, music aesthetics are contextualized within a theological, rather than an artistic framework of the Gothic- (architectural) and natural- (picturesque) sublime. In *The Roman Ritual and its Canto Fermo*, for example, Formby's theological analogy of the sublime is demonstrably vigorous. He premises his argument on the existence of an exemplar or pattern of musical perfection. An absolute standard does exist, he claims, if not innately, then through universal consensus, and the perception of the presence of such a standard in itself reflects its own presence in all things created. Creation, moreover, is the privileged work of God, and all things created by him or his creation (man) therefore contain and are by analogy representative of God. The various presences of God are tokens of real divine essences, and by virtue of these relationships created works of man can be judged to participate in divine activity. Quoting from Staudenmaier he writes 'The world is God's idea of the world brought into being, and the perfection of the original world consisted in the fact, that it absolutely corresponded to

the Divine idea',[22] and in his own words 'The idea of the Creator is to
man, as well as to the angels, the exemplar, or pattern, of his perfection'.[23] The divine exemplar of the creative ideal (the Ideal) is in fact the
very incarnation of the Son of God, the Eternal Son, whose sacred
humanity brings the knowledge of the Divine Exemplar to the minds
and hearts of Christians. In his presence and absence the apostles of the
Eternal Son disseminated the instruction of the Church, with it becoming a continuation of Christ. 'And thus with the question of Christian
song',[24] says Formby, 'the intellect must at once feel that it needs a
guide, and cannot be safely entrusted to itself. Nor can this guide be any
other than the Divine idea'.[25] Music, and especially Christian music,
requires not only a divine analogy for its true perception and spiritual
realization but an appropriately sublime apostolic pedigree as well. It
would, furthermore, be wholly dishonest and 'a manifest impiety for a
human mind to attempt to construct, a priori, an idea of music, and
then to call its own work the Divine idea'.[26] Musical invention in this
context must be perceived as emanating, at least in its conception, from
the Divine idea, rather than from the achievement (or approximation)
of the Divine idea through the greatness of human creation. Just as the
Divine idea can nevertheless subsist in objects of the world as it exists
and has existed, likewise it can be found in Christian church music
through the same course of its apostolic history.

Music, in the hands of Formby, has become a theologically historicized
sublime, with the apostolic/divine inheritance acting as its aesthetic
determinate. The mystification/awe process characteristic of the natural
picturesque sublime is couched in theological terms, with apprehension
of the Divine idea essentially replacing conventions normally associated
with the perception of nature. Natural mystification becomes divine
mystery, and sempiternality becomes the continuum of creation. In
Formby's writing the sublime is also characteristically an imposed uni-
versality (or catholicity). The notion of the sublime as forcibly
embracing its perceivers through its powers of inspiring universal and
all-encompassing awe is also paralleled in music, especially because
individual tastes, according to Formby, are 'if not wholly devoid of
rule, still do not go by any rule sufficiently clear, to be made the
subject of formal controversy'.[27] The personal apprehension of the

[22] Cited in Henry Formby, *The Roman Ritual and its Canto Fermo*, London, 1849, p. xi.
[23] Ibid., p. xiii.
[24] Ibid., p. xvi.
[25] Ibid.
[26] Ibid.
[27] Ibid., p. 3.

nature of music is, moreover, governed by principles of spiritual awareness. If music is the sublime, sacred music is the Gothic sublime, replete
with its apostolic resonances and efficacies. In this respect church music
is perceived by Formby to excel beyond any other music, owing to its
innate ideality and the absence of abstraction (through the necessity of
words). Song and truth are combined in church music, whereas other
music involves only song. In other words the element of personal aesthetic interpretation is ancillary to that of universal instruction. And in
this way church music mimics the sublime. Self-consciousness (or personal interpretation) is obliterated by the controlling powers of the
sublime, and man's consciousness of his context in relation to the object
is nullified. In this way he becomes greater than himself and more akin
to the object of his perceptions. In the case of Formby the realization of
this potential awareness is the Ideal. In music it is church music, and
only in church music is the individual forgotten and the barriers between object and subject self-consumed. Vijay Mishra, author of *The
Gothic Sublime*, as it so happens, describes the same type of relationship in his reading of Hegel's *Phenomenology of Spirit*, from which he
quotes the following: 'Self-consciousness exists in and for itself when,
and by the fact that, it exists for another; that is, it exists only in being
acknowledged.'[28] Here Mishray, like Formby in his music theology,
associates the sublime (or the Ideal) with the postulate of self-absence.
In this same light Formby writes that 'The human mind will not, and
indeed ought not, to submit to any mere human idea, but ought will-
ingly to accept the Idea of God; and hence, nothing but the Divine
idea'.[29] In terms of music, as Formby later attempts to prove, the
human heart and mind devolve in their humanity (and ultimately their
spiritual responsibility) when their creations are not conceived through
the Ideal, or God-sublime.

According to Formby's *Roman Ritual* sacred music, and in particular
plainchant, is the product of, or companion to, revelation. There follows as a result various of its denominators, including its authority,
both ecclesiastical and moral, its systemic and systematic completeness,
its moral and congregational fitness, its moral and spiritually medicinal
virtues, its durable popularity, its inherent security against abuse and its
companionship to doctrine. Of these it is perhaps the multifarious
notions of authority which most strongly embrace conventional decli-
nations of the sublime. In this case Formby proffers a distinction between
'positive authority' and 'absolute monopoly', citing the possibility of
modern music enjoying 'just toleration' under a regime of otherwise

---

[28] Cited in Vijay Mishra, *The Gothic Sublime*, Albany, NY, 1994, p. 149.
[29] Formby and Pugin, *The Roman Ritual*, p. 9.

Gregorian music. In Formby's estimation, however, the 'positive authority' is made more absolute through the frequency of its application in
ritual books of the church. In this way liturgical tradition becomes a
channel through which sacred song lives in a continually remembered
past, and realizations in the present, add credibility through successive
use. Authority, therefore, comes not just through origin but through
transmission. The Church endorses its music through tradition and
decree, and the reception of sacred music in itself confirms and perpetu-
ates its own authority. In other words, according to Formby, the divine
idea (primary authority) propels legislative authority (secondary authority), which in turn influences practice and reception (tertiary
authority). Thus the stream of revelation precipitates authority in an
ever repercusive pattern of ecclesiastical history. As for sacred music's
moral concomitant, authority, Formby lays this clearly in the roots of a
musical-apostolic succession beginning with Gregory the Great and
Gregorian chant. He then proceeds to the idea that the authority of
ritual song (Gregorian chant) is based, to some extent, on its incapabil-
ity of application to modern music. In other words, ritual music is
incapable of being updated, owing to (a) its exclusive application within
ritual, and (b) its 'static' or fully codified *oeuvre*. Modern music, on the
contrary, depends upon pleasure for use and is changing constantly
within itself and developing.

One convention of the sublime which can be traced throughout
Formby's work, as well as in many others', is the view that antiquity
represents a higher level of order than is immediately available in the
present. This synonymously involves despair towards the new. Formby
writes in this regard that 'If in the Divine idea of the Christian song,
there is necessarily contained the notion of a working and efficient
system, the simple truth is, that there is no such system, either in the
works of modern music themselves, or in the manner of their use.'[30]
The system to which Formby refers represents the interrelationship
between the textual complex of liturgy and its traditional rendering in
plainchant. All elements of the musical corpus are organized through a
textual hegemony, and personal choice in the application of it is irrel-
evant. Formby even goes so far as to describe as chaos the freedom with
which modern church music (i.e. Mozart, Haydn and Beethoven) is
indiscriminately chosen.[31] Ritual music, as well, is 'not every thing or
any thing that is beautiful in music, nor merely a work of art. It is,
strictly speaking, a Sacrificial Song',[32] and in this respect ritual music is

---

[30] Ibid., p. 22.
[31] Ibid.
[32] Ibid.

seen as comprising a higher order than music alone. Here the music of ritual is brought into the present and exceeds art and beauty, in perhaps the same way that the picturesque sublime exceeds the natural. The awe-sublime elevates its own object beyond itself, ineffably beyond comprehension, yet within revelatory perception. To adapt Formby's words, the sublime 'is not every thing or any thing that is beautiful in *itself*, nor merely a work of art'. Ritual music, therefore, necessitates a greater system, a greater order and consequently a greater perception and interpretation than works of art (i.e. modern music). This does not represent an antipathy towards modern music in Formby's estimation, just simply an apprehension of ritual decorum. The order which he assigns to ritual music is not, however, merely an opposite or obverse to that of modern music. It is one founded on the historical primacy of chant and its perpetual antiquity as a parallel to Christ's perpetual sacrifice. The matrix of past and present is for Formby evidence of the higher order of ritual chant and is not relevant to modern music. Modern music is by nature lacking in history and to speak of it in terms of order is therefore absurd. If authority is bound up in history and order precludes history, then modern music is without authority. To take it one step further, as Formby does, it is chaos, the very absence of order.

Prevailing throughout Formby's conceptions of history is the assumption that antiquity (in this case apostolic) proceeds through time from relevance to relevance regardless of parallel developments outside of its sphere. In the same way, perhaps, that he adjures the great cathedrals and churches continuing to present an active historical presence, he speaks of the 'durable' popularity of Gregorian chant[33] and repeatedly places its growth in uniform opposition to that of modern music. Ancient music, or ritual music, in this sense, enjoys a pedestalled insularity in comparison to the rather lowly modern music, which meanders along devoid of direction. Indeed, as the argument continues, there appears to be an increased synchronisity between the ontological divinity of ancient music and the spiritual deprivation of modern repertoire. Numerous writers on music, including Rousseau, Martini and Baini, to name but a few, are introduced to support this idea, and the principal strand of the argument begins to wax polemical. Writing on plainchant, for example, Rousseau is quoted as saying that

> There remains to it [plainchant] enough of its former charms to be far preferable, even in the state in which it now is for the use to which it is destined, than the effeminate and theatrical, frothy and flat, pieces of music which are substituted for it in many churches,

---

[33] Ibid., p. 44.

devoid of all gravity, taste, and propriety, without a spark of respect for the place they dare thus to profane.[34]

Similar views are espoused frequently in Formby's work and it is
largely the same which form the kernel of his disagreement with
modern music, outlined in 'a reply to some of the popular objections
brought against the ritual song'. Of course, in his reply Formby re-
sponds to criticism specific to the genre of chant rather than to its
innate historicity or modern relevance, claiming that it is precisely its
historicism which gives its performance its appropriateness and that
chant's own home is even more suitably placed in its historical context, the medieval cathedral.

Although Formby's views are not entirely unique for the time, what
marks him out from the rest of his contemporaries is the degree to which
he synthesizes the aesthetic and theological analogy into a Christological
musicology. Another writer working on similar principles is the archi-
tect and Christian apologist A. W. Pugin, whose *An Earnest Appeal for
the Revival of the Ancient Plain Song* defines the revival of chant in
terms of the Gothic revival in church architecture. Again, as in Formby,
the principal argument revolves characteristically around the dichoto-
mous relationship between validating an idealized historical presence
and historicizing modern ritual practices. As a concomitant to this,
Pugin, like Formby, rails initially against notions of populism, claiming
that 'It is, indeed, seriously proposed to chant the whole nature of the
divine services of the Catholic Church, under the specious pretext of
rendering them more popular and adapting them to the spirit of the
age',[35] and in this regard he speaks of 'the trumpery display of a toy-
shop and the vocal entertainment of a concert-room'.[36] As it so happens,
however, Pugin's conception of liturgical dignity is not just bound up
with an antithetical attitude towards modernity (as could be said of
Formby), but with his views on ecclesiastical aestheticism. For although
Pugin is essentially dominated by his view of catholicity as a religious
aesthetic armoury – i.e., that ecclesiastical historicism protects us from
modern aesthetic abuse – he also couches the various tiers of his argument in the language and symbolisms of the terror (or Gothic horror)
sublime, thus drawing down the conflict from that of an abstract
Christological sublime (as in Formby) to that of an actual moral and
aesthetical dramatization. At first, for example, Pugin writes of 'a growing appreciation of the glories of Catholic antiquity that will effectually

---

[34] Cited in ibid., p. 51
[35] Augustus Welby Pugin, *An Earnest Appeal for the Revival of the Ancient Plain
Song*, London, 1850, p. [3].
[36] Ibid., p. 4.

preserve us from the encroachment of modern innovations',[37] and of 'our rising to the high standard of ancient excellence and solemnity, and not by lowering the external of religious to the worldly spirit of this degenerate age'.[38] But in the same breath he speaks of 'monstrous' attempts at substituting vernacular for Latin and of it being 'time that every man who has a heart in the Catholic cause should testify his unbounded horror of so unhallowed an attempt to change the ancient offices'.[39]

Pugin's historicist dramatization does not stop with a conventional aesthetic dilemma regarding modernity, but proceeds to a notion which equates antiquity with purity and, hence, aesthetic health and superiority. Along these lines he speaks of 'the absolute necessity of restoring the ancient Chaunt in all its purity',[40] and this in contrast to the 'corrupt and artificial state of ecclesiastical music'[41] then current. As an extension of this Pugin also contrasts passivity with activity, or listeners with worshippers; 'the grand and edifying spectacle of priests and people uniting in one great act of adoration and praise' with 'a set of hired musicians, frequently heretics and infidels'; and 'the most solemn act of Christian worship' with 'a mere musical entertainment for the audience'. Thus Pugin provides antiquity with activity, unity and solemnity, even going so far as to suggest that there is 'a want of reality'[42] in modern service music. The 'miserable system' of modern music has thus 'completely cut off the people from taking part in the most solemn act of Christian worship, and degraded it in appearance to the level of a pageant'.[43] In other words the historicity of ritual is so all-encompassing that modernity is exclusive, or even peculiar, to it. Pugin views the historicity of the building in the same light, with example after example of new Gothic churches desecrated by modern music and modern architectural contrivances. He decries these latter as much as bad music, saying that

> that simple and divine song, which was created, like the architecture, by the influence of the Christian faith, and which alone assimilates and harmonises with its lofty vaults and lengthened aisles; without this the service and the fabric will be at utter variance, a most humiliating spectacle of ancient grandeur and modern degeneracy.[44]

---

[37] Ibid.
[38] Ibid.
[39] Ibid.
[40] Ibid., pp. 4–5.
[41] Ibid., p. 5.
[42] Ibid.
[43] Ibid., p. 6.
[44] Ibid., p. 8.

This last phrase – 'ancient grandeur and modern degeneracy' – summarizes not only the dialectical nature of Pugin's aesthetic historicism; it also emblemizes the characteristically inversionary nature of sublime symbolisms: open grandeur/confinement; freedom/slavery; community/isolation; and security/insecurity, to name just a few. For Pugin ancient music *is* the Gothic sublime, modern music its antithesis. Plainchant to him is the one pure universal reality-giving expression of music, modern music the fallen dismal corruption. Even unto the last Pugin prosecutes this view, praying thus:

> May He grant us to see a restoration, not only of the external glory of His temple, but of the reverent service which is alone suited to its ancient symbolism; and may our churches – which, for the most part, are so many stumbling blocks to our separated service – be purged from the disgrace of these modern performances, and become as shining beacons, not alone by the altitude of their spires, but by the purity and *reality* of the divine offices celebrated in them.[45]

Conclusion

As can be observed in Crotch's aestheticization, and Formby and Pugin's theologization, notions of the sublime had created a music historicism bound in definition by conventions of analogy. In Crotch's case the sublime informed not only his perception of musical progress, but it also redefined the hermeneutical nature of musicological perception. In Formby and Pugin's work the same principles apply, although these are directed to an essentially Christological end. For both of them divine history is as inseparable from music history as is art history for Crotch, and in each of these three cases the essence of their historicism is the extra-musical analogy. The nucleus of this analogy is the sublime, and it is through the analogy that music history in England was formulated in the middle part of the nineteenth century. It was, in fact, not until later in the century when evolutionary theory had been appropriated into a musicological context that the aestheticization and theologization of music history ceased to be as relevant. But even in that case it is possible to trace elements of the sublime in the most scientifically conceived historicism. For Crotch, Formby and Pugin, however, music history was nothing if not viewed from the vantage of the sublime, and as is shown in this chapter it was the sublime analogy which enabled them to define music history and its perception.

---

[45] Ibid., p. 10.

CHAPTER THREE

Parry as Historiographer*

Jeremy Dibble

Musical history and criticism as a discipline preoccupied Hubert Parry for the whole of his professional musical life – from roughly 1875 until his death in 1918. In his early career perhaps the most significant stimulus was the invitation to become sub-editor of the first edition of *Grove's Dictionary of Music and Musicians* to which he contributed over 100 articles. The success and productivity of this work led to his appointment as Professor of Musical History at the newly founded Royal College of Music (RCM) in 1883 and his historiographical work manifested itself in papers for the Musical Association, in lectures for the universities of Oxford, Cambridge and London, the RCM, the Royal Institution and other provincial literary and philosophical societies (notably in Birmingham, Leeds and Sheffield), in articles for numerous journals, and six books: *Studies of Great Composers* (London, 1887), *A Summary of Musical History* (London, 1893), *The Art of Music* (London, 1893), *The Music of the Seventeenth Century* (written for the Oxford History of Music, Oxford, 1902), *Johann Sebastian Bach* (New York and London, 1909) and *Style in Musical Art*, a compilation of his lectures while Heather Professor at Oxford between 1900 and 1908, published in London in 1911.

The important contribution Parry made to musical criticism strongly reflects the intellectual spirit of the later Victorian age: his political radicalism and profound belief in democracy, his fear of growing materialism, his rejection of orthodox religion, particularly in the wake of post-Darwinian science, his antipathy towards the aristocracy and his own personal austerity. Deeply entrenched in his thinking were many of the principle ideas of the time – the relationship between morality and art, the notions of culture, race and nationality – and, strongly connected with the latter, the concepts of evolution. That Parry constantly remained drawn to controversial thought of the time is evident from the reading lists he included at the end of his 54 years of diaries. We know crucially that he read Darwin's *The Origin of the Species* in 1877 and in

---

* This essay is an expansion of ideas first discussed in a paper, 'Parry, Stanford and Vaughan Williams: The Creation of Tradition', published in *Vaughan Williams in Perspective*, L. Foreman (ed.), Aldershot, 1998, pp. 25–47.

the following year *The Descent of Man*. Works by other writers such as
Carl Engel, James Sully, Edmund Gurney, J. S. Mill, William Pole,
Edward Burnett Tylor, Thomas Huxley, Henri Bergson and Benjamin
Kidd were widely read. The historical writings of Froude, Lecky, Carlyle
and Hallam figure prominently as do the literary works of Gissing,
Samuel Butler, Morris, Zola, Dickens, Hardy and George Eliot, reflect-
ing his concern with issues of class and social justice.[1] But most
quintessential to Parry's critical acumen was his admiration for Herbert
Spencer's *Synthetic Philosophy* which, more than any other, helped to
articulate his views of musical history.

Before discussing Parry, Spencer and evolutionism, it is also important to note the influence of Ruskin's doctrine of the morality of art
under which Parry fell during his time as an undergraduate at Oxford
between 1867 and 1870. Parry attended Ruskin's lectures which attempted to confront the issues of art and its relationship to religion and
ethics. After graduating from Oxford Parry read Ruskin's lectures on
Greek mythology published as *The Queen of Air* (this appears in his
reading list for October 1870). In these writings Ruskin made it clear
that music was the most directly ethical of the arts (pp. 58–9):

> Exactly in proportion to the degree in which we become narrow in
> the cause and conception of our passions, incontinent in the utter-
> ance of them, feeble or perseverance in them, sullied or shameful in
> the indulgence of them, their expression by musical sound becomes
> broken, mean, fatuitous, and at last impossible; the measured waves
> of the air of heaven will not lend themselves to expression of
> ultimate vice, it must be for ever sunk into discordance of silence.
> And since, as before stated, every work of art has a tendency to
> reproduce the ethical state which first developed it, this, which of
> all the arts is most directly ethical in origin, is also the most direct
> in power of discipline; the first, the simplest, the most effective of
> all instruments of moral instruction; while in the failure and be-
> trayal of its functions, it becomes the subtlest aid of moral
> degradation.

Parry remained firmly allied to Ruskin's moral aesthetic throughout his
life. Indeed it is potently evident in his later articles such as 'The
meaning of ugliness in art' delivered at the International Musical Congress in London in May 1911 and 'Things that matter' written for
Oscar Sonneck's new *Musical Quarterly* in 1915. In his first book,
Studies of Great Composers (1887), actually a compilation and expansion of short articles written for *Every Girl's Annual*, Parry needed no

---

[1] As a vivid illustration of his admiration for the evolutionist narratives of George
Eliot's novels, his two daughters, Dorothea and Gwendolen, were named after characters
in *Middlemarch* and *Daniel Deronda* respectively.

prompting in idolizing Beethoven as the embodiment of Ruskin's ideal
(p. 156):

> One of the most interesting things about the history of music is the
> way in which it invariably illustrates in some way or other the state
> of society, and the condition of thought of the people among whom
> it is produced. Second-rate composers illustrate the tone of mind
> among second-rate people, and the greatest masters of their art
> express things which are characteristic of the best and foremost of
> men of their time; and, yet further, when some exceptionally splen-
> did genius appears, who is fully in sympathy with the best tendencies
> of his day, and capable of realising in thought the conditions and
> feelings which men are most prone to in their best and truest
> moments, he becomes as it were a prophet, and raises those who
> understand him above themselves, and ennobles and purifies at
> least some of those traits and sympathies which combine to make
> the so-called spiritual element in man; and so comes to be a leader,
> instead of a mere illustrator, of contemporary emotion.

Words and phrases such as 'sincerity', 'genuineness of expression', 'earnestness', 'nobility of character and thought', 'exalted emotions' are
prominent components of Parry's Ruskinian vocabulary. This is nowhere more clear than in the final paragraphs of Parry's conclusion to
Studies which is effectively a personal declaration of his devotion to
Ruskin's ideals (p. 376):

> During the lives of great artistic workers of all sorts public judg-
> ment is constantly misled by personal considerations. One man has
> the gift for contriving or even organising success; another has an
> equally remarkable gift for preventing his own attainment of it.
> One man catches a fashionable taste and is adored, another wages
> war upon it and is vilified. But when they have passed away men
> begin to ask in more judicial mood what their works represent
> artistically. Do they open up any new vista? Do they show mastery
> of any new resource? Do they put things in a light never thought of
> before? Do they lead any whither? But mixed up with such ques-
> tions are still more important ones. Men ask what is the quality of
> the things they utter; whether they express great and noble traits of
> character and thought, whether they appeal to noble sympathies
> and arouse healthy and exalted emotions.
>   In literature, fine language, clearness of expression, mastery of
> design and power of laying out an argument, craftsmanship, and
> even correctness, all count for a good deal; but in the long run the
> man who has the noblest thoughts takes the highest place. And so
> it is in music. Finished art, mastery of resource, clearness of
> expression, all go for something; they are in fact indispensable;
> but however remarkable in their way they cannot atone for levity
> and shallowness. The great composers are not those who merely
> entertain us and make us for a while forget boredom and worry
> in trivial distraction; but such as sound the deepest chords in our
> nature and lift us above ourselves; who purify and brace us in

times of gladness, and strike no jarring in the time of our deepest
sorrow.

The conclusion to *Studies of Great Composers* underlines this artistic
quest for the high and noble which is exemplified by the then unfin-
ished work of Brahms. Other elements of Ruskin's work, notably his
political interpretation of art – one thinks particularly of his chapter
on Turner's *The Garden of Hesperides* – which Landow has perti-
nently described as 'an index to the spiritual condition of contemporary
England',[2] did not leave Parry unmoved. Class consciousness, a recurrent feature of his writings, is invoked in his denunciation of the
aristocracy's 'external culture' (to use Matthew Arnold's phrase from
Culture and Anarchy) which he continued to voice throughout his life,
reinforced no doubt by the attitudes he experienced from members of
his own class and that of his wife's.[3] As a composer too, Parry's sense
of social and artistic conscience is evident from the overtly ethical
series of choral works written between 1898 and 1908 (such as *A
Song of Darkness and Light*, *The Love that casteth out Fear*, *The
Soul's Ransom*, *Beyond these Voices there is Peace* and especially *The
Vision of Life*) and the late symphonic works, the Fourth and Fifth
Symphonies, the symphonic poem *From Death to Life* and the valedic-
tory *Songs of Farewell*.

Parry's preoccupation with the moral element of musical criticism
resulted in major prejudices elsewhere. Florid song, coloratura and a
large proportion of opera was frequently the subject of vehement denunciation. In *The Art of Music*, Parry early on described ornament as
'the part of anything which makes for superficial effect' (p. 59) and
went even further in 'Things that Matter' by saying that:

> The worst kind of such decoration is afforded in the horrible
> inanity of what is called 'coloratura' in Italian operas from almost
> the earliest days till the first half of the nineteenth century. Such
> decorative adjuncts have generally no meaning at all, and were
> introduced for no other purpose than to show off the vocal vanity
> of the singers. Some of the worst and most aggressive are in
> Meyerbeer's operas. (p. 318)

Indeed Parry had personal problems with opera generally and remained
uncomfortable about the role of opera in Britain's musical development

---

[2] Landow, G. P., 'Ruskin', in *Victorian Thinkers*, K. Thomas (ed.), Oxford, 1993, p. 157.

[3] Parry was born into the landed gentry, his father, Thomas Gambier Parry being a
wealthy Gloucestershire landowner who had inherited a considerable fortune from his
grandfather. In 1872 Parry married Lady Maude Herbert, the second sister of George
Herbert, thirteenth Earl of Pembroke. Both families vigorously opposed his aspirations
to become a professional musician.

as a nation, as is evident from a vituperative entry in a notebook of 1918 (Shulbrede Priory, Sussex):

> Opera is the lingering descendant of the paltry amusements of the courtly classes of the 17th, 18th and 19th centuries. Was there anything so fatuous as the entertainment called an Italian Opera? French Grand Opera was only a whit less fatuous, because its extravagant artificiality was one of the phenomena of industrial ingenuity. No composer who was independent and sincere could ever write an opera. Beethoven's one attempt was defeated because he was sincere. He wanted to set music to a drama which was genuine and moving and had qualities which people who had any discernment could recognize as human and not theatrical sham – and that would not be opera, and opera people would not have it ...

Parry believed that the true inner life of man's emotions could be equated with notions of organic coherence, the fusing of older methods with new and formal involution through intellectual application. This naturally led towards the German triumvirate of J. S. Bach, Beethoven and Brahms for whom his criticism is almost always conspicuously positive, not to say reverential. However, it is important to recognize that Parry also maintained a tempered admiration for Wagner.[4] This was principally owing to his acceptance of Wagner's artistic descendance from Beethoven as he expounded in *Studies*:

> As he [Wagner] himself said, even before he wrote *Tristan and Isolde*, 'It seemed feasible to realise my idea by leading the whole rich stream into which German music had swollen under Beethoven into the channel of the musical drama.' It was the general development of the language of music and its instrumental resources, in symphonies, overtures, sonatas, and quartetts and so forth, that made his attempt possible. The infinite variety of melody, and the gradual expansion of forms, enabled him to wed music to words without sacrificing sense or dramatic propriety; and the development of the dramatic story enabled him to dispense with the regular systematic outlines, which are necessary in pure instrumental music, and in their place admitted a freer emotional form, depending on a balance of emotional crises – moments of passion alternating with moments of comparative quiet in infinite gradations. (pp. 355–6)

In his first period of maturity as a composer, Parry gave much time to the study of Wagner's music dramas. We know this not only from his

---

[4] As a composer, Parry's interest in Wagner was considerable in the 1870s and early 1880s, but it is clear that his prejudice against opera in later years, strengthened by the failure of his one operatic venture for Carl Rosa, *Guenever* (1886), did much to moderate his enthusiasm. His writings on Wagner in *The Art of Music* are nevertheless highly engaging, particularly with regard to his insights into Wagner's formal and harmonic experiments seen as descending directly from Bach and Beethoven.

diaries but also from his sessions with his teacher and mentor Edward Dannreuther. It was after all Dannreuther,[5] the principal champion of Wagner in London during the 1870s, who had produced some of the most important elucidations of Wagner's operatic ideology in *Richard Wagner: His Tendencies and Theories* (London, 1872) and *Richard Wagner and the Reform of the Opera* (London, 1873) and several articles,[6] writings that Parry keenly imbibed.

After leaving Oxford in 1870, Parry's intellectual life was stimulated amongst a small group of college friends. They met regularly as part of an informal essay and discussion club in which the most recent developments in philosophy, art, science, the social sciences and politics were discussed. As a result of his degree at Oxford in modern history (as well as law), works such as Lecky's two-volume *Rise and Influence of Nationalism in Europe,* the same author's *History of European Morals,* Carlyle's *Chartism* and *Past and Present* and Draper's *Intellectual Development of Europe* demonstrate Parry's continued interest in current historical thought.[7] In the sphere of literary criticism he read Matthew Arnold's *Literature and Dogma* and *Culture and Anarchy* and a fascination for natural history – Parry owned and actively used his own microscope – led to a study of botany (which included Darwin's *Naturalist's voyage round the world* read in 1874 and *Vegetable mould and earthworms* in 1881), physiology and physics.[8] Christianity and religious debate feature prominently in his diaries during the early 1870s. John Stuart Mill's *Three Essays on Religion*, F. W. Newman's *Phases of Faith,* Strauss's *Das Leben Jesu,* the Duke of Somerset's *Christian Theology and Modern Sceptics* and Greg's *Creed of Christendom* symbolize the struggle with traditional religious dogma which he finally rejected in 1873. At this juncture the predominant subject material was that of the

---

[5] Parry began to study with Dannreuther in 1873. It is clear from his diaries and letters that discussion on the philosophy of history and culture took place between them, but the influences that were brought to bear on Dannreuther's own historical writings appear to be German (reflecting his Leipzig education and Teutonic background) such as Schopenhauer and Comte (who is openly quoted on the title-page of his book *Wagner and the Reform of the Opera*). The influence of Darwin and Spencer seems less overt by comparison.

[6] See also Dannreuther's two seminal articles on Wagner: 'The opera: its growth and decay', *Macmillan's Magazine*, 32, May (1875), 64–72 and 'The Musical Drama', *Macmillan's Magazine*, 33, November (1875), 80–85

[7] The booklists of Parry's later diaries also show that he was an avid student of the new *Cambridge Modern History*, all eleven volumes of which he read by 1911.

[8] Parry's study of the physical sciences stimulated his interest in sound. Already familiar with Tyndall's *On Sound* and Sedley Taylor's *Sound and Music*, he gave his earliest public lecture, 'A Lecture on the Science of Sound', at the Town Hall, Chertsey on 7 September 1875.

British empiricists, namely the essays of Locke, Hume, Huxley and John Stuart Mill. Mill's Utilitarian Rationalism lies at the very heart of Parry's embarkations into philosophy and ethics, and this was to act as the foundation of his artistic and moral outlook. Between 1870 and 1875 he read no less than eight of Mill's works;[9] *Utilitarianism*, Mill's seminal work, Parry read twice, first in 1872 and again in 1875 and Huxley's works, namely the *Lay Sermons* and *Critiques and Addresses* (read in 1873), emphasize his shift towards agnosticism (to coin Huxley's term). However, although utilitarianism played a prominent part within the formation of Parry's credo, it was evolutionism, already a potent feature of intellectual orthodoxy in Britain, Europe and America, that figured most robustly. Central to the deliberations was Spencer's 'Social Darwinism' in which the tenets of evolution could be applied equally to social and cultural phenomena. Parry was enormously impressed with Spencer's *Synthetic Philosophy* as evidenced by his reading lists during the 1870s which includes other of Spencer's writings such as *First Principles of Philosophy* (London, 1862) and *Social Statics* (London, 1855) read in 1871, *The Study of Sociology* (London, 1861) read in 1874 and *Data of Ethics* (vol. 1, part I of *Principles of Ethics*, London, 1879) read in 1879.

When considering the principle of evolution, and Spencer's theoretical writings within its bounds, it is worth remembering that, out of the Enlightenment and the Scientific Revolution had emerged hope and belief in progress, the improvement of the human condition and of upward change whereby faith in social and cultural amelioration translated easily into the conviction that the world of life and existence was also in a state of upward development. This was very much a symptom of 'the Romantic preference for analogy and metaphor as the means of conveying, or rather suggesting, ultimate truths'[10] favoured both by Auguste Comte in his positivistic philosophy and by the German *Naturphilosophs*, the latter of whom were influential in the development of British empiricist thinking in the first half of the nineteenth century. Central to the thinking of the *Naturphilosophs*, which was essentially historical, was the 'law of parallelism' i.e. the 'parallel between man's individual history, or gestation, and the universal history'[11]

---

[9] The following works by Mill appear in Parry's booklists between 1870 and 1875: *Political Economy* (1870); *Utilitarianism* (1872, reread 1875); *Autobiography* (1873); *Subjection of Women* (1874); *Three Essays on Religion, On Liberty, Essays on Civilization* and *System of Logic* (all 1875).

[10] E. Richards, 'Metaphorical Mystifications: The Romantic Gestation of Nature in British biology' in *Romanticism and the Sciences*, A. Cunningham and N. Jardine (eds), Cambridge, 1990, p. 130.

[11] Ibid., p. 132.

and the notion of *Entwicklungsgeschichte* where man and nature shared a common history of development. This mode of thinking dominated *Naturphilosophie* during the first decades of the nineteenth century and is perhaps best represented by Lorenz Oken's *Lehrbuch der Naturphilosophie* (Jena, 1809–11) which found its way into English translation in 1847 as *Elements of Philosophy* (London, 1847).[12] The influence of Oken and his adherents was considerable and it was not long before Romantic culture absorbed its metaphorical terminology:

> As it came to fruition within German Romantic philosophy, the metaphor of the gestation of nature encapsulated the organicism, the uncompromising developmentalism, anthropocentrism and insistence on the fundamental unity of all nature, of the Romantics. The Romantic universe being metaphorically an immense animal, it was animal-like in its functions and constitution, and even in its methods of procreation. Romantic literature abounds with references to this 'universal gestation of nature' – to the 'impregnation of the terrestrial womb', the 'pregnancy' of the world, the generation 'generation', 'gestation', 'growth' or 'development' of nature. Above all, through the metaphor of gestation, biological and historical thought could be united so that the rules and concepts of the one could be applied to the other, and this is epitomized in Oken's very definition of *Naturphilosophie* as 'the generative history of the world'.[13]

Oken's work as an embryologist and that of his contemporaries in Germany, Döllinger, Pander, Von Bär, Rathke and Remak, and in France, Prévost and Dumas became a prime focus for the illustration of 'parallelism' even though in fact much of the symbolic language rendered the philosophy obscure and imprecise to those who ventured to comprehend it. Nevertheless the work of Oken and Von Bär proved to be highly influential on the impressionable Thomas Huxley and equally so on Herbert Spencer whose writings Huxley was to describe as 'the spirit of Descartes in the knowledge of our own day, and may be regarded as the "Principes de la Philosophie" of the nineteenth century'.[14] During the 1850s Spencer was to develop his own evolutionary philosophy in *Social Statics* (London, 1850) and *Principles of Psychology* (London, 1855); and once Darwin and Wallace's 'On the Tendency of Species to Form Varieties and on the Perpetuation of Varieties and Species by Natural Selection: Proceedings of the Linnaean Society' (1858)[15] and

---

[12] L. Oken, *Elements of Physiophilosophy*, trans. A. Tulk, London, 1847, printed for the Ray Society (C. and J. Adland).

[13] Ibid., pp. 131–2.

[14] Huxley, T. H., 'Evolution in Biology', in *Science and Culture and Other Essays*, London, 1881, pp. 297–8.

[15] Reprinted in C. Darwin and A. R. Wallace, *Evolution by Natural Selection*, Cambridge, 1958.

Darwin's *Origin of the Species* (London, 1859) were published, his theoretical work gathered further momentum in a series of treatises beginning with *First Principles* (London, 1862).

By the end of the 1860s, Spencer, Huxley and other Darwinians 'were virtually running British science from the epicentre of the influential X-Club and recruiting social support from an increasingly secular and "progressive" middle class'.[16] It was at this very time that Parry, an impressionable student, was leaving Oxford and it is therefore no surprise that early in the 1870s, living in London and moving in the city's intellectual circles, he should have been swept along so vigorously by the wave of British empirical investigation and criticism. At the Gloucester festival of 1874 Parry had the opportunity to meet Spencer for the first time. 'I had a few words with him on casual subjects,' he wrote excitedly in his diary, 'and felt quite overwhelmed by the honour, so that I could hardly speak without trembling.'[17] Indeed Parry's admiration for Spencer was to remain a potent driving force for his own ruminations on music and other matters throughout his creative life. Spencer, for his part, also took an active interest in music and, late in his life, deferred to Parry's historical writings in support of his own thoughts on the subject.[18]

Spencer's influence on Parry's view of musical history can be felt in various ways. As a main and guiding principle, it was claimed that the evolution of man's biological past found a parallel in human social and intellectual history, and that music as part of that history could not be excluded. Evolution also strengthened the notion that the development of music was dependent on changing environmental conditions. It was vital to consider the circumstances under which composers lived, the historical position in relation to the musical genres in which composers chose to work, and the importance of individual and national character.[19] But perhaps most telling of all, the adoption of evolutionary and

---

[16] E. Richards, 'Metaphorical Mystifications', pp. 139–40.

[17] Quoted in Graves, C. L., *Hubert Parry*, London, 1926, vol. 1, p. 146.

[18] An indication of the wide-ranging influence of Spencer's writings can be gauged from a collective letter (dated 16 December 1896) written to Spencer congratulating him on the completion of his *System of Synthetic Philosophy*. Parry's name is of course among the list. The signatories also became subscribers to a portrait that was subsequently painted by Sir Hubert von Herkomer.

[19] Writing about Wagner in *Studies of the Great Composers*, such thinking loomed large:

> People commonly speak and write as if they thought that works of art and imagination, and all products of what they call genius, sprang by inspiration from nowhere, and were the independent creations of their originators. They can understand how natural laws work elsewhere; that a plant will

hence scientific theories within the province of music history bolstered the notion that music historians had a scientific earnestness which was different from the more arbitrary journalistic musings of the past. It is significant that *The Art of Music* of 1893, published in a revised edition three years later as *The Evolution of the Art of Music* (to clarify its 'scientific' intention) formed, as volume 80, part of Kegan Paul's strongly Darwinian *Scientific Series*, rubbing shoulders with works by Huxley, Tylor, Spencer and Walter Bagehot. Huxley's book, *Science and Culture*, published in 1881, and which Parry read in 1886, was almost certainly significant in that it argued for scientific methods of enquiry to be applied to areas other than the physical sciences. In this regard, too, Parry was very much aware of other scientifically based writings such as William Pole's *The Philosophy of Music* of 1877 (read in 1890) and Helmholtz's *On the Sensations of Tone as a Physiological Basis for the Theory of Music* of 1875 (read in 1878).

It is clearly evident from an article written about himself, probably as a draft for the first edition of *Grove's Dictionary*,[20] that his allegiance to Darwin and Spencer was formed early in the 1870s and that his first published historical writings, those for the dictionary, were imbued with Spencer's theories. In particular Spencer's notion of evolutionary movement from the 'general' to the 'special', or more precisely expressed in *First Principles* as the passing 'from a state of homogeneity to a state of heterogeneity' (derived essentially from Wolff and Von Bär), proved to be the backbone of Parry's concept of historical theory.[21] After a large proportion of the Grove articles were written which, concentrating on generic issues of form, technique, style and structural design, were essentially testing grounds to expound his developing historiographical theory,[22] Parry more publicly declared his evolutionary stance in a paper for the Musical Association in November 1884 entitled 'Some bearings of the historical method upon music'. In his paper Parry made clear his wish to seek an understanding of music as a steady growth in which the works of the 'great masters' – who

---

not grow unless the seed is put where it can germinate, and that it requires light and heat and moisture and nourishment to bring it to mature perfection. But they seem to think it is quite different with art and things which grow in the human mind. (p. 322)

[20] This article lies among the letters from Parry to Dannreuther, Bodleian Library, Oxford, *Ob* MS Eng. Letters e.117.

[21] See Andreski, S. *Herbert Spencer: Structure, Function and Evolution*, London, 1971, p. 78.

[22] For a full list of Parry's articles for the first edition of *Grove's Dictionary of Music and Musicians*, see Dibble, J., *C. Hubert Parry: His Life and Music*, Oxford, 1992, p. 525.

previously had been viewed largely in isolation – could be comprehended afresh. 'And it seems' he wrote,

> that if we observe the facts which lie ready to our hands carefully, and endeavour to frame our conclusions from them patiently without allowing preconceived ideas or prepossessions to get the better of us, we ought to find many things which will be of the most inestimable service in criticism, theory and even the application of such abilities as we have to execution and composition. (p. 2)

In avoiding the historicism of the isolated 'great masters', Parry's shaping of musical history took place through musical genres, their stages of development and the contributions made by individual composers. 'The study of isolated instances' he wrote,

> is merely bewildering, and the very greatness of some men when separated from their context is so dazzling that it almost numbs the judgement. But if we could study the successive steps, and follow the progressive stages up to the great achievements, we should not only understand those achievements better, but see how to direct our own footsteps accordingly. (Ibid., p. 7)

Though Darwinian evolution is mentioned in Parry's paper, a full declaration of his indebtedness to Herbert Spencer was not made until 1890, in a lecture 'Evolution in Music' delivered at the Royal Institution. At the outset of his lecture he stated categorically:

> As far as I can discover, not much has been said on the subject before us as yet; and as there is a great deal to be said, my only preliminary will be to remind you of one of Mr Herbert Spencer's definitions of evolution, which happens to be most apt to our subject.
> The formula in question is as follows: Evolution is a 'change from indefinite incoherent homogeneity to a definite coherent heterogeneity,' accompanying the dissipation of motion and integration of matter; which, for present purposes, I may expand into – a change from indefinite chaos to an aggregate of clearly-defined separate entities or organisms, each with functions well determined.[23]

This lecture attempted to embrace as many aspects of musical history as possible – genres, forms, harmony and orchestration, and in so doing acted as the bedrock for *A Summary of Musical History* and more importantly for *The Art of Music*.

The Art of Music is most representative of Parry's philosophy of musical history. The views expressed in it were to recur again and again in his lectures for the Royal College of Music (a teaching commitment he continued even after becoming Director of the RCM in 1895) and

---

[23] A typescript of Parry's unpublished lecture is located at Shulbrede Priory, Sussex.

during his tenure as Professor at Oxford. In acknowledging the influence of Spencer and the work of the famed explorer, Harry Johnston, Parry included a chapter entitled 'Preliminaries' on the music of savages, folk music and medieval music. This chapter, intended to demonstrate man's 'instinctive desire to convey impressions and enjoyments to others, and to represent in the most attractive and permanent forms the ideas, thought, and circumstances, scenes or emotions which have powerfully stirred the artists' own natures', was no doubt influenced by Spencer's essay 'The Origin and Function of Music', first published in *Fraser's Magazine* in October 1857 (one which had excited a debate with both Darwin and Gurney[24]) and Spencer's much later article on evolution and music published in *Mind* in 1890.[25] It is also very likely that Parry was receptive to the work of Edward Burnett Tylor, Oxford reader in Anthropology, whose *Primitive Culture* of 1871 Parry had read in 1885. Tylor's work and theories were to be particularly conspicuous in *Style in Musical Art*.

From the expressive cries and gestures of savages, Parry moved on to a discussion of scales and folk music in which he must have drawn on the work of Carl Engel as well as that of Hipkins whom he acknowledged. From Chapter IV, 'Incipient Harmony' and the music of the early Christian Church, Parry embarked fully on his conception of musical history as a continuous progression. Most common to his description are words like 'instinct', 'phase', 'stage', 'step' and the two watchwords of Spencer: 'homogeneity' and 'heterogeneity'. Here is an extract from Chapter V 'The Era of Pure Choral Music' – an era regarded by Parry as the 'babyhood of modern music':

> The manner in which the inevitable homogeneity of an early stage of art presents itself is still discernible from every point of view. The most comprehensive fact is that almost all the music of these two centuries [i.e. the fifteenth and sixteenth centuries] is purely choral – that is, either written for several voices in combination without independent accompaniment, or devised upon methods which were invented solely for that kind of performance. It followed from this general fact that the methods of art were also homogeneous; for the processes which are fit to be used by voices alone are more limited in range and variety than those which can be employed by instruments ... (p. 103)

---

[24] For a fuller account of the debate between Spencer, Darwin and Gurney, see Kivy, P., 'Charles Darwin on Music', in *The Fine Art of Repetition*, Cambridge, 1993, pp. 214–25.

[25] It is perhaps significant that Parry and Spencer were in correspondence at this time, principally as the result of Parry's request for information about the music of primitive peoples for *The Art of Music*.

Other watchwords were 'expression' and 'design' both ubiquitous to Parry's critical vocabulary. The relationship and equilibrium between these two elements, between form and content, becomes fundamental to Parry's thesis as his book develops. In consequence, we find that generative processes of form, notably instrumental form, and the expansion and increasing sophistication of structure, are venerated and seen as culminating in the sonata works of Beethoven. In this respect Parry is consistent with the views of other evolutionary writers such as James Sully who presented a similar exposé in his *Sensation and Intuition: Studies in Psychology and Aesthetics* published in London in 1874. In Chapter XII, 'The Balance of Expression and Design', Beethoven is discussed at length to the detriment of both Haydn and Mozart.

One of the most conspicuous of Parry's critical criteria, stemming again directly from Spencer's suggestions about race and culture, is the attempt to connect artistic attributes to racial types.[26] Though this stance has now been categorically rejected by the scientific community, Parry believed in the connection between race, style and national character. This belief gave rise to a cultural hierarchy in which Teutonic art held sway. The idea is introduced in his discussion of 'Folk Music' and further polarizations are evident in his deliberations on the music of the seventeenth century in which northern composers are seen as superior to their southern counterparts. This was an objection voiced later by Dent in his criticism of Parry's contribution to the Oxford History of Music – *The Music of the Seventeenth Century* – in which he saw that century primarily as a preparation for J. S. Bach.[27] Parry confessed himself an out-and-out pro-Teuton in one of his RCM addresses, though ironically it was delivered within the context of the First World War when he felt himself betrayed by German militarism.

Parry's other major literary work, *Style in Musical Art*, was published in 1911. The title of the book was taken from his inaugural lecture as

---

[26] Parry's preoccupation with ethnocentrism may also have been influenced by Huxley's essay 'On the methods and results of ethnology' and 'On some fixed points in British ethnology', in *Critiques and Addresses*, London, 1873, pp. 134–80.

[27] In *The Music of the Seventeenth Century* this polarization is clearly made as follows:

> The Northern composers, dwelling with intense and loving concentration on every detail of their work, brooding on its deeper spiritual meaning, and glorifying it by the full exercise of intellectual as well as emotional qualities; where the Southern composers, taking things more lightly and with little exercise of self-criticism, fall into trivialities, conventionalities and purely mechanical artifices, and in a branch of art which requires any copious exercise of intellect, are speedily left in the lurch. (pp. 118–19)

Oxford Professor in March 1900, which was shortly afterwards published in pamphlet form. The content of the book was derived from his Oxford lectures between 1900 and 1908. Parry took style to be 'mainly an external attribute – a means to an end, and in no wise comparable to actual qualities of character or action in man, or the thought embodied in what is said in poetry, or the idea embodied in art' (p. 2). It could be used, however, as criterion for judging whether the content of a work was well expressed. 'Differences in style', Parry concluded, 'are the outcome of the instinct for adaptation. In art the most perfect style is that which is most perfectly adapted to all the conditions of presentment' (ibid.). These conditions of presentment, in choral and instrumental work, to form, national influences, texture, thematic material and quality became the basis of Parry's study through which evolutionary thought runs as a central vein.

Style in Musical Art was Parry's last published volume concerned with historiography, though he did produce a large monograph, typically entitled *Instinct and Character*, tenaciously pursuing Spencerian principles, though this time inspired largely by Kidd's *Social Evolution* (which he read in 1918) and by the anthropological work of Tylor. Written at the end of his life, chiefly during the First World War, Parry hoped to bring his artistic beliefs into a wider focus of social behaviour and ethics. It was offered to Macmillan in 1918 but it was turned down, much to Parry's disappointment.

After the First World War, Parry's view of musical history as both culminative and progressive was rejected by the anti-evolutionists, among them Ernest Newman, not least because evolutionary thought presupposed that 'progress' and the metaphor of 'growth' in the development of music carried with it the perspective of value. Beethoven was seen as superior to Mozart (a point made by Shaw), Bach to his Italian forbears, and early music, notably that of the medievalists was reduced to crudity and primitiveness. Parry's distinct ethnocentrism, his prejudices for German art (to the detriment of French and Italian), his elevation of absolute instrumental music and his mistrust of opera weaken his standpoint considerably. Parry believed implicitly in the importance of tradition, of inherited values and techniques as part of his evolutionary philosophy, a stance which tended to underestimate experimentation and iconoclasm. This tended to colour his view of composers such as Purcell and Berlioz. Similarly, with his bias on organicism, he tended to dismiss the extended works of Schubert. However, as Dent pointed out in his review of 'Parry as Musical Historian' in the *Athenaeum* in September 1919, Parry's strengths lie not in his powers as an historian, but in his abilities as a critic. Although he was well read in both German and English monographs, his own judgements are so often refreshingly independent, especially his critical analyses of music that obviously interested him. This is true of his writing on Monteverdi, which shows signs of development and reassessment, especially his Musical Association paper of 1916, and the more discursive articles for *Grove*, such as 'Harmony', 'Form', 'Variations', 'Sonata' and 'Symphony' which exhibit, even now, an acute insight into structure and design. Dent significantly pointed out that the value of Parry's approach to musical history was as a composer (a fact emphasized by the young Elgar's admiration for them), and certainly his writings help to illuminate the nature of his own works, particularly his views on Beethoven, Schumann and Brahms.

Parry's work as a musical historian was nationally of great importance. His insights set his work apart from early histories in English, those by Naumann (trans. Ouseley), John Hullah and Rockstro, and an indication of the influence of his writings has to be measured by their longevity. In 1931 *The Art of Music* reached its tenth edition supplemented by further chapters based on evolutionary theory by Colles who succeeded Parry as lecturer in music history at the RCM in 1919. Colles also supplemented Parry's *Grove* articles for the third edition of the dictionary in 1927 and drew heavily on Parry's ideas for his own *The Growth of Music*, written between 1912 and 1916. Others too, such as Hadow, Fuller Maitland and Vaughan Williams, continued to fly the flag of evolutionism during the first half of the twentieth century, and one may argue still that, in spite of its numerous flaws and criticisms, the evolutionist model persists as the view of music history.

PART THREE
Instruments and
Performing Ensembles

CHAPTER FOUR

Who bought Concertinas in the Winter of 1851? A Glimpse at the Sales Accounts of Wheatstone and Co.[1]

Allan W. Atlas

When the master mystery writer Wilkie Collins placed the concertina in the hands of the aristocratic Count Fosco and the aspiring young lawyer Mr Pedgift, jun., in *The Woman in White* (1860) and *Armadale* (1866), respectively, he was portraying the instrument's social status at the time with pinpoint accuracy.[2] To be sure, such upper-crust company does not square with present-day images of the concertina, which tend to connect the instrument with the likes of morris dancing, street musicians, whaling ships and music halls, yet these associations came to predominate only in the final quarter or so of the nineteenth century.[3] Prior to that time, the story of the concertina – especially the 'English' concertina[4]– was quite different. Indeed, beginning in the late 1820s, when it was developed by

---

[1] For their help with various aspects of this chapter I should like to thank Professors Stanley Boorman, New York University, and Stuart Prall, Queens College/Graduate School, The City University of New York. I am also indebted to Mr Neil Wayne, former Director of the Concertina Museum, Belper, Derbyshire; Dr Frances Palmer, Keeper of Musical Instruments at The Horniman Museum, London; and Mr Stephen Chambers, Dublin.

[2] For the passages in question, see *The Woman in White*, J. Symonds (ed.), (Harmondsworth, 1974, p. 250; *Armadale* (New York, 1977), pp. 220–23, 227, 231; both passages are quoted in A. W. Atlas, *The Wheatstone English Concertina in Victorian England* (Oxford, 1996), pp. 2–3, 5. I am currently preparing an article on music in Collins's writings.

[3] Even in these venues, the concertina fell into relative obscurity after the Second World War. On the rebirth of what has been called 'concertina consciousness' in the 1970s, especially in the field of folk music, see Stuart Eydmann, 'The Concertina as an Emblem of the Folk Music Revival in the British Isles', *British Journal of Ethnomusicology*, 4 (1995), 41–9.

[4] Briefly, there are three different types of concertinas: (a) the 'English', a double-action (each button produces the same pitch regardless of the direction of the bellows), fully chromatic instrument with a range (for the treble model) of g-c'''' (48 buttons) or g-g'''' (56 buttons) and with successive notes of the scale alternating between the left and

the physicist Sir Charles Wheatstone (1802–75),[5] through its first great success on the concert stage at the 1837 Birmingham Festival, to the Collins novels of the 1860s, the concertina was most comfortably at home in England's leading concert halls and upper-class drawing-rooms, where its repertory included music by such respected composers as John Barnett, Julius Benedict, George Alexander Macfarren and Bernhard Molique, as well as by a number of concertina virtuosos. In fact, one estimate has it that, during its first four decades of production – from the 1830s into the 1860s – Wheatstone and Co., the most prestigious manufacturer of the concertina, sold approximately 80 per cent of its instruments to men and women of social privilege: titled aristocrats, 'professionals', the well-to-do among those 'in trade', high-ranking military officers and members of the clergy.[6]

My purpose here is to go beyond this generalization and draw a somewhat more precise – if still limited – profile of those who purchased Wheatstone concertinas during one brief period at the very middle of the century: January–March 1851, when Wheatstone and Co. sold, rented, loaned and exchanged 263 concertinas to/for some 140 customers,[7] their names carefully entered in one of the sales ledgers that

---

right sides of the instrument; (b) the German-derived 'Anglo' or 'Anglo-Continental', a single-action instrument (each button produces two pitches, one with the bellows drawn out, another with the bellows pushed in) and primarily diatonic (but with some chromatic capabilities on 'expanded' models); and (c) the 'duet', double-action and fully chromatic, but with its range of up to five octaves split into separate bass and treble registers (with some overlap) on left and right sides, respectively. See Atlas, *The Wheatstone English Concertina*, pp. 13–18, and 'Concertina', in the forthcoming revised edition of *The New Grove*; J. Pilling, 'Concertina', *The New Oxford Companion to Music*, D. Arnold (ed.), (Oxford, 1980), vol. 1, pp. 459–62; O. Heatwole, 'Types of Concertinas', *Concertina*, 1 (1), (1983), 5–15.

[5] Wheatstone developed a number of other musical instruments, some of which were very much the product of his combined inventor-curious mind and P. T. Barnum-like personality. Thus his acoucryptophone (also called the Enchanted Lyre) and Grand Central Diaphonic Orchestra never ventured beyond his own musical museum, founded in 1822; see R. Altick, *The Shows of London* (Cambridge, MA, 1978), p. 360. Still another invention, the Symphonion, led directly to the concertina; see Atlas, *The Wheatstone English Concertina*, pp. 29–32.

[6] See N. Wayne, 'The Concertina Revival', *Folk Review*, 3 (5), March (1974), 5; Atlas, *The Wheatstone English Concertina*, p. 5.

[7] The number of customers is subject to variation of perhaps one or two in either direction, since buyers whom I have considered to be one and the same despite variations in the ledgers' entries for them may in fact be different persons (and vice versa).

We might put the sale (rentals, loans, exchanges) of 263 concertinas in three months into perspective as follows: five years earlier, in 1846, Wheatstone's sales for the entire year came to 173 concertinas; the total for 1841 was 58. Thus Wheatstone more than quadrupled its business in one decade. See N. Wayne, 'The Wheatstone English Concertina', *Galpin Society Journal*, 44 (1991), 130.

record the company's transactions in virtually unbroken, day-by-day fashion from 1835 to May 1870. These ledgers, preserved for many years at the Concertina Museum (Belper, Derbyshire), were acquired – together with that museum's spectacular collection of concertinas and other Wheatstone-related items – in spring 1996 by The Horniman Museum, London, where they now await cataloguing.[8]

The discussion that follows focuses mainly on identifying some of the people who bought concertinas, and then concludes with some brief comments about the instruments themselves and the prices paid for them. Finally, Appendix A offers a day-by-day summary of the three months' transactions, while Appendix B lists the buyers in alphabetical order, with cross-references to Appendix A.

We can most easily develop our profile by placing the buyers into various social and occupational categories.

Professional concertinists

At least seven professional concertina players and self-styled 'Professors' of the instrument bought concertinas during our three months. And though they constitute only 5 per cent of the 140 or so buyers, they formed the core of Wheatstone's business; for as teachers of the instrument, they played a major role in developing a clientele for it.

By far the most notable among them was the famed virtuoso Giulio Regondi (1822/23–1872),[9] who was in and out of Wheatstone's work-

---

[8] There are eight such ledgers, with a break in the records only for 1849–50. A ninth ledger, organized by instrument serial number and without buyers' names, extends the coverage through 1891. In addition to these nine sales ledgers, there are two account books that record payments to Wheatstone employees for the years 1845–46 and 1848–49. Finally, upon acquiring the collection, The Horniman Museum received two additional sales ledgers, donated by Mr Stephen Dickinson, that I have not seen.

Although I examined the 11 ledgers that were housed at the Concertina Museum in 1993, this chapter is based mainly on a set of cross-referenced transcripts provided by Mr Neil Wayne (see Appendix A for a description of their contents) and a transcription in the style of a diplomatic facsimile prepared by Dr Frances Palmer. I am happy to acknowledge their kind assistance (see footnote 1), as well as Mr Wayne's generosity in opening the doors of the Concertina Museum to me in 1993.

The ledger containing the accounts for our three months was catalogued as C 1047 at the Concertina Museum and, in its entirety, covers the period from 1 January 1851 to 23 October 1852. For a summary of the ledgers that were at the Concertina Museum, see Wayne, 'The Wheatstone English Concertina', 144; and Atlas, *The Wheatstone English Concertina*, p. 3, n. 10, and p. 146, where the closing date for item C 1053 should read 1870 not 1873.

[9] On his life and career (he was also a virtuoso guitarist), see D. Rogers, 'Giulio Regondi: Guitarist, Concertinist or Melophonist? A Reconnaissance' [pts i–iii], *Guitar*

shop at 20 Conduit Street seven times with as many concertinas between 14 January and 12 March. That Regondi was picking up some,
perhaps all, of these instruments for his students can hardly be doubted.
Thus on 17 February, Regondi borrowed a concertina with the serial
number 2587, which, a few weeks later, on 12 March, was rented to a
Miss Binfield, who can be identified as either Hanna or Rosa Binfield,
both of whom were students and friends of Regondi (see below).

Regondi was one of the founding members of the Concertina Quartet, which had made its début to favourable reviews on 12 June 1844.
So too were Richard Blagrove (c. 1825–95) and George Tinckler Case
(1823–92). And while Blagrove is mentioned only in a marginal note in
connection with a Miss Kirkby, probably one of his students, Case
himself purchased two expensive instruments during this period.[10]

The five other professional concertinists who left Wheatstone's workshop with instruments were: Joseph Warren, whose *Grand Fantasia* on
a theme from Bellini's *Norma* was one of the works with which Regondi
established the concertina as a concert instrument at the 1837 Birmingham Festival; Wardle Eastland Evans, another member – though not
one of the original four – of the Concertina Quartet; one of the Pelzer
sisters – either Anné or Catherina Josepha – both of whom composed
and arranged for the concertina; and finally, Lindley Nunn and T. J.
Dipple, who both turned out transcriptions for the instrument.[11] Together, then, the seven professional concertinists were directly or indirectly
responsible for the sale or rental of 17 instruments.[12]

Review, **91**, Fall 1992, 1–9; **92**, Winter (1993), 14–21; **97**, Spring (1994), 11–17, which
concentrates on his career as a concertinist (a fourth instalment is in preparation); S.
Button, *The Guitar in England, 1800–1924*, Outstanding Dissertations in Music from
British Universities, New York, 1989, pp. 100–13 and 126–30, which emphasizes his
guitar playing; Tom Lawrence, 'The Guitar in Ireland, 1745–1861', PhD, University
College, Dublin (1998) and 'Giulio Regondi and the Concertina in Ireland', *International Concertina Association Newsletter*, **411** (July 1998), 21–5, which present newly
discovered documents about Regondi's performances on the concertina in Ireland in
1834; and for a capsule summary and further bibliography, Atlas, *The Wheatstone
English Concertina*, pp. 48–54.

[10] On Blagrove (the younger brother of the violinist Henry Gamble Blagrove), Case
(who also had concertinas manufactured under his name), and the Concertina Quartet,
see Atlas, *The Wheatstone English Concertina*, pp. 52, 54–7.

[11] On Warren, Evans and the Pelzer sisters, see Atlas, *The Wheatstone English
Concertina*, p. 1 n. 4, and p. 57; there is an edition of Warren's *Fantasia* on pp. 88–97;
on Nunn, whose arrangement of *The Carnival of Venice* was published by Wheatstone
and Co., see J. D. Brown and S. S. Stratton, *British Musical Biography*, London, 1897;
reprint, New York, 1971), p. 300; Dipple's *12 Operatic Solos for Concertina*, which
draws on melodies from Bellini and Donizetti, was published by Rock Chidley, himself a
concertina manufacturer and one-time employee of the Wheatstone firm.

[12] There might have been an eighth professional concertinist. On 27 February, the

There is an interesting phenomenon to be seen among the professional concertinists. Most, perhaps all, of them came to the concertina from other instruments. Regondi and Catherina Josepha Pelzer (also known as Madame R. Sidney Pratten) were virtuoso guitarists.[13] Blagrove played viola in the Philharmonic Society and taught that instrument at the Royal Academy of Music (RAM). Warren and Nunn were organists, while Case was a violinist at the Royal Opera House and a good enough pianist to serve as Regondi's occasional accompanist.[14] Yet among those who adopted the concertina as a second instrument, only Regondi really made it his primary one. Clearly, there was always a living to be made, and this was probably difficult to do on an instrument that – even during the mid-century 'concertina craze'[15] – always lived precariously close to the margin of non-respectability among many 'serious' musicians.[16]

---

ledger records the sale of two concertinas to a Mr Henry Lee. If, perhaps, 'Lee' is a slip of the pen for – or my misreading of – 'Lea', we may identify the buyer as Henry Lea of 8 Park Terrace, Camden Town, London, 'Professor of the Concertina', who arranged a number of operatic overtures for the instrument and compiled three tutors for it; see the title-page of his *Boieldieu's Overture to the Caliph of Bagdad*, British Library, Music Division, h.2336.20–37.

If, however, 'Lee' is correct, perhaps the buyer was the music seller Henry Lee, who would purchase the Liverpool-Dublin firm of Hime and Son in 1879; see D. W. Krumel and S. Sadie (eds), *Music Printing and Publishing*, The Norton/Grove Handbooks in Music, New York, 1990, p. 288.

As for the concertinist Henry Lea: perhaps we may futher conjecture that he is related to the later Thomas *Lea* Southgate, who presented a lecture on free-reed instruments in 1904 in which he proved himself knowledgable about both the English concertina and the symphonion; see T. L. Southgate, 'The Regal and its Successors: The Harmonica', *English Music (1604 to 1904), being the Lectures given at the Music Loan Exhibition of the Worshipful Company of Musicians held at Fishmongers' Hall, London Bridge, June–July, 1904*, 2nd edn, London, 1911, pp. 381–416.

[13] This side of Madame Pratten's career is covered in Button, *The Guitar in England*, pp. 113–17 and 133–9, and see footnote 9, above; see also, F. M. Harrison, *Reminiscences of Madame Sidney Pratten: Guitarist and Composer*, Bournemouth, 1899.

[14] See Atlas, *The Wheatstone English Concertina*, pp. 54 and 76. Case claims to have accompanied Regondi on the title-page of his own *Air by Himmel with Introduction & Variations*, Op. 9 (published by Wheatstone in the 1840s).

[15] I borrow the term from Maria Dunkel, 'Harmonikainstrumente', in *Die Musik in Geschichte und Gegenwart*, 2nd revd edn, ed. L. Finscher, Kassel, 1996, *Sachteil*, iv, col. 201.

[16] On the critical reception of the instrument, see Atlas, *The Wheatstone English Concertina*, pp. 72–5.

Music dealers

Wheatstone and Co. found an equally lucrative pool of customers among music and instrument dealers throughout the British Isles, since they often bought in bulk. Thus our three months saw the publisher-piano manufacturer Cramer and Co.[17] purchase nine concertinas within a period of two weeks, while Joseph Higham, the Manchester-based manufacturer of brass instruments, bought a like number on three occasions in January and March.[18] Other music dealers who figure in the ledger during this period are the London firms of Robert Cocks (1 instrument), Hale and Son (2?), and Keith, Prowse (1) – the last of which sometimes sold Wheatstone concertinas under its own label – as well as the Edinburgh/Glasgow dealers Hume and Son (4), Paterson and Roy (1), and Wood and Co. (8).[19]

In addition to the eight music dealers, there were three commercial buyers who seem, at least on the surface, to have had no special ties to music: Grindlay and Co., probably the bankers (1 instrument), a still unidentified Leicester and Sons (2), and the buyer listed simply as 'Brown's' – perhaps the well-known hotel, then located on Dover Street – which bought no fewer than 11 instruments on 17 January.[20]

---

[17] This, of course, is the firm of the pianist J. B. Cramer, which, in 1851, would more properly have been known as Cramer, Beale and Chappell; see Krummel and Sadie, *Music Printing and Publishing*, p. 208.

[18] On Higham, who founded his firm in 1842 and became 'Maker to the Army' in 1852, see L. G. Langwill, *An Index of Musical Wind-Instrument Makers*, 6th edn, Edinburgh, 1980, pp. 78–9.

[19] On these firms, see Krummel and Sadie, *Music Printing and Publishing*, pp. 203, 307, 359, 482; J. A. Parkinson, *Victorian Music Publishers: An Annotated List*, Detroit Studies in Music Bibliography 64, Warren, MI, 1990, pp. 55–6, 114, 213, 300–301; Brown and Stratton, *British Musical Biography*, pp. 312, 456. Cocks also published a tutor for the instrument: *Robert Cocks' & Co.'s Hand Book of Instructions for the English Concertina, with 32, 40 and 48 Keys* (1855). We should note that the presumed sale to Keith, Prowse is recorded in the ledger only as 'Mr W. Prowse'; on that company's activity as manufacturers of concertinas, see N. Wayne, *The Wheatstone Story: The Life and Works of Charles Wheatstone* (forthcoming). Finally, perhaps there were two other music dealers; see footnotes 12 and 33, and the identification of 'Mr Hinton' (below).

[20] I offer two possible identifications for 'Brown's', both of which are speculative and problematical: (a) The more likely identification is that the buyer was the fashionable Brown's Hotel, founded by James Brown and his wife in 1837 (and today having its main entrance around the corner on Albemarle Street). It was from Brown's that Alexander Graham Bell made the first telephone call in England in 1876, and it was there that Theodore and Franklin Roosevelt and their wives spent their honeymoons in 1886 and 1905, respectively; over the years the hotel has been home to J. P. Morgan, Rudyard Kipling and a bevy of visiting – often exiled – royalty.

Two problems: first, the ledger notes that Brown's is in Bloomsbury; yet Dover and Albemarle Streets are in Mayfair. Could the ledger be mistaken? Second, why should the

Thus the winter of 1851 saw as many as 11 business enterprises in England and Scotland purchase 48 concertinas from Wheatstone, with

---

hotel have purchased 11 concertinas in the first place? Was it with the intent of placing them at the disposal of its guests? If so, we might even imagine that the 11 instruments were not all standard trebles, but included some tenors, baritones and basses, the better to let the guests form small concertina ensembles. We might also note that Brown's was only a few minutes walk from the soon-to-open Great Exhibition, at which Wheatstone and Co. displayed six concertinas, and for whom Brown's would therefore have been a convenient venue at which to place concertinas into the hands of prospective visitors. On Brown's, see Christopher Matthew, *A Different World: Stories of Great Hotels*, London, 1976, pp. 113–17; and Mary Cathart Borer, *The British Hotel through the Ages*, London, 1972, pp. 163–4 and 201–3. I am grateful to Professor Stanley Boorman for the initial suggestion that 'Brown's' might be the hotel.

(b) Among the major banks of the time was the London-Liverpool enterprise of Brown, Shipley and Co., founded in 1810 and headed by William Brown (1784–1864), who served in Parliament from 1846 to 1859 and became a baronet in 1863. William Brown was also the chairman of the Atlantic Telegraph Co., in which capacity he would eventually work closely with Charles Wheatstone in 1859–60, when he and Wheatstone – whose great scientific interest was telegraphy – served together on a government commission that considered the laying of transoceanic telegraph cables. Thus Brown had interests that coincided closely with those of Wheatstone, and perhaps they already knew one another prior to their joint service on the commission, with that friendship whetting Brown's appetite for the concertina.

To thicken the plot: on 14 March 1851, a 'Mr W. Brown' purchased a concertina with the serial number 3162, the same instrument that Giulio Regondi had carried off just two days earlier without paying for it. That Regondi was taking the instrument in order to show it to Mr Brown seems evident, and our Mr Brown was probably Regondi's student.

Given these circumstances, then, we might hazard that the ledger's 'Mr W. Brown' is the William Brown who headed both Brown, Shipley and Co. and the Atlantic Telegraph Co.; that he shared similar and highly specialized scientific interests with Charles Wheatstone; that Brown, Shipley and Co. is the 'Brown's' recorded in the Wheatstone ledger; and that the firm bought the concertinas with the intention of selling them in the normal course of their commercial affairs, probably exporting them to the United States, where the English concertina had made its début on the concert stage in 1847, and with which Brown, Shipley and Co. controlled approximately one-sixth of the trade at mid-century.

Three problems: first, though I have yet to locate Brown, Shipley and Co. at a specific address, Bloomsbury would have been an unlikely location, since most of the major banking houses operated out of 'the City'. Second, if Brown, Shipley and Co. is the 'Brown's' of the Wheatstone ledger, it is the only time that a commercial customer is listed in a style other than the formal '———— & Co.'. Third, the ledger fails to describe Mr W. Brown as the 'Hon.', which title should have been used for a Member of Parliament, and is in fact used in the ledgers on other occasions. On William Brown, his company and his association with Wheatstone, see A. Simpson, *Anatomy of Britain*, New York, 1962, pp. 379–81, and B. Bowers, *Sir Charles Wheatstone, FRS, 1802–1875*, Science Museum, London, 1975, p. 151. On the concertina's 1847 début in the United States and its appearance at the Great Exhibition of 1851, see Atlas, *The Wheatstone English Concertina*, p. 8 n. 54, and p. 39 n. 10.

eight of these firms standing among the best established music dealers of the period.[21]

Two musical families

Wheatstone also found exceptionally good customers in two families that played leading roles in English musical life outside London: the Binfields of Reading and the Aylwards of Salisbury.

On 12 February and 12 March, the ledger records transactions with a 'Miss Binfield', while another pair of entries on 5 and 14 March lists sales to a Mr W. Binfield. The two entries for Miss Binfield must refer to Hannah and/or Rosa Binfield, the second pair to a still unidentified relative.[22] By 1851, the connection between the Binfields and the concertina was an old one, reaching back at least to June 1838, when one of the Binfield ladies bought what might have been the family's first concertina.[23] And one year later, now as the organizers of the Berkshire eleventh Triennial Musical Festival at Reading, the Binfields invited the teenage Regondi to appear as soloist. Regondi later repaid the Binfield's faith in him by dedicating three of his major compositions for concertina to members of the family, while Hannah, herself a pianist, harpist and the organist at Reading's Church of St Laurence, turned out a number of transcriptions for the instrument. In all, the Binfield–Regondi relationship extended beyond that of student–teacher, and Regondi maintained a lifelong friendship with the family.[24]

As for the Aylwards of Salisbury, a Mr W. P. Aylward purchased four concertinas on 15 February, and then bought three more on 10 March.

---

[21] If the sales to Henry Lee (see footnote 12) and J. Hinton (see below) are also to the music dealers with those names, the numbers rise to 13 firms, 52 instruments, and ten music dealers.

[22] The precise relationships are not altogether clear: Hannah (1810–87) was the daughter of Richard Binfield, and took over the family music business at Reading when Richard died in 1839; Rosa (also called Louisa) was probably her sister; Hannah definitely had three brothers: John Bilson, Thomas Sears (d. 1840), who was a member of the Royal Society of Musicians, and 'R.L.', none of whose initials, then, match those in the ledger; see Brown and Stratton, *British Musical Biography*, p. 47.

[23] On 22 June; see Wayne, *The Wheatstone Story* (forthcoming).

[24] On Regondi and the Binfields, see Rogers, 'Giulio Regondi', pt ii, pp. 16–17; Atlas, *The Wheatstone English Concertina*, p. 80. The three works that Regondi dedicated to members of the Binfield family are: *Introduction and Variations on an Austrian Air*, Op. 1, to Hannah; *Serenade*, to Rosa; and *Remembrance*, for unaccompanied baritone concertina, to Thomas Sears Binfield. Rogers has recently recorded the *Serenade* and *Remembrance* on *The Great Regondi*, vols 1 and 2, Bridge Records, BCD 1039 and 1055; there is an edition of the *Serenade* in Atlas, *The Wheatstone English Concertina*, pp. 123–37.

Surely, the buyer is William Price Aylward, who, with seven children, all of whom were musicians, seems to have been intent on outfitting the entire family with concertinas.[25]

Thus the Binfields and the Aylwards purchased 11 concertinas in a little more than a month. We can only wonder about how many other such concertina-playing families dotted the English countryside.

Members of the titled aristocracy

Business with the titled aristocracy proceeded as usual at the beginning of 1851, with sales to at least two such customers. On 16 January, Lady Catherine Loftus exchanged one concertina for another, paying a 'step-up' fee of 2 guineas in the process. Lady Catherine, whose full name was Catherine Henrietta Mary Tottenham, was the daughter of John, second Marquis of Ely.[26]

The second titled buyer, also a woman, was Lady Elizabeth Fuller, who bought a concertina on 12 March. Though I cannot identify her quite as precisely, we may assume, given the title 'Lady' followed by her own Christian name, that she was the daughter of a duke, marquis or earl, and married – below her rank – into the then untitled Fuller family of Neston Park, Wiltshire.[27]

More than respectable gentlemen

The Wheatstone ledger for our three months adds the seemingly ubiquitous 'Esquire' – a tribute that by the mid-nineteenth century was rather short on precise meaning – after the names of 13 customers. Here I should like to speculate about the identity of one of them: 'John Ellis,

---

[25] On the Aylwards, see Brown and Stratton, *British Musical Biography*, p. 19.

[26] *Burke's Genelogical and Heredilary History of the Peerage, Baronetage and Knightage*, 105th edn, ed. Peter Townend, London, 1970, pp. 941–2.

[27] On the Fullers, who would obtain a baronetcy in 1910, see *Burke's Peerage*, pp. 1054–5. For an exceptionally clear and concise explanation of the different contexts in which the title 'Lady' is used and the rank it denotes depending upon that context, see D. Pool, *What Jane Austin Ate and Charles Dickens Knew*, New York, 1993, p. 330. Perhaps there was a third titled customer, the Hon. William Farquarson, who purchased his concertina on 13 March. I cannot say whether he 'earned' the title as a Member of Parliament, or whether it was of the 'courtesy' type, bestowed upon the son of a viscount or baron, a younger son of an earl, or given his likely Scottish origins, the offspiring of a 'Thaine of the Estate'. On the use of the term 'honourable', see Pool, *What Jane Austin Ate*, p. 322; my thanks to Professor Stuart Prall for calling my attention to the Scottish title.

Esq.', and suggest that he is none other than Alexander John Ellis (1814–90), best known to musicians as the translator of Hermann Helmholtz's *Die Lehre von den Tonempfindungen*, to which, in the second edition of the translation (1885), he added notes that summarized his own research on tuning and acoustics.[28]

I lean towards him for two reasons. First, the Wheatstone ledgers list a Mr Ellis on at least three prior occasions, with entries on 4 October and 1 November 1839, and 10 September 1847, recording sales to one 'A. J. Ellis', and with the second of these entries adding the designation 'Esq.' after his name.[29] And while there could certainly have been two concertina players named Ellis, one John and the other A[lexander] J[ohn] (as I would expand the initials 'A. J.'), it strains our sense of coincidence a bit. Second, when Alexander John Ellis added the results of his own research to the second edition of his Helmholtz translation, he discussed the concertina's 'old' – that is, pre-1860s – meantone tuning, and did so with a sense of familiarity that one would hardly expect from someone who had only a casual acquaintance with the instrument.[30] In all, Alexander John Ellis, musician-mathematician-philologist, is precisely the type of customer that Wheatstone and Co. strove to cultivate.

Some men of science and/or their relatives

On 14 March, the ledger records a sale to one 'Mr Trevithick'. This is probably a relative of the Richard Trevithick (1771–1833) who played a major role in the development of the steam engine, perhaps one of his four sons.[31]

Eleven days later, on 25 March, Wheatstone and Co. sold a concertina to a gentleman whom I would identify as a notable scientist-inventor in his own right: Mr Alexander Bell. I believe that the entry refers to Alexander Melville Bell (1819–1905), father of Alexander Graham of telephone fame. Like Charles Wheatstone, Alexander Melville was interested in the physics of sound. Moreover, he was especially drawn to

---

[28] The translation, entitled *On the Sensations of Tone as a Psychological Basis for the Theory of Music*, first appeared in 1875.

[29] These appear in the ledger that was catalogued as C 1046 in the Concertina Museum; they are reported in Wayne, *The Wheatstone Story* (forthcoming).

[30] A. J. Ellis, *On the Sensations of Tone*, 6th edn, New York, 1948, pp. 321, 434, 446; on the question of the concertina's meantone tuning, see Atlas, *The Wheatstone English Concertina*, pp. 39–47.

[31] For a biography of Trevithick, see Francis Trevithick, *Life of Richard Trevithick*, 2 vols, London, 1872.

the work that Wheatstone had carried out in the 1830s on the mechanical imitation of human speech, and not only borrowed books from Wheatstone, but visited him (with the 16-year-old Alexander Graham in tow) in 1863 (if not before).[32]

Finally, that same shared interest – with Charles Wheatstone, that is – in the science of sound leads me to risk identifying another customer of 25 March: could the Mr Hinton who bought two concertinas that day be James Hinton (1822–75), the most well-known aural surgeon of the period? Hinton, we know, was passionately fond of music, and even dabbled at composition.[33]

In the end – and assuming, of course, that my identifications of Messrs Ellis, Bell and Hinton are correct – we might conjecture that all three men were drawn to the concertina, at least initially, more out of their intellectual sympathy for the scientific work and inventions of Charles Wheatstone, than by their love of the instrument itself (though I should like to think that familiarity bred passion).

Women, military officers and clergymen

Of the 140 or so people who purchased concertinas during our three-month period, 33 were women. Thus women constituted almost 25 per cent of Wheatstone's trade that winter. In addition, the ledger makes it clear that at least three instruments purchased or rented by men definitely found their way into female hands, while any number of others may have shared the same destiny. Indeed, Wheatstone and other concertina manufacturers marketed the concertina as an instrument especially suitable for women. Their strategy finds clear expression in Alfred B. Sedgwick's tutor, *Complete System of Instructions for the Concertina*, which, after describing some of the instrument's advantages, states: 'To Ladies it is particularly recommendable from its extreme elegance and portability, as also on account of its being the only *wind*

---

[32] See R. V. Bruce, *Bell: Alexander Graham Bell and the Conquest of Solitude*, Boston, 1973, *passim*.

[33] In a letter of March 1851 to his future wife, Margaret Haddon, Hinton writes: 'I send you some music to copy. It is a chant of my own composing ... '; see Ellice Hopkins, *Life and Letters of James Hinton*, London, 1878. That the ledger refers to him as 'Mr' instead of 'Dr' is in keeping with the custom of the time; see Pool, *What Jane Austin Ate*, pp. 250–51, 379.

As inviting as this identification is, there is another, equally strong – perhaps even stronger – candidate: J. Hinton, the Birmingham 'Maker and Repairer' of instruments; see Wayne, *The Wheatstone Story* (forthcoming).

instrument at their command.[34] One contemporary writer, William
Cawdell, was simply enchanted by female concertinists:

> I must not omit to speak of lady concertinists; I have heard of the
> dangers of *Croquet* to young men of a susceptible turn of mind,
> but I think that those perils cannot be compared to the fascination
> of a group of young ladies in a magic semicircle practising selec-
> tions on several Concertinas. I remember once being present at
> such a scene, and I went home suffering from heart affection and
> Concertina on the brain combined. I recovered entirely from the
> first, but the effects of the latter have not quite disappeared.[35]

One of the women who visited Wheatstone and Co. was Mrs Newman
Smith, who rented a concertina on 25 February. That she continued to
enjoy – and apparently promote – the instrument is evident both from
her studies with Regondi and from the appearance of her name as
'dedicatee' on the title-pages of three pieces for the concertina: Julius
Benedict's *Andantino* (1858) and Bernhard Molique's two sets of six
miniatures, *Flying Leaves*, Op. 50 (1856) and *Six Characteristic Pieces*,
Op. 61 (1859).[36]
As for the military and the clergy: the former was represented by a
colonel, three captains and a lieutenant. The association between the
concertina and the officer corps was a strong one. As that devotee of
female concertinists, William Cawdell, put it:

> [the concertina] … has been regarded as fit only for a parting
> present to some cadet fresh from Sandhurst about to embark for
> India who might in the retirement of his bungalow at Muddle-a-
> poor-head, learn to draw out the notes of 'Home! Sweet Home',
> while yearning for the realization of the idea.[37]

---

[34] A. B. Sedgwick, *Sedgwick's Complete System of Instructions for the Concertina*,
London, [1848?], p. 1; Sedgwick was one of the founding members of the Concertina
Quartet (see above) and was among the first to introduce the concertina to the music
halls, this no later than April 1851; see Atlas, *The Wheatstone English Concertina*, p. 57,
n. 45.
By November 1851 at the latest, Sedgwick had emigrated to the United States, settling
down in Brooklyn. There and throughout the greater New York area he continued to
perform on the concertina, though this took second place to his career as a composer for
the musical theatre; see Michael Meckna, *The Collected Works of Alfred B. Sedgwick*,
Nineteenth-Century American Musical Theater, 7, New York, 1994, pp. xiii–xvii.
[35] W. Cawdell, *A Short Account of the English Concertina, its Uses and Capabilities,
Facility of Acquirement, and other Advantages*, London, 1865, p. 17. This 23–page
'history' seems to be the first extended apologia for the instrument. That Cawdell
thought it necessary to write one shows, perhaps, that the shift in the concertina's social
status was already under way.
[36] On Mrs Smith's studies with Regondi, see Rogers, 'Giulio Regondi', pt i, p. 3, n. 5.
[37] Cawdell, *A Short Account of the English Concertina*, p. 14.

On the other hand, the accounts for the three months include no one who can be securely identified as a clergyman.[38]

A family affair

As already noted, both the Aylwards of Salisbury and the Binfields of Reading were concertina-playing families. Although they were involved in music as a profession, the notion of the concertina as a family instrument seems to have appealed even more strongly to households in which, so far as I can tell, music was a purely recreational pursuit. Thus the ledger acounts for sales to one 'Mr-Mrs-Miss' threesome, two 'Mr and Mrs' pairs, three combinations of one parent plus offspring, one pair of sisters, and perhaps a pair of brothers. Further, at least 40 gentlemen for whom I can find no obvious ties to music as a profession bought concertinas by the pair, presumably one for themselves and one for another member of the family.

In all, to the extent that I can identify Wheatstone and Co.'s customers during the winter of 1851 with some confidence, what we see is a mid-century clientele drawn exclusively from Victorian England's privileged élite: members of the titled aristocracy; distinguished men of science, letters and commerce; soldiers of officer rank; patrons and organizers of musical life; as well as professional musicians, respected music publishers and instrument dealers, and even, perhaps, one of London's most fashionable hotels. Bearing in mind the adage that a picture is worth a lot of words, I can think of nothing that better depicts the 'English' concertina's upper-class social standing than the frontispiece to the third edition of Edward Chidley's *Instructions for the Concertina*, published in London in 1854. It is Wheatstone's sales ledgers come to life pictorially (see Plate 4.1).

With respect to the concertinas themselves, I shall offer three brief observations. First, although the ledger does not describe the concertinas sold,[39] we can probably assume that the vast majority of the instruments traded were 48–button trebles which, by the middle of the century, had become the standard type; in fact, only three of them are definitely known to have been anything else.[40] Second, according to the serial

---

[38] On the use of the concertina by members of the clergy, see Atlas, *The Wheatstone English Concertina*, pp. 6–7; Percy Scholes, *The Mirror of Music: 1844–1944*, vol. 2, Oxford, 1947, p. 814.

[39] There is one ledger that does so: C 1054, to use its old catalogue number at the Concertina Museum, which covers the period March 1866–December 1891; unfortunately this ledger does not name the buyers.

[40] Concertina No. 105 was a 28–button treble, originally sold to one Reverend J.

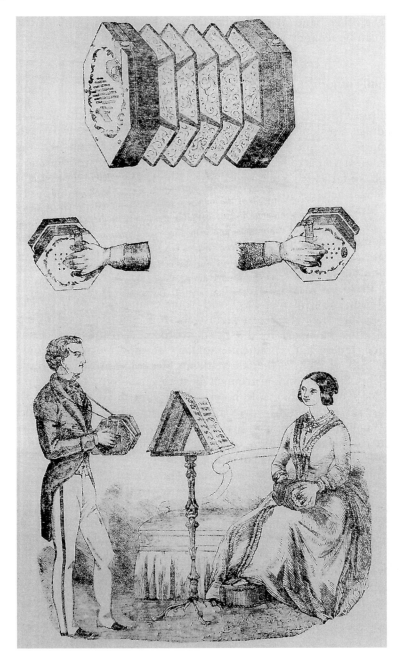

Plate 4.1   Edward Chidley, *Chidley's Instructions for the Concertina*, 3rd edn (London, 1854), frontispiece

numbers of the instruments, the overwhelming majority of the concertinas were relatively new, that is, manufactured within the last year or two.[41] If anything, it is difficult to say why the three customers who purchased the concertinas with the serial numbers 105, 344 and 759, would have wanted them; they date, at the very latest, from 1836, 1839 and 1843, respectively,[42] and would probably have had their original reeds of nickel alloy instead of the then current brass.[43] Third, buyers were not at all adverse to purchasing second-hand concertinas, as witness the 17 instruments that were sold, returned and sold again during the three months.[44]

Finally, a note about prices:[45] the most expensive concertina sold during our three-month period went for 14 guineas and would have looked rather like the slightly later (1858) instrument shown in Plate 4.2. And though Wheatstone and Co. sold only one such instrument at that price during the three months, they sold as many as 26 for between £10 and 13 guineas.[46] By far the most popular instruments, however, were those that cost either six guineas or £7 17s. 6d., of which 70 and 49, respectively, were sold, often as a pair.[47] As for the bottom of the price range: this is less well defined, since one must always wonder, when the price dips to £3 or below, if the entry is simply failing to note that the transaction was an 'exchange', with the recorded price then

---

Craig on 25 October 1836; No. 759 was a 44–button tenor; No. 2891 was a 48–button baritone, now part of The Horniman collection. My thanks to Stephen Chambers for the information about these instruments.

[41] For guides that offer approximate correlations between serial numbers and date of manufacture, see Richard Carlin, 'Dating Wheatstone Concertinas', *Mugwumps*, 7, (1), (1981), 16–18; Nigel Pickles, 'Dates for Wheatstone Concertinas', *Concertina and Squeezebox*, 14–15 (1987), 69.

[42] The dates are based on what seems to be their earliest appearance in the ledgers. On Nos 105 and 759, see footnote 40.

[43] Brass would soon be supplanted by steel, which is still used for the reeds of the concertina.

[44] Two instruments were even marketed three times, though the second and third of these transactions resulted from the two-step process in which Giulio Regondi first picked up an already used concertina for a student and then passed it on to him/her, with the student then paying for it in a separate transaction.

[45] I have considered only those that the ledger records in absolutely unambiguous fashion; at times the prices of two or more instruments will be lumped together in such a way that the price of any individual instrument is not altogether clear.

[46] Perhaps some of the most expensive instruments were baritones; see footnote 48, below.

[47] Perhaps we may speculate that, when sold as a pair, they were often intended for husband and wife, and that the extra £1 11s 6d. for the more expensive instrument – meant for the woman(?) – was for something 'cosmetic', such as a little extra gold tooling or inlay, or a more elaborate design on the bellows.

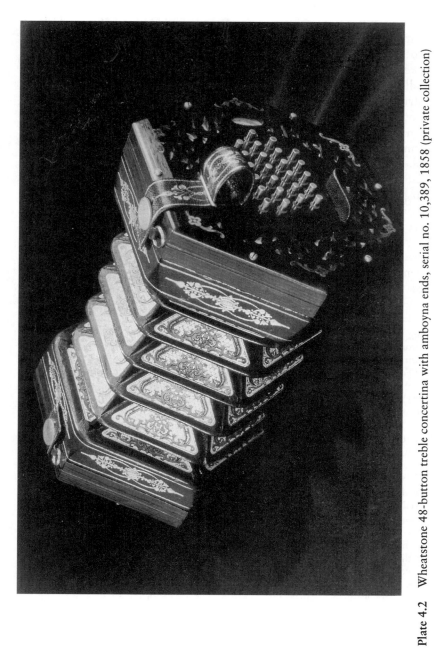

Plate 4.2 Wheatstone 48-button treble concertina with amboyna ends, serial no. 10,389, 1858 (private collection)

representing a 'step-up' fee as one instrument was swapped for a more expensive one.[48]

In all, Wheatstone's prices go a long way in explaining why the concertina enjoyed the social status that it did. Given an average working man's salary of about 15s. a week,[49] even Wheatstone's 'popular' concertina at 6 guineas would have cost the equivalent of about two months' wages, and then only if the wage earner and family deprived themselves of life's necessities. Only in the 1860s, when Louis Lachenal and other manufacturers began to master the art of mass production and – with the likes of Lachenal's 2-guinea 'People's Concertina' (see footnote 48) – peg prices to less affluent wallets, did the present-day image of the concertina – the 'English' included – as an instrument of the working classes begin to take shape. And only after another decade or so during which it was something of an instrument for 'all classes' did the concertina finally relinquish, once and for all, its proud place among Victorian England's social élite.[50]

Appendix A

Appendix A provides a summary of Wheatstone and Co.'s concertina sales, rentals, exchanges and loans for the period January–March 1851. Though I examined the original sales ledger that records the transactions when it was still housed at the Concertina Museum, Belper (catalogue No. C 1047), the summary is based primarily on computer generated, cross-referenced transcripts – by date, alphabetical list of names and instrument serial number – kindly provided me by Mr Neil Wayne (see

---

[48] On the other hand, the range of prices may have stretched to under £3. A decade later, in 1862, the manufacturer Louis Lachenal, then Wheatstone's main competitor, would issue a catalogue in which prices ranged from as little as 2 guineas for his 'People's Concertina' with mahogony ends to 22 guineas for an amboyna, ivory-topped baritone concertina; see *The International Exhibition of 1862: The Illustrated Catalogue of the Industrial Department*, vol. 2, London, 1862, p. 112, and Atlas, *The Wheatstone English Concertina*, p. 6, n. 19, and p. 10. Lachenal, a one-time employee of Wheatstone, set up his own workshop in 1859; see Wayne, *The Wheatstone Story* (forthcoming).

[49] J. F. C. Harrison, *The Early Victorians: 1832–1851*, New York, 1971, p. 66; P. Howarth, *The Year 1851*, London, 1951, p. 83.

[50] George Gissing caught the situation accurately in his novel *The Netherworld* of 1889. Describing one of the central characters, Bob Hewett, who earns his living as a die-sinker, Gissing writes: 'Then he was clever in a good many other ways. He had an ear for music, played (*nothing else was in his reach* [my italics]) the concertina ... ' (in the World's Classics edition, ed. Stephen Gill [Oxford, 1992], p. 70. How striking a difference with the characters who play the concertina in Wilkie Collins's novels of about a quarter of a century earlier!

footnote 8 above), whose generosity I should like to acknowledge once again. I am also grateful to Dr Frances Palmer, Curator of Musical Instruments at The Horniman Museum, London, who provided me with yet another transcript. Finally, my thanks to Mr Stephen Chambers of Dublin for information about instruments 105, 759, and 2891.

The six columns provide the following information:

No.: the entry nos are editorial.
Date: the date given holds until succeeded by another one.
Customer: successive transactions by the same buyer are signalled with ditto marks; the ledger's 'Mr' is retained only when gender might otherwise be in doubt.
Serial No.: each instrument had its own serial number, which was customarily recorded in the ledger.
Price: I have omitted this for both rentals and exchanges, as well as for 'bulk' sales in which the price of an individual instrument is not entirely clear.
Comments: while these serve mainly to identify the buyers, they also draw attention to such matters as multiple sales of the same instrument, exchanges of instruments, rental and 'step-up' fees (the latter when an instrument was exchanged for a more expensive one); finally, they refer the reader to appropriate places in the text.

The bibliographical references and their sigla are:

AltickS	R. D. Altick, *The Shows of London*, Cambridge, MA, 1978.
AtlasW	A. W. Atlas, *The Wheatstone English Concertina in Victorian England*, Oxford, 1996.
BMB	J. D. Brown and S. S. Stratton, *British Musical Biography*, London, 1897; reprint, New York, 1971.
DNB	*The Dictionary of National Biography*, 22 vols, ed. L. Stephen and S. Lee, London, 1963–64.
HopL	E. Hopkins, *Life and Letters of James Hinton*, London, 1878.
LangI	L. G. Langwill, *An Index of Musical Wind-Instrument Makers*, 6th edn Edinburgh, 1980.
MMP	*Music Printing and Publishing*. The Norton/Grove Handbooks, eds D. W. Krummel and S. Sadie, New York, 1990.
ParkV	J. A. Parkinson, *Victorian Music Publishers: An Annotated List*, Detroit Studies in Music Bibliography, 14, Warren, MI, 1990.
WayneW	N. Wayne, 'The Wheatstone English Concertina', *The Galpin Society Journal*, 44 (1991), 117–490.

WayneWS   N. Wayne, *The Wheatstone Story: The Life and Works of Charles Wheatstone* (forthcoming).

Page numbers follow sigla in the sixth column.

No.	Date	Customer	Serial No.	Price (£ s. d.)	Comments
1	January 1	Grindlay & Co.	3144	6.6.0	Perhaps the banking firm of that name
2	2	Miss Tattersall	2311		See Nos 19, 47; perhaps related to William DeChair Tattersall (1752–1829), compiler of psalm collections (*BMB*, 405; *DNB*, vol.19, 388–9); instrument subsequently returned and sold twice; see Nos 77, 98
3		John Ellis, Esq.	2319	6.6.0	Alexander John Ellis; see text
4		Thomas Birt	2828	7.17.6	
5		"	2829	7.17.6	
6	3	Miss Jane Long	?		Rental for a fee of 1 guinea
7	6	Mrs Hughes	2343	5.5.0	There is a 'B' in the margin; its meaning is not clear
8		[Mr] Ashe	3149	6.6.0	From Exeter; see Nos 74–5
9	January 7	Mr Earles	3212	6.6.0	
10		[Mr?] Wood	3150	6.6.0	He (?) was from Cambridge
11		[Mr?] Wood	2838	7.17.6	
12	8	John St Claire	3089		Rental
13		"	2210		Rental
14		Dr Simpson	2895		Rental and exchange; he had purchased a concertina on at least one earlier occasion (WayneWS)
15		Wood & Co.	2850	7.10.0	The Edinburgh music publisher-instrument dealer (ParkV, 301; *MMP*, 482); they had been buying concertinas for at least a decade; returned the instrument, which was subsequently sold again; see No. 188; see Nos 144–6
16		"	2851	7.10.0	
17		"	2852	7.10.0	

No.	Date	Customer	Serial No.	Price (£ s. d.)	Comments
18		"	2853	7.10.0	
19	9	Mrs Tattersall	2334		Rental; see Nos 2, 47
20		Hale & Son	3213	6.6.0	Charles Hale & Son, music publisher-dealer (ParkV, 114)
21		Charles Bowyer, Esq.	2840	10.10.0	Probably related to Capt. Bowyer; see No. 38; related to the well-known miniature-painter Robert Bowyer?
22		Mrs Dundas	2897		= Dandas/Dandar? exchange
23	11	[Mr] Hutcheson, Esq.	2898	12.12.0	Possibly Charles Hutcheson (1792–1852), founder of the Glasgow Dilettanti; published *Christian Vespers*, a collection of harmonized hymn tunes (1832) (*BMB*, 213–14); returned the instrument by 14 Jan.; see No. 40; it was later rented by Mrs Newman Smith; see No. 169
24		Mrs Winstanley	2719		Rental at 5s.; returned instrument before 3 Apr.
25		Mr F. Wright	1978	12.12.0	
26		Miss Kirkby	2858		Exchange with fee of 2 guineas; a student of Blagrove (?); see No. 184
27		Miss Holland	2862		Exchange with fee of 2 guineas; marginal note: 7 weeks; daughter of the Hollands who bought instruments on 16 Jan. and 17 Feb.; see Nos 44, 132
28	January 13	Mr F. Povey	2846	7.17.6	
29		Mr Gib	1998		This and next transaction were exchanges at 2 guineas
30		"	2687		Wardle Evans would buy this instrument on 30 Jan; see No. 84
31		Thomas Beswick	3004	10.4.9	Instrument returned and sold again on 8 Feb.; see No. 106
32		"	2841	7.17.6	
33		"	2843	7.17.6	Returned instrument by 5 Feb.; see No. 102

No.	Date	Customer	Serial No.	Price (£ s. d.)	Comments
34		"	2260	6.6.0	Instrument returned by 1 Feb.; see No. 87; he thus returned three of the six instruments purchased
35		"	2444	6.6.0	
36		"	1692	5.10.0	
37	14	Miss Badger	2856	7.17.6	
38		Captain Bowyer	2855		Probably related to Charles Bowyer, Esq.; see No. 21; exchange with fee of 3 guineas
39		Lieutenant Dymok	3006	13.13.0	= Dymoke (?)
40		[Mr] Hutcheson, Esq.	3003		Exchange for No. 2898, with fee of 1 guinea; see No. 23
41		Miss Hulse	2701		Rental and exchange; instruments returned by 27 Jan.; see No. 79
42		Signor Regondi	2898		Giulio Regondi; see text; first of seven entries for him; instrument borrowed
43	16	Lady Catherine Loftus	2847		An exchange with fee of 2 guineas; on Lady Catherine, see text
44		Mrs Holland	2068		See Nos 27, 132; instrument returned by 25 Feb.
45		George Field	3152	6.6.0	
46		"	2839	7.10.0	
47	January 17	Miss Tattersall	2615	9.9.0	See Nos 2, 19
48		Brown's	2158		See text and n. 19
49		"	2159		
50		"	2160		
51		"	2161		
52		"	2162		
53		"	3188		
54		"	2925		
55		"	3170		
56		"	3171		
57		"	3172		
58		"	3173		
59	18	Hume & Son	3115	6.6.0	Firm of Alexander Hume & Son, Liverpool and Glasgow-Edinburgh (BMB, XX); all sales to Liverpool branch
60		"	3116	6.6.0	
61		"	3217	6.6.0	For this and the next transaction, marginal note 'S', meaning unclear
62		"	3218	6.6.0	

No.	Date	Customer	Serial No.	Price (£ s. d.)	Comments
63		[Mr?] Smith	3174	3.18.9	Resided in Liverpool
64		"	3153	6.6.0	
65	22	Mr Gib	2899		An exchange; after returning two instruments, he kept this one; see Nos 29–30
66		Mr J. W. Holder	?	7.17.6	He bought two more instruments on 1 Apr.
67		Thomas Reynolds, Esq.	833	6.6.0	Purchased for Miss Rome; there was a Thomas Reynolds, bandmaster of the '2nd Light Infantry' (BMB, 342); see No. 164
68	24	[Mr] C. Barrington, Esq.	759		Rental for Miss Perse
69	25	Miss Humphreys	2632		Rental
70		Lindley Nunn	2805	7.17.6	Professional concertinist; see text
71	January 27	Mr Higham	3219	6.6.0	Surely Joseph Higham (see Nos 220–21), the Manchester instrument dealer; see text
72		"	3220	6.6.0	
73		"	2869	7.17.6	
74		"	2876	7.17.6	Instrument returned by 6 Mar.
75		Mr Ashe	2859	7.17.6	See No. 8
76		"	3154	6.6.0	
77		Henry St John, Esq.	2311	4.8.0	Instrument previously had by Miss Tattersale, No. 2; returned by 4 Feb., see No. 98; he also purchased a flute; Wheatstone's father had been a flute maker (LangI, 168; WayneW, 118, 148); see No. 80
78		Mr Newman	1463		Rental; resided at 122 Piccadilly
79		Mr Dipple	2701	7.17.6	The concertinist T. J. Dipple; see text
80	30	Henry St John, Esq.	2848		Exchange with fee of 2 guineas; see No. 77
81		Signor Regondi	2837	10.10.0	Second of seven transactions
82		Mr Case	2000	9.10.0	The noted virtuoso, George Tinkler Case; see text; he will purchase another instrument on 25 Mar.; see No. 172

No.	Date	Customer	Serial No.	Price (£ s. d.)	Comments
83		Cocks & Co.	2135	3.15.0	Robert Cocks & Co., music publisher-dealer (*MMP*, 203; ParkV, 55–6); see text
84		Wardle E. Evans	2687	7.17.6	Professional concertinist; see text; instrument first purchased on 13 Jan. by Mr Gib; see No. 30
85	31	John Haseldine	3175	5.5.0	
86		Ernest Peste	2896	13.13.0	
87	February 1	Miss Campbell	2260		Rental and exchange; instrument first purchased on 13 Jan. by Mr Beswick; see No. 34
88		Thomas Stratford	2802	7.17.6	
89		"	3177	3.8.9	
90		"	3221	6.6.0	
91	February 4	Mr Rose	2224	6.6.0	From Bedford, where there was an organist named Robert Rose at St Paul's (*BMB*, 355)
92		"	2864	7.17.6	
93		Mr Fritchler	3223	6.6.0	= Tretschler?
94		"	2861	7.17.6	
95		Mr Field	2857	7.17.6	No doubt the Joseph Field who made two purchases on 16 Jan.; see Nos 45–6
96		Mr Palmer	2842	7.10.0	Presumably T. L. Palmer, who returned this instrument and bought two others on 3 Mar.; see Nos 207–8; could he be related (father?) to Thomas Palmer, organist-conductor-composer, who graduated from Cambridge in 1879? (*BMB*, 307)
97		Miss Gardner	2734	9.9.0	An exchange; for her probable father, see Nos 195–6
98		Mr J. Brinsmead	2311	5.5.0	Third and final time this instrument was sold; see Nos 2, 77
99		"	3222	5.5.0	
100		[Mr?] Burkingyoung	2748	7.17.6	This and next instrument shipped 13 Feb.
101		"	2749	7.17.6	

No.	Date	Customer	Serial No.	Price (£ s. d.)	Comments
102	5	Mr Errol	2843	7.10.0	Instrument purchased earlier by Mr Beswick on 13 Jan.; see No. 33
103		Mr J. L. Clark	2849		Exchange with fee of £3 15s. 0d.; probably the James Clark who bought an instrument on 22 Feb.; see No. 153
104	7	Miss Poole	2868		Exchange with fee of £1 11s. 6d.
105	8	Miss Fletcher	2952	13.13.0	Returned the instrument by 23 Feb.; see No. 163
106		Mr A. Zanzi	3004	9.9.0	Instrument first purchased by Mr Beswick on 13 Jan. for £10 4s. 9d.; see No. 31
107		Colonel Dunn	3225		Exchange with fee of £4 10s. 0d.
108	10	Mr Simms	3226	6.6.0	Perhaps a member of the Simms family that produced generations of organists (BMB, 373–4)
109		"	2885	7.17.6	
110		Mr Wigley	3228		Wheatstone employed a Mr Wigley at least in 1848–49 (WayneWS); perhaps related to the Charles Wigley who made wind instruments in 1799–1825 (LangI, 189) and who is probably to be identified with the jeweller of that name who ran 'Wigley's great Promenade Room' (AltickS, 72); this instrument and the next provided as 'samples'; this one returned within two days; see No. 113
111		"	2886		
112	February 12	Miss Binfield	2891	9.9.0	Hannah or Rosa; see text and Nos 216, 236, 241; a baritone concertina
113		Mr Hale	3228		Exchange with fee of 1 guinea; Charles Hale of Hale & Son?; see No. 20; had Wigley taken the instrument to show it to him?; see No. 109

No.	Date	Customer	Serial No.	Price (£ s. d.)	Comments
114	13	Signor Regondi	3203	10.10.0	Regondi's third instrument
115		Mr W. Prowse	2888	9.9.0	See text, fn. 19
116	14	Mr Henry Bridger	2866	7.17.6	
117		"	2884	7.17.6	
118		Mr F. Greenwell	2464	5.2.6	
119		Mr J. D. Morris	3231	6.6.0	
120		"	3232	6.6.0	
121	15	Mr W. P. Aylward	2872	7.17.6	On the Aylwards of Salisbury, see text
122		"	2873	7.17.6	
123		"	3233	6.6.0	
124		"	2874	7.17.6	
125		Cramer & Co.	2880		The music publisher-dealer Johan Baptist Cramer (*MMP*, 208; ParkV, 62–63); see text; total sale = £42
126		"	2881		
127		"	2882		
128		"	2871		
129		"	2877		
130		"	2878		
131	17	Miss Lang	3237		Rental
132		Mr Holland, Esq.	2875	10.0.0	His daughter and wife had purchased instruments on 11 and 16 Jan.; see Nos 27, 44
133		Mr Silmond	2312	5.5.0	
134		Signor Regondi	2587		Fourth appearance; instrument loaned to him, and later rented by his student, Miss Binfield, 12 Mar.; see No. 236 and text
135	February 18	"	3204	10.0.0	Fifth appearance
136		Mrs Drake	2883		Exchange with fee of £3; probably the wife of Mr Drake; see No. 243
137		Mr Patch	2790		
138		John Renton	3251	6.6.0	An organ builder of that name in Edinburgh (LangI, 144)
139		"	3252	6.6.0	
140		"	2466	5.2.6	
141		"	1649	5.10.6	
142		[Mr] F. Thompson	2467	5.2.6	
143		"	3179	3.18.9	
144		Wood & Co.	3234		Total sale = £18
145		"	3235		
146		"	3236		

No.	Date	Customer	Serial No.	Price (£ s. d.)	Comments
147	19	Mrs Ling	3238	6.6.0	
148		"	2860	7.17.6	
149		Mr Lenter	3239	6.6.0	= Lesiter?
150		"	2941	7.17.6	
151		Miss Tilney Long	2887	10.0.0	
152		Mr Duncan	?	6.6.0	Two musicians named Duncan – Alexander and Arthur – active in Scotland at the time (*BMB*, 180–81)
153	22	James Clark	3242	6.6.0	Probably the J. L. Clark who exchanged an instrument on 5 Feb.; see No. 103
154		Mr J. H. New	3240	6.6.0	
155		"	3241	6.6.0	
156	23	Mr J. Spary	3244	6.6.0	
157		"	2943	7.17.6	
158		Mr P. J. Hellyer	3246	6.6.0	
159		"	2950	7.17.6	
160		John Beasley	1563		Rental
161		Miss Hulme	2961		Exchange with fee of 2 guineas
162		Paterson & Roy	3247	6.6.0	The Edinburgh music publisher-dealer (*BMB*, 312; *MMP*, 359); in the ledger spelled 'Patterson'
163		Captain Cowry	2952	10.10.0	Instrument purchased earlier by Miss Fletcher, who paid 3 guineas more for it; see No. 105
164		Mr Reynolds	2956	7.17.6	Probably the Thomas Reynolds who purchased an instrument on 22 Jan.; see No. 67
165	February 25	Mr Hinton	3248	6.6.0	Possibly the noted aural surgeon, James Hinton; see text (*DNB*, vol. 9, 581; HopL, 56); or possibly instrument maker J. Hinton; see text (WayneWS, 45)
166		"	2744	7.17.6	
167		Mr Treakell Senior	3253	6.6.0	= Trelkell?
168		"	2944	7.17.6	
169		Mrs Newman Smith	2898		Rental; instrument first purchased on 11 Jan. by Mr Hutcheson, who returned it by 14 Jan.; see Nos 23, 40; she was a student of Regondi and

No.	Date	Customer	Serial No.	Price (£ s. d.)	Comments
					the dedicatee of pieces by Benedict and Molique; see text
170		C. E. Ward, Esq.	3207		Exchange with fee of £6; possibly Cornelius Ward (b. 1814), composer, organist, teacher at Speen, Buckinghamshire (BMB, 431); probably related to W. H. Ward; see No. 180; are they both related to John Charles Ward (1835–1919), organist, concertinist, and one of the founders of the Henry Leslie choir? (AtlasW, 81)
171		Mr Mortimer	2443		Rental; his wife buys an instrument on 18 Mar.; see No. 247
172		George Case	2931	9.10.0	See No. 82
173		Miss Scudamore	2068		Rental
174		Captain Hopper	2942		Exchange with fee of 3.3.0
175	February 26	Mr W. H. Moore	2940	7.17.6	
176		"	3254	6.6.0	
177		"	2852	7.17.6	
178		"	3245	6.6.0	
179		Miss Anson	2966	10.10.0	Returned the instrument by 18 Mar.; see No. 248
180		W. H. Ward, Esc.	2946		Exchange with fee of 5 guineas; probably related to C. E. Ward; see No. 170
181		Mr B. Wells	3206	10.5.0	A Benjamin Wells (b. 1829) of Cambridge; taught flute at the RAM after studying there with John Clinton, who collaborated on occasion with Regondi (BMB, 439)
182		Mr Alexander	3201	10.5.0	Two tempting identifications: (1) James Alexander, who published Book of Instructions for the Accordion in 1845; (2) Lesley Alexander of 29 Campden Grove, Kensington, who stamped name and address on arrangements for concertina ensembles of

No.	Date	Customer	Serial No.	Price (£ s. d.)	Comments
					tunes from *La traviata* and *La Fille du regiment*; perhaps both identifications are undermined by the note that the buyer was residing in Paris
183		Lindley Nunn	2969	7.17.6	Purchased for a Mr or Mrs Freidach, probably a student; see text
184		Miss Kirkby	1919	6.6.0	Second instrument for her; see No. 26; a note mentions Richard Blagrove (her teacher?)
185	27	[Mr] W. J. Bodgett	3257	6.6.0	With 14 sales, the busiest day of the 3–month period
186		"	3258	6.6.0	
187			2954	7.17.6	
188		Henry Lee	2850	7.17.6	Could the name be 'Lea'?; see text, n. 12; one of the instruments that Wood & Co. purchased on 8 Jan. and then returned
189		"	3255	6.6.0	
190		Robert Darling	3261	6.6.0	
191		"	3262	6.6.0	
192		Cramer & Co.	3259	6.6.0	Had already bought 6 instruments on 14 Feb.; see Nos 125–30; these three sales to the Brighton branch
193		"	3260	6.6.0	
194			2959	7.17.6	
195		Mr L. Gardner	3263	6.6.0	Probably the father of the Miss Gardner who bought an instrument on 4 Feb.; see No. 97
196		"	3263	6.6.0	
197		Mr J. Tucker	3265	6.6.0	
198		"	3266	6.6.0	
199	February 28	Mr Neibour	2745	7.17.6	
200		"	3267	6.6.0	
201		Mr W. H. Sutton	3256	6.6.0	
202		"	3269	6.6.0	
203		"	2951	7.17.6	
204	March 1	Mr E. Lord	3160	9.9.0	Returned instrument by 20 Mar.; see No. 249
205	4	Mr J. Warren	3227	6.6.0	Certainly the Joseph Warren whose works for the concertina were performed by Regondi at

No.	Date	Customer	Serial No.	Price (£ s. d.)	Comments
					the 1837 Birmingham Festival; see text
206		"	2962	7.17.6	
207	5	Mr T. L. Palmer	3271	6.6.0	See No. 95
208		"	3272	6.6.0	
209		Mr W. Norfill	3270	6.6.0	
210		"	2955	7.17.6	
211		Mr W. Loof	3268	6.6.0	
212		Miss Fulton	2968	10.10.0	
213		Leicester & Sons	2069		Rented; see text
214		"	3202	13.13.0	
215		Samuel Hatchard	2324	6.6.0	Resided in Hertford; related to the publishers-bookseller Hatchard & Son, who, however, have no prominent Samuel among them? (*DNB*, 9, 150)
216		Mr W. Binfield	3200	10.5.0	See text and Nos 112, 236, 241
217	March 6	Mr Huchinson, Esq.	3159	12.12.0	Probably the T. Huchinson, Esq., who purchased a concertina a decade earlier, on 23 Jan. 1841
218		Mr Peckler	2876		Wheatstone and Co. employed a Mr Peckler at least in 1848–49 (WayneWS); instrument first purchased on 27 Jan. by Joseph Highham; see No. 71
219		"	2842		Instrument first bought by Mr Palmer on 4 Feb.; see No. 95
220	7	Joseph Highham	2971	7.17.6	See No. 71
221		"	2972	7.17.6	
222		Miss Verburen	1812		Rental and exchange
223		Mrs Frederick Brand	2965	7.17.6	Purchased for Mrs Rackmarsh
224	8	Signor Regondi	3158	9.9.0	Sixth visit to the shop
225		Mr Peckler	3273	6.6.0	Probably the Wheatstone employee, though he usually did not pay for the instruments (see also Nos 218–19, 234–5)
226	10	Joseph Sowerey	3161	6.6.0	
227		Mr Aylward	3274	6.6.0	See No. 121
228		"	105	4.0.0	Instrument (with 28 keys) was sold at least as early as 25 Oct. 1836, when it

No.	Date	Customer	Serial No.	Price (£ s. d.)	Comments
					was purchased by the Revd J. Craig, and is the oldest instrument traded during the three months; purchased for 'Addison'
229		"	2146	2.7.6	Exchange with a 'step-up' fee?
230		Mr Peckler	1996		See No. 218; marginal comment reads: 'To make stands to'
231		"	1999		
232	11	Mr Molyneux	3275	6.6.0	
233		"	3276	6.6.0	
234		"	3277	6.6.0	
235		"	3278	6.6.0	
236	March 12	Miss Binfield	2587		Hannah or Rosa; see No. 112 and text; rental; Regondi had borrowed this instrument for her on 17 Feb.; see No. 134 and text
237		Signor Regondi	3162		Seventh and final visit during this period; instrument taken for Mr W. Brown; see No. 240
238		Lady Elizabeth Fuller	2983	10.0.0	See text
239	14	Mr Trevithick	2963	10.10.0	A relative (son?) of Richard Trevithick, the famous engineer? see text
240		Mr W. Brown	3162	9.4.0	A student of Regondi, who had taken the instrument for him two days earlier (No. 237); on his possible identity, see text, note 19
241		Mr W. Binfield	2283		See text
242	15	Wardle E. Evans	3279	6.0.0	See text and No. 84
243	17	Mr Drake	2883		Rental; probably the husband of Mrs Drake; see No. 136
244		Mr R. Purdie	3280	6.6.0	Not Robert Purdie, the Edinburgh music dealer-publisher, who died in 1837 (MMP, 382); BMB, 332, lists him as active until c. 1887, but probably confuses him with his son John; perhaps this Purdie is another son

No.	Date	Customer	Serial No.	Price (£ s. d.)	Comments
245		"	3281	6.6.0	
246		"	2964	7.17.6	
247	18	Mrs Mortimer	2976	10.10.0	Probably the wife of Mr Mortimer; see No. 171
248		Hon. William Farquarson	2966		See text; the fee of 5 guineas covered an exchange; instrument first purchased by Miss Anson; see No. 179; he returned the instrument by 2 Apr., when it was purchased by Mr L. Hyde, Esq., at the same 10 guineas paid by Miss Anson
249	20	Joseph Higham	3160	9.9.0	See text and No. 71; instrument first purchased by Mr Lord on 1 Mar.; see No. 204
250		Joseph Higham	2755	7.17.6	
251		"	2756	7.17.6	
252	March 21	Dr J. W. Calvert	2967	10.0.0	
253		Miss W. Prowse	2927		Probably the daughter of William Prowse of the firm of Keith, Prowse; see No. 115; a marginal comment: 'sale'
254	25	Miss Tudor	2973		Also rented concertina 3773
255		Alexander Bell	3282	7.4.0	Probably Alexander Melville Bell; see text
256	26	Joseph Woodward	3457	6.0.0	
257	27	Miss Pelzer	2757		Anné or Catherine Josepha; see text; exchange with fee of £2 3s. 0d.
258		Matthew Liddell	2313	5.0.0	
259		"	3301	2.12.0	Exchange?
260		Thomas Myron, Esq.	3208		Exchange
261	28	A. J. R. Stewart, Esq.	3209	14.14.0	
262		Thomas Guest	3458	6.0.0	
263		"	344	4.10.0	

Appendix B

Appendix B provides an alphabetical list of those who purchased concertinas from Wheatstone and Co. during the period January–March 1851. The reference numbers guide the reader to the appropriate entries in Appendix A.

Alexander, Mr 182
Anson, Miss 179
Ashe, Mr 8, 75–6
Aylward, Mr W. P. 121–4, 227–9
Badger, Miss 37
Barrington, Esq., C. 68
Beasley, John 160
Bell, Alexander [Melville?] 255
Beswick, Thomas 31–6
Binfield, Miss [Hannah and/or Rosa] 112, 236
Binfield, Mr W. 216, 241
Birt, Thomas 4–5
Bodgett, [Mr] W. J. 185–7
Bowyer, Esq., Charles 21
Bowyer, Captain 38
Bridger, Henry 116–17
Brind, Mrs Frederick 223
Brown, Mr W. 240
Brown's [Hotel?] 48–58
Burkingyoung, [Mr?] 100–101
Calvert, Dr J. W. 252
Campbell, Miss 87
Case, George Tinkler 82, 172
Clark, James L. 103, 153
Cock's & Co. 83
Cowry, Captain 163
Cramer & Co. 125–30, 192–4
Darling, Robert 190–91
Dipple, Mr [T. J.?] 79
Drake, Mrs 136
Drake, Mr 243
Duncan, Mr 152
Dundas [= Dandas/Dandar?], Mrs 22
Dunn, Colonel 107

Dymok [= Dymoke?], Lieutenant 39
Earles, Mr 9
Ellis, Esq., [Alexander?] John 3
Errol, Mr 102
Evans, Wardle Eastland 84, 242
Farquarson, Hon. William 248
Field, George 45–6, 95
Fletcher, Miss 105
Fritchler, Mr 93–4
Fuller, Lady Elizabeth 238
Fulton, Miss 212
Gardner, Miss 97
Gardner, Mr L. 195–6
Gib, Mr 29–30, 65
Greenwell, Mr F. 118
Grindlay & Co. 1
Guest, Thomas 262–3
Hale, Mr 113
Hale & Son 20
Haseldine, John 85
Hatchard, Samuel 215
Hellyer, Mr P. J. 158–9
Higham, Joseph 71–4, 220–21, 249–51
Hinton, Mr [James? / J.?] 165–6
Holder, Mr J. W. 66
Holland, Miss 27
Holland, Mrs 44
Holland, Esq. 132
Hopper, Captain 174
Hughes, Mrs 7
Hulme, Miss 161
Hulse, Miss 42
Hume & Son 59–62
Humphreys, Miss 69

Violin Pedagogy in England during the first half of the Nineteenth Century, or *The Incompleat Tutor for the Violin*

David J. Golby

The subject of English, or for that matter British violinists is seldom discussed, largely because there are very few prominent figures associated with the instrument and native to this country who readily spring to mind.[1] There are, of course, some notable exceptions from the present century, but it would seem that the achievements of individuals prior to this generally give little cause for national pride. Although it is not unique to the violin (my own instrument), it is useful to investigate this situation as a symptom of broader trends and to take a look at the reasons why English performers in general were unable to make an impact in England before the latter part of the nineteenth century, and why those who were active before this time remain for the most part a footnote in history.

Significantly, two of the most recent and popular books containing biographical information on violinists, by Boris Schwarz and Margaret Campbell respectively,[2] begin sections devoted to British exponents with mention of foreign violinists. Schwarz, at the beginning of his chapter entitled 'The British School' writes: 'Traditionally, foreign violinists have always been received in England with great hospitality and warmth, but little encouragement was given to gifted British young men and women to pursue music as a profession' (p. 482). Campbell, opening a chapter devoted to Albert Sammons, writes in much the same vein:

---

[1] This area has received some attention recently with 'a look at the wider string scene in Britain' in 'the first STRAD issue of its kind' ('Britain in focus', *The Strad*, February (1998), 101) and the series of events organized under the title 'The British Violin' (Royal Academy of Music, 31 March to 11 April 1998); but the emphasis is firmly on violin-making and organology in both cases.

[2] B. Schwarz, *Great Masters of the Violin*, London, 1984; M. Campbell, *The Great Violinists*, London, 1980.

For well over two hundred years extending until the 1930s, Britain
was dominated by foreign musicians. The public fancied the British
lacked the charisma that surrounded the imported artist. Violinists
were the breed most affected by this prejudice. Spohr, Paganini,
Ysaÿe and Kreisler were all names with magical connotations. The
only alternative open to the British artist was to study abroad for a
couple of years, and return with a 'ski' or an 'ini' added to his
name. (p. 144)[3]

The predilection of British audiences for foreign musicians and the
resulting lack of encouragement for native aspiring instrumentalists had
far-reaching consequences, not least for the standard of education and
training offered, albeit within a vibrant, cosmopolitan cultural centre
with unrivalled concert and publishing activity. There was no shortage
of teachers, as the vast majority of performers (through choice or
financial hardship) supplemented their income in this way, and we have
no reason to believe there was a shortage of talent; but the opportunities to reach the highest level of practical musicianship were lacking,
along with the organized and systematic approach to pedagogy found
elsewhere at the turn of the nineteenth century, which was vital if the
situation was to be remedied.

The low status of music education in England during the first half of
the nineteenth century is hard to refute, but the period does provide
very rich sources of information on how this situation gradually changed
and how an awareness of the need to nurture native talent emerged.
Written instruction methods of the time are of course only part of the
story, but they do provide us with a unique insight into the practices
and priorities of the time, combining the practical and theoretical, as
documented by those teachers and theorists who were inclined to put
their ideas down on paper. Accepting the general nature of the sources
and their shortcomings, the violin treatises discussed here, in addition
to their own intrinsic value, therefore reflect the changes evident on a
much broader scale. The technical details that arise, specific to the
violin, are more properly dealt with in a catalogue of pedagogical
works, such as that I am in the process of compiling. The broad intentions of the authors and the purpose and status of the treatises in
question are more relevant to the present discussion.

During the eighteenth century in England tutor books appeared
in abundance and were often written for adult beginners from the
upper classes.[4] The vast majority were completely inadequate for self-

---

[3] Henry Roth's *Violin Virtuosos From Paganini to the 21st Century*, Los Angeles,
1997, makes only passing reference to Sammons and British players.

[4] The sources for the violin and related repertoire published in England during the
second half of the eighteenth century are discussed in D. J. Golby, 'Technique and

instruction and merely satisfied the demands of 'dabblers' for 'easy and fast results', as referred to by Leppert.[5] Elementary methods written at the beginning of the eighteenth century or even earlier often formed the basis of works published much later, with little modification or revision. These sources provide little more than the basics of notation and fingering, and a collection of dance tunes and popular airs. In the case of the violin, numerous treatises appeared, some as late as the beginning of the nineteenth century, based unashamedly on the Fifth Part of Prelleur's *The Modern Musick-Master* of 1731, itself originating in 1695 as *Nolens Volens or You Shall Learn to Play on the Violin Whether You Will or No*, published in London by Thomas Cross. These were therefore neither 'New' or 'Compleat' as the title-pages often claimed; but many were attributed to Geminiani and contained his table of embellishments, fingering exercises and section on bowing from *The Art of Playing on the Violin* of 1751. The second half of the eighteenth century in England witnessed, as a result of the growing interest in the instrument, the rise of 'a "do-it-yourself" movement in violin instruction',[6] with no recognized guiding force other than perhaps the work of Geminiani and his disciples. A pupil of Corelli, Geminiani and his followers ensured that the 'stabilizing and refinement'[7] that he brought to violin playing and performance style continued well into the nineteenth century.[8] Geminiani's significant and famous treatise, the first intended for advanced students, remains an odd synthesis of material and does not display the systematic thoroughness and technical detail of Leopold Mozart's treatise of 1756. It is an example of a method, albeit

---

Performance on the Violin in England c.1750–c.1800', MPhil, Oxford University, 1995. For earlier works, David D. Boyden's bibliography of violin treatises published in England 1658–1731 can be found in 'A Postscript to "Geminiani and the first violin tutor"', *Acta Musicologica*, 32 (1960), 40–47; and a selective listing of British violin treatises *c.* 1760–1840 is given in R. Stowell, *Violin Technique and Performance Practice in the Late Eighteenth and Early Nineteenth Centuries*, Cambridge, 1985, pp. 372–4.

[5] R. Leppert, *Music and Image: Domesticity, Ideology and Socio-Cultural Formation in Eighteenth-Century England*, Cambridge, 1988, p. 68.

[6] K. M. Stolba, *A History of the Violin Etude to about 1800*, Fort Hayes, 1968–69, p. 17.

[7] Ibid., p. 24.

[8] The widespread influence of Corelli and the popularity of his works as pedagogical tools, particularly among amateurs, during the eighteenth century and beyond is discussed in W. Weber, *The Rise of Musical Classics in Eighteenth-Century England*, Oxford, 1992, pp. 77–89. On the particular importance of the Violin Sonatas, Op. 5 as teaching pieces see N. Zaslaw, 'Ornaments for Corelli's Violin Sonatas, op. 5', *Early Music*, February (1996), 95–115. G. Hogarth wrote: 'These, to this day, are considered among the best compositions that can be put into the hands of a young performer on the violin, for the purpose of forming both his hand and his taste' (*Musical History, Biography, and Criticism*, 2nd edn, London, 1838, p. 155).

advanced and fascinating from a technical perspective, that has little concern for the needs of the student using it and is therefore intrinsically flawed as a teaching too. in itself. Teachers protected their own interests and publishers satisfied the requirements of the wealthy and fashion conscious. Pedagogy and serious instruction through written material were seldom a concern and the firmly established role of the master and the apprenticeship system naturally excluded those with the desire to learn but without the financial means or family connections required, which prevented them from advancing beyond the most basic level.[9]

The second half of the century brought one or two more enlightened publications, most notably one by Stephen Philpot, a pupil of Michael Festing who was in turn taught by Geminiani. His *An Introduction to the Art of Playing on the Violin* (published in London probably in 1767)[10] is indebted to Geminiani but, unusually, is quite explicit and honest about for whom it is intended. The title-page continues: ' ... AN / ENTIRE NEW PLAN, / Calculated for Laying a / REGULAR FOUNDATION for YOUNG BEGINNERS, / Explained by Such Easy / RULES and PRINCIPLES as will enable a SCHOLAR to acquire a proper / METHOD for performing on that INSTRUMENT ... ' It omits the usual collection of elementary compositions and instead provides useful exercises, for changing position and developing different bow strokes for example. It is indeed 'an entire new plan' that aims to inform and help the student to practise and progress. Jeffrey Pulver, in his article 'Violin Methods Old and New', describes it as 'sane, sound, and solid' and proposes that it is perhaps 'more useful as a skeleton guide for teachers than as a self-instructor for the young student himself',[11] which was equally desirable and rare at this time. Edward Heron-Allen refers to it as a 'glimpse of what ordinary tuition really amounted to in the middle of the last century',[12] which is perhaps more optimistic than accurate. Philpot explains that learning an instrument is 'An Advantage to Youth' and a worthwhile alternative to 'Gaming, Drinking, or other

---

[9] The research I have undertaken for the *New Dictionary of National Biography* (to be published by Oxford University Press early in the twenty-first century), covering over 120 prominent nineteenth-century musicians (either British or with established British ties) in various fields, has confirmed the vital importance of money and/or family ties in determining opportunity and success.

[10] British Library, *GB-Lbl* g. 490.

[11] J. Pulver, 'Violin Methods Old and New', *Proceedings of the Royal Musical Association (PRMA)*, 50 (1923–24), 114.

[12] E. Heron-Allen, *De Fidiculis Bibliographia: Being an Attempt towards a Bibliography of the Violin and All Other Instruments Played with a Bow*, London, 1890–94, vol. 1, pp. 155–6.

expensive Diversions' (p. 4) (again, perhaps optimistic), and so laments 'the Want of proper Rules for young Beginners' and expresses genuine concern that,

> except the excellent one of *Geminiani* (which is too difficult for Children or young Beginners to attempt till they have made a good Progress in playing) there has not appeared any rational Treatise upon this Subject, that has been of any other Use, than as a Gamut to shew the Notes, and something of the different Sorts of Time. (pp. 5–6)

Philpot's comments are significant. True, his criticisms of others serve in part to promote his own work; but his claims are genuine and the dissatisfaction he expresses at the situation as he sees it is evidently pertinent and justified, at least as far as the situation in England during this period is concerned.

With the arrival of the nineteenth century, there are signs that attitudes in England towards music education were beginning to change, pre-empted by writers such as Philpot. Not that a great deal was being done to transform the legacy of the eighteenth century, but the overwhelming complacency previously evident in this area was at least beginning to subside. The situation in France was very different, with moves being made to improve standards and methods in education on a large scale, and in musical performance in particular. As Cynthia Gessele has stated, '[the] Conservatoire's enduring legacy was the centralization of musical training in Paris and the standardization of teaching methods in France ... [concentrating] on its pedagogical programme, rather than on a national programme of music education'.[13] The creation of the Paris Conservatoire was largely inspired by the feeling that a musical nationalism needed to be enforced and as a result foreign musicians actively discouraged. Consequently, the teaching there was firmly based on texts written by professors employed by the institution. In the case of the violin, this meant the *Méthode de violon* (Paris, 1803) of Baillot, Rode and Kreutzer, and later Baillot's *L'Art du violon* of 1834, both of which played an important part in reaffirming the dominant position of the French violin school and its technical innovations during the period. This is in marked contrast to the diversity that characterized English culture and its influences at the time. Some in England acknowledged that the situation was detrimental to the standards of native performers but, aware of the tastes of the increasing concert-going public, chose to press the need to aspire to the achievements of the foreign musicians

---

[13] C. M. Gessele, 'The Conservatoire de Musique and National Music Education in France, 1795–1801', in M. Boyd (ed.), *Music and the French Revolution*, Cambridge, 1992, p. 191.

and compete with them, assimilating their practices and ideas, rather than seeking to discourage their presence. An essay entitled *Sketch of the State of Music in London* written in May 1823 refers to 'the great ascendancy gained by foreign talent, and the apparent disinclination of our countrymen to combat with energy and vigour for the honours of pre-eminence'.[14] The need to 'stand up for the right of English talent to its full share of consideration' (ibid., p. 246) is identified, although it is conceded that 'to establish a British school is neither to be done at a stroke nor in a season. Time and patience, as well as labour and encouragement will be required' (ibid., p. 250).

As the need to raise the standard of instrumental performance and 'prevent an inexorable slide into mediocrity'[15] was identified, at least by a few, a more critical attitude towards pedagogical literature emerged. An article in the 1820 edition of the *Quarterly Musical Magazine and Review* (*QMMR*) includes a commentary on the nature of 'Elementary treatises' in general (pp. 100–103). Significantly, it expresses the need for more effective methods of 'instilling' information and 'a positive determinate series of lessons', as opposed to an apparently random collection of disparate parts.

The same, new-found critical approach is evident in reviews of individual treatises. Richard M. Blagrove's *A New and Improved System to the Art of Playing the Violin* is reviewed in the *QMMR* in 1828, the writer remarking: 'What there is that deserves to be called "new" in this system, we have not discovered' (p. 109).

The established late seventeenth-/eighteenth-century treatise format is, remarkably, still in evidence, although it is now acknowledged to be woefully anachronistic and insufficient. The more advanced and comprehensive continental tutors began to find their way to England and several eventually appeared in translation, including the works by Rode et al. (first in 1823, 20 years after it was first published) and Campagnoli. It is also worth mentioning that short sections from the pioneering treatises of Leopold Mozart and L'abbé *le fils* were issued during this period.[16] These

---

[14] *Quarterly Musical Magazine and Review*, 5 (1823), 241–75, 241.

[15] C. Ehrlich, *The Music Profession in Britain since the Eighteenth Century: A Social History*, Oxford, 1985, p. 83.

[16] B. Campagnoli, *Metodo per violino*, ?Milan, ?1797. English trans. *c.* 1830; 2nd edn, 1834 and 1856; L. Mozart, *Versuch* … , Augsburg, 1756, trans. as *Mozart's Violin School on the Art of Bowing, shewn by a Variety of Examples, with directions & Examples on the different Orders of Shifts* … [an abridgement], London, *c.* 1812, 18 pp. (British Library, *GB-Lbl* h. 1753.j.); L'abbé le fils [Joseph-Barnabé Saint-Sevin], *Principes du violon* … , Paris, 1761, trans. as *An Easy Method of Producing on the Violon, the harmonic Sounds in all the major & minor Keys*, 2nd edn, London, *c.* 1828, 3 pp. (British Library, *GB-Lbl* h. 1753 p. (7.)).

set the new standards, and those producing teaching material in England gradually appreciated the need to assimilate the advances made elsewhere, with regard to both content and presentation. Jean Jousse, in the Preface to his *The Theory and Practice of the Violin* (published in London in 1811 and dedicated to J. P. Salomon)[17] states that his work: ' ... contains the precepts of the greatest Violin-masters Italian, French and German, viz; Mozart, Geminiani, L'Abbé, Rodes [*sic*], Baillot, Kreutzer &c[.] I have read attentively what these Authors have written on the subject, and from their Ideas and my own, formed this method' (p. V). This work has received some attention in violin research,[18] largely because of Jousse's rejection of vibrato,[19] which, if taken at face value, is perhaps as unrepresentative of general practice as Geminiani's often quoted universal advocation of the effect.

A review from 1824 of a translation of the method by Rode et al.[20] refers to Jousse's work and John David Loder's *A General and Comprehensive Instruction Book for the Violin* (published in London probably in 1824), which was widely used and republished as late as 1911.[21] The review begins with a comment on the French approach: 'it appears that the French school has proceeded upon a system, the aim of which is, to reduce and consolidate all the parts of the science into one relative and compact body of institutes' (ibid., p. 528). It continues:

> The two best modern books of instruction for the violin with which we are acquainted are those of Mr. Jousse and Mr. Loder. The former is in a good measure founded upon that of the conservatory, and upon foreign works at large, which renders it the more valuable, as we esteem it, because it renders it the more copious, and because it embraces the opinions and experience of the larger number of eminent men. Mr. Loder's is the more original, and standing upon the eminence he does, it may well be conceived to be excellent. It is indeed very excellent, on account of the examples – by which art is said to be 'best taught.' They carry the pupil through a vast body of progressive practice. (Ibid., pp. 529–30)

A review of Thomas Howell's *Original Instructions for the Violin* (published in Bristol in 1825 and dedicated to Nicholas Mori)[22] also reveals how treatises began to be judged in the nineteenth century on their

---

[17] British Library, *GB-Lbl* h. 1034. c.

[18] For example Stowell, *Violin Technique*, pp. 89 and 210.

[19] J. Jousse, *The Theory and Practice of the Violin*, London, 1811, pt 1, 48.

[20] *QMMR*, 6 (1824), 527–31.

[21] A third edition ('Considerably enlarged & improved') appeared in 1837 (Bodleian Library, Oxford, *GB-Ob* Mus. Instr. I, 160 (10)) and a fifth in 1841 (Bodleian Library, Oxford, *GB-Ob* Mus. Instr. I, 160 (11)).

[22] *QMMR*, 7 (1825), 507.

usefulness as teaching tools, complementing the role of the teacher, and
on how accessible they were to those outside the upper classes:

> Here we have a new method from Mr. Howell, whose object
> appears to be, to begin his structure from the very foundation, and
> to proceed upon his own plan step by step, in the closest manner,
> as far as the elementary principles are concerned. This book leaves
> far less for oral instruction than any other similar treatise that we
> are acquainted with. Its comprehensiveness, its systematic arrange-
> ment, and its cheapness (10s. 6d.) are all strong recommendations.

Even if the writer is 'flying the flag' to a certain degree, the violin
treatises published in English during the early part of the nineteenth
century are generally a great deal more substantial than the equivalent
examples from the eighteenth, displaying a genuine and growing concern for the systematic development of technique. They provide written
information on the instrument, its origins and maintenance, and present
carefully constructed exercises, often scored as duets, to help develop
both right- and left-hand technique. Howell's other treatise, *Practical
Elementary Examples for the Violin*, published in London in around
1827,[23] exemplifies the new approach and priorities of these treatises.
The art of bowing is given detailed textual explanation with comprehensive exercises, using principles employed by Leopold Mozart[24] and
ideas which later played an important part in Baillot's writings.[25]

The legacy of the eighteenth century left writers in England during
this transitional period unsure of their market and reluctant to commit
themselves to a completely modern approach overnight. As a result, the
sources are, as Pulver states, 'a curious blending of ancient and
modern methods'[26] as well as an amalgam of different continental
schools. For example, Loder's treatise from 1841 still feels the need to
specify the old 'rule of the down bow' (i.e. a down bow at the beginning
of each bar), with the use of an up bow in the same context very much
an exception, at least in theory (p. 4). This is the case even though the
treatise as a whole is conceived with the modern Tourte-model bow in
mind, with its far more even distribution of weight and pressure, and
with the *marcato* bowing style, characteristic of this type of bow, specified elsewhere (ibid., p. 31 for example). There are numerous sources

---

[23] Bodleian Library, Oxford, *GB-Ob* Mus. Instr. I, 126 (11).

[24] The bow divisions employed by Mozart (1756, ch. 5, sects 4–7, English trans. pp.
97–9) are used by Howell as a point of departure (pp. 6–9).

[25] The need to 'proportion the pressure [applied to the bow] to the Velocity' referred
to by Howell (p. 1) is part of Baillot's pioneering approach to bowing (as found in his
1834 treatise), in which bow speed is fundamental to articulation and tone quality.

[26] Pulver, 'Violin Methods Old and New', p. 117. This comment is made with reference
to Jousse's *The Modern Violin Preceptor*, London, ?1805.

from the whole of the nineteenth century (and into the twentieth) that
betray their origins in the standard eighteenth-century format, with its
brief written explanations, limited musical examples (including the
gamut) and a relatively large collection of short pieces added at the
end.[27] However, the essential difference is that some of these examples
do not claim to cater for the whole range of ability and provide all that
the student will ever require; but are targeted at the beginner, supplying
the need for a foundation before more advanced material is introduced.
Consequently, they are more successful and effective as teaching tools
and often present new and novel ideas, such as Paine's 'Bow Guide'.[28]

Nevertheless, the need for a central teaching institution for music in
England remained. These sources provide a fascinating insight into the
influences and attitudes of the time, but also reflect the lack of a
coherent approach to the teaching of the instrument, there being little
sign of a clear sense of purpose and a central, influential driving force in
this area. This situation prompted Fétis in 1829 to note that 'musical
science in England ... is still in its infancy'.[29] Discussing the Royal
Academy of Music (RAM), he remarks:

> All the parts of musical execution in this school are not in an equal
> state of prosperity, and I am of the opinion that what is defective
> ought to be charged to the account of the professors rather than of
> the pupils. There is no school of the violin in England, though Viotti
> resided here so long. The most celebrated violinists in London are
> Messrs. F. Cramer, Mori, Spagnoletti, and Oury. These four profes-
> sors give lessons in the Royal Academy of Music ... [which] might
> be productive of the most happy effects in regard to English music,
> provided the Government were to grant such assistance as to enable
> instruction to be given gratuitously. (Ibid., pp. 236–9)

National allegiances aside, the less than flattering picture of the new
institution that the Frenchman paints is significant. The feeling ex-

---

[27] For example J. Paine, *A Treatise on the Violin*, London, ?1819 (*GB-Ob* 8° N 146
(2) BS), written in the old-fashioned dialogue format; H. Farmer, *Instructions for the
Violin*, London, n.d., the content of which was republished under various titles (including *New Violin School* and *Tutor for the Violin*) from 1847 until at least 1903; and J. A.
Hamilton, *The Universal Violin Tutor*, London, *c.* 1850, one of many instrumental
methods and several examples for the violin by the same author, who also issued editions
of treatises by Campagnoli, Baillot and Rode. These last two examples form part of a
richly diverse collection of pedagogical material from the period for a whole range of
instruments in The Bate Collection of Musical Instruments, Faculty of Music, University
of Oxford.

[28] Paine, *A Treatise on the Violin*, p. 47.

[29] These comments originate in a letter to his son on 21 May 1829, later reproduced in
the *Revue Musicale*, 5, (18), May (1829), 409–17. Extracts are translated in W. W.
Cazalet, *The History of the Royal Academy of Music, Compiled from Authentic Sources*,
London, 1854, pp. 230–39. It is this source that is referred to here.

pressed, rather than one of self-satisfaction, appears to be that of regret, that the opportunity is at this time not being taken to rectify a situation that had been allowed to exist and deteriorate for far too long. He highlights the particular plight of the violin, which is seen to exist in spite of the great names that had been active in London (although it was probably in no small part attributable to them), and also the consequences of the RAM's meagre financial backing for prospective students. Musical training there was 'absurdly limited', to quote Ehrlich, with no 'corporate identity or coherent purpose'.[30] Time for instrumental lessons was very limited and each professor instructed 'according to his own system',[31] unlike in Paris. Those in charge were unable to provide the stable and supportive teaching environment and pedagogical system essential if standards were to improve on a significant scale, and RAM-trained natives were unable to pose a challenge to foreign musicians.[32] In this sense, the existence of the institution at this stage was more symbolic than revolutionary for instrumental teaching.

These frequently superior foreign musicians 'continued to visit or emigrate to London throughout the 1830s and 1840s', although 'the best RAM graduates assumed leading roles in British musical life'[33] and were able to take advantage of the limited opportunities offered. The RAM also provided opportunities for native teachers to impart their ideas, and the London-born Nicholas Mori, taught by Barthélemon and Viotti, was appointed the first violin professor there.[34] J. D. Loder, the first Englishman to lead the orchestra at the Philharmonic Society of London (from 1817), had become a professor in 1840.[35] Henry Blagrove, in the words of Ehrlich 'one of the few nineteenth-century British violinists to achieve more than a modest competence',[36] was one of the

---

[30] Ehrlich, *The Music Profession*, p. 84.

[31] W. W. Cazalet, 'Rules and Regulations to be observed by the Professors of the Royal Academy of Music, Article 1', in his *The History of the Royal Academy of Music, Compiled from Authentic Sources*, London, 1854, p. 342.

[32] See D. A. Rohr, 'A Profession of Artisans: The Careers and Social Status of British Musicians 1750–1850', PhD, Pennsylvania, 1983, pp. 167–76.

[33] Ibid., p. 173.

[34] Hogarth admitted that 'England has produced few great performers on the violin', but selected Mori as 'Our only native violinist, of long established reputation as a concerto-player ... a pupil of Viotti, and one of the preservers of his pure and admirable school' (*Musical History*, p. 265). However, he was succeeded in 1845 by the Frenchman Prosper Sainton, who was trained by Habeneck in Paris.

[35] Two copies (hardback and paperback) of J. T. Carrodus's edition (London, ?1884) of Loder's treatise referred to above are still housed in the RAM library (shelfmark 65.01).

[36] Ehrlich, *The Music Profession*, p. 85. Blagrove is the only nineteenth-century English violinist that H. Davey mentions by name in his *History of English Music*, 2nd edn,

first students to be admitted to the RAM in 1823, where he was taught by Cramer (having already received tuition from Spagnoletti) and later studied with Louis Spohr in Germany. Blagrove acted as a 'sub-professor' at the RAM after he had 'been given up by Mr. Cramer as an advanced pupil'[37] and then became a professor in 1831, writing studies and other teaching material and performing widely as a leader and chamber musician. He is one of the few success stories of the early RAM as far as the violin is concerned, although it is significant that his father (R. M. Blagrove) had been a prominent violin teacher and writer on the instrument in Nottingham.[38]

The library of the RAM contains perhaps more copies of Louis Spohr's violin treatise in its various editions than any other, at least from the nineteenth century. A central figure for various reasons, there is not space here to do justice to the role and importance of Spohr in English music; but in the context of violin pedagogy, he is as important to the nineteenth century as Geminiani and the school of Corelli are to the eighteenth. His *Violinschule* (1832) became very popular in England and was available in an English translation (by Rudolphus) as early as 1833. This is possibly because of its relatively conservative approach to violin technique, which never places display above expression and prefers 'a more "classical" on-the-string bowing technique and singing tone'[39] compared to some virtuosi and teaching methods. It is highly significant that Spohr's performing style, as far as it is reflected in his treatise, was based on the technical and expressive qualities of the earlier French school of Viotti and his disciples (and in particular Rode), rather than the contemporary, more virtuosic French style (especially with respect to the use of springing bowings) that Baillot represented and documented comprehensively, partly reflecting the innovations made by Paganini in the interim.[40] Viotti himself and his compositions had of course been received with great enthusiasm in England from the end of the eighteenth century and his virtues were still being extolled in the 1830s:

New York, 1969, describing him as 'perhaps the best' of the 'few of eminence' (p. 440). Hogarth, after mentioning the 'highly distinguished' orchestral leaders 'Francois Cramer, Weichsell, Mori, Loder of Bath, and T. Cooke' (*Musical History*, p. 265), comments on Blagrove's position among 'our younger violinists' and how he 'has acquired great reputation by his talents both as a solo-player and a leader' (ibid., pp. 265–6).

[37] See his short autobiography in W. W. Cazalet, *History of the Royal Academy of Music*, pp. 285–7.

[38] His treatise (1828) is referred to above.

[39] R. Stowell, 'The pedagogical literature', in R. Stowell (ed.), *The Cambridge Companion to the Violin*, Cambridge, 1992, p. 227.

[40] For a fascinating study of the performing style of Spohr set in context, see C. Brown, 'Bowing Styles, Vibrato and Portamento in Nineteenth-Century Violin Playing', in *Journal of the Royal Musical Association (JRMA)* 113 (1988), 97–128.

As a musician, it may be truly said, that though the virtuosi of the present day execute difficulties which were not attempted in his time, yet, in all the highest qualities that belong to performance, he has never been surpassed. His compositions for the violin ... still furnish, when performed by the surviving disciples of his school, one of the most delightful treats which a lover of the great and beautiful in music can receive.[41]

One of his 'disciples', Spohr, and the anachronistic style that he promoted found favour with the English in the nineteenth century in much the same way that Corelli and his school had in the eighteenth. This could indeed be viewed as a continuation and consistency of style, as it is possible to trace the lineage of teacher–pupil relationships from Corelli, through Somis and Pugnani, to Viotti and hence to Spohr. Hogarth believed that his reputation as 'the first violinist of the age' was justified and noted that he 'was particularly distinguished for his pure and delicate tone, the smoothness and facility of his execution, his expression, and the vocal character of his style'.[42] The writer is not alone in highlighting the refinement and beauty in Spohr's performing style. It is common for both contemporary and present-day commentators to view Spohr's art as the very antithesis of that of Paganini, characterized by its extreme bravura and virtuosity.[43] Paganini did enjoy, of course, much success in England in the early 1830s, but he was admired for the magical qualities and technical brilliance of his technique,[44] rather than respected as an honourable man and consummate artist. His performances were without doubt thrilling experiences, but his was not an appropriate style for young native artists to aspire to. Spohr, on the other hand, provided the ideal model.

A faithful and complete translation of the Spohr treatise, by John Bishop, appeared in 1843, and was endorsed by the author himself and dedicated to Edward Taylor, a close friend of Spohr in England. It is significant that the Committee of Management of the RAM became patrons of this edition in 1843 and placed a copy in the library of the academy.[45] Many other translations, editions and reprints followed, including selections from the studies and duets in the method, and

---

[41] Hogarth, *Musical History*, p. 177.

[42] Ibid., 187.

[43] Spohr himself was critical of the frivolous and extreme elements in Paganini's style (see Schwarz, *Great Masters*, p. 184). Henry Roth is typical of modern writers in his description of Spohr as 'a pillar of respectable musicianship', while focusing on Paganini's technical accomplishments (*Violin Virtuosos*, p. 14).

[44] See Schwarz, *Great Masters*, pp. 186–7.

[45] A letter to this effect from the Secretary of the RAM to the publishers is reproduced in G. Dubourg, *The Violin*, 4th edn, London, 1852, pp. 3–4.

Spohr's treatise became an important part of violin teaching in England during the rest of the century and into the twentieth, long after his popularity as a composer had waned. In addition to the Bishop edition, there are three copies of the version edited and revised by Henry Holmes in the RAM library.[46] Henry and his brother Alfred were English violinists who received at least some instruction from Spohr, who dedicated some violin duets to them. The Holmes edition of the treatise contains various additions and amendments that demonstrate differences of approach and a desire to include some aspects of technique that Spohr had rejected when compiling the original work, most notably springing bowings. Although the substantial part of the work remains faithful to the practices of Spohr, it was perhaps considered expedient to reflect contemporary style and incorporate technical developments made half a century earlier.[47] Nevertheless, the tradition of Spohr's teaching continued in England, through Blagrove at the RAM and the Holmes brothers, Henry becoming the violin professor at the newly founded Royal College of Music (RCM) in 1883.[48]

The use of the Spohr treatise as a teaching tool is another issue. *The Young Violinist's Tutor and Duet Book … For The Use of Beginners … By a Professional Player* is one of a number of anonymous violin tutors from the second half of the nineteenth century which were in fact written by W. C. Honeyman.[49] It is interesting for a number of reasons, including its use of exercises by Loder, comments on Spohr and his

---

[46] This edition (translated by F. Marshall) was issued in 1878. The library also contains another copy of the Bishop edition and one of the Rudolphus.

[47] Spohr's pupil Ferdinand David, who also enjoyed success in England, included springing bowings in his own *Violinschule* (Leipzig, 1864), as part of an attempt to bring German violin playing up to date. See Brown's discussions in 'Bowing Styles', p. 108 and C. Brown, *Louis Spohr: A Critical Biography*, Cambridge, 1984, pp. 212–14.

[48] The Violin Concerto of Beethoven is a work that perhaps benefited from the cultivation of Spohr's approach over a long period in England, even if the two figures were not always complimentary about each other's music. As with Spohr's style, the concerto's origins and inspiration lie in the French school of Viotti and his followers and, championed by Joachim (who shared a great deal of Spohr's musical heritage and artistic temperament) in London in 1844, the work was for the first time fully appreciated. It was finally accepted and valued by performers and a public less concerned with virtuosity and bravura, who identified with and desired such restraint and refinement in their music-making: qualities epitomized by Spohr. See R. Stowell, *Beethoven: Violin Concerto*, Cambridge, 1998, for a detailed discussion of the issues surrounding the work.

[49] The copy discussed here is in The Bate Collection of Musical Instruments, Oxford and is the third edition, published in Edinburgh and London but not dated. The British Library has a copy of the fifty-fourth edition which is dated *c.* 1900. Honeyman's other works include *The Violin: How to Master it* (Edinburgh, 1880), and his writings and life are discussed in B. W. Harvey, *The Violin Family and its Makers in the British Isles*, Oxford, 1995, pp. 177–80.

school and the progressive attitude it shows towards written pedagogy generally. He stresses the need to acquire 'a thorough knowledge of the system of bowing elaborated by Spohr and David in their great schools of Violin playing' (p. 3), but is conscious of the need to provide 'a stepping-stone to the standard Violin Tutors' (p. 4):

> Teachers in every branch have, within the last twenty years, consid-
> erably modified the old modes of imparting knowledge to the
> young, and I know of no good reason why this healthy progress
> should not extend to music and the Violin. On the contrary, my
> wonder is that the change has not taken place sooner, or been
> inaugurated by some one with more talent and time than I can
> command. (Ibid.)

The role of Spohr, reflecting his central position in this area, receives special consideration and criticism under the title 'Spohr and the Young':

> To put before a young violinist a book like Spohr's great 'Violin
> School,' is as stupid and cruel as it would be to put Euclid instead
> of a First Primer in the hands of an infant. Everything in its proper
> place. For the advanced student and the professional player there is
> no book better than Spohr's, for the young Violin player – and all
> Violin players *must* begin young – no book could be worse ... If
> ever any one made a delightful study dry and repellent to the
> young, and failed to adapt Violin studies to their limited powers,
> that man was Louis Spohr. (Ibid.)

The writer mentions the fact that Spohr was aware of his own lack of experience when it came to elementary instruction and asked in the 'Author's Preface addressed to Parents & Teachers' to his treatise for 'instructive hints' relating to the first half of the work.[50] It is significant that the shortcomings of Spohr's work are highlighted in this way, especially by a native (in fact Scottish) violinist and writer, and that similar (if less defamatory) criticisms were made by Philpot with regard to Geminiani's treatise (see above), the other seminal work in this area. This critical approach displays a progressive attitude towards pedagogy, and, as in the case of examples based on eighteenth-century models mentioned above, an increasing number of methods appeared in the nineteenth century that responded to a real need as well as a gap in the market. This more effective targeting of treatises provided the beginner and, perhaps for the first time, the intermediate player with relatively cheap material to complement practical tuition or serve as an alterna- tive to it when it was not accessible.

The uniquely 'international', or at least 'pan-European' approach to music-making and specifically violin-playing evident in England during

---

[50] *Louis Spohr's Celebrated Violin School*, trans. Bishop, London, 1843, p. iii.

the nineteenth century, along with the prevailing attitudes of the time, meant that its pedagogy was far from systematic and a distinct national 'school' would fail to emerge. However, as the century progressed a better quality of teaching material began to appear. Much of it was intended for the more advanced student, including both translations of continental treatises and original works in English, often eclectic in nature.[51] The result of this was a general improvement in the standards and consistency of instrumental performance, even if the achievements of the continental virtuosi were beyond native musicians at this point. George Bernard Shaw makes a few observations on the subject in his own inimitable way, although his opinions were undoubtedly far from unique to him. On 25 March 1891 he writes:

> It may be that my early experience of amateur and apprenticed violinists, especially young women, was unfortunate; but I cannot help thinking that there has been an enormous improvement in them since my boyhood. At that time the sight of a fiddle-case in a drawing room filled me with terror: it boded all that was insufferable, infirm, and ridiculous in amateurism. But it was not alone the amateur that was to be dreaded. Even in good professional orchestras, a few bars of solo for the leader, the obbligato to Salve dimora! or the like, was an infliction which you bore sitting back, with your teeth set, and a grin of indulgent resignation on your drawn lips. I can remember thinking the violin a noxious instrument, and wondering why people played it. My astonishment when somebody took me to hear Sivori was boundless: I perceived that the thing could be played after all, but concluded that it took a magician to do it.[52]

On 22 November 1893:

> I continue to be amazed at the way in which the younger generation plays the fiddle. Formerly there were only two sorts of violinists: the Paganinis or Sivoris, and the bad amateurs whose highest flight was an execrable attempt to scrape through a variation or two on The Carnival of Venice ... Nowadays all that is changed in the most bewildering manner. Europe appears to be full of young ladies between twenty and thirty who can play all the regulation concertos – Beethoven, Mendelssohn, Brahms, Bruch, and Saint-Saëns – and throw in Bach's chaconne in D minor as a solo piece at the end of the concert.[53]

---

[51] For example, A. Wilhelmj and J. Brown, *Modern School for the Violin*, London, 1898, and K. Courvoisier, *The Technics of Violin Playing on Joachim's Method*, London, 1899. Significantly, Wilhelmj was a pupil of Ferdinand David (Spohr's pupil) at Leipzig (as was Joachim), and became principal violin professor at the Guildhall School of Music, London in 1894.

[52] G. B. Shaw, *Music in London 1890–94*, London, 1932, vol. 1, pp. 153–4.

[53] Ibid., vol. 3, p. 92.

Some lessons (possibly more useful than the instrumental ones) were learned at the RAM in its early years, and a large number of music colleges began to appear towards the end of the century,[54] including the 'College of Violinists Ltd.', founded in 1889, at which Albert Sammons later became a professor.[55] Following the achievements of John Carrodus,[56] Sammons 'did much to elevate the status of the British performer'[57] but, like Paganini and Bull, he was largely self-taught. Therefore, rather than education and teaching methods being the issue, perhaps it could be argued that a native violin virtuoso was just more feasible due to changes in taste at this time; or perhaps the previous lack of a similar figure was more down to temperament and typical English modesty and self-depreciation, and the public were right: native performers lacked the 'charisma' required and referred to above[58] and it was far easier (and more convenient) to accept imported brilliance than identify the issue, confront the problem and attempt to nurture our own. Without doubt, an approach that failed to encourage and nurture native talent through all the stages of its development would result in very few success stories, and those exceptions would be determined mainly by chance and privilege.

Positive changes did eventually occur, however, particularly with regard to the early development of instrumentalists and the provision of materials for beginners.[59] The opinions and aspirations of writers such

---

[54] See Ehrlich, *The Music Profession*, pp. 105–20 and 238.

[55] Sammons was also a professor at the RCM and wrote two violin treatises, including *The Secret of Technique in Violin Playing* (London, 1916), a copy of which is in the RAM library. The performing style of Sammons in the twentieth century, as revealed in his recordings, with its *discreet* use of portamento and a quite fast *continuous* vibrato, is the opposite of what was prescribed in many nineteenth-century methods, including those of Spohr and his followers. See R. T. Philip, *Early Recordings and Musical Style: Changing Tastes in Instrumental Performance, 1900–1950*, Cambridge, 1992, and Brown, 'Bowing Styles', pp. 110–28.

[56] A pupil of Molique (who had received some lessons from and whose style was influenced by Spohr, and who lived and taught in London from 1849 to 1866), Carrodus's playing impressed Spohr and he 'contributed much to raising the level of string playing in Victorian England' (Schwarz, *Great Masters*, p. 482). In addition to editions of the treatises of Loder and Spohr already mentioned, he published his own *Chats to Violin Students on How to Study the Violin*, London, 1895, and taught at the National Training School (established in 1876 and the precursor of the RCM), the Croydon Conservatoire of Music (established in 1883) and at the Guildhall School of Music and Trinity College, London.

[57] Campbell, *The Great Violinists*, p. 144.

[58] Ibid.

[59] As instrumental teaching became more established in schools at the end of the nineteenth century the violin, due to its size and the commercial skills and opportunism of a few individuals, established itself as the main school instrument, with school

as Honeyman (quoted above), reflect a more serious and (morally if not always financially) supportive environment in which native talent could be encouraged and appreciated.[60] Allied to the emergence of and the need for English nationalism in music as the twentieth century loomed large, instrumental pedagogy became a more important consideration for society generally. These changes in the late nineteenth century originated in the developments made in written teaching material outlined above by those who, despite the widespread apathy shown towards native musicians during the period, anticipated the need to foster growth and progress in this area. The nature of the material and of the learning process generally meant that results were only apparent after a significant period of time, as confidence and proficiency began to proliferate through society.[61]

The pedagogical literature from the nineteenth century is more individual and diverse than that of the eighteenth, allowing it, as demand increased, to cater for specific markets and the whole range of ability. In fact, as shown above, individual examples and writers began to be judged on their success at satisfying the need for a coherent and systematic approach. It is highly significant that the models that were firmly established, accepted and considered appropriate for violin teaching and performance in Britain from the eighteenth century through to the twentieth, namely the schools of Corelli (mainly through Geminiani) and Viotti (mainly through Spohr) in their respective periods, are part of a continuous tradition which emphasizes the vocal, refined and 'tasteful' expressive qualities of the instrument rather than the full extent of its technical capabilities.

---

orchestras often comprising little else. For a discussion of this trend and the role and importance of the 'Maidstone System' in introducing violins and violin tuition into schools, see D. Russell, *Popular Music in England, 1840–1914: A Social History*, 2nd edn, Manchester, 1997, p. 54.

[60] New periodical publications such as the *Strad* (beginning in May 1890); *Violin Times* (from November 1893); *The Violin Monthly Magazine* (1890–94); and *The Violin* (1889–94), involving distinguished writers such as Eugene Polonaski and Edward Heron-Allen, reflect the new popularity of the instrument and the serious attention paid to the different subjects connected with it.

[61] It is regrettable that present-day thinking in this area appears to signal a regression to an essentially élitist system.

CHAPTER SIX

The Practice and Context of a Private Victorian Brass Band

Trevor Herbert

The outline history of British brass bands is easy to plot. Most were a product of the commodification of piston valve brass instruments, which in the middle of the nineteenth century, with the emergence of sophisticated production techniques and lower raw material costs, were considerably cheaper to produce and buy than brass instruments had ever been before. These instruments were easy to play, and the most successful designs were invented almost exactly at the same time as key economic, social and demographic factors came together to provide an ideal environment for their mass-marketing.

Prominent among these favourable factors were population growth, urbanization and efficient marketing strategies. In addition, a new mass leisure industry was developing as many working-class people began to enjoy the benefits of better financial circumstances, hire purchase agreements, access to recreational time and railway travel.

The higher orders of society encouraged the participation of the working class in music-making, subscribing to the widespread belief that communal music-making might prove to be a panacea for the social crisis which many perceived to be looming.[1] This 'crisis' was more imagined than real, but it was no less a cause of concern because of that. Not only demographics, but also systems of belief and social order were changing. Moral reformers preached the merits of 'rational recreations' and 'self improvement'. The acquisition of deft musical skills by members of the working classes was encouraged, in the belief that this would facilitate the development of a mass working-class population possessing tastes and values in harmony with those of the dominant class. However, though such sentiments and intentions contributed to the background of the development of brass bands, in

---

[1] There were, of course, several dimensions to this. Eric Mackerness, in *A Social History of English Music*, London, 1964, has put forward the view that any form of communal music-making was interpreted as virtuous, because it relied on co-operation. In fact, the issues were more complex and involved matters such as the status of different types of music.

reality, the primary causes of bands becoming a mass activity were deeply commercial.

By the 1880s there were many thousands of brass bands, and they were distributed throughout the country. It was one of the most widely experienced forms of popular music. Indeed, in some respects, brass bands provide the classic illustration of the relationship of music-making to the buoyant producer–consumer dynamic of the Victorian period. But how should we position brass bands in British music history? Do they offer an example of musical continuity, or of change? Above all, how similar to or different from each other were brass bands? Should the term 'brass band' refer to a range of types, rather than a single genre?

This chapter will focus on a case study of the Cyfarthfa Band, and on the extent to which understanding the context and culture of such a band is the key to understanding its musical behaviour. But because the Cyfarthfa Band was not typical of Victorian brass bands, we need first to consider Victorian amateur brass bands in general.[2]

The formation of most brass bands was financed by public subscription or through a hire purchase agreement. In such agreements, an employer usually acted as the guarantor for the loan. Indeed it was common for band magazines and other publications to print 'model letters' which entreated groups of workmen to acquire such loans.[3] Petitions requesting a guarantee for a loan were often accompanied by a deferential request for permission for the band to carry the name of the relevant mill, factory and so on; contrary to popular belief, few employers actually set up and directly financed works bands merely as an act of philanthropic benevolence.

When a band *was* set up, it soon became, in most practical senses, independent of the agency that had supported its foundation – whether that agency was an employer, a mechanics institute, a church or whatever. It was precisely this feature – the speed with which bands became independent of their sponsors, their capacity to become discrete musical institutions – that caused William Booth to go to elaborate lengths to separate Salvation Army bands from the rest of the brass band movement in the 1870s. The *Orders and Regulations for Field Officers* of the Salvation Army drew officers' attention to 'the advantages and dangers'

---

[2] A version of this chapter was given at the Historic Brass Society's Festival and Symposium at Amherst, MA, in August 1995. It was published as Trevor Herbert, 'The Reconstruction of Nineteenth-Century Band Repertory: Towards a Protocol', in the proceedings of the event, *Perspectives in Brass Scholarship*, ed. Stewart Carter, New York, 1997.

[3] Such a letter is printed in Algernon Rose's *Talks with Bandsmen*, London, 1890, pp. 303–4.

of brass bands. Indeed Booth's directives in this respect were specific and consistent: 'The F.O. [Field Officer] must be ready to check the first beginning of anything like a separate feeling betwixt the Band and the Soldiers.'[4]

Booth's concern stemmed from his observation of the growing independence and ambition of brass bands outside the Salvation Army. It was common for them to put administrative infrastructures in place (sometimes with the help of lawyers) to emphasize and guarantee their independence and autonomy. Such infrastructures were almost always democratic but, paradoxically, most bands devolved powerful – almost autocratic – authority to a small group of members to guide the band musically and sustain discipline and propriety. The most ambitious bands focused upon contesting as their *raison d'être*, but almost all brass bands seem to have drawn pride from a sense of independence and self-ownership. They offered an alternative focus to that which members experienced in their working lives. The respect which men enjoyed as players affected the way they were seen and the way they saw themselves. Spheres of authority were different from those at work and, of course, there was the sense of collective identity which found expression in routine procedures and activities such as rehearsal nights, committee meetings and regular community obligations. Bands often further emphasized their collective and community identity through other rituals or gestures. The wearing of uniforms is an example of such a gesture. Uniforms signified and emphasized coherence and permanence; they also demonstrated the wealth of a band. Uniforms were often flamboyant demonstrations of collective pride. Brass bands did not wear them merely as show business props.

Some bands were recreational, but many had great ambitions. As the century progressed, a set of standard orthodoxies became evident. But equally evident were differences, and these differences often reflected local practices and preoccupations.

The advent of the brass band contest was the most influential agency in the process of standardization. The move towards a standard brass band instrumentation came about because of the need for bands to compete on equal terms. The brass band format which has been maintained until present times was put into place in the late 1880s, because the three most important conductors of competing bands, John Gladney, Alexander Owen and Edwin Swift, started using it consistently. Lesser bands imitated this format, and soon it was standard among publishers

---

[4] *Orders and Regulations for Field Officers*, London, 1888, p. 54. These orders and regulations were also disseminated to soldiers through other publications such as *The War Cry*.

of brass band music. The performing style of the best bands was imitated too, and it is evident from the brass band magazines which appeared in the 1880s that by the end of the century there was a shared understanding of what the brass band idiom actually was.

The cultural identity of the Cyfarthfa Band

The Cyfarthfa Band, the main subject of this chapter, provides an interesting and important example of how some highly developed bands did not fit into the most commonly encountered stereotype. On the face of it, it might seem to be a typical example of a British brass band. Its name appears frequently in secondary sources for Welsh social history. All such sources refer to it as having been founded in 1844, in Merthyr Tydfil in the county of Glamorgan, South Wales. Many brass bands originated in the 1840s. Indeed, the development of the amateur brass band movement can be said to have started in 1844, when the Distins, the family troupe of English brass virtuosos, encountered the inventor Adolphe Sax in Paris, and negotiated the British franchise for his design of piston valve instruments. This is why many early bands were called 'saxhorn bands' – a generic term apparently invented by Henry Distin rather than Sax himself. Distin was a keen entrepreneur, who went on to establish important instrument manufacturing and music publishing concerns; the name 'saxhorn' was effectively a marketing ploy.[5] There was no widespread amateur brass band movement in Britain before about 1844; where brass bands existed, they were small bands, usually professional – such as circus bands.

However, other aspects of the sources for the Cyfarthfa Band did not fit the usual pattern for amateur brass bands, or the development of the brass movement generally. Keyed instruments seemed to have been in use much longer at Cyfarthfa than they were elsewhere. Also, the repertory – even in the earliest part of the band's existence – was considerably more sophisticated than that of other bands of the same period. Another important factor – perhaps *the* most compelling one – which made the Cyfarthfa Band appear different from others, concerned the social context of the town in which it was formed.

---

[5] The patents registered by Adolphe Sax in Paris include one for a 'Saxhorn', but this was for a specific instrument rather than a group of instruments. It was Sax's usual practice to prefix the word 'Sax' to whatever instrument he was working on ('saxotromba', for example). Since the nineteenth century, the word 'saxhorn' has been used generically to describe valved, conical-bore brass instruments which have the bell pointing upwards – such as the tenor horn and euphonium. The word is used yet more freely in the USA.

Merthyr Tydfil is about 30 miles north of Cardiff and the south-east coast of Wales. It is the most northerly point in the southern industrial belt of Wales. North of Merthyr, up to the northern coast of Gwynedd and Clwyd, is the mountainous hinterland of central Wales, which is almost entirely agricultural. In the nineteenth century, Merthyr was by far the largest Welsh town, and one of the most important industrial centres of the British Empire. In 1851 it had a population of 46 378, compared to the next largest town, Swansea, with a population of 21 378. The present Welsh capital, Cardiff, had a population of 18 351 in 1851, and did not pass Merthyr in size until the 1880s.[6]

The growth and importance of the town came from a series of geological coincidences which made it possible for iron to be mined and smelted there cheaply and in vast quantities. For a period in the early Victorian era, one in every five tons of iron produced in the world was produced in the Merthyr area. The iron industry both of the district and of Wales was dominated by four families, each of which owned massive ironworks. The largest ironworks was the Cyfarthfa works which was established in the eighteenth century by the Crawshay family. The Crawshays were one of the most prosperous families in Britain. In 1821, William T. Crawshay had built a mock castle – Cyfarthfa Castle – overlooking the ironworks, as the family home. By the beginning of Victoria's reign, the incumbent was his son, Robert Thompson Crawshay. Cyfarthfa Castle is a large, imposing and impressive, if ostentatious, edifice which still stands and dominates most vistas of the town. It was set in several acres of well-stocked grounds with a large fishing lake. The interior of the castle was fitted and decorated with appropriate opulence.[7]

In contrast, the inhabitants of Merthyr, despite the town's industrial success, had no trappings of luxury, and seem to have experienced conditions comparable to the worst slums of London or Glasgow. In 1851, T. W. Rammell, an inspector for the Board of Health, submitted his report on conditions in Merthyr. It was as damning as it was graphic:

> From a small village it has in half a century grown into an extensive town with a flourishing and busy population of more than 40,000 inhabitants, but without the existence of a single regulation promotive of the good order or well being of the community, or a

---

[6] The 1851 Census, quoted in Harold Carter and Susan Wheatley, *Merthyr Tydfil in 1851*, Cardiff, 1982.

[7] Cyfarthfa Castle is now a museum owned and run by Merthyr Tydfil County Borough Council in association with the Council of Museums for Wales. Some reception rooms have been carefully restored to their nineteenth-century state.

single constituted authority by whom such regulations, if existing, could be carried into effect. In a word, for all intents and purposes of civic government, Merthyr Tydfil is as destitute as the smallest rural village in the empire ...[8]

In fact, 'the smallest rural village in the empire' was probably considerably less destitute. Page after page of Rammell's report produces evidence that Merthyr was lamentably lacking in any of the most common benefits that other towns of it size and station enjoyed. Three years later, William Kay's *Report of the Sanitary Condition of Merthyr Tydfil* provided more evidence of squalor: '[We observed] without surprise, street after street of low, confined tenements, with roads unformed, without footpaths, undrained, presenting a mass of mud and filth, and destitute of the slightest provision for carrying off the refuse of a teeming population ... '[9] While this may not necessarily present an accurate picture of the town as a whole, it remains true that Merthyr had few features in common with other places where amateur brass bands were formed. Most such places were small industrial villages on the edge of larger conurbations. Bands often had affiliations with a factory or some other source of employment that provided a collective focus. The ironworks provided a focus in Merthyr, but these other places manifestly shared a single feature of which virtually every contemporary commentator observed the absence in Merthyr Tydfil: a developed or even embryonic sense of *community*. As Rammell remarked, in Merthyr, 'whenever a man made a little fortune, or even a sufficiency for the supply of his future days, he took leave ... [for] ... a more healthy and agreeable place'.[10]

Thus Merthyr was clearly not the type of place which, mainly through the raw endeavours of its ordinary inhabitants, would have produced a virtuoso amateur brass band, and the extant repertory and unusual instrumentation raised further questions about the date when the band was founded.

Important evidence surviving in the Crawshay archives at the National Library of Wales shows that the band had indeed been established before 1844. A bill of sale to Robert Thompson Crawshay for '3 Eight Key'd Bugles with Tuning Slides', from Charles Pace and Son, is dated 21 March 1840.[11] Though piston valve instruments were widely available, Crawshay was buying keyed instruments. It therefore seems likely

---

[8] T. W. Rammell, *Report to the Board of Health on a Preliminary Inquiry into ... the Sanitary Conditions of the Inhabitants of Merthyr Tydfil*, London, 1850, p. 12.

[9] W. Kay, *Report of the Sanitary Condition of Merthyr Tydfil*, Merthyr Tydfil, 1854, pp. 68–9.

[10] Rammell, *Report*, p. 11.

[11] National Library of Wales Cyfarthfa Papers (NLW Cyf.), Box XIV.

that the players who were to perform on them could already play, as it was valve instruments that were being promoted for players to learn on. That the band had been established in 1838 was further confirmed by a detailed account of the formation of the band printed in Crawshay's obituary.[12]

The first band – formed in 1838 – was amateur and (apparently) incompetent, so it was immediately wound up and re-formed with professional players from London, and touring show and circus players. Even in its first year, this new band was musically literate and technically competent.[13] The first conductor, a Mr Gratian, was a London theatre musician. In the early 1840s he was replaced by a man from a similar musical background, Ralph Livesey. He and his son George were directors of the band for the rest of the century. Players were enticed to Merthyr with promises of abundant playing opportunities, good secure jobs and housing. Crawshay also employed a French arranger, a man named George D'Artney, whose only responsibility was to transcribe and arrange music for the band to play.[14] The establishment of the band was motivated by the same sentiments that led to the building of Cyfarthfa Castle. It was part of the construction of an oasis of culture. The evidence clarifies the identity of the Cyfarthfa Band: unambiguously, this was a functional private band.

Throughout its existence it was entirely separate from the rest of the brass band movement. It seldom entered brass band contests. One important exception was the contest held at the Crystal Palace at Sydenham in the summer of 1860, where it won the second day's competition with a performance of the overture to Verdi's opera *Nabucco*. The 1860 Crystal Palace brass band contest was not a run-of-the mill event, and though it only existed in this manifestation (the contests were revived in 1900) for four consecutive years, it can in many senses be taken as something of a milestone in the history of brass bands.[15]

---

[12] *The Merthyr Express*, 17 May 1879.

[13] A typescript copy of a manuscript kept at Cyfarthfa Castle, which appears to give the start of a history of the Crawshay family, relates the story of the earliest days of the band. The information in this typescript is different from, but consistent with, the story given in Crawshay's obituary.

[14] D'Artney figures prominently in all writings about the band including, for example, David Morgans's *Music and Musicians of Merthyr and District*, Merthyr Tydfil, 1922. But leaving aside the band part books which are presumably in D'Artney's hand, there is no primary source material which casts light on his origins or background. Morgans claims that he was recruited from France and given accommodation on the Crawshay estate, and that he was a notorious and incurable drunkard.

[15] The contest was held over two consecutive days in 1860 and 1861, the first day being called the National Contest, the second the Sydenham Amateur Contest. There seems to have been little material difference between the two events, and most bands

The Crystal Palace Company commissioned the Hull-based impresario and musician Enderby Jackson to run the contest, following the success of similar ventures at Hull and at the Belle Vue Zoological Gardens in Manchester. It drew 39 bands, most of which contested on two consecutive days. Vast crowds supported the event, which attracted much attention from the London press because it was the first large-scale brass band contest to be held in southern England. Jackson's contests provided the model if not the prototype for all brass band contests. They were carefully organized open air events, with a wide variety of attractions – such as balloon ascents – running simultaneously. Central to Jackson's organization of these contests was his liaison with the growing railway network. Bands indicated their point of embarkation on their contest application forms, and he corresponded with the railway companies to set up the novel idea of cheap day excursions.

Crawshay almost certainly put his band forward for this contest because of the distinctive nature of the event. That it was beaten by the Black Dyke Mills Band on the first day may have been a surprise as well as a disappointment. The Cyfarthfa Band did not enter many subsequent contests and seems to have been, in effect, an isolated institution, serving one sponsor and his needs. The band is mentioned by the brass band press, but it is obvious that it was regarded as special. Indeed, a correspondent writing a summary article on brass bands in Wales paid homage to the virtuosity of the Cyfarthfa Band but observed, somewhat caustically, that it could hardly be cited as a Welsh band because it was made up almost entirely of imported Englishmen.

Crawshay died in 1879, by which time the family fortunes were in terminal decline. The band did not last as a major force for long after his death; it seems to have been on the wane by the 1890s. It was during Crawshay's lifetime that the band was at its zenith. It had no democratic structures and was always led by a professional conductor who took his instructions from Crawshay, the sole sponsor. Many of the players too were professionals who, when they joined the band, took other more secure and better paid jobs, most of them in the ironworks. Some younger players joined the band during this period, but all were the offspring of the first generation members. However, some new, outstanding players were brought in, such as the great ophicleidist Sam Hughes, who, during his sojourn in Merthyr Tydfil, ostensibly worked as a 'railway agent'. In fact, Hughes may have been working in London as a professional player with Julien's orchestra and at Covent Garden,

---

entered both of them. The 1862 and 1863 contests were held on one day only. The contest was then discontinued until 1900, when it was held annually without a break until 1936.

in addition to his engagements with the band.[16] It is probably fair to class the players as amateurs – but only just. Hughes was just one of a group of players who were highly accomplished and sophisticated musicians before they ever came to Merthyr.

The repertory

No brass band repertories from the nineteenth century are known to have survived intact and very few have survived in a state which makes their performance possible. The Black Dyke Mills band books, which probably date from 1855, are kept at the band's headquarters at Queensbury, Yorkshire, but less than half of the part books survive, and there is no full score. More complete sets survive in the library of the Besses o' th' Barn Band near Bury in Lancashire but these are later, dating mainly from the 1880s/1890s, and are written in the hand of Alexander Owen, their distinguished conductor. A number of smaller collections survive which do not contain virtuoso music.[17] An abundance of printed music survives in the form of published 'journal' music, but this type of source is much less interesting than handwritten part books, which testify to the musical identity of a group of players at a particular time in history.

Though the Cyfarthfa repertory is not complete, it is by far the largest and most comprehensive brass band music library to have survived. It is also, as far as is known, the repertory which covers the longest period in the existence of any one band – it appears to have been used persistently for almost half a century. The repertory is contained in 104 part books, all handwritten.[18] Most of the copies are done by two hands, almost certainly those of D'Artney, the arranger, and Livesey, the conductor. There are six sets of part books with between 13 and 20 parts in each. A label on the cover of each book identifies the set, or series, to which the book belongs: 'B', 'G', 'H', 'I', 'J', 'L'. Another label gives the name of the instrument, or part, contained in that book. Both labels are printed rather than handwritten (see Table 6.1).

Two ledgers survive which were obviously compiled by a band librarian a considerable time after most of the music was transcribed. They

---

[16] See Trevor Herbert, 'The Virtuosi of Merthyr', *Llafur: The Journal of Welsh Labour History*, August (1988), 60–69; and Trevor Herbert, 'A Lament for Sam Hughes: The Last Ophicleidist', *Planet: The Welsh Internationalist*, July (1991), pp. 66–75.

[17] Among such collections are the 'Goose Eye' band books at Keighley, Yorkshire, and part books used by the W. L. Marriner's Band.

[18] A list of the works in the repertory is given in Herbert, 'Reconstruction'.

Table 6.1   Instrumentation in the Cyfarthfa part books

1	2 B	3 G	4 H	5 I	6 J	7 L
Soprano Cornet				Db	Db	Db
Soprano Cornet						Db
Cornet 1	Ab / Bb	Ab	Ab	*		Ab
Cornet 2	Ab	Ab	Ab	Ab	Ab	Ab
Cornet 3			Ab		Ab	Ab
Repiano Cornet						Ab
Bugle 1	Db / Bb	Db	Db	Bb	Db	
Bugle 2	Bb	Bb	Bb	Db	Bb	
Bugle 3	Ab					
Repiano Bugle	Db	Db	Db			
Flugel Horn						Bb
Saxhorn 1	Db / Eb	Eb	Eb	Eb	Eb	Eb
Saxhorn 2	Db / Eb		Eb	Eb	Eb	Eb
Alto Tbn	*					
Tbn 1	*	*	*	*	*	*
Tbn 2	*	*	*	*	*	
Tbn 3		*	*	*	*	
Tbn 4		*	*	*	*	
Valve Trombone		*				
Valve Trombone		*				
Baritone		Bb	*	Bb	*	*
Baritone				Ab		
Baritone			*			
Euphonion [sic]			*	*	*	
Euphonium						*
Euphonium						Bass
Ophicleide 1	*	*	*	*	*	
Ophicleide 2		*	*	*		
Bombardon	*	*	Bb Bass		BBb	BBb
F Bass		*		*		*
Bassi		*	*	Eb	Eb	Eb
Drum		*	*	*	*	*

Key: Column 1 gives the names of instruments which appear on labels on the covers of all part books. In Columns 2–7, an instrument pitch or an asterisk indicates the instruments named in specific series of books. The asterisk means that an instrument name appears without an instrument pitch. The table should be taken as no more than an impression of the instrumentation of the band at various points of its existence. The labelling was probably not always accurate and most sets of books seem to have been used simultaneously after the 1860s even though the instrument had changed.

do not contain a comprehensive list of all pieces in the repertory, but rather an index by genre – marches, waltzes, overtures and so on – of the music that the band performed most often when the ledger was compiled. It is evident from this catalogue that other sets of music are now lost. However, the five sets that survive seem to be those which were most frequently used, as they contain most of the more important and interesting pieces in the repertory. In all, the six sets contain something in excess of 350 pieces. Because the pieces are unique, bespoke arrangements, they are an important testimony of the technical ability of the band. The authors of the arrangements and the original works knew the players, and it was for them that they wrote. It would have made no sense for them to have written parts that were beyond the capabilities of their players.

There is little evidence of the band having played from printed music, and given that published journal music at this time was extremely simple and undemanding, it is easy to understand why. One of the prizes for the 1860 Crystal Palace contest was a set of military journals. These survive, but it appears that they were never used.[19]

The part books were used for the entire period of the band's existence, but they need to be read with caution, because their use changed in two important respects. First, the repertory was continuously being added to. It is almost certain that the arrangers did not routinely finish all pages of any one set of books before starting another. After all, most of the books were in day-to-day use – the contents of each set grew simultaneously; the five sets do not represent a single chronological sequence revealing the growth of the repertory. Second, the instrument named on the front of a book may not accurately indicate which instrument played that part at any given time. Indeed, it is doubtful whether the labelling was ever entirely accurate. The instrumentation of the band changed several times. For example, parts originally written for ophicleide were played by euphonium players by the mid-1870s, and keyed bugle parts were eventually played by cornets. No new parts were made for new instruments or their players. However, markings on individual leaves inside the books provide clues about a series of changes in instrumentation. It is clear, however, that the mix of keyed and valve instruments continued for much longer than it did elsewhere. After all, the players were expert keyed instrument players when they arrived at Merthyr. They had no need to acquire valve skills.

The greatest part of the repertory can be divided into three groups or types of pieces. The first served the band's function as a surrogate orchestra, and contains a large selection of music from the classical

---

[19] The military journals are archived at the Merthyr Tydfil Public Library.

repertory. *Complete* symphonies by Beethoven, Mozart and Haydn were arranged, but derivatives from opera, particularly contemporary Italian opera, are the most prevalent sources for arrangements. Italian opera selections and overtures were performed in transcription by brass bands in Britain very soon after their first performances. The sources for these arrangements were probably short score publications such as those found in the Novello catalogues.

The second group of pieces served the band's function as a dance band. The Crawshays held elaborate banquets and balls which were famously popular among the well-to-do of South Wales and the West of England.[20] The part books contain a large selection of quadrilles, polkas and waltzes. In common with practices elsewhere, some of the dances, particularly polkas, were elaborated to make virtuoso solos for cornet players. But the form – very long series of repeated sections – indicates that the music was played to be danced to, not merely used as concert pieces.

The third group, which is smaller, is made up of miscellaneous pieces that do not fit easily into the other two categories. It includes some original works, none of which seem to be paralleled in other repertories. Among them is *The Tydfil Overture*[21] by Joseph Parry, the most important Welsh figure in the world of nineteenth-century art music. This is almost certainly the earliest original work for brass band by an established composer, and perhaps the earliest instrumental art-music work for ensemble by any Welsh composer. Other interesting works include an arrangement of 'The Triumphal March'[22] by Charlotte Sainton-Dolby – probably the first arrangement for brass band of a work by a woman composer. Apart from their intrinsic musical interest, these works point to the fact that the band had a status which was quite different from that of other bands of the time, in that it seems to have been the focus of attention from some of the most prominent establishment figures of the day.

---

[20] Watercolour paintings of these occasions by the Welsh artist Penry Williams survive at the Cyfarthfa Castle Museum.

[21] The work is undated, but it is likely that Parry composed it in the late 1870s, following his return from the USA, and prior to his appointment as first Professor of Music at the University College of Wales, Aberystwyth. The parts are headed 'Composed and arranged expressly by Joseph Parry for the Cyfarthfa Band'.

[22] The 'Triumphal March' is part of Sainton-Dolby's cantata *The Legend of St Dorothea* (1876).

Performance practice

The surviving instruments, the part books, contemporary documentary commentaries and photographs all represent sources for the performance practice of the band, but none of these types of source on its own provides conclusive evidence. The earliest surviving photograph, probably taken by about 1850, may well be the earliest photograph of any British brass band. The new 1838 band had 20 players, and played a mixture of keyed and valve instruments, together with trombones and percussion. In 1841 Crawshay bought the three new keyed bugles mentioned above. The 1850 photograph shows a mixture of keyed and valve instruments. The only other picture taken before the end of the century that is of any research value was taken in 1873, and shows the band in attendance at a Crawshay family wedding.

At some time, probably in the late 1840s or early 1850s, Crawshay bought a number of new valve instruments. Many of these survive and are engraved with the Crawshay name. He did not buy British-made piston valve instruments which were easily available, but rotary valve instruments imported from Vienna. Why these instruments were chosen when instruments based on the Sax designs were easily available is difficult to understand – the use of such instruments in Britain is probably unique. Crawshay, like other people of his station, kept an account with a series of leading London trade houses. His supplier of musical accoutrements was Charles Pace. It is possible that he instructed Pace, one of the longest established suppliers, to obtain the best foreign instruments. A simpler explanation is that the purchase of exotic Viennese instruments was one of Crawshay's typically extravagant gestures. It further signified the exclusive and private nature of his band, at a time when piston valve instruments of the Sax design must have been commonly seen in the hands of amateurs. Despite the acquisition of rotary valve instruments, ophicleides and keyed bugles appear to have been used until well into the 1860s. Sam Hughes was with the band in 1858.

Conclusions

The idiomatic repertory of the British brass band has only really developed in the twentieth century, though the standard instrumental format has its origins a little earlier. During the twentieth century the standard brass band sound – mellow and homogenous – has provided a soundscape for a number of television and film images, because it summons up instant resonances of the Victorian working class. This stereotype of the idiom is easily drawn, because the orthodoxies of the brass band have become so firmly fixed. But in the nineteenth century, such standardizations took some time to become established. A variety of circumstances and a multiplicity of musical and social functions must have produced several very different models of brass band. In the densely populated areas of Lancashire and Yorkshire similarities might have emerged very quickly. But elsewhere bands must have developed largely oblivious of what was to become known as the brass band 'movement'. The Cyfarthfa Band is a vivid example of such a phenomenon, but it may not be the only one. Other private bands are known to have existed, and despite the ascendancy of northern bands, the 1863 Crystal Palace contest was won by a band from Blandford in Dorset.

It is not just the twentieth-century peddlers of sound-bites who have characterized Victorian brass bands as a standard species. The Victorians themselves were eager to fashion the brass band into a a series of stock images which substituted for the truth. In 1850, Charles Dickens published an article under the title 'Music in Humble Life', in *Household Words*, the magazine he owned and edited. The article took the Cyfarthfa band as a convenient model:

> [Another] set of harmonious blacksmiths awaken the echoes of the remotest Welsh Mountains. The correspondent of a leading London newspaper, while visiting Merthyr, was exceedingly puzzled by hearing boys in the Cyfarthfa iron works whistling airs rarely heard except in the fashionable ball-room, opera house, or drawing room. He afterwards discovered that the owner of the works, Mr Robert Crawshay, had established among his workers a brass band ... I had the pleasure of hearing them play and was astonished by their proficiency.[23]

The article properly signifies the repertory and quality of the band, but the characterization of it as a 'workers' band, the product of generous philanthropy on the part of Crawshay is thoroughly misleading. It may have suited the moral and social posture of Dickens and his associates, but it disguises the true identity of this remarkable band.

---

[23] *Household Words*, 1, (7), 11 May (1850), 161. Article written by George Hogarth and W. H. Wills.

PART FOUR
The Wesley Family

CHAPTER SEVEN

The Obituary of Samuel Wesley

Philip Olleson

Obituary notices are important, if problematical, sources of information for the biographer and historian. As considered summings-up of
their subjects' lives and achievements, published soon after their death,
they claim to speak with authority. But they are also subject to a
number of conventions and constraints – familiar in broad outline from
present-day examples – which can hamper and circumscribe them and
make them less than wholly truthful and reliable. In addition, despite
their outward appearance of objectivity and detachment, they are inevitably subjective and personal documents, expressing the opinions and
the assessments of their (usually anonymous) authors. For all these
reasons, they need to be treated with particular care. In order to gain
the maximum information from them we need to be sensitive to their
particular features: where to trust them, where to read between the lines
and where to listen attentively to their silences.

The obituary of Samuel Wesley which appeared in *The Times* on the
day after his death on 11 October 1837 is a case in point. It is an
extraordinary document, which for a number of reasons repays close
attention. First, it is an important biographical source, containing a
wealth of detailed information, some of it found nowhere else, and all
of it needing careful evaluation. Second, the very fact of its publication
is a matter for comment and explanation, for lengthy obituaries of
creative artists in the daily press were exceptional at this time, and – as
we shall see later – it is likely that peculiar circumstances were involved
in its writing and appearance. Third, because Wesley's highly unconven-
tional life is well documented in personal letters and papers, it is possible
to compare the account given in the obituary with what is known from
other sources, and thus to gain a particularly good insight into the
obituarizing process.[1]

I am grateful to Christina Bashford and Leanne Langley, discussions with whom
have helped to clarify my thinking on some of the issues of authorship dealt with in this
paper.

[1] The *Times* obituary was substantially reprinted in *Gentleman's Magazine*, 8, n.s.
(1837), 544–6. See also 'Professional Memoranda of the late Mr Samuel Wesley's life',
Musical World, 7 (1837), 81–93, 113–18.

Before considering the obituary itself, a brief sketch of Wesley's life and career will be in order.[2] Samuel Wesley (1766–1837) was the son of the Methodist hymn-writer Charles Wesley (1708–88) and the nephew of John Wesley (1703–91), the founder of Methodism. He therefore came from a distinguished and extremely well-known family. Like his elder brother Charles (1757–1834) he began his musical career as a child prodigy, and was hailed at the age of eight by William Boyce as 'an English Mozart'. Later, he and Charles were to organize several series of private subscription concerts at the family home in Marylebone, intended by their father as opportunities for them to practise music while avoiding exposure to the moral dangers of appearing at public concerts.

In 1778, at the age of 12, Wesley started attending services at Roman Catholic chapels. This development cannot have pleased his father, even though the initial reasons for his interest appear to have been musical rather than religious. But in 1784 he converted to Roman Catholicism, and this was in part the cause of his deep estrangement from his father and from the other members of his family.

Wesley's private life was highly irregular. His marriage to Charlotte Louisa Martin, contracted in the teeth of family opposition in 1793, broke down after years of unhappiness in early 1810. Wesley then set up house with his servant Sarah Suter: he was 42, she was 15 or 16. Their first child was Samuel Sebastian, born in August 1810; he would later eclipse his father in fame. Divorce at this time was not an option for any except the very wealthy, so Wesley and Charlotte had no option but to remain married, and all of the numerous children of the second family were illegitimate.

During all this time, Wesley was making his living as a musician. His bread-and-butter work was teaching at private schools, which he hated and regarded as 'ABC drudgery', but which brought in a regular basic income. His composing and his involvement in London's concert life proceeded by fits and starts, periods of great energy and productivity alternating with periods of depression and almost complete inactivity.

The most successful and active period in Wesley's career was from around 1808 to 1816, when he was active in almost every field open to a London musician of the time: as a composer, a performer on the piano and organ, and as a journalist, critic and lecturer; in his spare time, he also found time to be involved in Roman Catholic church

---

[2] For published accounts of Wesley's life, see G. J. Stevenson, *Memorials of the Wesley Family*, London, 1876, pp. 490–538; J. T. Lightwood, *Samuel Wesley, Musician*, London, 1937. The account here draws substantially on unpublished family letters and papers.

music as the unpaid assistant of Vincent Novello at the Portuguese Embassy chapel. This period was also the time of his discovery of the music of J. S. Bach, of his many performances of Bach's music, and his editions of the organ trio sonatas and the 'Forty-Eight'. He must at this time have presented a picture of abundant and at times manic energy, fitting an almost unbelievable number of activities into his life as a busy freelance musician. But in May 1817 he suffered a serious mental breakdown which resulted in his confinement in an asylum for a period and his complete absence from the musical scene for almost two years. He had a further period of good health and high activity from around 1823 to 1830, but was then affected by a further period of depression from which he emerged only shortly before his death. The last time he appeared in public was on the occasion of Mendelssohn's recital at Christ Church, Newgate Street on 12 September 1837, when he was persuaded to play. Mendelssohn was generous in his praise, but Wesley could only say, 'Sir, you have not heard me play. You should have heard me 40 years ago'.

Wesley was best known as an organist, and was generally acknowledged as the finest player of his age. He was particularly noted for his improvisations, which were of unparalleled brilliance and inventiveness. This brilliance also applied to his conversation and his intellect. But he also had a reputation for plain speaking which often crossed the line into rudeness and intolerance, and a marked disrespect for all those in positions of authority.

These characteristics cannot have helped to advance his career. His scandalous private life would not have endeared him to the parents of prospective pupils, who may well have preferred to send their daughters to a teacher more solid and respectable, if less gifted. His colleagues in the musical profession may have been more tolerant of the irregularity of his domestic arrangements, but advancement there still depended on maintaining harmonious relationships with one's fellow professionals, and Wesley's outspokenness and disregard of conventional niceties of behaviour must have counted against him. In consequence, he stands somewhat apart from the rest of musical London of his time as a maverick figure, never fully part of the small group of professional musicians who ran London's concert life at the time, and never rewarded with the official appointments and honours which went to others with only a small fraction of his musical abilities.

Provided with that overview of Wesley's life, we can now turn to his obituary in *The Times*. How much of what we know from other sources about his life appears in the obituary? How accurate and authoritative is it? To what extent can we believe what it tells us, and to what extent are we to treat it with caution?

The *Times* obituary, under the byline of 'a Correspondent', reads as follows:

It is with unfeigned regret that we have to announce the death of this accomplished scholar and extraordinary musical genius. Mr. Samuel Wesley expired yesterday afternoon, about 20 minutes past 4 o'clock. Although he had been for about a month an invalid, there were no anticipations of so speedy a termination of his mortal career until Tuesday morning last, when it became 5
evident to his family and friends that the long continuance of his disorder (that of diarrhoea) was more than his enfeebled frame could withstand. Exhausted nature rapidly gave way, and the sufferer passed from time to eternity without a struggle. His last moments were engaged in imploring the blessing of the Almighty on his children, and he expired in the effort of bidding them an 10
affectionate farewell.

Mr. Wesley was born on the 24th day of February, 1766, being the same day and month on which Handel came into the world. He was consequently in his 72d year. When only three years old he could play and extemporize freely on the organ, and before he was five had taught himself to read and write a print 15
hand from his unremitting study of the oratorio of *Samson*, which he committed entirely to memory. He also learned by heart within a month the whole of Handel's overtures, and before he was eight years of age had composed and written out an oratorio which he entitled *Ruth*, and presented to Dr Boyce, who acknowledged the compliment in the following terms: – 'Dr 20
Boyce presents his compliments and thanks to his very ingenious brother-composer, Mr. Samuel Wesley, and is very much pleased and obliged by the possession of the oratorio of *Ruth*, which he shall preserve with the utmost care as the most curious product of his musical library.' Before he reached the year of his majority he had become an excellent classical scholar, a fine 25
performer on the pianoforte and organ, and unquestionably the most astonishing extemporaneous player in Europe. His prospects in life were unfortunately clouded by a dreadful accident which befel him in the year 1787. Returning home one evening from a visit to an intimate friend (one of the oldest members of the Madrigal Society), in passing through Snow-hill, 30
he fell into a deep excavation which had been prepared for the foundation of a new building. There he lay insensible, until day-light disclosed his situation, and he was conveyed home. His head had received a most serious injury, and the medical attendants wished to perform the operation of trepanning; but Wesley obstinately refused his consent, and the wound was permitted to heal. 35
This he ever after regretted; for it is supposed that in consequence of some portion of the skull adhering to, or pressing upon, the brain, those periodical states of high nervous irritability originated, which subsequently checked and darkened the splendour of his career. For seven years immediately following his accident he remained in a low desponding state, refusing to cultivate his 40
genius for music. On his recovery he prosecuted the science with the utmost ardour, bringing to light the immortal works of Sebastian Bach, then alike unknown here and on the Continent. In 1815, when on his journey to conduct an oratorio at Norwich, he suffered a relapse of his mental despondency, and for another seven years he retired from public life, endeavouring to find relief 45
in constant attendance upon public worship, and living with the austerity of a hermit. In 1823 he recovered, and up to 1830 composed many excellent pieces, and was much engaged in public performances on the organ. He then relapsed into his former state, but in August last partially recovered his health and spirits. It soon became evident, however, that his constitution was 50
undergoing a great change. When at Christ Church, Newgate-street, about

three weeks since, he rallied, passed a delightful day, and spoke in the evening of Mendelssohn and his 'wonderful mind' in terms of the strongest eulogy. On Saturday last he played extemporaneously to a friend, and composed some psalm tunes. On Monday he endeavoured to write a long testimonial for an old pupil, but which his strength only permitted him to sign, and in the evening retired to his room with a presentiment which the event of yesterday has but too accurately verified.

As a musician his celebrity is greater on the Continent than in his own country. His compositions are grand and masterly; his melodies sweet, varied, and novel; his harmony bold, imposing, unexpected, and sublime. His resources were boundless, and if called upon to extemporize for half-a-dozen times during the evening, each fantasia was new, fresh, and perfectly unlike the others. His execution was very great, close, and neat, and free from labour or effort, and his touch on the pianoforte delicate and *chantante* in the highest degree. His favourite contemporaries were Clementi and Woelfl; his models in early life were Battishill and Worgan on the organ, and subsequently Sebastian Bach. Of young Pinto, who was taken away in the prime of life, he always spoke in terms of rapture, and thought him the Mozart of this country. The amateur Mr. Goodbehere, son of Alderman Goodbehere, he also remembered in high terms of admiration. Mr. Wesley was remarkable for great energy, firmness, nobleness of mind, freedom from envy, penetration, docility, approaching almost to an infantine simplicity, and unvarying adherence to truth These characteristics were united with a credulity which exceeded, if possible, that which marked his uncle, the celebrated John Wesley. His passions were exceedingly strong, and from a habit of always speaking his mind, and his having no idea of management or the *finesse* of human life, he too often by the brilliancy of his wit, or the bitterness of his sarcasm, unthinkingly caused estrangements, if not raised up an enemy. His conversation was rich, copious, and fascinating; no subject could be started which he could not adorn by shrewd remarks, or illustrate by some appropriate and original anecdote. For many years it has been his constant habit to study the Bible night and morning, and, as no meal was taken before he had offered up his orisons to Heaven, so he never lay down without thanksgiving. He disclaimed ever having been a convert to the Roman Catholic Church, observing, that although the Gregorian music had seduced him to their chapels, the tenets of the Romanists had never obtained any influence over his mind. He was regarded with peculiar solicitude by his uncle, John Wesley, who writing in reference to his supposed conversion to Popery observed: 'He may indeed roll a few years in purging fire, but he will surely go to Heaven at last.' Mr. Wesley was accustomed to relate that his father (the Rev. Charles Wesley) when dying called him to his bedside, and addressed him in these words: '*Omnia vanitas et vexatio spiritus: praeter amare Deum, et illi servire*', and blessing him said, 'We shall meet in heaven'. Mr. Wesley has left a large family, nearly all of whom are distinguished for their talents and acquirements. The younger branches, although of very tender years, display evident indications of fine intellect and that exquisite sensibility which characterized the parent. The musical profession has lost its brightest ornament. Since the days of Henry Purcell no British composer has evinced so much genius and learning, developed with such variety and sensibility, or has displayed so much energy and industry in the composition of memorials as lasting as they are extraordinary. Flourishing at a period when composers met with less encouragement than at any epoch in the history of the art, he pursued his course without reference to the applause of the day, resting on the certainty that the time must come when his works would receive that justice which the then state of the art forbade. He cared nothing for the public opinion respecting his compositions: with him the art was all in all, and like Sebastian Bach, Handel, and Mozart, he affords

another instance of the remark, that it is the prerogative of genius to look
forward with a calm but assured expectation that posterity will award that   110
meed of approval which must ever attend its bright and beautiful creations.

Many of the questions arising from a reading of Wesley's obituary
concern aspects of its authorship. Who wrote this obituary? How well
did he (for the author was almost certainly a man) know Wesley, and
how close was he to his family and professional circle? If we can
establish authorship, we will be in a better position to assess the authority and reliability of the obituary; conversely, the degree of authority
and reliability that it possesses may help us to identify the author.

It is clear from many passages in the obituary that its author was
someone close to the Wesley family: see, in particular, the account of
Wesley's meeting with Mendelssohn and of his final illness. Elsewhere
in the obituary there are other references to Wesley's own opinions and
views: see lines 33–9, describing Wesley's head injury and reporting
Wesley's regret that he did not submit himself to the operation of
trepanning; lines 85–8, reporting his denial that he had ever been a
convert to Roman Catholicism; and lines 91–5, reporting his father's
deathbed words to him. Together, these pieces of evidence help to build
up a picture of the obituarist's position as someone in a particularly
privileged and authoritative position as far as the factual information in
the obituary is concerned. We will return later to investigate further the
question of his precise identity.

The next step in establishing the accuracy and authority of the obituary is to check the facts it contains with the information we have from
other sources. If we can establish its accuracy or inaccuracy in those
areas where we have corroborative evidence, we can come to a better
assessment of its reliability in those areas where we do not. In addition,
the pattern of the obituary's accuracies and inaccuracies can itself tell us
more about the author's background and give us further clues about his
identity.

On the whole, the details in the obituary agree very well with what
we know of Wesley's life from other sources; where there are discrepan-
cies, they are easily explicable and do not seriously compromise the
authority of the obituary as a whole. The dates given for Wesley's
extended periods of depression are for the most part remarkably accurate. Admittedly, in line 43 the writer dates Wesley's collapse while on a
visit to Norwich as having happened in August 1815, whereas we know
from Wesley's letters that it occurred a year later. But this incident had
happened over 20 years earlier, and the error is in any case hardly
important: the sort of mistake which can easily be made when attempting to remember the events of the relatively distant past. On the other
hand, the dates of 1823 given for Wesley's recovery and of 1830 for his

subsequent relapse agree precisely with what we know from family letters and papers. The conclusion once again must be that the author was to a remarkable degree well informed about the intimate details of Wesley's life, and this again points to someone close to the family.

Reaching this conclusion about the obituary's overall authority helps us to interpret a specific passage within it: the account in lines 33–47 of Wesley's head injury, and of the effect that this accident is supposed to have had. The story of Wesley's fall into a building excavation is a famous one, included in every biographical account of his life, usually without any attempt to examine its credentials or its provenance. Surprisingly, the *Times* obituary is the first place in which it appears. It is not mentioned in family letters and papers, copious quantities of which have been preserved, and where one might expect to find at least some mention of such a momentous event and its equally momentous consequences. In view of this late appearance of the story and the apparent lack of corroborative evidence from other sources, it seems appropriate to ask some searching questions about the incident. Are we to take the account in the obituary at its face value? And is the fall likely to have had the effects claimed for it?

The first inclination in the light of the lack of corroborating evidence is to treat the account of the fall with a considerable amount of scepticism. As we have seen, however, the author of the obituary was evidently someone close to the Wesley family, and his information about Wesley's life is for the most part accurate and reliable. Furthermore, as we have seen, the obituary on a number of occasions cites Wesley's own views and opinions, and appears to do so here. The clear implication both from the wording of the account and from the large amount of detail it contains is that the story came from Wesley himself. If this is the case, we can confidently accept that the event did indeed happen, and that it became associated in Wesley's mind with the first onset of the attacks of depression which were to afflict him for the rest of his life. We can be more sceptical about the year given: it was a very long time in the past, and as we know from Wesley's manuscript *Reminiscences*,[3] Wesley could be very inaccurate about dates. Perhaps we should understand '1787' as indicating some time or another in Wesley's early adulthood. Whether Wesley was correct in identifying the fall as the cause of his bouts of depression is an entirely different question. All that can usefully be said here is that this was what Wesley believed, and that it was in these terms that he explained his bouts of depression both to himself and to others.

---

[3] British Library, Add. MS 27593.

So far we have been looking at purely factual matters. But we also rely on an obituary to give us a snapshot of the personality and character of its subject. This is a more problematic area, of course, where the obituarist's desire to be authoritative can often be in tension with his or her desire not to speak ill of the dead. To this end, less attractive features of the subject's character or activities are routinely omitted, glossed over, or softened by understatement or euphemism, and the reader needs first to identify and then if possible penetrate the lack of candour which is likely to be present.

The main description of Wesley's character begins in line 71:

> Mr. Wesley was remarkable for great energy, firmness, nobleness of mind, freedom from envy, penetration, docility, approaching almost to an infantine simplicity, and unvarying adherence to truth. These characteristics were united with a credulity which exceeded, if possible, that which marked his uncle, the celebrated John Wesley.

This statement is clearly intended to present Wesley's character in the most positive terms. Hard on its heels, however, comes a statement intended to convey its less attractive features (l. 77):

> His passions were exceedingly strong, and from a habit of always speaking his mind, and his having no idea of management or the *finesse* of human life, he too often by the brilliancy of his wit, or the bitterness of his sarcasm, unthinkingly caused estrangements, if not raised up an enemy.

This gives a tolerably clear picture of Wesley's legendary outspokenness and rudeness, but is still considerably understated: we know from other sources that his behaviour at times went far beyond the bounds of what was tolerable in polite society. But it is probably as candid a summing-up of Wesley's character as was permissible in an obituary notice, or indeed any printed account, at the time.

As it happens, we can compare this account with a rather more outspoken assessment of Wesley's character in a private, unpublished, source: a fragment of a letter from Mary Sabilla Novello, the wife of Vincent Novello, to the bass singer Henry Phillips. She is writing a few years after Wesley's death, apparently in response to an enquiry from Phillips about Wesley's character, and is not hampered by the restraints which clearly would have applied had she been writing for publication. She evidently did not share her husband's high opinion of Wesley; indeed, as the mistress of a literary and artistic salon whose members included Charles and Mary Lamb, Leigh Hunt, Shelley, Keats and other notable figures, she probably considered him socially beyond the pale. In her letter she makes no attempt to conceal her disapproval of him; her sketch none the less conveys Wesley's character with a frankness and immediacy which would have been impossible in an obituary:

> I have great pleasure in sending you two of Wesley's letters which are particularly interesting, as shewing the mind of a man in its opposite extremes of mad fun and excessive depression, to which alternations Wesley always was subject. I knew him unfortunately, too well; pious Catholic, raving atheist, mad, reasonable, drunk and sober – the dread of all wives and regular families, a warm friend, a bitter foe, a satirical talker, a flatterer at times of those he cynically traduced at others – a blasphemer at times, a puleing Methodist at others ...[4]

So far, we have concentrated on what Wesley's obituary has told us, and have said nothing about what it leaves out. The most striking omission, of course, is of any discussion of Wesley's private life: there is no mention of his marriage, let alone of its breakdown, or his subsequent relationship with Sarah Suter. We may note in lines 96–8, however, an allusion to the children of his second family (the 'younger branches'), who are described as displaying 'evident indications of fine intellect and that exquisite sensibility that characterized the parent'. Mentioning these illegitimate children at all, however obliquely, was probably straining the bounds of what was permissible in an obituary; but there was no escaping the celebrity of Samuel Sebastian, by this time well established in his career as a cathedral organist and already eclipsing the fame of his father.

The silence of the obituary about Wesley's private life is precisely what we would expect, and hardly merits comment: discussion of a failed marriage, let alone of an extra-marital relationship and illegitimate children, would have been out of the question in an obituary notice in the early nineteenth century. We may note in passing that Wesley's later biographers felt the same reticence, and that the first mention in print of Sarah Suter and the role she had played as Wesley's partner for the last 26 years of his life was as late as 1899, in F. G. Edwards's article in the *Dictionary of National Biography*. There was no question here of a cover-up or deliberate concealment of the facts; it was simply a matter of the proprieties of what could and what could not be expressed in print.

The summing-up of Wesley's achievement and significance is left until the end of the obituary. This section, like everything that has preceded it, needs careful consideration. How much of the assessment is considered judgement, and how much is mere empty panegyric? And to what extent can we regard the obituarist's assessment as a representative one?

The perspectives already offered on the authorship of the obituary helps to provide some answers. As we have seen, the author was

---

[4] Mary Sybilla Novello to Henry Phillips, British Library, Add. MS 31764, f. 34. The letter can be dated from internal evidence to around 1841.

someone close to the family circle, and his account can be seen as representing the assessment held there, and among Wesley's friends and musical associates. It seems unlikely, however, that the obituary's confident description of Wesley as the greatest English composer since Purcell would have found widespread agreement outside his own circle. To most musicians and concert-goers, by the time of his death Wesley was a half-forgotten figure from the past who had long since ceased to play any significant part in London's musical life, and whose music had been superseded by more up-to-date styles. Those in the music profession, particularly those involved in organ and church music may have had a rather different view of Wesley's significance. But most of them, too, would have found the assessment of the obituary absurdly overstated. For those in Wesley's closest circle, on the other hand, and particularly for those in his musical circle, the general assessment would probably have seemed just, and the picture of Wesley as a neglected genius would have appeared as nothing less than the truth.

But this concluding section of the obituary goes further than merely presenting the understandably partisan views of those closest to Wesley, and a view of his importance that would have appeared inflated to most readers. With its assertion that Wesley 'cared nothing for the public opinion for his compositions' (l. 107) the obituary attempts to claim Wesley as an archetypal Romantic artist. In this detail, the obituary is demonstrably false: Wesley cared greatly for public opinion, and his attitude to worldly fame was far from that attributed to him here. He may at times have affected a lordly unconcern at the lack of public interest in his largest and most ambitious works such as the *Confitebor tibi, Domine*, composed in 1799 and only performed once in his lifetime, but only the most naïve observer would have taken this stance at its face value.

We may conclude by returning to the question of authorship. The first point to address is the appearance of an obituary notice at all. At this time, the obituary section was not the regular feature of newspapers that it is today, and obituaries were few and far between. Thus, although the deaths of such nationally famous figures such as Lord Byron (d. 1824) and Sir Walter Scott (d. 1832) received extensive treatment, those of less prominent figures in the worlds of literature, the fine arts, and music frequently received only the briefest of mentions. There was, for example, no obituary in *The Times* for Wesley's contemporary, Thomas Attwood, who died in the year after Wesley and who as organist of St Paul's Cathedral and composer to George IV was a public figure in a way Wesley never was. We need to ask how it was that Wesley received an extensive obituary, when a figure as famous as Attwood did not.

The obvious answer is that Wesley's obituary appeared through personal intervention. Although there is no explicit information on how this came about, there is a good deal of circumstantial evidence which points to a close connection between members of Wesley's circle and a senior figure at *The Times* who was able to secure the insertion, first of the obituary, and then, six days later, of an equally detailed account of the funeral service and burial.

The contact at *The Times* was Thomas Massa Alsager (1779–1846), the manager of the paper's office and one of its proprietors.[5] He was also a prominent amateur musician, an occasional writer on music in *The Times* and elsewhere and an influential patron of music, the importance of whose role in London music is only now beginning fully to be recognized.[6] He had been responsible for organizing the first performance in Britain of Beethoven's *Missa Solemnis* at his house on Christmas Eve 1832, and he was later to play an important part in the promotion of the music of Beethoven and in the foundation of the Beethoven Quartet Society.[7] He was also a friend of Mendelssohn, who was a frequent visitor at his house. Significantly for the present discussion, he had strong links with Vincent Novello and his family and professional and social circle. Several members of the Novello family had taken part in his *Missa solemnis* performance: Vincent Novello himself played the organ, Novello's daughter Clara and son Alfred were the soprano and bass soloists, and his son Edward, his daughter Victoria and her husband Charles Cowden Clarke sang in the chorus.[8] Given his Novello connections, Alsager would almost certainly have met Wesley and no doubt shared Novello's high opinion of him. In addition, his senior position at *The Times* would have ensured that he could readily secure the insertion of an obituary notice written by a friend of the family.

We can now construct a hypothetical sequence of events for the preparation of the obituary. At some point, presumably in the final month of Wesley's life, when according to the obituary he was an

---

[5] For Alsager, see *The Times*, *The History of The Times. Vol. 1: The Thunderer in the Making, 1785–1841*, London, 1935, pp. 415–16. Alsager joined *The Times* in 1817 as City Correspondent, founded the City office in Birchin Lane and inaugurated the 'City' article; he was made a manager in 1821.

[6] See David B. Levy, 'Thomas Massa Alsager, Esq.: A Beethoven Advocate in London', *19th-Century Music*, 9 (1985), 119–27; Leanne Langley, 'The English Musical Journal in the Early Nineteenth Century', PhD, University of North Carolina at Chapel Hill, 1983; Christina Bashford, 'Public Chamber-Music Concerts in London, 1835–50: Aspects of History, Repertory and Reception', PhD, University of London, 1996.

[7] Bashford, 'Public Chamber-Music Concerts in London', pp. 180–88.

[8] Levy, 'Thomas Massa Alsager, Esq.', pp. 121–2, citing programmes at the British Library (Add. MS 52347, f. 1) and the Fitzwilliam Museum, Cambridge.

invalid, an approach would have been made to Alsager at *The Times* and agreement reached about the inclusion of an obituary notice. The bulk of the obituary would then have been written at leisure, by someone who knew Wesley well and possessed the necessary journalistic skills. The detailed sections about Wesley's early musical life came directly from the account by Wesley's father which had first been published in 1781[9] and had subsequently been reprinted several times, most recently in 1834 in the *Wesleyan Methodist Magazine*;[10] other sections would have been compiled from information gathered from a variety of family and other sources. As soon as the critical nature of Wesley's condition became apparent (on the morning of 10 October, according to the obituary), *The Times* would have been alerted of his impending death. Following the death, at 4.20 p.m. on 11 October, the final details would have been added and the completed article taken to the offices of *The Times* for inclusion in the following day's paper.

Who was the author of the obituary? Given Wesley's close links with journalistic and literary circles, it could have been one of a number of people. One strong candidate is Vincent Novello, who as one of Wesley's closest friends and professional associates over a long period was certainly the best placed to speak authoritatively about him. Another is Charles Cowden Clarke (1787–1877), Novello's son-in-law and the first editor of the *Musical World*, who had been responsible the previous year for commissioning an article from Wesley for its first number.[11] Yet another is Henry John Gauntlett (1805–76), a pupil of Wesley and the organist at this time of Christ Church, Newgate Street, where Wesley and Mendelssohn had had their famous meeting in the month before Wesley's death; he was at this time a frequent contributor to *The Musical World*, which he was later for a time to edit.

Novello, Gauntlett and Cowden Clarke all came from the world of music and musical journalism. On the other hand, the wealth of the references to Wesley's Methodist background might suggest that the author may have come from a Methodist quarter, or at least that someone from the Methodist community had a significant hand in the content of the obituary. The most obvious candidate here is the Reverend Thomas Jackson (1783–1873), the editor of the *Wesleyan Methodist*

---

[9] Included in Daines Barrington's 'Account of Master Samuel Wesley', in his *Miscellanies*, London, 1781, pp. 291–310.

[10] 'Anecdotes of the Early Life of Samuel Wesley, Esq.', *Wesleyan Methodist Magazine*, 13, 3rd series (1834), 596–9, 670–74.

[11] 'A Sketch of the State of Music in England from the Year 1778 up to the Present', *Musical World*, 1 (1836), 1–3. For the circumstances of the publication of this article and the non-appearance of its projected continuation, see Philip Olleson, 'Samuel Wesley and the European Magazine', *Notes*, 52 (1996), 1097–1111.

Magazine, who was later to include a substantial account of parts of Wesley's life in his biography of Wesley's father.[12] He and Wesley had known each other since November 1826, when Wesley had approached him about the publication of an edition of hymn-tunes by Handel to words by Wesley's father, and they had had subsequent business dealings in connection with the publication of a collection of hymn-tunes by Wesley himself.[13] More recently, Jackson had been in regular contact with the family in connection with the payment of the allowance made to the Wesley family by the Book Room in respect of the copyright in Wesley's father's hymns; on the death of Wesley's brother Charles in 1834, this allowance had passed to Wesley, and it had helped to ease the poverty of his final years.[14] Jackson was present at Wesley's bedside during his final hours if not actually at his death, and attended his funeral.[15] If he was not the overall author of the obituary, it is probable that he contributed the information on which the part dealing with Wesley's Methodist background was based.

Establishing the precise identity of the author of the obituary, however, is relatively unimportant. As we have seen, more than one person may have been involved in its writing, and it was certainly put together from information gathered from a variety of sources. What is important is to recognize the quarter from which it came, and its status as essentially a family memoir, with all that this implies for the reliability of its factual statements on the one hand, and the inevitably partisan nature of its assessment of the importance and significance of Wesley and his music on the other.

---

[12] Thomas Jackson, *The Life of the Rev. Charles Wesley, M.A.*, 2 vols, London, 1841, vol. 2, pp. 329–76.

[13] *The Fitzwilliam Music, never published. Three Hymns, the Words by the late Revd Charles Wesley, A.M. of Christ Church College, Oxon, and set to Music by George Frederick Handel, faithfully transcribed from his Autography in the Library of the Fitzwilliam Museum, Cambridge, by Samuel Wesley, and now very respectfully presented to the Wesleyan Society at large*, London, 1826; *Original Hymn Tunes, adapted to every Metre in the collection by the Rev. John Wesley*, London, 1828.

[14] Thomas Jackson, *Recollections of my Own Life and Times*, London, 1874, pp. 231–2. A number of letters from Wesley to Jackson relating to the payment of this allowance are preserved at John Wesley's Chapel, Bristol.

[15] Jackson, *Recollections*, p. 232.

CHAPTER EIGHT

The Unknown Wesley: The Early Instrumental and Secular Vocal Music of Samuel Sebastian Wesley

Peter Horton

Despite the recent growth of interest in nineteenth-century British music, large areas of the repertory still remain almost unknown, among them the group of works for the concert hall, theatre or domestic use by Samuel Sebastian Wesley. Yet these were the pieces which not only initially dominated his output but were also the means by which he first gained recognition as a composer. Indeed, as the Appendix to this chapter shows, for most of the 1830s compositions for church use formed but a small part of an extensive series of songs, glees, choral, orchestral, piano and organ works. It is to some of these, their place in his output and their relationship with his better known works for the church that the following pages are devoted. A glance first at Wesley's background, however, will help to set the scene.

Although born into an educated, respectable middle-class family, Wesley's childhood was anything but conventional. His father, Samuel, was the younger son of the great hymn-writer Charles and the great-nephew of John, the founder of Methodism, but despite being one of the foremost composers and organists of his time he knew little fame and rather less fortune. Indeed, his individual approach to morality (influenced by the radical views on marriage of Martin Madan), impatience with those in a position of authority, early conversion to Catholicism and manic-depressive personality had all contrived to prevent him from obtaining employment worthy of his talents, and his only regular income came from teaching in a girls' school, an occupation he loathed. An unfortunate marriage had brought little happiness and although it survived until 1810, it had been punctuated by several periods of separation from his wife: the final, irrevocable rift was caused by Samuel's liaison with their new teenage housemaid, Sarah Suter, whose first child, Samuel Sebastian, was born in August 1810. The couple thereafter lived together as man and wife but, with the added burden of a considerable maintenance award to his estranged wife, Samuel found it even harder to make ends meet and in 1817, during a particularly severe attack of depression, threw himself from an upstairs window to escape from imaginary creditors. During his subsequent detention in a private asylum well-meaning friends sought to help provide for his family, and it was probably as a result of their exertions that Samuel Sebastian was accepted as one of the Children (choristers) of the Chapel Royal, St James's Palace. For the next eight and a half years the house of William Hawes, Master of the Children, was to be his home, and the latter's influence on his own development as a musician was to be considerable.

Hawes was a man of many parts. In addition to his responsibilities at the Chapel Royal he was also Master of the Choristers, almoner and lay vicar at St Paul's Cathedral, lay vicar at Westminster Abbey, music publisher, conductor of the Madrigal Society and responsible for the music at many city banquets (for which he would use his choristers and pocket most of their fees); he was later to be music director of the English Opera House and conductor of the Lent Oratorio Concerts. Not surprisingly, he did not wish to lose the services of his former chorister (whom he described as 'the best boy he had ever had')[1] when his voice broke in 1826, and from 1828 (if not before) involved him in the work of the English Opera House as 'pianist and conductor of the chorus' – presumably a *répétiteur*-like role; in 1830 he also obtained for him the post of organist at the oratorio concerts and a year later published his earliest compositions. Although Wesley concurrently held a series of organists' posts at London churches and was influenced by the playing of Thomas Adams at St George's, Camberwell, and on the large organ at the Appolonicon, it was undoubtedly his work with Hawes at the English Opera House which was to have the greatest influence on his subsequent development as a composer.

In his choice of repertory Hawes was nothing if not adventurous and included a wide range of recent works. Weber's *Der Freischütz* had been given in the 1824 season and in subsequent years London audiences were introduced to an adaptation of Winter's *Das Unterbrochene Opferfest* (*The Oracle; or, The Interrupted Sacrifice*), arrangements of Mozart's *Così fan Tutte* (as *Tit for Tat; or The Tables Turned*) and *Don Giovanni*, Ries's *Die Räuberbraut* (*The Robber's Bride*) and *The Sorceress* and Marschner's *Der Vampyr*, as well as many shorter pieces by native composers. We can see the results of Wesley's exposure to these and similar compositions in a number of works dating from the early 1830s, not least the overture and 'melodramatick music' he contributed in 1832 to Edward Fitzball's melodrama *The Dilosk Gatherer*.[2] Given a

[1] G. J. Stevenson, *Memorials of the Wesley Family*, London, 1876, p. 545.
[2] Produced at the Olympic Theatre, 30 July 1832.

run of 12 performances, it failed to impress the critic of *The Theatrical Observer* who noted that although 'Messrs. Hawes and S.S. Wesley claim the honour of composing the music ... to our thinking, it is scarcely to the reputation of either gentlemen'.[3] Independent corroboration of the skills he acquired is provided by H. J. Gauntlett who, in 1835, commended his 'perfect knowledge of the extraordinary combinations to be met with in the modern Opera'.[4]

Wesley's other main platform in the capital had been the annual Lent Oratorio Concerts at Drury Lane and Covent Garden Theatres where, for three seasons from 1830, he acted as organist. Here, too, he had the opportunity to introduce works of his own, playing his *Variations on 'God save the King'* for organ in 1831 and accompanying a setting for vocal quartet and organ of the 'Benedictus qui venit' a year later. It was against such a background of involvement at the forefront of musical life in London that Wesley embarked upon his career as a composer, and with this in mind his choice of those forms for which there were opportunities for performance or publication becomes more readily understandable. So, too, does his custom of dedicating works to those with influence or the potential to assist him: J. B. Cramer, Mrs Hawes, Vincent Novello, Henry Mullinex (his piano teacher at the Chapel Royal) and Robert Glenn (organist of Christ's Hospital and later to become his brother-in-law).[5] Embracing all genres except chamber music, they provide evidence of his complete grasp of the contemporary early romantic idiom and, in a number of works, an increasingly idiosyncratic use of it. Such characteristic features as strong diatonic dissonance, a fondness for plunging into remote keys and contrapuntally inspired textures (including simultaneous false relations and variations on the 'English' cadence) are all present, while the use of similar motifs in both sacred and secular works makes for some fascinating comparisons.

By 1832 Wesley had also received several favourable reviews of his published compositions and it therefore seems the more strange that, within a few weeks of the production of *The Dilosk Gatherer*, he should have chosen to forsake London for the rural isolation of Hereford. There can be no doubt that he little suspected what a profound

---

[3] See [F. G. Edwards], 'Samuel Sebastian Wesley', *The Musical Times*, 41 (1900), 299.

[4] Exeter Cathedral Library MS D & C Exeter 7061/Wesley papers/2. (Also quoted by J. T. Lightwood, 'S.S. Wesley – A Sad Story', *The Choir and Musical Journal*, 32 (1941), 101.)

[5] Glenn, who had already provided financial assistance to Samuel Wesley, was comfortably off and when Samuel Sebastian submitted his anthem 'The Wilderness' for the Gresham Prize Medal the possibility of Glenn being willing to buy it from him was clearly in his mind (as he wrote to his mother): 'If I get the gold medal will Glenn *buy* it, it is worth 5 guineas.' British Library, *Lbl* Add. MS 30519, f.14.

effect such a move would have on his career, nor that for one used to the standards of one of the foremost musical centres in Europe it was a rude awakening:

> Painful and dangerous is the position of a young musician who, after acquiring great knowledge of his art in the Metropolis, joins a country Cathedral. At first he can scarcely believe that the mass of error and inferiority in which he has to participate is habitual and irremediable. He thinks he will reform matters, gently, and without giving offence; but he soon discovers that it is his approbation and not his advice that is needed. The Choir is 'the best in England,' (such being the belief at most Cathedrals,) and, if he give trouble in his attempts at improvement, he would be, by some Chapters, at once voted a person with whom they 'cannot go on smoothly,' and 'a bore.' The old man knows how to tolerate error, and even profit by it; but in youth, the love of truth is innate and absorbing.[6]

He had probably been enticed to Hereford by the recently appointed dean, Dr John Merewether, formerly incumbent at Hampton where for two years he had held the post of evening organist. The prospect of an enhanced status and professional independence doubtless proved irresistible and it was not until he had been there for several months that the full extent of his isolation, both physical and musical, began to sink in. An immediate consequence, however, was the completion of the work which effectively marked the start of his career as a church composer – the anthem 'The Wilderness'. First performed at the reopening of the rebuilt cathedral organ in November 1832, its confident use of an unashamedly contemporary idiom (within the framework of a traditional verse anthem) represented a radical new departure for English church music and also provides an early example of that fruitful stylistic cross-fertilization seen in his music during the 1830s. What the Hereford congregation made of such passages as the sequential modulations and clashing contrary motion parallel thirds in the section 'For in the wilderness', the dramatic recitative 'And a highway shall be there' or the affecting chromaticism of the concluding verse 'And sorrow and sighing' can only be imagined, for nothing remotely like it had been heard in an anthem before. The composition of 'The Wilderness' also marked the beginning of a period of some ten years during which sacred music came gradually to dominate his output. Whether this would have happened had circumstances been different remains a moot point, and his later comment that he 'left London when very young ... intending to compose chiefly for the Church'[7] should probably be treated with some

---

6 S. S. Wesley, *A Few Words on Cathedral Music and the Musical System of the Church*, London, 1849, pp. 11–12.
7 British Library, *Lbl* Add. MS 35019, ff. 124–5.

scepticism. Indeed, within two months of the completion of the anthem we find him writing to his friend W. H. Kearns about the possibility of submitting two works for one of the Philharmonic Society's 'Trial' nights: 'I ... am now going to address you on a subject very near my heart as you will know. I saw an account of Mendelssohn's intended proceedings at the Philharmonic. *I will send something* ... I shall *send* ... an Overture and my Benedictus newly *scored* ... '[8]

From a letter to the secretary we can sense his irritation at the way Mendelssohn was fêted:

> I take the liberty of troubling you with two compositions of mine ...
> I am not unacquainted with the suspicious view with which the Musical writings of Englishmen are [sic] received by your Society. I cannot but admit that those suspicions are most fully founded, but from the liberal patronage you have lately bestowed on a foreigner, 'of distinguished merit, truly' I have ventured to hope, that even the accompanying productions may not be thrown aside *unexamined*.[9]

Sadly he was to be disappointed. Although the Overture was accepted for rehearsal on 31 January (which, he wrote to Kearns, 'pleased me much for should it be succesful I shall receive a *spur* which may be highly useful to *me*')[10] it was not given a concert performance and this was to be the last occasion on which one of his purely orchestral works was heard in the capital. The award later that year by the Gentlemen's Glee Club, Manchester, of a gold medal for his five-part setting of 'I wish to tune my quiv'ring lyre' must have been some compensation, as was the opportunity to programme three of his own works at the 1834 Hereford Festival. Yet despite some favourable comment in the press none of these – a setting of the Sanctus for chorus and orchestra, a sacred song for baritone and orchestra ('Abraham's Offering') and an overture – was ever heard again. Neither was a short cantata for four solo voices, 'Millions of Spiritual Creatures' (to verses from *Paradise Lost*), given at Gloucester a year later. Coinciding with his move to Exeter – and away from the opportunities for performance which the Three Choirs Festival had provided – this effectively marked the end of his attempts to gain recognition as a composer outside the relatively specialized fields of church and organ music. Indeed, after completing a number of works for the piano and organ during the later 1830s and early 1840s, he wrote no further instrumental works for some 20 years and no more than a handful of pieces other than for church use during the remainder of his life.

---

[8] British Library, *Lbl* Add. MS 69435, f. 5v.

[9] British Library, *Lbl* Loan 48/13/35 (Royal Philharmonic Society Letters Vol. 35).

[10] British Library, *Lbl* Add. MS 69435, f. 9.

Given that many of the works have either remained unpublished or have not been reissued since their original publication in the 1830s or 40s, it is not surprising that even their existence should have been almost forgotten. Yet better acquaintance with this sizeable part of Wesley's *oeuvre* not only enables us to see – and hear – his church music in truer perspective but also reveals a number of pieces which rank among his best. One of the earliest to reveal his distinctive voice is a set of Variations for organ on 'God save the King' (see Example 8.1), completed when he was 19 and first heard in October 1829 at the opening of the rebuilt organ in St Mary Redcliffe, Bristol. Full of the vitality of youth, it stands as a monument to his considerable playing technique: 'This is, in many respects, an extraordinary composition'[11] declared *The Harmonicon*, noting in particular 'the uncommon use made of the pedals' (for which Wesley had provided a third stave) and asking who, apart from him, could cope with such writing. The interest of the work, however, lies as much in its musical content as in its technical demands. The carefully differentiated textures, with the two manuals and pedals frequently characterized by distinctive tonal colours, the use of contrasted blocks of sound and bold harmonic effects all betoken a composer with an ear for colour and a feeling for drama. Particularly effective is the *minore* slow variation with its plentiful diminished 7ths and arresting Neapolitan harmony before the final cadence.

Although the Variations provide little hint of that independence of harmonic thought so characteristic of Wesley's mature music, their free use of such features as augmented triads, augmented 6ths, diminished 7ths and that other device he so loved, the simultaneous false relation, provides ample evidence of a free-thinking composer, ever willing to experiment. The same boldness is found in the first edition of *A Selection of Psalm Tunes Adapted Expressly to the English Organ with Pedals* (published in 1834 but probably written a year or two earlier), although here the occasional harmonic waywardness suggests that novelty, not musicality, was sometimes his primary concern. Harmonic innovation of a different order is seen in one of the short numbers which make up the 'melodramatic' music for *The Dilosk Gatherer* (see Example 8.2). Depicting a moment of great drama when Fergus, the hero, is climbing a precarious ruined tower to rescue his infant child from an eagle's nest, its musical structure is founded on a descending whole-tone scale in the bass. Harmonized by a series of minor triads and diminshed or dominant 7ths, its conception is remarkable for so youthful a composer and must surely represent one of the first uses of such a scale in this country, if not in Europe.

---

[11] Review of Samuel Wesley's 'God save the King', *The Harmonicon*, 20 (1831), 196.

Example 8.1   Variations on 'God save the King' (Variation 6)

Elsewhere the score contains numerous reminders of Wesley's exposure to the music of Weber, Spohr and their contemporaries and, in the Overture (see Example 8.3), includes a well-constructed movement in A B A form. One of its most striking features is the sense of breadth conveyed by the long harmonic paragraphs of the first section, whether at the opening where sustained harmonies, ostinato figures in the first violin part and a slow-moving solo horn conjure up a vision of the gently rocking sea by which the work opens, or in the equally expansive second subject group. Ominous string temolandi presage a change of mood and introduce the central Allegro agitato (in the tonic minor), dominated by a vigorous passage of imitative counterpoint (which recurs in a later number), before slowly falling woodwind chords over an inner pedal lead to a silent pause and the recapitulation of the opening.

Long series of sustained harmonies characterize another contemporary work, the Overture in E (see Example 8.4). Here, however, the almost continuous quaver movement in the string parts (which gives the music its compelling forward drive), the general lightness of touch and the deft orchestration are all reminiscent of Mendelssohn and imply, moreover, that this could have been the overture Wesley submitted to the Philharmonic Society in 1833. In fact its history is something of a mystery and its survival purely as a set of professionally copied orchestral parts (simply labelled 'S. Wesley') has led to its having been hitherto attributed to Samuel Wesley.[12] That the watermark date of the paper is 1834, that the copyist (I. Hedgley) was the one employed by Samuel Sebastian for the 1834 Hereford Festival at which an overture of his composition was performed, that it contains echoes of both the song 'There be none of beauty's daughters' and the Rondo in C for piano, that the style of the music with its strong romantic leanings is at variance with Samuel's other late works and that he had written no orchestral music since c. 1815 suggest that it is much more likely to be by the younger Wesley than his father.[13] Scored for a larger orchestra than *The Dilosk Gatherer* (double woodwind, four horns, two trumpets, three trombones, timpani and strings), it is an impressive work, nowhere more so than in the coda where rapid figuration in the violin parts and rising arpeggios for the trombones combine to reinforce the

---

[12] See British Library, *Lbl* Add. MS 35010, ff. 39–100.

[13] Further circumstantial evidence includes the fact that no overture by Samuel Wesley is known to have been performed in 1834 and that the work was excluded from the list of works appended to the article on Wesley in the first edition of Grove's *Dictionary of Music and Musicians* (although his other overtures were included). As the list had been compiled with the assistance of the composer's daughter Eliza, one would not have expected her to have omitted a work apparently performed when she was 15.

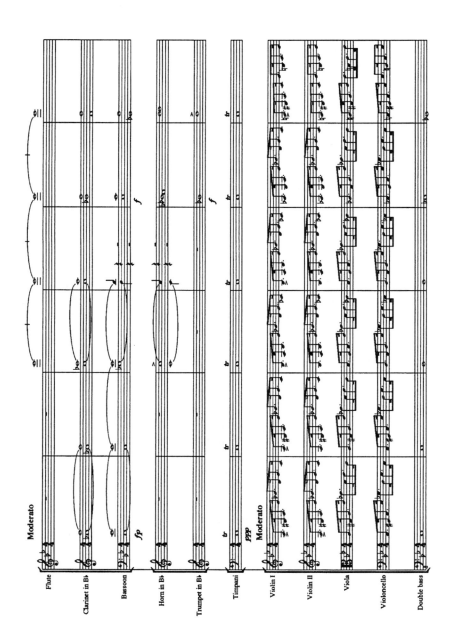

8.2a

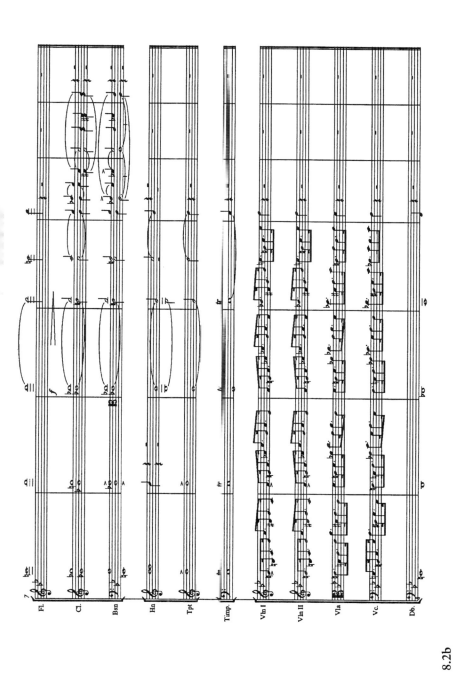

8.2b

Example 8.2 *The Dilosk Gatherer*, no. 16 (British Library Add. MS 33819)

insistent subdominant harmony and give the music an almost Brucknerian grandeur.

The one-movement Symphony (see Example 8.5) is another work whose history is obscure. Surviving solely as a somewhat hastily written autograph score, much of it on paper dated 1834, it could theoretically be the work played at Hereford that year, although the existence of a set of parts for the Overture makes this unlikely. Indeed, the only suggestion that it might ever have been performed is a note on the score that a hairpin *crescendo* and *diminuendo* should be added to all the parts. (That Wesley should have written a work for which there was no immediate chance of performance is not as unlikely as it might sound, with one of his finest anthems, 'Let us lift up our heart' (c. 1836), apparently never having been sung before its publication in 1853.) In contrast to the overture's clear, essentially homophonic textures and economy of thematic material, the Symphony is remarkable both for its consistently contrapuntal nature and for its wealth of musical ideas. It also reveals a new-found harmonic inventiveness, with a number of examples of that typically Wesleyan feature of a sustained dissonant inner pedal point (particularly a dominant pedal sustained through an interrupted cadence in the relative minor). In his handling of chromaticism Wesley is also bolder than in the overture. One of the most exciting sections occurs near the end of the development where a slow-moving, almost chorale-like phrase for the woodwind and brass (heard earlier in the movement), leads into a vigorous passage of double counterpoint and finally a series of wonderfully bold harmonic sidesteps which sweep the music rapidly through the keys of E, F, D♭, D minor, B♭, B minor before reaching a degree of stability in the tonic, C minor.

An intriguing aspect of the score is the entirely incidental similarity of certain phrases – the scalic passages, the insistent use of dotted rhythms – to later orchestral works by Wesley's exact contemporary, Robert Schumann. Even the frequently thick orchestral texture is not dissimilar and suggests, moreover, the influence of a third figure, Louis Spohr. Not only was the latter one of Wesley's most revered composers, but he was also to praise his handling of the orchestra many years later[14] (and frequently included the overture to *Jessonda* in his organ recital programmes).

Few of Wesley's works from the early and mid-1830s – whether sacred or secular – do not reveal some evidence of Spohr's legacy, and

---

[14] In his diary entry for 6 January 1866 Hubert Parry recorded a discussion with Wesley about writing for the orchestra: 'He told me that the reason why Spohr so excelled was because he could bring such a marvellous tone out of his orchestra. Mendelssohn could not be sure of it.' (Shulbrede Priory, Lynchmere, Sussex.)

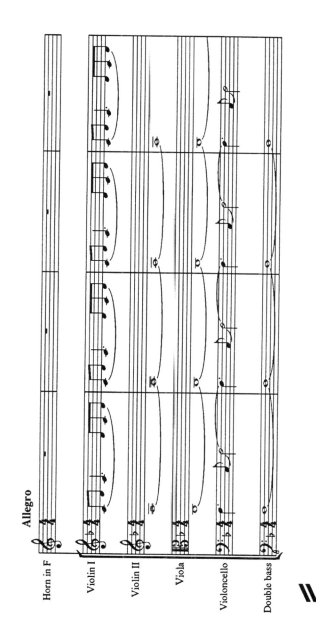

8.3a

Example 8.3   Overture to *The Dilosk Gatherer* (British Library Add. MS 33819)

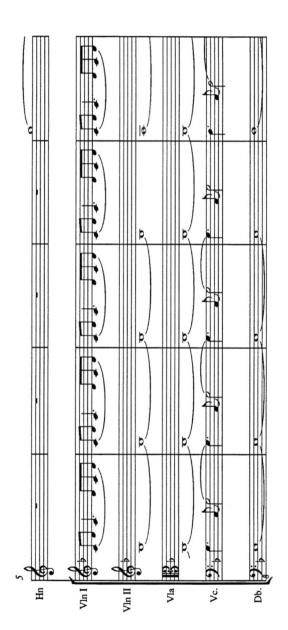

8.3b

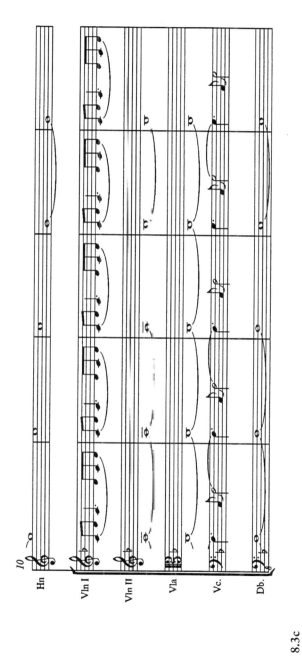

8.3c

Example 8.3 Overture to *The Dilosk Gatherer* (continued)

8.3d

Example 8.3   Overture to *The Dilosk Gatherer* (continued)

8.3e

Example 8.3   Overture to *The Dilosk Gatherer* (continued)

8.3f

the influence of his music is certainly felt in the sacred song for baritone and orchestra, *Abraham's Offering* (see Example 8.6). The text, by Wesley's acquaintance W. H. Bellamy, tells the story of God's call to Abraham to sacrifice his son Isaac and evoked a ready response from Wesley, resulting in a work of great emotional power whose consistently contrapuntal texture provides a secure foundation for a dramatic large-scale structure. From its brooding, gloom-laden opening in E flat minor, through the soloist's recitative entry to the dissonant final climax and hushed arioso which concludes the first section, the flow of the music is controlled by a skilled hand. The build-up to the phrase 'Spare mighty God' is especially effective. After a dominant (B^b) cadence, the outer parts diverge chromatically against a sustained inner dominant pedal, creating considerable passing dissonance but demonstrating impeccable logic in the part-writing. The overall effect is splendid.

Here and throughout the work Wesley makes much of simultaneous false relations, and it was doubtless his liberal use of these and other strong dissonances, not to mention his adventurous chromatic harmony, which caused problems for the soloist, Henry Phillips. As the local press tactfully reported, 'Mr. Phillips was evidently new to the subject, which circumstance was much against the effect of the performance'.[15]

Similarly circumspect criticism greeted Wesley's short cantata 'Millions of spiritual creatures' (a setting for solo quartet of verses from *Paradise Lost*) on its performance at the 1835 Gloucester Festival. Described by *The Musical Magazine* as a 'singular composition ... [which] possesses much originality',[16] it is imaginatively scored and includes some highly effective modulations, but is weakened by a dependence upon homophonic writing and regular, short phrases which largely preclude the possibility of building up the broad paragraphs so characteristic of *Abraham's Offering*. Paradoxically, it is to the glees for unaccompanied men's voices, written for the Gentlemen's Glee Club, Manchester, that one must turn to find examples of extended contrapuntal writing. The opening movements of 'I wish to tune my quiv'ring lyre' and 'When fierce conflicting passions rend the breast', in particular, possess the same exhilarating vigour as the best writing in the church music and, like that, are sustained in their forward flow by a liberal use of suspensions and appoggiaturas. But it was their harmony which most appealed to the reviewer in *The Musical World* (Edward Holmes?). Describing them as being 'conspicuous for well conceived design, feeling, and a graceful melodious spirit', he especially appreciated

---

[15] *The Hereford Times*, 13 September 1834, 3.
[16] *The Musical Magazine* (10), October, (1835), 154.

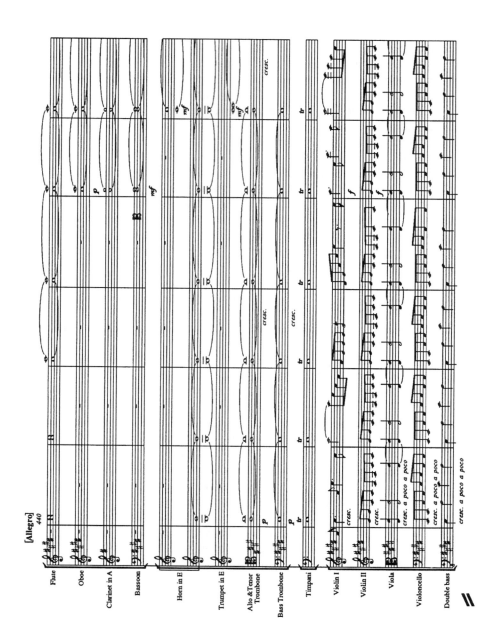

8.4a

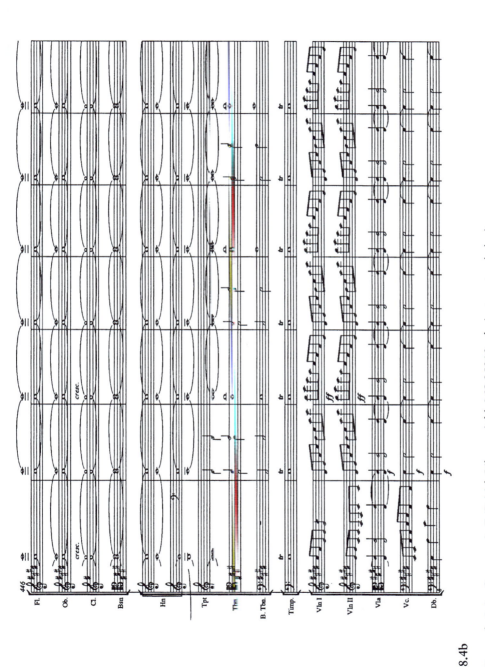

8.4b

Example 8.4 Overture in E (British Library Add. MS 35010: clarinet parts missing)

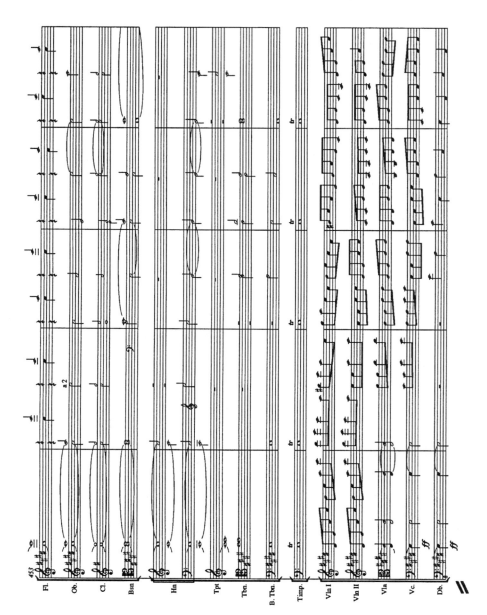

8.4c

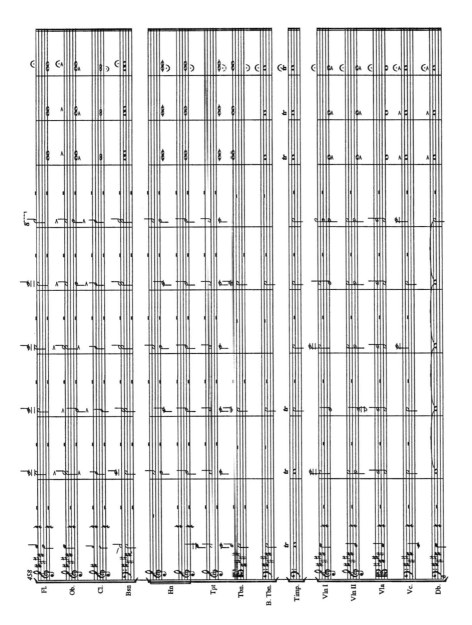

8.4d

Example 8.4　Overture in E (continued)

8.5a

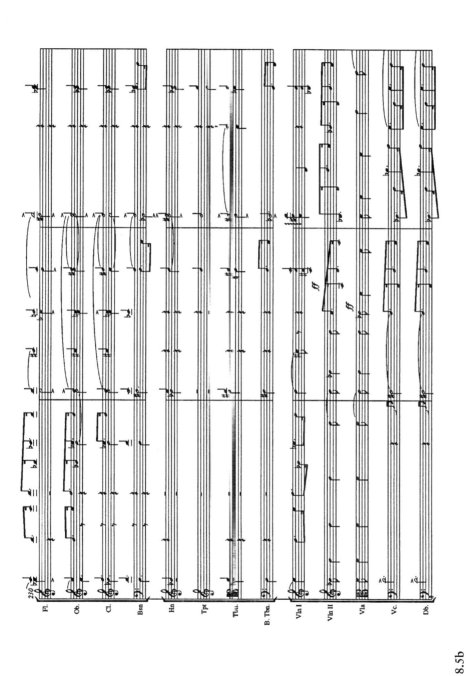

8.5b

Example 8.5   Symphony (Royal College of Music MS 4033)

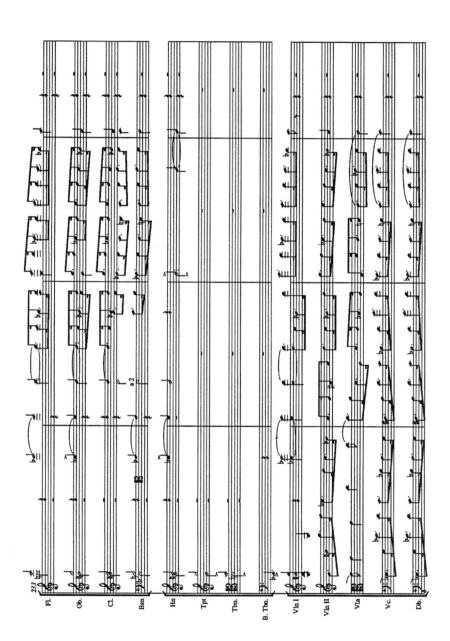

8.5c

Example 8.5   Symphony (continued)

Wesley's free use of 'modern German harmonies' and only regretted that 'the modern Germans ... are likely to know nothing of this collection'.[17] An intriguing observation was that the second movement of 'When fierce conflicting passions' (see Example 8.7), a $^6_8$ Allegretto in F$^\#$ major, contained 'such writing as one would expect in the slow movement of a double quartet by Spohr arranged for voices'. If Wesley had written for a chamber ensemble would it have sounded like this?

'When fierce conflicting passions' and 'I wish to tune my quiv'ring lyre' both set translations from the classics by Byron, to whose verses Wesley had also turned for the texts of four songs. In this, as in his choice of poems by Shelley and Scott (and lack of interest in the work of earlier poets), Wesley showed himself to be among the more forward-looking composers of his generation and his songs with piano accompaniment form a significant contribution to the relatively new tradition of the English art-song. The pieces themselves range from strophic settings of moderate difficulty to through-composed works whose vocal range and technical demands require the skill and stamina of a professional singer. Among the latter may be mentioned 'Blessed are the dead', a dramatic two-part setting for high voice of verses from Byron's *Poems* of 1816. Wide leaps in the voice part and unexpected changes of harmony combine in the slow introduction to create a sense of expectation which is fulfilled in the ensuing *Allegro* where gradually expanding melodic intervals and fast scale passages in the accompaniment bring the work to an exciting conclusion. Another Byron setting, 'There be none of beauty's daughters' (see Example 8.8), is less exuberant but, in its central section, contains some of Wesley's most poetic writing (Plate 8.1). Opening with a sudden plunge from the tonic (E major) to the mediant (G$^\#$ major), a long pedal point depicts the 'Charm'd ocean's pausing' while later, at the words 'The waves lie still and gleaming', a magical effect is achieved by fluctuating piano chords which weave a delicate filigree around the vocal line. 'Did I possess the magic art' is another delightful song, while mention must be made of two minor key settings, 'By the rivers of Babylon' and 'Orphan hours', whose melancholic sentiments brought out the best in Wesley. Links between the former and the eloquent bass solo 'Thou, O Lord God' from the anthem 'Let us lift up our heart' are at once apparent and serve as a reminder, if one is needed, that there is no clear dividing line between Wesley's church and non-church styles. Indeed, much of the solo writing in that group of early anthems in E^b, 'Blessed be the God and Father', 'Trust ye in the Lord' and 'O give thanks', is stylistically indistinguishable from that of contemporary songs in the same key

---

[17] *The Musical World*, 11 (1839), 211–12.

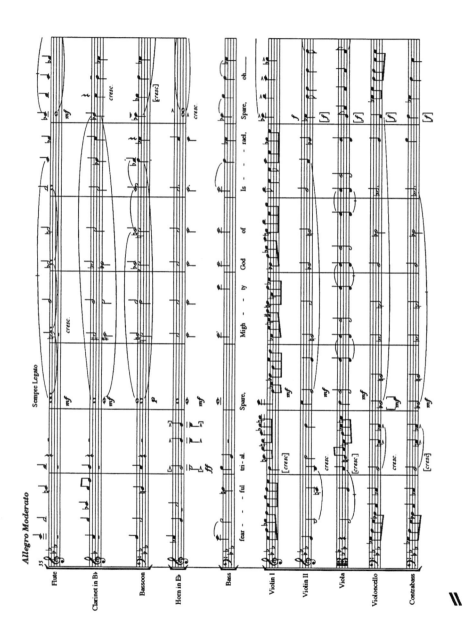

8.6a

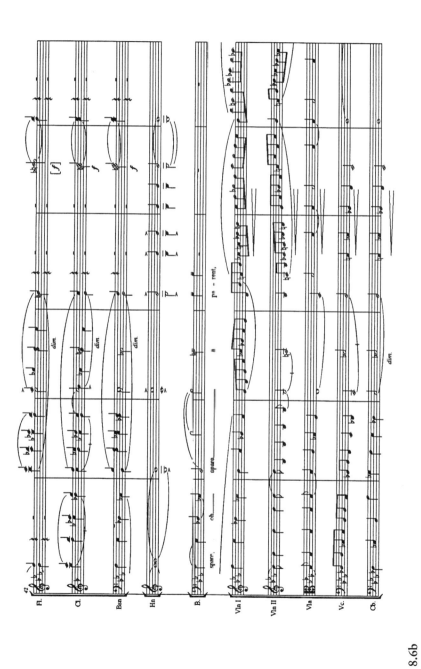

8.6b

Example 8.6　*Abraham's Offering* (Royal College of Music MS 4030)

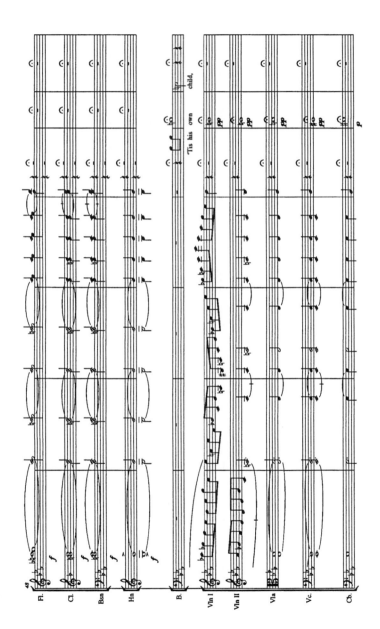

8.6c

Example 8.6 *Abraham's Offering* (continued)

('Blessed are the dead' and 'The smiling spring'), while the opening of 'By the rivers of Babylon' sounds rather more church-like than the early and very operatic treble solo in the Creed of the Service in E.

Hitherto most of the examples of cross-fertilization between secular and sacred have been from the former to the latter but, with the growing dominance of church music in Wesley's output in the late 1830s and 1840s, there are a number of examples of the reverse process. One of the most striking is to be found in a virtuoso concert work for the piano, the Rondo in C (see Example 8.9). Published with its companion March in C minor in 1842, it is the most substantial piano work of Wesley's maturity to have survived and, like the Symphony, is overflowing with musical ideas. Among these is a D minor theme (in the bass) which is introduced towards the end of the development section. Driven inexorably forward by insistent dotted rhythms, it immediately causes the emotional temperature to rise and builds up to a powerful climax preceding the return of the rondo theme (in the subdominant). But underneath the tremolando figuration or bravura arpeggios the harmony has a diatonic purity, not so dissimilar to the passage for men's voices 'The darkness is no darkness with thee' in the anthem 'Thou wilt keep him in perfect peace'.

How, or whether, Wesley might have pursued this line of development further must remain speculative, as the March and Rondo were to be his last instrumental works intended primarily for the concert hall. Indeed, for some 20 years he was to write very little that does not fall into the broad category of sacred vocal music, whether service settings, anthems, hymn tunes or sacred songs. Among the latter is one substantial work for baritone and orchestra, 'I have been young and now am old' (Plate 8.2, and see Example 8.10). Written in 1848 while he was recuperating from a compound fracture of the right leg, it is a setting of verses from various Old Testament sources and, as the last of his 'early' works for voices and orchestra, forms an obvious conclusion to this brief survey. First performed at the 1850 Gloucester Festival by Wesley's old acquaintance Henry Phillips it (like *Abraham's Offering*) failed to impress, with the critic of *The Musical World* complaining of an 'absolute want of phrase or melody' and 'strange harmonies and excessive modulation'.[18] Yet to modern ears the first of its three movements emerges as one of Wesley's most impressive achievements: a deeply felt rhapsodic structure (whose form is dictated by the carefully compiled text), dominated by the eloquent main theme. The latter's first entry – where it is heard in an imitative dialogue with the cellos – is at a moment of sudden stillness, as the rapid harmonic movement of the

---

[18] *The Musical World*, 25 (1850), 589.

8.7a

Example 8.7 'When fierce conflicting passions'

8.7b

Allegro Moderato

8.8a

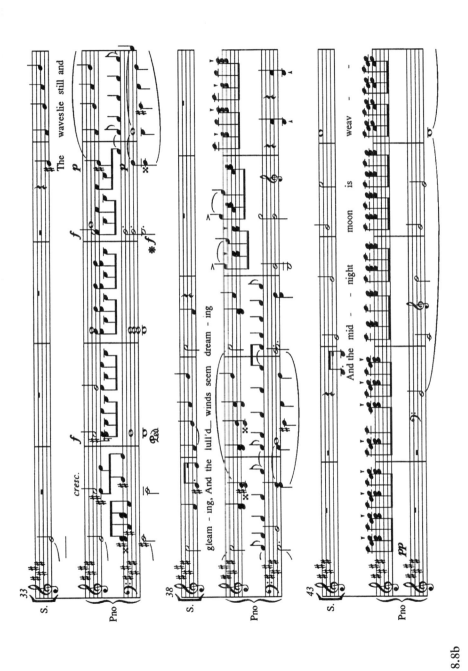

8.8b

Example 8.8   'There be none of beauty's daughters'

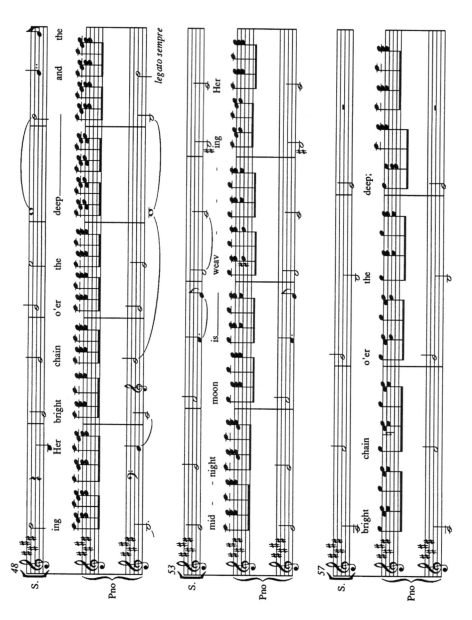

Example 8.8 'There be none of beauty's daughters' (continued)

8.8c

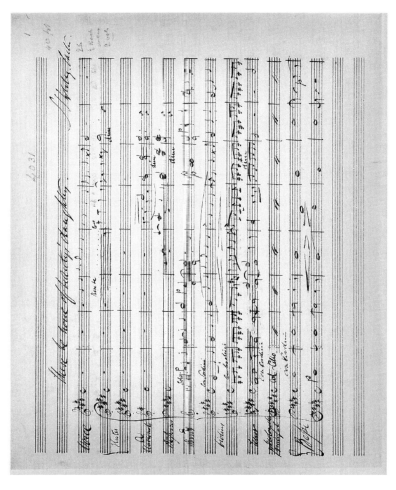

Plate 8.1   The opening of Wesley's orchestral version of 'There be none of beauty's daughters' (Royal College of Music MS 4031)

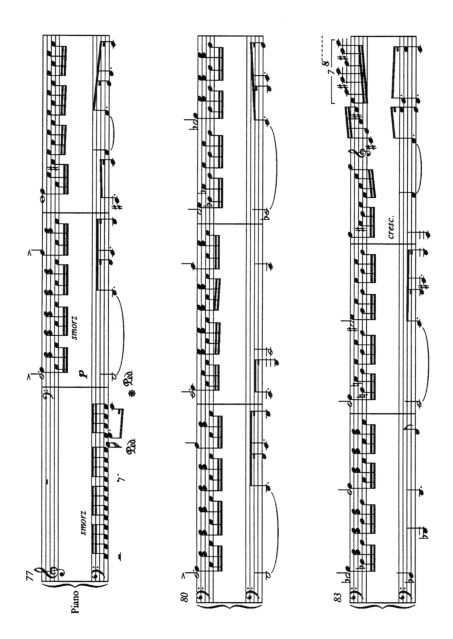

8.9a

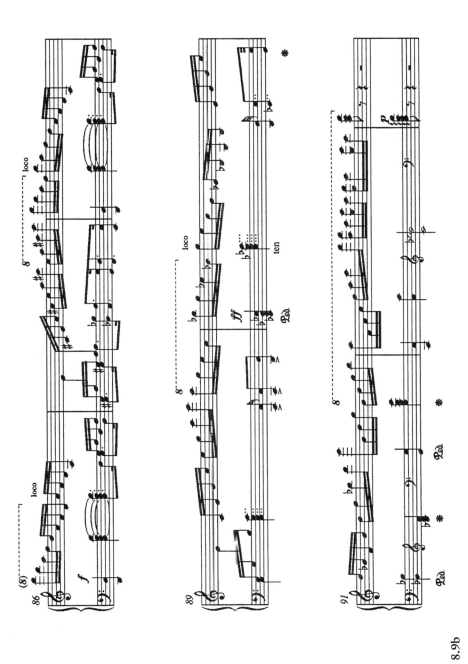

8.9b

Example 8.9 Rondo in C

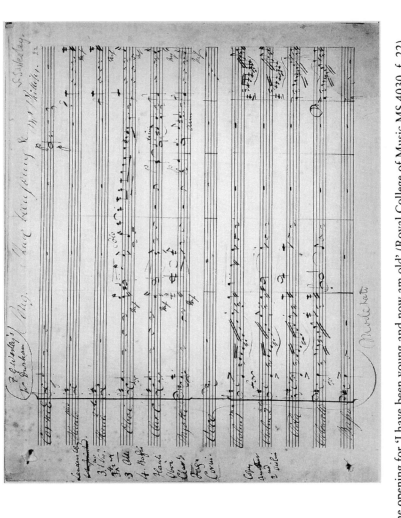

Plate 8.2   The opening for 'I have been young and now am old' (Royal College of Music MS 4030, f. 22)

orchestral introduction gives way to long-sustained chords. Here, indeed, is a demonstration of how far Wesley's music had evolved from the dense, chromatic writing of *Abraham's Offering*. Not only is the harmonic foundation very simple – a series of diatonic triads – but it also invites comparison with contemporary anthems, particularly 'Cast me not away from thy presence', and in doing so neatly encapsulates the way in which Wesley's music had moved full circle, from works for the church which were influenced by the concert hall to those for the concert hall which were indebted to the church. But more than that, it reminds us that at any one time Wesley made little stylistic differentiation between sacred and secular, church and non-church music.[19]

Despite having made such a promising beginning, writing music for the concert hall or home had brought Wesley neither fame nor fortune. Yet the experience of writing such works – particularly in the early 1830s – had had a powerful influence on his development as a composer. Not only had it encouraged him to employ a similar style in his church music, thereby (to quote Watkins Shaw) 'placing it once more in touch with the progress of musical composition',[20] but it had also – among other things – introduced him to the idea of thinking orchestrally. It was, I believe, from his early experience of orchestral music that he gained that insight into the importance of musical texture which subsequently bore such good fruit in his church music. One has only to look at the keyboard accompaniments to the solo movements in the anthems to see how multilayered they often are, while other, more fully scored movements – the Service in E being a good example – exploit the orchestrally derived resources of texture, colour and effect. But perhaps the best demonstration of such thinking is to be found in 'The Wilderness'. Written in 1832 when the echoes of the English Opera House were still ringing in his head, its organ part is wholly orchestral in conception and, as his own orchestration of 1852 so ably demonstrates, transferred effortlessly from one medium to another.

Whilst it would be idle to claim that all of Wesley's non-church music is on the same exalted plane as his best anthems or the Service in E, the finest works (among them the two orchestral songs, the Symphony, the Overture in E, the March and Rondo, the glees and a number of songs) fully deserve to be known in their own right. More than that, they also demonstrate that their composer made a small but significant contribution to that little known corpus of English Romantic music.

---

[19] There are, of course, occasional exceptions to this generalization, among them the set of 'Quadrilles à la Herz', *Jeux d'Esprit* (1846) and the part-song 'Shall I tell you whom I love' (1862), neither of which make any pretence to seriousness.

[20] Watkins Shaw, 'The Achievement of S.S. Wesley', *The Musical Times*, **117** (1976), 304.

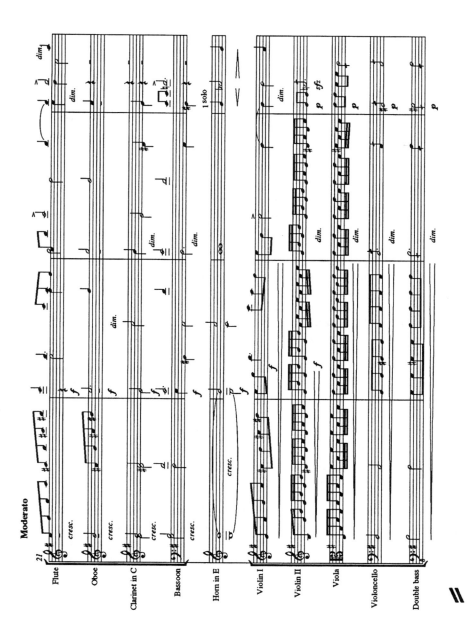

8.10a

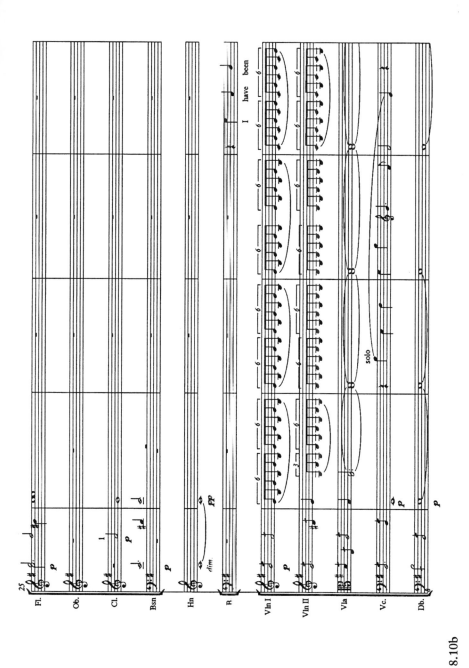

8.10b

Example 8.10 'I have been young and now am old' (Royal College of Music MS 4030)

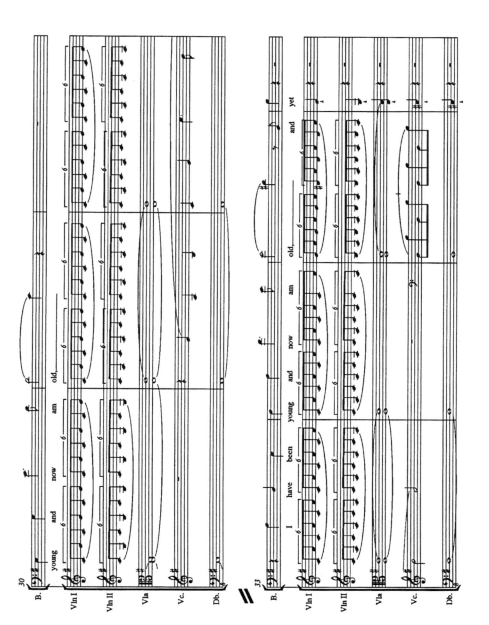

Example 8.10 'I have been young and now am old' (continued)

8.10c

Appendix: S. S. Wesley – chronological work list to 1848

Title	Date of composition	Date of publication
Incidental music	c. 1825	—
Tho' round thy radiant throne on high	c. 1827	—
Waltz (piano)	1828–29?	1830
Andante in A (organ)	1828–30?	Posthumous
Variations on 'God save the King' (organ)	1829	1831
Young Bacchus in his lusty prime (male voices & orch)	c. 1829	—
March in Bb (orchestra)	c. 1830	—
Gloria in Excelsis (choir & orchestra)	c. 1830	—
Agnus Dei (voice & orchestra)	1830–32?	—
Choral Song and Fugue (organ)	1830–32?	1842
Introduction & Rondo ... Spohr's *Azor & Zemira* (piano)	1831?	1831? [lost]
You told me once (song)	1831?	1831
Original air with variations (piano)	1831?	1832 [lost]
Glory to God on high (choir and organ)	c. 1831?	—
O God whose nature and property	c. 1831?	1831
Benedictus qui venit (vocal quartet & organ)	1832	—
Overture &c for *The Dilosk Gatherer*	1832	—
The Wilderness	1832	1853 [1840]
When we two parted (song)	1832?	1832
The smiling spring (song)	1832?	1832
Wert thou like me (song)	1832	1835
Rondo 'La Violette' (piano)	c. 1832?	Before 1842 [lost]
Blessed are the dead (song)	1832–35?	1835
Did I possess the magic art (song)	1832–35?	1835
There be none of beauty's daughters (song)	1832–35?	1835
I wish to tune my quiv'ring lyre (glee)	1833	1839
There breathes a living fragrance (song)	1833	—
Selection of Psalm tunes (organ)	c. 1833	1834
Dance (piano)	1833–34	—
Sanctus (?choir & orchestra)	1833–34	— [lost]
Abraham's Offering (baritone & orchestra)	1833–34	—
Creed and Kyrie (no 2) in E	1833–34?	1845
Blessed be the God and Father	1833 or 34	1853
Overture in E	1834?	—
Symphony in C major/minor	1834?	—
At that dread hour (glee)	1834	1839
Fill me, boy as deep a draught (glee)	1834	—
The bruised reed (song)	1834	1840
Piano piece in E minor	1834	—

Appendix continued

Title	Date of composition	Date of publication
Presto in C minor (piano)	1834	—
Rondo in G (piano)	1834	1835
Millions of spiritual creatures (vocal quartet & orchestra)	1835	—
Introduction and Fugue in C# minor (organ)	1835?	1836
Trust ye in the Lord	*c.* 1835?	—
O give thanks unto the Lord	*c.* 1835?	1853
Larghetto in F minor (organ)	1835–36?	Posthumous
Sanctus in E	1835–36?	1845
Orphan hours (song)	*c.* 1836	1867
Let us lift up our heart	*c.* 1836	1853
O Lord, thou art my God	*c.* 1836	1853 [1840]
To my request and earnest cry	*c.* 1836	[1840]
When fierce conflicting passions (glee)	1837	1839
[Glee in honour of Sir John Rogers]	1838	— [lost]
Wash me throughly	*c.* 1840	1853
March and rondo (piano)	1840–42?	1842
Andante in F (organ)	1840–42?	1842
Andante in E♭ – First set (organ)	1840–42?	1842
Andante in G (organ)	1842	1842
Larghetto in F# minor (organ)	1842	1842
Andante in E♭ – Second set (organ)	1842	1842
Te Deum, Jubilate, Magnificat, Nunc Dimittis and Kyrie (no 1) in E	1842–43	1845
Man that is born of a woman	*c.* 1845	1853
Chant Service in F (evening)	1845–46	1851
Jeux d'esprit (piano solo or duet)	1846	1847
Gloria in Excelsis in C	1846–47	1869
Cast me not away	1848	1853
The face of the Lord	1848	1853
I have been young and now am old (baritone & orch)	1848	—
Almighty God, O give us grace (song)	1848	1848
Most blessed Lord (song)	1848	1848
Lord Jesus Christ, thou who at thy first coming (song)	1848	1848

Note: Works for church use are distinguished by the use of italics; square brackets are used to denote the projected collection of six *Anthems*, incomplete proof copies of which were printed in 1840.

PART FIVE
Local Music History

Musical Life in the 'second city of the Empire'[1] during the 1870s as reflected in T. L. Stillie's contributions to the *Glasgow Herald*

Stuart Campbell

Introduction

This chapter[2] pretends to be no more than a pebble cast into a deep and murky pool. That pool is the history of art music in Scotland during the nineteenth century. The period from the Renaissance up to the end of the eighteenth century has furnished music's scholars with a number of Scottish composers who are at least interesting creative figures and at their best are fit to be considered alongside European contemporaries working in the tradition of Western art music, and their works have reached publication in editions worthy of their composers' standing.[3] The advent of the CD has brought fresh attention to music from the second half of the nineteenth century and later, written by composers of Scottish birth

---

[1] The description of Glasgow as 'the second city of the Empire' refers to the size of its population. *The Guide to the Glasgow and Ayrshire Railway*, Glasgow, 1841, made the claim, which held good until 1951 when Birmingham's population narrowly overtook Glasgow's. This information is drawn from Joe Fisher, *The Glasgow Encyclopedia*, Edinburgh, 1994, p. 296.

[2] The article is an expanded version of a paper of the same title read at the conference. I am grateful to Bennett Zon for his helpful comments, and to John Gormley for his practical help. A related article entitled 'Wagner and the *Glasgow Herald* in the 1870s' is to appear in the first *Yearbook of the Wagner Society of Scotland* under the editorship of Derek Watson.

[3] *Music of Scotland, 1500–1700*, being volume 15 of *Musica Britannica*, London 1957, 1964, and latest edition 1975, edited by Kenneth Elliott has recently been complemented by a new series under Dr Elliott's General Editorship; Musica Scotica so far extends to vol. 1: *The Complete Works of Robert Carver*, Glasgow, 1996, vol. 2: *Sixteenth-Century Scots Songs for Voice and Lute*, Glasgow, 1996, and vol. 3: *The Complete Works of Robert Johnson*, Glasgow, 1998. Other editors, notably the late Isobel Preece (née Woods), have worked in this earlier period, and David Johnson has made editions of eighteenth-century compositions. Music from the earlier period has been issued in recorded form, especially on the ASV Gaudeamus label.

who sought musical education elsewhere and usually pursued their careers there – mostly in London: Sir Alexander Campbell Mackenzie (1847–1935), William Wallace (1860–1940), Learmont Drysdale (1866–1909, though he spent the last five years of his life in Scotland), Hamish MacCunn (1868–1916) and John B. McEwen (1868–1948).[4] The fact that these Scots left their homeland in pursuit of musical ambitions seems to confirm that at that time Scotland promised little for a composer.

The greater part of the nineteenth century, however, is relatively barren territory, both in good composers and general musical activity – or so it has been depicted by its historians. The most extensive account remains that provided by Henry George Farmer in his *A History of Music in Scotland* (London, 1947, repr. New York, 1970) where Part VII 'The Nineteenth Century' occupies something approaching a third of the whole text (pp. 347–538); that is the best starting-point for anyone seeking information about education, performers, composers, institutions, etc. Frederick Rimmer deals much more briefly (perforce) with the period in his contributions 'The Nineteenth Century (1800–1880)' and 'The Late Nineteenth to Mid-Twentieth Centuries (1880–1950)' (pp. 59–63 and 63–77 of Kenneth Elliott and Frederick Rimmer: *A History of Scottish Music* (London, 1973). John Purser's *Scotland's Music. A History of the Traditional and Classical Music of Scotland from Early Times to the Present Day* (Edinburgh, 1992) considers the nineteenth century in Chapters XVI 'The Withdrawing Room and the Concert Hall (1820–1920)' (pp. 211–28) and XVII 'Sea, Field and Music Hall (1820–1910)' (pp. 229–42) before putting art music of the nineteenth century in its place with the title of the next chapter, no. XVIII 'The Classical Takes Root (1910–1970)' (pp. 243–59); Dr Purser has drawn welcome attention to a number of neglected composers and highlighted many areas which demand investigation.

The history of music is not, however, identical with the successive emergence of individual composers, whether continuously or in a broken line. The cultivation of performance goes on; listeners remain to attend to the work of performers. Music-making has persisted, whether in the home, the stately home, the public hall, the church or the theatre; if that statement is true of art music, it is at least equally true of folk music associated with the events of personal life, work and story-telling as well as the life of the community and society.

---

[4] Mackenzie, *Orchestral Music* (Hyperion CDA66764); *Violin Concerto, Pibroch* (Hyperion CDA66975); Wallace, *Symphonic Poems* (Hyperion CDA66848); *Creation Symphony* (Hyperion CDA66987); MacCunn, *Land of the Mountain and the Flood* (Hyperion CDA66815); McEwen, *Three Border Ballads* (Chandos CHAN 9241), and also CHAN 9345.

When it appears worthwhile to do so, scholars will undertake the dogged archival investigation which may bring light where before there was little. Detailed individual pictures – of the musicians who resided and of those who only visited, the performance series to which they contributed, the venues in which their performances took place, the repertory that was heard, the public who attended and how they responded to what was offered – may at length bring a greater degree of clarity about the musical infrastructure of the period. If few symphonies or operas are evident, then songs, partsongs, glees, hymn-tunes and other supposedly lower forms of musical life may illuminate the outlook and taste of the time.

Research into some specific topics from this period is already in progress. Leaving aside Jenny Burchell's work on aspects of musical life in Edinburgh,[5] it includes John Cranmer's dissertation on the same city,[6] Duncan Barker's on Mackenzie[7] and Valerie Carson's on Wallace.[8] A team based at the University of Glasgow are preparing an edition of all of the folksong arrangements commissioned from Haydn by George Thomson.[9] Recent final-year dissertations for the B.Mus degree there have taken Mackenzie[10] and Drysdale[11] as their subjects. Once progress has been made on these narrower fronts, it will be more rewarding to enter the more speculative field of why circumstances were so. That will entail evaluation of the part played by the Calvinist reformation and its consequences, the removal to London of the Scottish Court in 1603 and of the Scottish Parliament in 1707, the Jacobite uprisings of 1715 and 1745, the decline of aristocratic patronage, to say nothing of the factors which were considered to have dragged English music down to a level from which an English musical renaissance began its rescue.

When so much awaits investigation, some might consider it perverse to turn to a music critic as a point of departure. T. L. Stillie is, however a vivid personality, and his work in the *Glasgow Herald* is easy of access. His publications in that newspaper outline important developments in

---

[5] Jenny Burchell, *Polite or Commercial Concerts?: Concert Management and Orchestral Repertoire in Edinburgh, Bath, Oxford, Manchester and Newcastle, 1730–1799*, London and New York, 1996.

[6] John Cranmer, 'Concert Life and the Music Trade in Edinburgh c1780–1830', PhD, University of Edinburgh, 1991.

[7] PhD in progress, University of Durham.

[8] PhD in progress, University of Durham.

[9] Marjorie Rycroft, Executive Editor with Kirsteen McCue (Scottish Music Information Centre) and Warwick Edwards, are preparing the edition for publication by Henle Verlag for the Haydn Institut.

[10] Frances A. C. Grant, 'The Published Songs for Solo Voice of Sir A. C. MacKenzie'.

[11] Moira A. Harris, 'The Life and Work of Learmont Drysdale'.

musical institutions, present the opinions of an astute observer, and offer an instructive counterpoint to the progress of Russian music in the same decades which will remain at the centre of this author's interests.

The relationship between the existence of musical institutions and the presence of compositional talent is not a straightforward one, though it may reasonably be argued that significant original musical composition is most likely to flourish when the necessary infrastructure is there. One of those institutions is informed critical writing about the state of musical life and its events. The discovery in Glasgow University Library of four albums compiled largely from the notices published in the *Glasgow Herald* from the late 1860s to the early 1880s was the immediate stimulus to find out what light could be shed on Glasgow's musical infrastructure in the period.

Two aspects should be kept in mind: developments in Glasgow are most likely related in many ways to equivalent patterns in the United Kingdom as a whole, and especially in the large industrial cities such as Birmingham, Manchester, Leeds and Liverpool, with London setting the pace and style for all the lesser centres. There may secondly be features peculiar to Scotland, with its largest city, Glasgow, and its capital, Edinburgh, then as now engaged in rivalry which is at times friendly.

A further topic suggests itself: it was not in Scotland alone – indeed, perhaps not principally in Scotland – that original compositional voices were heard in the late nineteenth century where before there had been relative silence. Why it was that countries from Spain to Lithuania and Finland found stronger voices than they had recently listened to deserves enquiry, though it may turn out that a variety of disparate factors were at work. Speculation about these topics will not be attempted here.

T. L. Stillie

Every June the examiners' meeting in the Department of Music in the University of Glasgow concludes with decisions about prizes. Among these is an award made to the student of highest attainment in each of the first and second years of the general Arts course who is proceeding to the following year of the course, an award which is known as the Stillie Bursary. Like the Stillie Collection bequeathed to the University Library in 1884, this award commemorates the life of Thomas Logan Stillie, a Glasgow merchant much of whose time was dedicated to the cultivation of music. Born in Maybole in Ayrshire in 1932,[12] Stillie was

---

[12] *Glasgow Herald*, hereafter *GH*, obituary of T. L. Stillie, 8 June 1883, p. 6.

first an apprentice and later a partner in the Glasgow calico-printing enterprise of Messrs James Black and Co.[13] Later still he became the Glasgow representative of the Manchester firm of T. G. Hill and Co. He was at length in a position to retire from business and devote himself to music. His contributions to the *Herald* given evidence of extensive travel to musically significant destinations both in Britain and on the continent. A facility of languages may have advanced his career, and would certainly have eased problems of foreign travel. In those days certain overseas sojourns were reckoned beneficial to health, and Stillie may also have been abroad for that reason. He died in 1883.[14]

For a number of years Stillie contributed material about music to the principal daily newspaper in Glasgow – then, as now, the *Herald*: it has also at times carried the name *Glasgow Herald* or *Glasgow Daily Herald* on its masthead. An anniversary publication of the newspaper contained an account of music on its pages, and contains the claim that Stillie was the paper's first music critic.[15] From this evidence a portrait could be drawn of the state of music-making in the city and its environs from the 1860s to the early 1880s; musical forces and repertory could be examined and recorded; the reception of significant compositions could be assessed; evidence of the introduction of organs to the Presbyterian churches could be amassed. I do not aim here, however, to trace the history of the Paisley Tonic Sol-fa Institute, the Bellahouston Musical Association, the Hillhead Musical Association, the St George's Choral Union, the concerts of the Glasgow Abstainers' Union or the lectures on music of the Glasgow Association for the Higher Education of Women – indications of worthy musical activity though they be – nor shall I deal with the careers of eminent visiting performers, whether brought north by the operatic impresarios Gye and Mapleson or the concert promoter J. Muir Wood – not even with that of the bass singer Signor

---

[13] For information about this firm, see *Official Illustrated Guide to the Lancaster and Carlisle, Edinburgh and Glasgow, and Caledonian Railways*, London, 1859, sect. 'The Commercial Aspect of Glasgow', pp. 303–10.

[14] Biographical information is available in his obituary notice in the *Glasgow Herald* (see footnote 12 above) and in a less formal article in *The Bailie* of 9 March 1881, no. 438, pp. 1–2, from which the portrait reproduced here is also taken.

[15] Euphemia Gray, *The Music Makers, in The Glasgow Herald 1783–1958*, Glasgow, 1958, p. 70. I have worked throughout on the assumption that all the articles to which reference is made are the work of Stillie himself. He was in the period in question acknowledged as the paper's music critic, and at the very least it seems improbable that, in either the selection of topics for coverage or the general direction of opinion, material at variance with his approach or attitudes would have made its way into print. The newspaper has not been indexed for the period, and its present owners 'have no archives from last century' (letter from Ian Watson, Information Services Manager, Scottish Media Newspapers, 10 March 1998).

Campobello 'our countryman; and as he is the first Scotchman who has earned a prominent position on the Italian boards, we naturally feel proud of him, and at the same time anxious for his future success'[16] – preliminary to outlining helpfully his shortcomings in the role of the Count in *The Marriage of Figaro*: this Campobello was in fact Henry Maclean Martin, born in 1839 (Brown and Stratton, 1897, p. 273). (I am grateful to Jane Mallinson for pointing out this information.)

I shall instead mention the contents of the Stillie Collection as reflection of its owner's outlook; consider his view of Glaswegian musical life (at the metropolitan rather than the district level); refer to his efforts, as a journalist and as a practical man, to raise the level of musical infrastructure; and allude to his assessment of a few composers.

The Stillie Collection

'Bach, interwoven with Spohr and Beethoven'[17] certainly describes a significant part of the some 700 volumes of printed music and books about music which Stillie collected.[18] The Bach included the eight volumes of organ compositions published by Peters under the editorship of Roitzsch and Griepenkerl. Beethoven is represented by 24 volumes of the Breitkopf and Härtel edition published between 1862 and 1865, and by Lenz's book *Beethoven et ses trois styles* in its Paris form of 1866. Other composers of our canon are represented as follows:

● Handel, by the 12 volumes of the (English) Handel Society of 1843
● Haydn, by the symphonies published in the *Bibliothèque musicale* by Pleyel from 1802
● Mozart, by a first edition of Köchel's catalogue (Leipzig, 1862).

The operatic repertory of the time is abundantly represented by vocal scores, from Auber to Wagner and Balfe to Sullivan – indicating an enthusiasm fed not only by those works which could be heard in Scotland performed by visiting troupes or in London but also in European centres. His copy of Franz Hueffer's *Richard Wagner and the Music of the Future* (London, 1874) confirms a strong interest on Stillie's part, even if his ardour was stronger for what he called 'the music of the

---

[16] 24 February 1874, p. 4.

[17] *The Mikado*, 'My object all sublime'.

[18] See Michael Cormack, 'Guide to the Stillie Collection in Glasgow University Library' 1974, typescript; I am indebted to Mary Sillitto of that library for drawing my attention to this item.

present' (*Tannhäuser, The Flying Dutchman, Lohengrin*) than for 'the music of the future' (from *Das Rheingold* on). Composers' letters are also represented in published editions. Scholarly concerns are indicated by Burney's *A General History of Music* (4 vols, London, 1776–89), Fétis's *Biographie universelle des musiciens* (2nd edn, Paris, 1860–80 – eight volumes plus two volumes of supplement), and Coussemaker's *Histoire de l'harmonie au moyen-âge* (Paris, 1852) – so that Gilbert's 'series of masses and fugues and "ops"' are also there. The collections of Scots songs may have served Stillie in his contributions to the first editions of Sir George Grove's *A Dictionary of Music and Musicians (A.D. 1450–1883)*, an addendum to the entry on 'Scotish music' [*sic*] (vol. 3, London, 1883, pp. 449–52) and all of the entry 'Strathspey' (vol. 3, pp. 735–7).

The library is the collection of a musician who was abreast of the music of his own time, British and European, and who shared the by then common curiosity about the music of earlier periods. It indicates a willingness to spend money to support a hobby and its outgrowth in journalism. It confirms his scholarly interest in music, its technical dimension included, as indicated in frequent observations in his music notices in favour of the programme annotations supplied by Grove and Macfarren.

Glasgow's musical life

The anonymous writer of Stillie's *Herald* obituary declared that: 'He held strong opinions with respect to music, and was inclined to express them freely. There could be no doubt as to his earnestness, and we think it may also be said that he did good service by speaking out boldly with reference to musical matters at a time when frankness was much to be desired.'[19] H. G. Farmer referred to 'Stillie's vigorous but well-disciplined pen'.[20] When considering performing standards, Stillie could certainly display 'vigour' in condemning accounts of musical compositions for lack of resources, want of rehearsal or plain technical inadequacy. He saw no need to give unjustifiable encouragement to incompetent amateur attempts at music-making in public, and was rebuked for thus giving no quarter in a letter from a reader signing himself 'Flagellum' in the *Herald* of 11 February 1873, who reproved him for being the only person in the room to find no pleasure in the exertions of the Amateur Orchestra Society. In 1870 he had uttered the

[19] Cf. footnote 12 above.
[20] H. G. Farmer, *A History of Music in Scotland*, London, 1947, p. 428.

following denunciation of orchestral standards in reviewing a performance of *Samson* promoted by the Tonic Sol-Fa Society in which Sims
Reeves had participated:

> What can we say of the orchestra? It is indeed a weary and thank-
> less task to point out the imperfections of the 'scratch' orchestras
> we usually have in Glasgow. Last night – from whatever cause –
> the performance of the orchestra was, and we say it advisedly, the
> worst we can remember. The state of instrumental music in Scot-
> land is simply a disgrace to us, and unless very great improvement
> is made in this department of the art we must return to organ
> accompaniments when oratorio music is attempted. It was at times
> positively painful to hear the vocalists struggling against such a
> chaos of sounds as the instrumentalists produced last evening.[21]

In the mid-1870s, on the establishment of what was known as the
Glasgow Permanent Orchestra, one gains a sense from reading Stillie of
the listlessness induced by the efforts at conducting orchestral works of
a major local figure in choir-training, Henry Lambeth, efforts which led
to his eventual resignation, to be replaced by Hans von Bülow and
Arthur Sullivan. The Italian Opera's 1875 visit to the Theatre Royal in
Glasgow included the Glasgow première of any opera by Wagner.
Lohengrin was performed on 3 November 1875,[22] and Stillie observed,
after giving generous credit to Mdlles. Albani and D'Edelsberg, and
moderately complimenting Messrs Naudin and Maurel:

> The chorus at times was execrable. The orchestra, not complete at
> all points, was often successful in its endeavours. Too much praise
> cannot be bestowed on Signor Vianesi for his unwonted exertions.
> He was in turns conductor, stage-manager, prompter, and solo and
> chorus singer. But for his prompt action and intimate knowledge of
> the music, matters could not possibly have gone so satisfactorily as
> they did.[23]

Such was the excitement awakened by *Lohengrin* that it was repeated
on the following Saturday morning, when Stillie recorded some improvement, although

> The chorus was totally unfitted to give even a satisfactory indica-
> tion of Wagner's ideas. What could seven or eight female voices do
> in Wagner's intricate double choruses? The orchestra struggled
> manfully against heavy odds. They certainly did their limited best,
> and Signor Vianesi was a tower of strength amongst them. Wagner's
> score is one of the fullest, while the orchestra on Wednesday and
> Saturday was unusually incomplete; it was, therefore, simply

---

[21] *GH*, 13 October 1870, p. 4.

[22] The London première of a Wagner opera took place on 23 July 1870 when *The Flying Dutchman* was performed at the Drury Lane Theatre in Italian.

[23] *GH*, 4 November 1875, p. 4.

impossible that the composer's ideas could receive anything like justice. Now that Mr. Gye has tested the capabilities of Glasgow to provide a local orchestra fit to interpret difficult music, it may be presumed that on the occasion of another visit he will show more forethought in his arrangements.[24]

On the evening of the day on which he conducted *Lohengrin* in the morning, Vianesi conducted *Uno ballo in maschera* – with two cellos, one of which filled in the absent bassoon part.[25] The plague of opera companies which attracted audiences by advertising illustrious singers' names and then let them down with less famous vocalists, incomplete orchestras and reach-me-down sets and productions was not peculiar to Scotland: Tchaikovsky was complaining of it in the same decade in Moscow.[26]

Developments in musical infrastructure

In the 1870s Glasgow prospered, and Stillie (with others) was eager to see commercial success matched by equivalent artistic prowess. His press campaigns in support of various expressions of this desire concerned the Glasgow Musical Festival, a permanent orchestra and a new concert hall adequate for large-scale works. His opinions on these topics will now be considered.

On 19 February 1873 Stillie chaired a meeting, its proceedings reported in the following day's newspaper, about a proposed Glasgow Music Festival. A printed statement considered at the meeting opined that

> there could be no sufficient reason rendered why Glasgow, with its enormous population, its vast resources and increasing wealth, its cultivated taste, and undeniable musical enthusiasm, should not have its triennial musical festivals. The only festival hitherto held in Glasgow took place in January, 1860. Although pecuniarily disappointing, this festival proved artistically most successful, and gave an immense impetus to the study of music in Glasgow. Since that date the public taste in this direction has advanced at a rate truly astonishing, and it had therefore been thought that the time has now arrived when periodical musical festivals, on a scale still more important than that just referred to, might safely be organised in this city, with a fair prospect of receiving adequate support. It is proposed, therefore, to

---

[24] *GH*, 8 November 1875, p. 4.

[25] Ibid.

[26] See, for instance, Tchaikovsky's notice of 17 September 1872 (O.S.) translated in Stuart Campbell (ed.), *Russians on Russian Music, 1830–1880*, Cambridge, 1994, pp. 134–40.

hold in October, 1873, under the auspices of the Glasgow Choral Union, a Grand Musical Festival in aid of the funds of the Western Infirmary, and to give in all six concerts – viz., four grand concerts on the evenings of Tuesday, Wednesday, Thursday, and Friday, and two grand concerts on the mornings or afternoons of Wednesday and Saturday. The music to be performed will include some new and important compositions not previously heard in Glasgow, and also several of the well known and ever popular works of the great masters, including Handel's *Messiah* and Mendelssohn's *Elijah*. The necessary expenses of the festival will obviously be very considerable, and it is proposed to organise a guarantee fund, to which gentlemen of influence interested in the success of the undertaking, will be asked to subscribe.[27]

On 28 April 1873 Stillie stoked the fire of Glaswegian enthusiasm for the festival by outlining what took place elsewhere:

The gigantic gatherings of the Crystal Palace – the executants numbering about four thousand – possess their attractions, and many of the choral effects produced are strikingly grand. Still, from a purely artistic point of view, we have not much sympathy with these performances. The feeble effects produced by the solo singers are entirely disproportionate to the enormous volume of sound thundered out by thousands in the choruses, whilst these grand sounds, meandering amongst the long aisles and striking against the glass house, get broken amidst reverberations. Besides, the scheme is limited to the production of Handel's works. Anyone, however, who is desirous of witnessing a grand Vanity Fair show, and of studying the gaiety of fashionable England, should not miss the opportunity of doing so which is afforded at Sydenham. The Birmingham Festivals must be referred to in different terms. These every philanthropist must admire, because of the enormous sums which they have been the means of raising for charitable objects. Every lover of music, too, stands deeply indebted to them [... with] a gross total of over £100,000 of profits realised since the beginning. In regard to the art itself, the influence of the Birmingham Festivals cannot be over-estimated. Their records contain many glorious first productions of immortal compositions. Amongst these may [be] cited 'St Paul' and the 'Lob-Gesang' of Mendelssohn, given in 1837 and 1840, and the popular 'Elijah', specially written for Birmingham, and produced at the Festival of 1846 under the conductorship of Mendelssohn himself.[28]

Comments on choirs heard in London, Birmingham, Bristol and other centres seem to confirm that Stillie had some direct experience of musical life there.

The growth of plans, the eventual artistically successful festival and the final accounting may be traced through the press. The festival took

---

27 *GH*, 20 February 1873, p. 3.
28 *GH*, 28 April 1873, p. 4.

place in November, not October, 1873 and its repertory encompassed Costa's *Eli*, *Messiah* and *Elijah* as well as compositions by Smart, Lambeth and others, as summarized here:

4 XI (evening):	*Elijah* conducted by Henry Lambeth
5 XI (morning):	largely orchestral concert with some vocal and solo organ items conducted by Lambeth
5 XI (evening):	Costa: *Eli* conducted by the composer
6 XI (evening):	largely orchestral programme with some vocal and choral items
7 XI (evening):	Lambeth: Psalm 86; Smart: *Jacob* conducted by Lambeth
8 XI (morning):	*Messiah* conducted by Lambeth
8 XI (evening):	'extra popular concert' with orchestra, singers and W. T. Best as organist.

This Festival seems not to have any successors, perhaps because of one of the other matters which Stillie tackled.

In the early 1870s the Choral Union appears to have been Glasgow's principal permanent music-making institution. In a practice still familiar, a local chorus was joined by solo singers from outside and an orchestra gathered as opportunity allowed (referred to in this case as the 'Glasgow Scratch Orchestra').[29] For the 1873 Festival an orchestra formed of notable musicians from outside Glasgow was assembled for the purpose, and performed well through constant rehearsing. The example of Charles Hallé's orchestra, visiting Glasgow annually in the 1870s, however, readily convinced Stillie of the merits of an ensemble of skilled musicians accustomed to playing together. As Michael Kennedy records: 'In Manchester, after 1858, there was for the first time in British history a professional symphony orchestra with a personnel which remained relatively unchanged. Constant rehearsal ensured well-prepared performances'.[30]

It was soon after the Festival, in December 1873, that Stillie began to make the case for what he called variously the resident orchestra or the 'Glasgow Permanent Orchestra', outlining a considered scheme under which the orchestra would be administered by the Choral Union and would both support the choir's performances and give orchestral concerts on its own. Plans proceeded, an orchestra was engaged for a fixed term, and the first concert was reported on 4 November 1874 in the

---

[29] *GH*, 2 January 1874, p. 4.

[30] Michael Kennedy, *The Hallé 1858–1983. A History of the Orchestra*, Manchester, 1982, p. 5.

Herald. The first season was dogged by poor attendances and some dissatisfaction with the repertory. Dr Hans von Bülow was engaged as conductor for one concert instead of the unfortunate Mr Lambeth, and galvanized the players beyond recognition in a programme of Beethoven, Schumann, Wagner and Liszt.[31] The 'well-disciplined pen' allowed itself some freedom in reviewing this event: 'From the renown of this great artist much was expected. All preconceived expectations of excellence were more than realised; and it may be said with perfect confidence that last night's concert was the grandest ever given in Glasgow during the present generation.' Stillie hinted that Mr Lambeth either did not rehearse enough, or did not know the music of the orchestral repertory thoroughly enough, or else by his diffidence did not inspire sufficient enthusiasm in the players.

The following season's orchestra was conducted once by Costa but principally by Arthur Sullivan, of whose work Stillie reported on 1 December 1875:

> Now that Mr. Sullivan and his orchestra are *en rapport* – he knowing their individual as well as collective strength, and they understanding the slightest inclination of his baton – it would be impossible to name another conductor and orchestra in the country capable of producing equal effects. Especially noteworthy are the remarkable delicacy and purity of the *pianissimi*, which have certainly never been hitherto equalled in Glasgow. As to Mr. Sullivan's manner of conducting, it is perfectly undemonstrative, in which respect it might gain the commendation even of Berlioz. Accustomed as we have been in this city to less self-suppression on the part of the conductor, this may seem to argue want of earnestness, but it is not so.[32]

The orchestra continued to function on a similar basis, until almost the same pattern (of engagement for a season) was adopted by the new Scottish Orchestra from 1891.

The limitations of the City Hall (opened in 1841) were becoming increasingly obvious, as larger numbers of performers were required and superior facilities demanded. Stillie published a digest of London press comment on the hall on 15 November 1873 as a consequence of the Festival held that year, and kept readers informed of the progress of the project for a larger, superior auditorium. He described the planned arrangements for the laying of the foundation stone in May 1875, and reported on the inaugural *Messiah* on 13 November 1877 as well as reviewing many of the concerts held there subsequently; among those listed as present at the hall's opening are Mr and Mrs T.

---

[31] *GH*, 26 January 1875, p. 4.
[32] *GH*, 1 December 1875, p. 4.

L. Stillie.[33] This hall, known as the St Andrew's Hall – at the suggestion of Stillie, according to *The Bailie*,[34] was widely admired for its acoustic properties and served with distinction until destroyed by fire in 1962. If the Birmingham Festival served as the model for the Glasgow Musical Festival (in its combination of choral and orchestral concerts and its emphasis on raising funds for charitable purposes), it seems to have been the Philharmonic Hall in Liverpool which was kept in mind in the championing and planning of Glasgow's new hall. In noting Stillie's death, *Musical Opinion* observed: 'The deceased gentleman was the musical critic of the *Herald*, and was, further, the originator and helper of many of the flourishing institutions which now exist in that thriving northern town.'[35]

Bach, Schubert, Mendelssohn and Wagner

There is scope for only a small sampling of Stillie's opinions about individual composers and schools. Such is the volume of his writing, and so great his aural experience of music that a comprehensive survey of these views could quite easily be prepared. I have chosen four composers about whom he wrote vividly, and who stand for powerful currents in nineteenth-century music: Bach, Schubert, Mendelssohn and Wagner.

The following excerpts provide evidence for the author's uncommonly extensive experience of the musical repertory and musical life of his day. The first dates from 1871:

> Meyerbeer's 'Roberto' is one of my favourite operas, and one with every bar of which I am conversant. I had heard it years ago in Paris, when it was reproduced under the composer's immediate superintendence, and again there to give Mdlle Christine Nilsson an opportunity of appearing as *Alice*. I had heard it in London some time ago when Costa had full command in Covent Garden, and when Mario and Grisi were in the zenith of their powers. I had heard it repeatedly in Glasgow fifteen years ago, when Formes was in full possession of his grand powers, and but the other day in Drury Lane, under Mr. George Wood's management. I was therefore glad to have an opportunity of hearing the work in Berlin.[36]

Writing of *Elijah* at the Leeds Musical Festival of 1880, the *Herald*'s critic observes: 'Today's performance was one of great excellence. I

---

[33] *GH*, 14 November 1877, p. 4.
[34] Cf. footnote 14, reference above, p 2.
[35] *Musical Opinion and Trade Review*, 1 July 1883, p. 420.
[36] *GH*, 3 July 1871, p. 4.

cannot say that it was as good as that of Birmingham some five years ago, nor that of your own [Glasgow] Choral Union in 1860.'[37] These two extracts appear to confirm Stillie's authorship: who else is likely to have combined Glaswegian concert- and opera-going with attendance in all the other centres?

Support for the contention that it was Stillie and none other who did so much travelling, apparently in the cause of music journalism, is given by a number of articles sent from the post-war Paris of 1871 and signed 'S'. The first of them suggests the habitual business traveller which Stillie may well have been:

> I used to leave Glasgow by limited mail, and used to get to Paris within twenty-four hours. [...] The distinguished correspondent of the *Daily News*, a Scotchman, was, as your readers know, the first man to enter Paris after the armistice. I think I have a right to claim the honour of being first in who left Scotland for that purpose. If any other one should ask that distinction I shall gladly compare dates.[38]

The same signatory engaged, as Stillie might have done, 'in conversation with business people and artists'. Some of the former mentioned were precisely in his professional line:

> I met with several of the largest manufacturers and printers who have their works in Alsace, and who appeared to be apprehensive that they would be compelled to give up their houses in Paris and transfer their business to Berlin. This simply means that nearly the whole of the spinning, weaving and calico printing trade of France would be at one sweep transferred to Germany.[39]

Stillie's notice of the Scottish première of Bach's 'St Matthew Passion' conveys a sense of the awe which the critic felt on first confronting that composition, even if in our estimation he allowed himself to be carried away: 'It is without question one of the most stupendous examples of sacred music we possess, and no student of the art should miss the opportunity of hearing a work which is regarded as the finest production of the "Homer" of music.'[40]

> Last night's performance was on the whole a successful one, in the hearing of which one was enabled to begin the study of a work which will take many hearings before its powers can be thoroughly realised. On listening to it we felt still more forcibly than before the leading and vital force which was exhibited in nearly every bar we have heard of Bach's music. There is always so much earnest-

---

[37] *GH*, 14 October 1880, p. 5.
[38] *GH*, 25 February 1871, p. 2.
[39] *GH*, 2 March 1871, p. 3.
[40] *GH*, 1 April 1872, p. 4; the comparison of J. S. Bach with Homer was a favourite.

ness in it – not the flashing ardour of youthful genius, but an earnestness which can alone proceed from a man conscientious in his life, tranquil in his habits, and with his feelings and sentiments toned down by the experience of life. For it must be borne in mind that Bach published no composition before he was 40 years of age. To judge the value of Bach's music, we must not forget the age in which he wrote, nor how much the art as we now have it is indebted to his bold innovations. On a careful study of his works, it is amazing to find how much indebted to him are Handel and Mendelssohn, as well as a host of less distinguished musicians.[41]

Like Bach, Schubert was a composer whose works were progressively claimed for the repertory after his death. This aspect was treated as follows in 1869:

> Till very lately Franz Schubert, a contemporary of Beethoven, was almost unknown in this country, save through a few of his songs. Thanks to Mr. Manns, of the Crystal Palace, and Mr. Hallé, however, many of his works have lately been produced in England. [...] Poor Schubert wrote many works of great importance teeming with beauty and genius; from various causes, however, he heard scarcely any of them performed. He had no inducement whatever to wrote music, as he could neither get his works published nor performed. [...] In spite of every discouragement he could not help composing; there was that within which compelled him to do so. He lived in a garret, in absolute poverty, continuing to write day after day and stow away his creations in a cupboard. Many of his MSS. were used for lighting fires; those rescued from destruction are only now being given to the world by his nephew.[42]

What might be called a 'Romantic fallacy', the notion that the creation of great art depends upon chronic poverty compelling the artist to create in order to live, is apparent in reverse in Stillie's opinion of Mendelssohn (see below).[43]

Stillie viewed Schubert as endowed with a prodigious capacity for inventing musical ideas which he lacked the ability to discipline, control and channel suitably. This assessment is evident in remarks made about a concert conducted by Hallé in 1870:

> Schubert's Rosamunde music is slowly but steadily gaining an important position. This gifted but erring composer wrote the incidental music to Madame Helmina Chezy's drama in 1823, the authoress acting the principal part of the Princess Rosamunde. We should never have heard of the play had it had been for Schubert's magnificent music. In it he had given the world a profusion of lovely melodies, which, if they had been treated by a master more

---

[41] *GH*, 3 April 1872, p. 4.
[42] *GH*, 24 November 1869, p. 4.
[43] I am grateful to David F. Crichton for drawing attention to this point.

cunning in the art of composition, would have been been even more interesting.[44]

Stillie admired much in Schubert, but returned often to his complaint against his music, stated here in a review of a performance given by Neruda, Vieuxtemps and Hallé in January 1874:

> The trio in B flat reveals in a marked degree Schubert's one great weakness, which we have repeatedly alluded to – his want of concentration. The work teems with effects which are perfectly enchanting, with melodies pure and fervid, and with cunning counterpoint; and yet his most ardent admirers, amongst whom we class ourselves, are forced to confess that the ideas are often too much spun out.[45]

It is hardly necessary to point out how much of a god for Victorian Britain was Mendelssohn. Here is Stillie's verdict, one tempered to a more modern view: 'Mendelssohn […] in almost everything he wrote, shows the polished and highly educated gentleman, the child of fortune, the man of the world; and the master who, if never inspired by the true fire of genius, yet possessed consummate talent and profound erudition.'[46]

A negative tone frequently accompanies references to compositions by Mendelssohn: 'We do not profess to have an intense admiration of this composer's quartets, yet the work under notice [Op. 44 no. 1] contains many passages of great beauty'.[47] The same tone is struck in a comment prompted by the Scherzo from another's First Symphony: 'Gade's compositions do not indicate any great creative power, but remind us rather forcibly of Mendelssohn at his weakest.'[48]

> [The 'Italian' Symphony] does not greatly add to Mendelssohn's reputation. The idea has been started lately, both in this country and on the Continent, that Mendelssohn has during the last twenty years occupied a position somewhat beyond his merits as a musician. This opinion is confined for the most part to those who may be described as unorthodox on such a question, and, while we feel inclined to sympathise with it to some extent, we do not admit its entire soundness. Many causes have been referred to as accounting for what is deemed Mendelssohn's undue prominence in the musical world. He of all musicians that ever lived was a 'child of fortune'. Born of rich parents, he received the most perfect education which could be afforded. He never knew what it was to write one note save to gratify his own inclinations. Happy in his family

---

[44] *GH*, 14 February 1870, p. 6.
[45] *GH*, 13 January 1874, p. 3.
[46] *GH*, 3 December 1872, p. 4.
[47] *GH*, 9 January 1871, p. 4.
[48] *GH*, 18 February 1874, p. 4.

relations, he experienced almost no troubles unless they were of his own seeking. Petted and extolled wherever he went, it is not surprising that he was in some degree spoiled. He came to this country, and by reason of his connections and worldly position found all men eager for his embrace. Moreover he had the rare tact of making friends in high station, whose influence was often exerted on his behalf. But these personal advantages are no longer potential, and henceforth Mendelssohn's fame must rest on his own merits as a composer. Nor is it desirable that it should be otherwise, for art, to be high and pure, must be freed from all extraneous influences. In saying so much (which we have been betrayed into saying because of the existence of this heterodox opinion respecting Mendelssohn), we must beg not to be misunderstood. We heartily acknowledge that Mendelssohn was a great musician – a man possessed of enormous talent, cultivated to the highest degree. Who that knows his 'Elijah' or 'Scotch' Symphony can fail to acknowledge this? Yet his writings [i.e. compositions] exhibit so much head, but ordinarily so little heart, that we almost feel forced tremblingly to throw in our lot with those who hold that he was denied the sacred fire of inspiration so bountifully bestowed on Bach, Handel, Mozart, Gluck, Beethoven, and Schubert. Moreover, in judging of the relative merits of Mendelssohn's compositions, especially of his orchestral works, it must be borne in mind that the composers last named all lived prior to his time, and that he was much indebted to them and their productions. Nor should it be forgotten that Rossini had previously produced all his operas, and Meyerbeer some of his, with their brilliant instrumentation; and that although Mendelssohn was accustomed to under-rate those writers, their advanced and at times overwrought colouring in orchestral effects seems to have had its influence on him.[49]

Several references to Mendelssohn as 'the Hamburg Jew'[50] seem to display the matter-of-fact style of the period and are not a sign of anti-Semitism.

Stillie was sufficiently interested in the activities of Mendelssohn and his successors at the Conservatorium in Leipzig to visit that institution in 1871, possibly taking advantage of an introduction from Sullivan to Ferdinand David: he found it 'a most ricketty, dirty, and I may safely add disreputable, building. Surely a little paint, some soap, and a good deal of whitewashing might be judiciously applied to make something like decent the foremost school of music in the world'.[51] That assessment forms a strong contrast with his visit to Messrs Breitkopf and Härtel in the same city, where he was welcomed on the basis of an introduction from his friend, the Glasgow musical entrepreneur Mr J. Muir Wood:

---

[49] GH, 15 February 1871, p. 4.
[50] For instance, in GH 14 October 1880, p. 5.
[51] GH, 4 July 1871, p. 3.

I have seen not a few printing, engraving and lithographing offices, but never one approaching to the order and cleanliness there maintained. And, then, such workmanship. A page of one of their books or a sheet of their music is of itself a perfect picture. They well deserve the high position they have attained.[52]

The anonymous *Herald* obituarist mentioned only one composer by name in his eulogy of Stillie: 'He was, and had long been, an admirer of the genius of Wagner. As the musical critic of the *Herald* for several years, Mr. Stillie championed the music of Wagner when it was not so highly regarded as it is now.'[53] Stillie had no doubts about the qualities of Wagner's compositions before 1850. He wrote in the tone of a prophet in the wilderness on behalf of *The Flying Dutchman, Tannhäuser* and *Lohengrin*. He owned vocal scores of all the Wagner operas or music dramas from *The Flying Dutchman* to *Parsifal* (which are now in the Stillie Collection), and made some effort to come to terms with the works in that form. '[Lohengrin] happens to have been my chief study last winter [i.e. 1870–71, so that I was prepared to enjoy a representation of it.'[54] That representation took place in Leipzig in July 1871:

> It is impossible in a letter such as this to attempt a description of the music of 'Lohengrin'. That would require a very long notice. I may say, however, that it is essentially dramatic in character – not dramatic in the Italian sense of that world [i.e. melodramatic?], but truly so. Every situation, every change of sentiment, is carefully studied by the composer. Opinion must, however, differ as to whether he is correct in the ideas themselves, as well as the manner in which they have been carried out. Those who have been accustomed to regard the Italian and French operas as a perfect school of dramatic music cannot well admire Wagner's works, as there is in the latter such absence of flowing melody, and so many long heavily-scored recitatives. It is not that Wagner cannot write melody when that suits his ideas, as witness the glorious introduction to and much of the third act of 'Lohengrin' [...]. Let any of your musical readers get a copy of 'Lohengrin' and study carefully this chain of movements, and he will find that when Wagner chooses he can write glorious melodies.[55]

In reviewing a concert by 'Mr. Hallé's orchestra' in February 1872 Stillie wrote:

> These productions [*Rienzi, The Flying Dutchman, Tannhäuser* and *Lohengrin*] abound with solos, duets, ensembles and choruses overflowing with melody, at times breathing most tender passionate

---

[52] Ibid.
[53] Cf. footnote 12 above.
[54] *GH*, 4 July 1871, p. 3.
[55] Ibid.

love, at others expressing the accents of hate and fury, and anon
embodying in exquisite musical form the changing scenes and ac-
tions of romance and chivalry. In these his dignified melody, his
wondrous harmonies (not always in strict rule), and gorgeous instrumentation display the hand of a genius.[56]

Stillie's puzzlement on encountering Wagner's 'reform' operas is anticipated in a notice of November 1875 where he records the public success
of the first *Lohengrin* in Glasgow:

it cannot be too clearly understood that the four operas enumer-
ated above [see preceding paragraph] do not belong to the so-called
'Music of the Future', and that Wagner himself has repudiated
them as unworthy of his genius. That comes later on, culminating
in the 'Niebelungen' [*sic*] – a series of operas which take four
nights to perform, and which are to be brought out at Wagner's
own theatre at Beyreuth [*sic*] next year. Never having had an
opportunity of hearing any of the 'Music of the Future' on the
stage, we cannot give an opinion as to its effect when performed:
for home study it is most uninteresting and perplexing.[57]

The visit to Bayreuth reported in the *Herald* in August 1876 continues
this puzzlement, with only the more picturesque moments making an
immediate favourable impression. Despite his enthusiasm for certain
aspects of Wagner's music, Stillie's cold eye was still directed at others.

The extent to which he understood Wagner's aims is noteworthy. He
mentions the preferred choice of subject-matter (i.e. myth), the intended
subordination of music to drama (or poetry), the ideal sightlines, outstanding orchestral sonority and superb production facilities of the
Festspielhaus, and always acknowledges Wagner's powerful musical
gifts. He recognizes the emotional power of some of the music, but
complains of places which suffer from 'formlessness', lack of beauty –
sometimes reaching ugliness – and in particular about the presence of
'over-scored recitatives'.

Conclusion

This chapter has touched on some aspects of what may be learned from
reading the work of an informed and up-to-date writer about music. In
conjunction with archival investigation of concert programmes, the
reading of correspondence, contracts and other documents, this activity
could yield a more precise and detailed picture of infrastructure and
repertory than has yet been attempted for music in Scotland in this

---

[56] *GH*, 10 February 1872, p. 4.
[57] *GH*, 4 November 1875, p. 4.

period, providing a fuller context for the eventual emergence of distinctive compositional voices. This would be a useful contribution to the study of the least familiar period in Scotland's musical history for which evidence exists.

Select bibliography

Baptie, D., *Musical Scotland, Past and Present: Being a Dictionary of Scottish Musicians from about 1400 till the present time, to which is added a bibliography of musical publications connected with Scotland from 1611*, Paisley, 1894; repr. Hildesheim, 1972.

Brown, J. D. and Stratton, S. S., *British musical biography: a dictionary of musical artists, authors and composers, born in Britain and its colonies*, Birmingham, 1897.

Cormack, M., *Guide to the Stillie Collection in Glasgow University Library*, MS 1974.

Elliott, K. and Rimmer, F., *A History of Scottish Music*, London, 1973.

Farmer, H. G., *A History of Music in Scotland*, London, 1947.

———. 'Glasgow', *Die Musik in Geschichte und Gegenwart* (*MGG*), vol. 5, Kassel, 1956, cols 223–31.

Johnson, D., 'Glasgow', in *The New Grove Dictionary of Music and Musicians*, London, 1980, vol. 7, pp. 425–6.

CHAPTER TEN

Music in Nineteenth-Century Oxford

Susan Wollenberg

QUESTION: How many Oxford dons does it take to change a lightbulb?
ANSWER: *Change?*

The nineteenth century was very much a time of change in Oxford, as the relevant volumes of the new *History of the University of Oxford* show.[1] In this chapter I will identify, and explore briefly, some of the changing contexts in which music played a role in nineteenth-century Oxford. In doing so I will refer to contemporary writings as well as to the more familiar secondary literature.

First, I offer a sample of the view from 1856: 'Of all the progeny of Alma Mater, she alone [i.e. music] is allowed to grow up without training and education'.[2] Maurice's document comes from the period when Ouseley began to agitate for the reform of the music degrees. (For brief biographical details of Ouseley and others mentioned in this chapter, see the Appendix.) The rambling style of Maurice's disquisition should not be allowed to obscure the real importance of his question 'What shall we do with Music?', nor to detract from the validity of the arguments he presents at this early stage in what was to be a protracted and complex process of development. It is also important to recognize the novelty of this searching approach to music, in its historical perspective; as far as I am aware, eighteenth-century Oxford was devoid of any comparable enquiry, and of the reforming zeal that both prompted and flowed from it. A new role for music in nineteenth-century Oxford was as the focus of academic reform.

The impression given in the more recent literature is that Ouseley's innovations, introducing a written degree examination, constituted the sole manifestation of music's reformed status; and a single date is usu-

---

[1] Vols 6 and 7, Oxford: Clarendon Press. Vol. 6, ed. M. G. Brock and M. C. Curthoys, published 1997; Vol. 7 forthcoming.

[2] *WHAT SHALL WE DO WITH MUSIC? A letter to the Rt. H[on]. the Earl Derby, Chancellor of the University of Oxford, by Peter Maurice, D.D. Chaplain of New and All Soul's Colleges in Oxford*, London, 1856, p. 5.

ally assigned to the process. Thus Westrup's 'Until 1862, when a regular examination was instituted, candidates for degrees in music had merely to submit a musical composition ... '.[3] Apart from mention of the dates when the public performance of the 'exercise' in composition was abolished for the B.Mus. and D.Mus., the next date that appears in Westrup's account is 'after the 1914–18 war'. Any reference to the situation in between is largely negative.

Taking a longer view of the period of Ouseley's reforms, 1856–89, and their repercussions in the late nineteenth and early twentieth centuries, it is possible to trace a progressive redesigning and refining of the music degree syllabus, with each change tending to generate the need for further change. Among important stages in the process I will single out the following. First, after Ouseley's new examination scheme of the late 1850s, the next significant stage came in 1871, when the B.Mus. examination was expanded to encompass two parts, the first (in harmony and counterpoint) acting as a preliminary to the second, which tested not only more advanced harmony and counterpoint, but also history of music, form and set works. The new stiffening of the requirements must have affected the way the degree was perceived, both within and beyond the university.

The examination papers reflect some sense of a systematic study of the subject, and of a corpus of historical data, secondary literature and repertoire. Although some of the questions on musical history were designed to link up with the harmony and counterpoint studies, and with the church-music sphere in which most candidates still operated, in general they cover an impressively wide range of subjects, including continental and Catholic traditions, and with some emphasis on earlier (Renaissance and Baroque) periods. The feature that 'dates' these historical papers is a kind of 'trivia' question scattered among the more searching enquiries (for example, 'Can you mention any musical anecdote in connexion with King Louis XII of France' or 'Who first introduced unprepared dominant sevenths'). They are certainly not marked by a preoccupation with nineteenth-century music, although there are some challenging questions on Berlioz, Liszt and Wagner. But questions on organum, on early and exotic instruments, on the music of Dufay, Josquin, Frescobaldi, Monteverdi, Couperin, the sons of Bach and their influence, and some historiographical issues, show a breadth of outlook beyond the standard repertoire and require some sophisticated reading.

Papers of this sort could hardly have been offered to eighteenth-century candidates. By the nineteenth century, of course, Burney and

---

[3] Jack Westrup, 'Oxford', *New Grove Dictionary of Music and Musicians*, London, 1980, vol. 14, p. 38.

Hawkins had left their mark (already visible in Crotch's syllabus of lectures).[4] In Stainer's notes for candidates in music the recommended historical texts included both Burney's and Hawkins' *Histories*, and some more recent authors: Hullah and Naumann.[5] Hullah is best known for his educational contribution in the field of singing, but his historical writings evidently enjoyed some currency: the *History of Modern Music* was later translated into Italian (Ricordi, 1880). The writings of Naumann in Germany (a pupil of Mendelssohn, and Professor at the Dresden conservatory) belonged, together with those of English scholars such as Parry, to the series of general books that reflected the aftermath of the 'widening of interest in music history' in the third and fourth decades of the nineteenth century,[6] bringing together the information that was increasingly being gathered on specific areas. An important factor in the development of English musical scholarship in this period was the translation into English of major historical and scientific literature on music. In the five volumes constituting Ouseley's edition of Naumann's *History of Music*, the presentation of a remarkably comprehensive coverage of past traditions, and some consideration of 'The Present', is further amplified by Ouseley's addition of six chapters on English music balancing Naumann's continental perspective. Perhaps the work could then be more confidently recommended by the Oxford authorities to their candidates, who would find contained in it Ouseley's vigorous refutation of the assumption that England lacked music.

On the technical side, Ouseley's and Stainer's treatises on harmony, counterpoint and form, and Parry's *Grove* article on form, were listed. Without promoting exclusively local scholarship, Stainer's list gave due prominence to Oxford-based productions, especially on the technical side of the subject; it is noteworthy also that Ouseley's works were published by the Clarendon Press at Oxford. After 1871 the technical papers place less emphasis on theory and more on practical writing and analysis. What dates these papers is that the given material (to which parts were generally required to be added) is almost always unattributed to either a specific composer or a style. This anonymity only partly

---

[4] William Crotch, Syllabus of Oxford Lectures (1800–1804), Oxford Bodleian Library, MS Top. Oxon. d. 22/II and G A. Oxon. b. 19 (265).

[5] John Hullah, *The History of Modern Music*, London, 1862 (2/1875) and *A Course of Lectures on … Transition Period of Musical History*, London, 1865 (2/1876); Emil Naumann, *History of Music*, transl. F. Praeger, ed. F. A. Gore Ouseley, 5 vols, London, 1882–86. Listed in J. Stainer, *Directions for Candidates for Degrees in Music* [Oxford, 1891].

[6] 'Historiography', *New Grove Dictionary of Music and Musicians*, London, 1980, vol. 8, pp. 596–7 on the nineteenth century.

reflects the textbook literature; Ouseley's *Treatise on Counterpoint, Canon and Fugue* includes material by Gibbons, Handel, Reicha and others, with ascription to their authors. But the examiners' concern was primarily to test particular contrapuntal techniques (constructing species counterpoint or complex fugal answers) and harmonic grammar. The combination of textbook knowledge and its practical application created a new tradition of Oxford harmony and counterpoint in the later nineteenth century.

For the D.Mus. examination, which included the study of acoustics, the recommended authorities were Helmholtz, Pole, Stone and Sedley Taylor. Both Parry and Pole were musical graduates of Oxford. Stone was William Henry Stone (1830–91) who read Classics at Oxford, and then medicine, and was a scholar of physics and music. In the wake of Helmholtz (whose *Lehre von den Tonempfindungen* of 1863 was available from 1875 in A. J. Ellis's English translation as *On the Sensations of Tone*), again an Oxford-based contribution is discernible in the development of the subject of acoustics. Finally, in this outline of the academic scope of the Oxford degrees, the element of musical analysis should be mentioned as an increasingly noticeable component of the examination papers. Parry's *Grove* article on form[7] represented a major contribution to this area of enquiry, ranging widely over topics as diverse as the early Lutheran chorale, the Branle (from Arbeau's 'Orchesographie'), Corelli's chamber sonatas, the influence of Emanuel Bach on Haydn, and the rondos of Beethoven. Parry's approach is distinguished by a capacity for drawing together some crucial definitions (of form itself, or of coda, for instance) with exemplary clarity. In its breadth of reference his article complements the kind of range found in the general histories. The scholarly work of these three successive professors – Ouseley, Stainer and Parry – is itself complementary to the ways in which the Oxford musical degrees during this period had by stages acquired a new academic *gravitas*.

Yet Hadow, in one of a series of important writings on the subject around the turn of the century, referred to the Oxford B.Mus. and D.Mus. as 'still certificates of technical proficiency, not marks of university citizenship'.[8] A telling expression of concern for the academic status of the degrees had occurred in the evidence submitted to the Selborne Commission some 25 years earlier by Ouseley and Corfe:

> Those who study music, as well as those who teach it, have felt it as a continual discouragement of late years that the degrees in this

---

[7] George Grove, *A Dictionary of Music and Musicians*, vol. 1, London, 1879, pp. 541–55 (C.H.H.P.).

[8] H. Hadow, *FACULTY OF ARTS: Degrees in Music*, Oxford, *c.* 1900, Oxford, Bodleian Library GA Oxon b 41 (7).

subject, whatever be the amount of acquirement that they testify to, do not carry the weight that other Degrees do ... A small beginning has already been made in this matter by the requirement of passing an elementary examination in subjects other than technical music.[9]

This 'small beginning' referred to the university statute of 1876 requiring B.Mus. candidates who were not members of the university to show competence in English, Maths, Latin and either Greek or a modern language.

The other main concern throughout the period of reform was the traditional absence of any residence requirement for the musical degrees. This problem surfaced regularly and generated an extensive amount of (often eloquent) argument. Some of the most illuminating ideas were those expressed by Hadow during discussions of this perennial issue that took place in 1898.[10] The nub of Hadow's reasoning was based only partly on the Oxford perspective which showed in his regard for 'that essential part of Oxford education – the education gained from the daily life'. His argument was otherwise formed on a more general view. The proposed enhancement of the 'educational value of the degree' was perceived as a corrective to what Hadow described as the 'comparatively low standard of education ... hitherto ... accepted among musicians in this country ... '. Hadow observed that 'the musical profession in England is still, as a rule, somewhat behind other arts and other professions in point of general intellectual culture'; and 'that this standard should be raised' was, he suggested, 'the desire of almost all who are interested in the future of English music'.

It is possible that the wider climate influenced the reform of music in Oxford. Within the university, other disciplines such as medicine were moving in similar directions. And within the musical world an increased emphasis on educational standards was apparent. The Prince of Wales, 'at a meeting held in 1882 to float the scheme for a Royal College of Music' imagined it taking on 'the more extended function of a University'.[11] An important factor in Oxford's outlook on music was the

---

[9] *University of Oxford Commission* (1877, publ. 1881), supplementary evidence, pp. 374–5.

[10] University of Oxford, Hebdomadal Council: Minutes 3/16 (1898), pp. 35–46 *passim*. The quotations that follow are from pp. 38–9. Some aspects of this debate are discussed in H. Watkins Shaw, rev. and ed. Peter Ward Jones. 'The Oxford University Chair of Music, 1627–1947, with some account of Oxford degrees in Music from 1856', *Bodleian Library Record* (1998), vol. 16, pp. 233–70. For a general account of this and other issues see my chapter in the forthcoming *History of the University of Oxford*, vol. 7 and my forthcoming book *Music at Oxford in the Eighteenth and Nineteenth centuries*.

[11] E. D. Mackerness, 'George Bernard Shaw and the English Musical Renaissance', *Durham University Journal*, June (1987, p. 303.

possibility of links between music and theology. As Maurice[12] put it in 1856, Oxford was sending an 'academic population' out into the world as 'pastors' without sufficient musical training. It has been suggested that the call for the formation of a satisfactory musical school within the university was informed by an 'explicit ecclesiastical impulse'. Cuddesdon theological college had been founded in 1854, and Professor Hussey and others were probably concerned to prove 'that the university could supply all the training ... necessary for clergymen'.[13] (Hussey was Professor of Ecclesiastical History and a supporter of the reformed musical degrees.) A report of the seventh annual meeting of the University Motett and Madrigal Society in 1853 stressed that the course of instruction offered to members of the society by Dr Corfe would enable them to acquire skills in reading and singing at sight for their future involvement, as clergymen, with parish choirs. (It was felt around that time that it was inappropriate to appoint a Heather Professor who was not a church musician.) The growth in influence of the Oxford Movement was another important element in the prevailing climate.

The issues discussed so far affected hundreds of degree candidates during the second half of the nineteenth century. Examination records survive for approximately 369 successful B.Mus. candidates in the period 1854–1914. The anomalous non-residential requirements for the degrees produced a wide variety in individual patterns of achievement. Among the documentation of candidates are some remarkable instances of early application: Parry (b. 1848) had taken the B.Mus. examination in 1866, while in his teens and at Eton, before coming up to Exeter College, Oxford, where he took the BA in 1870 (when Stainer conducted the Exeter College Musical Society in the 1860s, Parry was active as a student member). Parry's D.Mus. (awarded 1884) was honorary. Stainer (b. 1840) had been awarded his B.Mus. in 1859, four years before he took the BA (1863); he proceeded to the D.Mus. in 1865. Under the unreformed (pre-Ouseley) statute, Leighton G. Hayne (b. 1836) of Queen's College had taken the B.Mus. in 1856; *Jackson's Oxford Journal* in its issue of 17 May 1856 noted that this was believed to be

> the first instance of an Undergraduate of either University graduating in music before his degree in arts, and it reflects great credit on a gentleman so young to have shown such proficiency in the science of music as to have been able to produce an exercise worthy

---

[12] Ibid., p. 9.

[13] I am indebted for this suggestion to Mark Curthoys, of the *History of the University of Oxford*.

of a degree, for it is a well-known fact that musical degrees are not obtained now so easily as in days gone by.

(How much more pertinent these words would have seemed by the 1880s when the efforts of Ouseley's reforms had become established.)

With the stiffening of the requirements for the examined degrees in the later nineteenth century came the regular award of the honorary D.Mus. from Oxford. (Before the mid-nineteenth century the examined D.Mus. had been comparatively rare, and the honorary D.Mus. even more so.) From 1879 a series of distinguished composers (with Arthur Sullivan one of the earliest, in that year) received the honorary doctorate from Oxford; some of these were similarly honoured by Cambridge also. Among the later honorands were Elgar (1905), Grieg (1906), Glazounov and Saint-Saëns (1907). University musicians also figured among those honoured, including Sir Herbert Oakeley (Christ Church; Professor of Music at Edinburgh from 1865 to 1891: hon. D.Mus. Oxon, 1879) and Charles Villiers Stanford (1883), later Professor at Cambridge.

By 1897, in a booklet filled with wise advice to candidates for the Oxford B.Mus., Stainer summed up the nineteenth-century developments. Referring to the presentation of an exercise in composition, still a central element in the examination for both the bachelor's degree and the doctorate in music, he remarked:

> It may be asked why more merit is demanded in the Exercise than formerly, say thirty or forty years ago. The answer is this. Musical education has made extraordinary strides during this period; lessons in Composition, which were then the luxury of the few, are now the commodity of the many. In my boyhood there was a distinct lack of good books, good teachers, good institutions for training in music. Old things have passed away, the mysteries of the art are laid bare to all-comers, instruction in Form is no longer reserved by a small group of experts as only suitable to a few ... it is dispensed wholesale to classes. This being the case, we are bound to confer our degrees only on students who are 'up to date' in intelligence and education.[14]

While these comments explain the background to the degrees at that particular stage of their evolution, they serve – together with Stainer's insistence, throughout this publication, on high standards of teaching and good habits of study – also as an indication of some of the motivating forces that led to the establishment of the Board of Studies in Music at Oxford in 1911, which itself can be seen as a sign that both the

---

[14] J. Stainer, *A Few Words to Candidates for the Degree of Mus. Bac., Oxon*, London and New York [1897], p. 19.

educational aspirations and the administrative mechanisms were in place
that were necessary for the eventual formation of a Faculty of Music in
the modern sense.

Appendix

Corfe, Charles William (1814–83)
B.Mus. 1847; D.Mus. 1852
Organist, Christ Church 1846; Choragus 1860–83

Crotch, William (1775–1847)
B.Mus. 1794; D.Mus. 1799
Organist, Christ Church 1790, St John's and University Church of St
Mary's 1797; Heather Professor 1797–1847; first Principal of the Royal
Academy of Music, 1822

Hadow, William Henry (1859–1937)
BA 1882; MA 1885; B.Mus. 1890
Fellow of Worcester College 1888

Ouseley, Frederick Arthur Gore, Bart. (1825–89)
BA 1846; MA 1849; B.Mus. 1850; D.Mus. 1854
Heather Professor 1855–89; Warden, St Michael's College, Tenbury
1856

Parry, C. Hubert Hastings (1848–1918)
B.Mus. 1867; BA 1870; MA 1874; D.Mus. 1884
Director, Royal College of Music 1894; Heather Professor 1900–1908

Pole, William, FRS (1814–1900)
B.Mus. 1860; D.Mus. 1867
Professor of Civil Engineering, University College London 1859–76;
Organist St Mark's, North Audley Street, 1836–66

Stainer, John (1840–1901)
B.Mus. 1859; BA 1863; D.Mus. 1865; MA 1866
Organist, Magdalen College 1859; Heather Professor 1889–99

All degrees given in this list are Oxford qualifications.

CHAPTER ELEVEN

Music-Making in a Yorkshire Country House

Caroline Wood

Burton Constable Hall is situated some 8 miles east of Hull, in the district known as Holderness, where the Constable family have been important landowners since the thirteenth century. Parts of the house date from medieval times, but the major enlargement of the original tower-house took place in the late sixteenth century. The Elizabethan house was modernized in the eighteenth century, and further extensive refurbishments took place in Victorian times.

A collection of sheet music there has recently been reassembled from the places in the house where it had languished for some time, and both this sheet music and bound volumes have been cleaned. Two of the Hall's band of volunteers, who had been helping to make an inventory of the Hall's entire contents, have turned their attention to the music. Accession slips are being completed, but there is still some way to go with the cataloguing process. There has been some sorting, separating out handwritten music, bound and unbound, and some grouping of certain categories of published sheet music, such as music for harp, guitar and concertina. The bound volumes of music have been cleaned but not accessed, nor their contents listed. Nevertheless, the contents of the collection as so far revealed can tell us quite a lot about the people who amassed the music, and the part that music played in their lives.[1]

Study of the music's background and context has included dipping into a very large archive of estate and family documents in the County Archive Office at Beverley. This consists of thousands of items ranging from bills and account books to maps, letters and legal documents, dealing not only with the house and the considerable estate in East Yorkshire but also with the Constable family's extensive properties and estates elsewhere.

---

[1] I am indebted to David Connell and Lorna Haysom of the Burton Constable Foundation for answering many queries and for permission to use illustrations from the Burton Constable collections, and to Paul and Muriel Scudamore, who are compiling accession slips for the collection, for their assistance.

The interest of historians in Burton Constable has chiefly centred upon the eighteenth century and a very considerable and important collection of material relevant to the study of the history of science. Detailed studies have been done on the acquisition of this cabinet of curiosities, as well as on the modifications made to the house and the acquisition of a considerable library of books and manuscripts, amounting by 1775 to nearly 9 600 items.[2] The only musical information so far uncovered relating to the house in the eighteenth century is from an inventory of its contents carried out for the purposes of probate in 1791.[3] In this extensive list, there are just two items of musical interest: one hand organ and one harpsichord, located in the Great Hall. It is not known when and how the harpsichord was acquired or what happened to it; the table top organ, by George Pyke of London, dates from around 1750, and was repaired in 1759 and 1794; it is still at the Hall (Plate 11.1). Although the presence of these instruments suggests some musical activity, it is not certain that any of the music belonged to members of the family living at Burton Constable at that time.

Just over 100 years later, another inventory was taken.[4] In the library are listed a violin, a guitar, described as 'very fine', a small harp, a tambourine, a mahogany grand piano by Erard, and two cases of violin and harp strings. In the theatre are a 'gilt harp', a 'base fiddle in green case' and a 'double base fiddle'. Various music stands, chairs and stools are also listed. In the description of the contents of the theatre the following appears: 'The orchestra filled with music stands covered with crimson cloth and the whole lined with crimson cloth brass nailed.' The house had been unoccupied for 25 years prior to this latter inventory being taken, and the major part of the music collection appears to have been assembled by the family members who lived at Burton Constable between about 1830 and 1870. When another generation of the family returned to occupy the house again, the music collection shows that there seems to have been a revival of musical interest.

In 1791, the year of the earlier inventory, the baronetcy passed from William Constable to his nephew, Edward, who was succeeded by his brother Francis. William's father Cuthbert had assumed the name Constable in order to continue the line; Edward and Francis Sheldon had to do the same. William, Edward and Francis died without issue. The succession then passed to Thomas Hugh Clifford, of Tixall in Staffordshire, who again added the surname Constable; only two years later he was succeeded by his son Thomas Aston Clifford Constable, who suc-

---

[2] Hall, I. and Hall, E., *Burton Constable Hall: A Century of Patronage*, Hull, 1991.

[3] East Yorkshire County Archive Service (hereafter EYCAS), DDCC 145/28.

[4] In private possession.

Plate 11.1   Organ by George Pyke of London at Burton Constable Hall

ceeded to the title in 1823, when he was 15 years old. Four years later, Thomas Aston Clifford Constable married his first cousin, Marianne Chichester, of Calverleigh in Devon, and shortly afterwards they moved to Burton Constable and began a programme of refurbishment and restoration. Marianne's older unmarried sister, Mary Elizabeth, known as Eliza, also came to live with them. On the evidence of the music collection, the marriage brought together two families with musical interests, and from the evidence of signatures on copies, the earliest music in the collection was probably brought to Burton Constable from the two family homes. After the death of Sir Clifford Constable in 1870, his successor and only child, Talbot, chose to live elsewhere and Constables did not live at Burton Constable for 25 years. On Talbot's death, the succession passed to the Chichester line of the family, Lieutenant-Colonel Walter George Raleigh Chichester assuming the name and arms of Constable in 1895; the house became lived in again and its music collection was further enlarged. This study concentrates on the period of the Clifford Constables, and looks at the music and performers of that generation.

The handwritten music consists of about 24 bound volumes and a box of unbound music, nearly 100 items in total. These 'items' range from a single leaf to a small bundle of individual parts sewn together or punched and tied with home-made ribbon bows. Some 750 accession slips have been written so far for items in the collection of printed sheet music, but those account for only perhaps three-fifths of this part of the collection. There are several boxes of such items as operetta scores, individual songs and piano music which date roughly from the 1880s to the 1930s, and reflect the musical tastes and acquisitions of later generations. The hard-bound volumes of printed music amount to approximately 230. A few of these may have been purchased in bound form, such as the volumes of 'Clarke's Handel'.[5] In the other volumes are bound together anything from three to 50 separate items, with a typical volume containing around 12 to 20 items on average.

Many of these volumes are handsomely bound, and labelled with some idea of their contents and owner; hence 'Violin and Piano Duetts' on the spine, and on the front 'Sir Clifford and Lady Constable'; or 'Violin and Flute Accompaniments' on the spine and 'Miss Chichester' on the front. In the last named of these are bound together all the optional parts provided for versions of operatic favourites found in solo or piano duet volumes. So in this particular case, for example, the first five items are a flute part for Airs from *The Barber of Seville*, a violin

---

[5] *The Vocal Works composed by G. F. Handel.* Arranged for the Organ or Piano Forte by Dr John Clarke, 6 vols, London [1820?].

part for an unspecified overture (the title *Demophon* has been pencilled in), a violin part for the overture to *La Gazza Ladra*, another for J. N. Hummel's *The Caliph of Baghdad*, and a flute part for the overture to *Zampa*, as arranged by Bochsa for harp and piano. At first sight this would seem to be an admirably systematic and practical way of organizing a large quantity of sheet music, but it is proving difficult to find matching volumes, and very few of the volumes are indexed. However, in several volumes the individual items within have been numbered by hand, presumably as an aid to the bookbinders.

The process of compilation started early, and it seems likely from the evidence of binders' stamps and labels that some of these volumes had been assembled before the Chichester sisters left Calverleigh and Sir Clifford left Tixall. Several volumes have a date on the spine; the latest one, 1870, has 'Lady Clifford Constable' on the front, but Marianne had died in 1862 and this was Sir Thomas's second wife, Rosina. It was she who was responsible for acquiring the Erard grand piano mentioned in the 1895 inventory, which is still at the hall. It was already, in modern parlance, a 'top of the range' model costing £255, but by the time Lady Rosina had had it 'customized' to match one of the cabinets in the house, the cost had rocketed to £787 10s. 0d.; the guidebook to the hall claims that this was the most expensive piano made by Erard up to that date.

The music collection shows that the members of the family could muster several instruments, though not a large ensemble without assistance from house guests or others. The permanent members of the household in the period between approximately 1830 and 1860 were Sir Clifford and Lady Clifford Constable, their son Talbot (born in 1828), and Lady Clifford's older sister, Eliza, usually referred to as Miss Chichester. (The two sisters died in the early 1860s, Sir Clifford remarrying in 1865 and surviving until 1870.) The family's principal instruments seem to have been the violin, for Sir Clifford, and the piano and harp, for his wife Marianne and sister-in-law Eliza; young Talbot learned the *cornet à pistons* and probably the piano and violin as well.[6] The collection includes tutor books for all the above, as well as for voice, flute, flageolet, guitar and banjo. The optional flute parts with which so many publications were provided seem to have been kept, but it is not clear who played these: possibly it was one of the relatives or other regular house guests. An anonymous lithograph at the house shows music-making in the gallery with one of the women playing the guitar (Plate 11.2) and we may assume that all would have sung (Eliza

---

[6] He even turned his hand to composition, publishing a polka for piano 'Rêve de la jeunesse' dedicated to 'Lady Chichester', probably around 1850 (Paris).

Plate 11.2   Music-making in the gallery, Burton Constable Hall, *c.* 1850 (artist unknown)

possessed two large volumes of Lanza's *Elements of Singing,* Parts I and II[7]). There is plenty of evidence that the music in this collection was not merely accumulated but was used: fingerings, indications for pedal changes on the harp music, well-thumbed and dog-eared pages and other wear and tear. In difficulty, the music ranges from elementary to the virtuosic. Members of the family were prepared to tackle the pyrotechnics of the innumerable fantasias and variations on operatic themes by such composers as Thalberg, Herz and Osborne which fuelled the public's insatiable appetite for display, alongside the studies of Cramer, Chopin and Liszt, the violin sonatas and piano trios of the classical period, and an extensive harp repertoire, all of which are well represented in the collection.

The theatre mentioned in the 1895 inventory consisted of a bedroom and a dressing-room converted for the purpose during the 1840s (prior to about 1850, plays were given in the gallery). One of these rooms formed the auditorium, the other the stage and fly-tower. In this century the rooms were converted again and are now the museum rooms, in which are displayed some of William Constable's scientific collection; there is no trace of their previous function. However, some scenery survives, together with playbills and scripts. The amateur theatricals which took place at the Hall are very much like those described by Wilhelmma Quirante Ramas in her study 'Private Theatricals of the Upper Classes in 18th Century England',[8] and several of the characteristics she describes are perpetuated in the somewhat later events at Burton Constable. The whole undertaking was taken extremely seriously, with a season of plays produced each year. Handbills detailing the performers were printed by a local firm. The main participants were members of the family and their house guests. There is the occasional suggestion of 'stiffening' from the professional theatre, although nobody of the calibre of the participants at places like Richmond House, where the most celebrated luminaries of the London stage might be drawn into the events. The custom of having an epilogue to the play or season of plays persisted here; so that the playbill for *The Sheriff of the County,* given on Saturday 14 April 1849 announces that 'After the play an epilogue composed expressly for the occasion by Sir Edward Bulwer Lytton, Bart., will be spoken by Mr. Gerard' (the stage manager).[9]

It is difficult to determine how much music there was in these productions. The 1895 inventory, which probably reflects the contents of

---

[7] Part I published for the author by Button and Whitaker, London, 1813; Part II by Chappell and Co., London, n.d.

[8] Unpublished dissertation, Fordham University, New York, 1970.

[9] EYCAS, DDCC17/13.

the Hall more or less as it was left when Thomas and Marianne's successor decided to live in one of his other houses, in the1870s, refers to 'The orchestra filled with music stands covered with crimson cloth'. A pencil drawing of the theatre at Burton Constable of unknown date shows a row of heads where we would expect musicians to be (Plate 11.3). The playbills do not mention music beyond something to the effect that 'The whole [evening] will conclude with a comic song sung by Mr. Chetwynd',[10] but we may assume that music had some part to play. However, the members of the family and some house guests who we know from other evidence to have been skilled musical performers had speaking parts in the plays, so there is some work to do to discover what music was used and who played it. However, a newspaper account may give a clue: in the *Hull Advertiser*, 17 February 1843, there is an account of 'Theatricals at Burton Constable' which ends 'The whole concluded with a quadrille. Mr. Giles's excellent band was in attendance for the occasion'. There is any amount of music in the collection which could have been used as incidental music to such plays as *The School for Scandal* and the comedies and farces which the entertainment comprised.

Quite a lot of the music dates from before the family moved to Burton Constable. There are several items signed 'Miss Clifford' or 'Miss Clifford's, Tixall'; these presumably belonged to Sir Clifford's sister. 'Master Clifford's, Tixall' probably means Sir Clifford, but could just be his father. There are even a few items which are signed in her maiden name by his mother, Mary McDonnell Chichester, who was born in 1768 and married in 1791. Elsewhere we find the name Calverleigh, the childhood home of the Chichesters. Marianne Chichester signs one item with her name and the date 1815 when she would have been 14 or 15; inside some volumes she signs 'Mary Ann Chichester her book' which suggests an even younger Marianne. There has to be just a little caution in assuming original ownership: a bound volume of six assorted items (two sets of Scots songs, some tunes for German flute, two songs in manuscript and a printed song and six trios by Giardini) is signed by Eliza Chichester, who was born in 1798, but at least two items in the collection were first published around 1760, so she may have put together some old music and had it bound.

The handwritten music shows some evidence of the family's fondness for travel. This is music written into books purchased as manuscript books, which served as 'commonplace books' into which the owner copied music for future reference. Where there is any indication, it

---

[10] Playbill for performance of *The School for Scandal*, Wednesday, 26 April 1843: EYCAS, DDCC17/13.

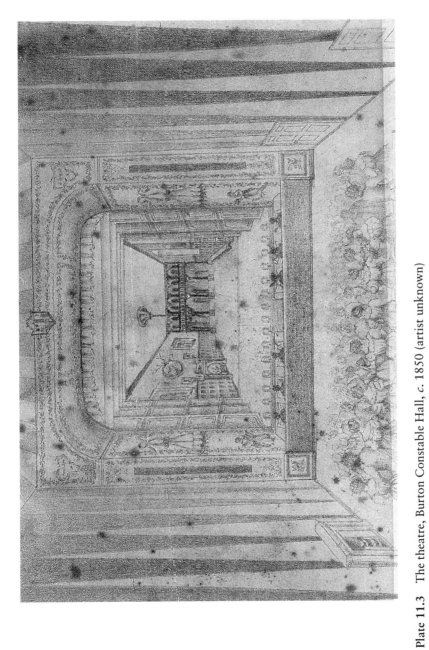

Plate 11.3   The theatre, Burton Constable Hall, c. 1850 (artist unknown)

shows that the manuscript books were purchased in London, Bristol, Bath, Paris and Hull. In nearly all cases, there is no evidence of any planning, and songs, piano music, guitar music and harp music are jumbled together. In several cases, a few left-over pages at the end are used up for exercises or, in one case, 'a method for tuning the double action harp'. Only relatively infrequently is a composer mentioned by name. Occasionally the writer has dated the piece; where there are such dates, they show that the books were added to over a number of years. In one book, a sequence of dates begins with April 1827; it continues with items marked successively with dates between 1829 and 1834 and place-names from Brussels to Paris via Coblentz, Rome and Harrogate. One other conclusion which these books suggest is that their owners were comfortable with several languages: songs in French, German, Italian, Spanish, Portuguese, Welsh and a Swiss dialect are to be found.

Music for dancing forms a significant part of the collection. There are huge quantities of quadrilles, waltzes, polkas and the like; these appear in both the printed and the handwritten music. The works of Philippe Musard and Charles D'Albert are conspicuous. Their quadrilles and other items were bought in arrangements for various instruments, and some of them were copied out by hand. Musical members of the family may have played for dancing on informal occasions, but for their formal balls musicians were imported. On Monday 5 October 1840 a grand ball was held at Burton Constable, with a quadrille band directed by 'Mr. Weippert'. This seems to have been held as a preliminary to the Hull Musical Festival of 6–9 October 1840, of which Sir Clifford was a patron and to which he no doubt took some of his distinguished guests. The Hull-born musician and impresario Enderby Jackson (writing in 1896 about events in 1845) describes himself as having been the flute player of a 'select Burton Constable quadrille band' under 'Mr. George Leng, bandmaster to the barony'.[11] A dance programme for a formal ball of 1861 mentions 'Mr Acey's Quadrille Band'.[12] John Bernard (or Burnham) Acey appears in local trade directories in which he is variously described as a music teacher and a dealer in music. The embossed stamp J. B. Acey, Music Seller, Savile Street, Hull, is found on some items of sheet music in the Burton Constable collection, and in *A Musical Pilgrimage in Yorkshire*, J. Sutcliffe Smith reports that one John

---

[11] Jackson, E., 'The Origins and Promotion of Brass Band Contests', *Musical Opinion*, November (1896), 101–3. Jackson describes having played to accompany 'a series of showy pageants and pictures by the house guests in costumes illustrating historical events' in 1845; this supports the suggestion that the musicians of such local quadrille bands were imported for theatrical performances.

[12] EYCAS, DDCC17/16.

B. Acey was a violinist and leader of the orchestra of the Hull Subscription Music Society in 1855.[13]

The musical connections between the inhabitants of Burton Constable and the city of Hull were not all one-way. Members and guests of the Burton Constable gave a concert in Hull in 1858 in the Music Hall, part of what was then known as the Public Rooms, recently built by public subscription, which subsequently became the New Theatre (still the city's theatre). The list of performers in this concert includes names already mentioned: Sir Clifford Constable, his wife Lady Clifford Constable, and his sister-in-law Miss Chichester. Lady Wolseley and Major and Mrs Gage were relatives of the family. The names Wolseley and Goldsmid appear also in the surviving playbills, as do those of Talbot and Charles Searle. The last named of these made pastel sketches of several members of the house parties who performed plays and music. This concert was something of a novelty, and featured prominently in the 'Local Gossip' column of the *Hull Advertiser* for 20 and 27 March. The first of these articles informed readers that it was not to be a 'professional like concert' but was to see 'a transference of the drawing-room of Burton Constable to the Hull Music-hall'. This was to be achieved both through the informality of the performers, who were to avoid 'all appearance of singing or playing to an audience', and through fitting up the stage with 'the richest furniture and the choicest articles of *vertu*'. The column in the following week commented on the pedigree of the performers and the 'class of music selected', which was to be 'of the highest order and such as is only attempted by first-class musicians' (Plate 11.4).

The programme is a typical mixed bag. The first and last items were presumably played in the reduced scoring easily available. The overture to *Figaro* is in the music collection in an arrangement by Masi in the series 'Mozart's Grand Overtures' for two violins, flute, two tenors, cello and double bass (or two cellos) published by Cocks and Co. On the first violin part is written the name 'Colonel Stephen'. There is any amount of material on the lines of the Duett 'Don Juan' and the pianoforte solo in the collection. The concertina music in the collection is signed by Marianne's brother Charles, who served abroad in the army and as acting governor of Trinidad, then in Canada. He married his first cousin, Mary Barbara, sister of Sir Clifford Constable, and one assumes they visited Burton Constable when back in this country. He is presumably the Captain Chichester, later Major Chichester, who features in the

[13] Smith, J. S. S., *A Musical Pilgrimage in Yorkshire*, Leeds, *c.* 1928, p. 286. I am grateful to Norman Staveley for sharing the fruits of his researches on the history of the music and musicians of Hull.

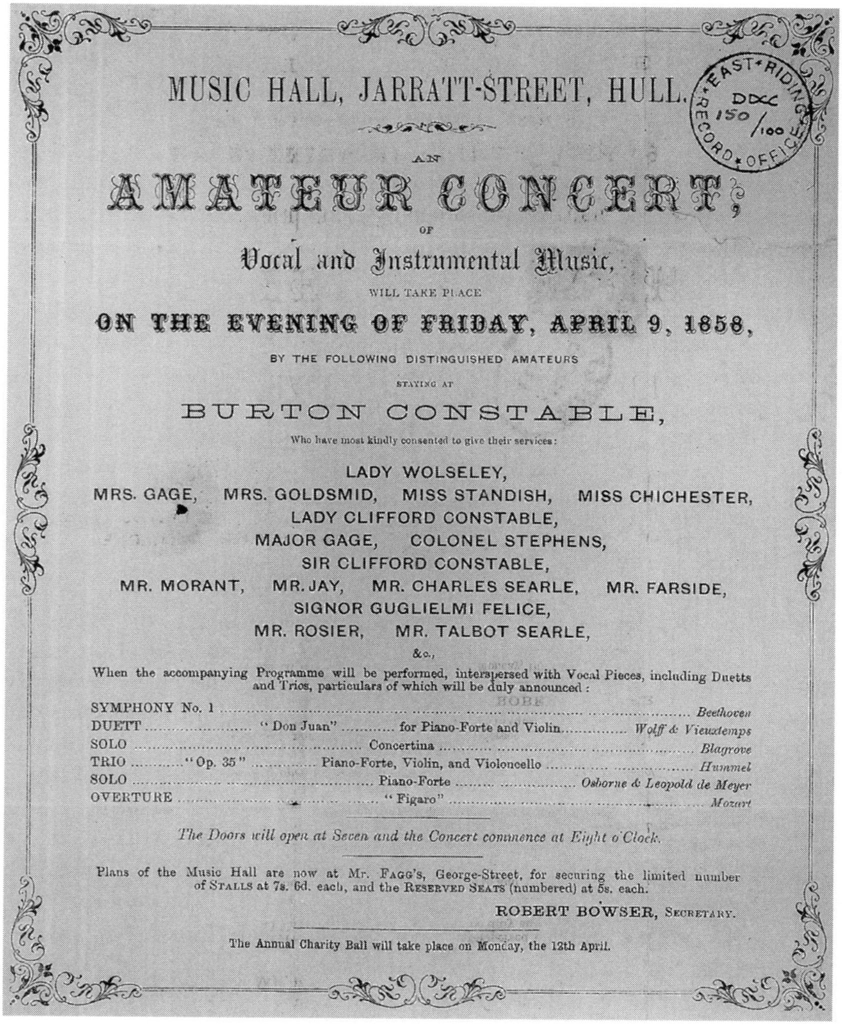

MUSIC HALL, JARRATT-STREET, HULL.

AN

AMATEUR CONCERT,

OF

Vocal and Instrumental Music,

WILL TAKE PLACE

ON THE EVENING OF FRIDAY, APRIL 9, 1858,

BY THE FOLLOWING DISTINGUISHED AMATEURS

STAYING AT

BURTON CONSTABLE,

Who have most kindly consented to give their services:

LADY WOLSELEY,
MRS. GAGE, MRS. GOLDSMID, MISS STANDISH, MISS CHICHESTER,
LADY CLIFFORD CONSTABLE,
MAJOR GAGE, COLONEL STEPHENS,
SIR CLIFFORD CONSTABLE,
MR. MORANT, MR. JAY, MR. CHARLES SEARLE, MR. FARSIDE,
SIGNOR GUGLIELMI FELICE,
MR. ROSIER, MR. TALBOT SEARLE,
&c.,

When the accompanying Programme will be performed, interspersed with Vocal Pieces, including Duetts and Trios, particulars of which will be duly announced:

SYMPHONY No. 1			*Beethoven*
DUETT	"Don Juan"	for Piano-Forte and Violin	*Wolff & Vieuxtemps*
SOLO		Concertina	*Blagrove*
TRIO	"Op. 35"	Piano-Forte, Violin, and Violoncello	*Hummel*
SOLO		Piano-Forte	*Osborne & Leopold de Meyer*
OVERTURE		"Figaro"	*Mozart*

The Doors will open at Seven and the Concert commence at Eight o'Clock.

Plans of the Music Hall are now at Mr. Fagg's, George-Street, for securing the limited number of Stalls at 7s. 6d. each, and the Reserved Seats (numbered) at 5s. each.

ROBERT BOWSER, Secretary.

The Annual Charity Ball will take place on Monday, the 12th April.

Plate 11.4 Handbill advertising the concert by the Distinguished Amateurs of Burton Constable at the Music Hall, Hull, 1858

amateur theatricals. However, according to the newspaper account, the concertina solo in the concert, based on airs from *Il Trovatore*, was performed by 'Mr. Morant'. Parts for several chamber compositions of Hummel are scattered about in various bound volumes. The review in the *Hull Advertiser* of 10 April is fulsome in its praise of the performances, expressing the hope that the event would be repeated, but this does not seem to have happened.

The Clifford Constables were, as befitted their social position, looked to as patrons of many local charitable societies and cultural events. In his book *A History of Hull Organs and Organists*, published around 1910, Dr G. H. Smith describes the formation of the Hull Choral Society in 1823, in succession to other earlier societies. The words 'Patron: Sir Clifford Constable, Bart.' appear in an advertisement for a Hull Choral Society concert in the *Hull Advertiser* of 5 January 1833 and first appeared on the society's programmes on 21 January 1835.[14] In Smith's words:

> Sir Clifford Constable, the munificent patron of the society, became also the cause of its undoing. At the beginning choral music was kept well to the fore, the rehearsals were well attended, and the society prospered. Later, a miscellaneous element was introduced and, principally at the instigation of Sir Clifford, star vocalists and other artists were engaged for the concerts.
>
> He was never more happy than when dispensing the almost regal hospitality of Burton Constable to musicians, some of European fame; and Mario, Lablache, Grisi, Thalberg and many other celebrities thus appeared at the concerts of the Society. But the interest became focused upon them, with the inevitable consequence that chorus singing came to take a subordinate place in its work; so much so, indeed, that its name, the Hull Choral Society, became a misnomer.[15]

It may not be fair to lay all the blame for what Smith describes as the Choral Society's 'process of painless extinction' at the door of its patron, but concerts involving celebrity soloists began around the time at which his patronage was acknowledged, and he may well have had a hand in securing their services. A concert billed as a 'Grand Selection of vocal and instrumental music' took place in October 1833, and each Choral Society concert after that had guest soloists. At the concert held on 10 December 1834, the principal performers were the German harpist and composer Franz Stockhausen and his wife Margarethe, a singer. The programmes of the Choral Society bear out the appearance of the famous names Smith mentions, and others: Mr (later Sir) Henry Bishop and his wife, the singer Anna Riviere, Clara Novello, Charlotte Sainton-Dolby, Michael Balfe, and another distinguished harp virtuoso and composer, Nicolas Bochsa.

Whether through extending their 'regal hospitality' or through their travels abroad, the Clifford Constables met several composers. One name crops up several times in the music collection, that of Mme Oury, née Anna de Belleville, daughter of a French nobleman. Among her

---

[14] Hull Central Library, L784.

[15] Smith, G. H., *A History of Hull Organs and Organists*, London, *c.* 1810, pp. 56–7.

published compositions are a 'Grande Fantaisie Brillante sur l'opéra de *Martha*', for piano, Op. 46, which bears a printed dedication to Lady Clifford Constable, and on the copy of her Andante Capriccioso in the collection, she has written 'Lady Clifford Constable, with Madame Oury's compliments', dating the inscription 29 June 1853. The 'Grand Duo for piano and violin on motifs from *The Barber of Seville*' by G. A. Osborne (1806–93) and Charles de Beriot (1802–70) is dedicated 'À Sir Clifford et Lady Constable'. Several items by the Polish composer and arranger Edouard Wolff (1816–80) are to be found in the collection, among them a 'Duo brillant sur des motifs de l'opera *Il Trovatore*' Op. 198, for piano duet, dedicated to two of his pupils, nieces of Marianne and, in manuscript, a piece for harp, 'Souvenir de Paris; grand valse brillant, Op.173', described as having been 'composed expressly for Lady Clifford Constable by her devoted professeur Edouard Wolff'. There are similar items by local composers. Among the presentation copies in the collection is a volume of scores of nine string quartets by John Lodge Ellerton, inscribed 'Lady Clifford Constable, presented by the Author, Burton Constable, December 20th 1856'.

One of the artists in the Burton Constable 'Distinguished Amateurs' concerts is of particular interest. 'Mr. Jay' was Stephen Octavius Jay, the steward at the Hall; in other words, the most senior male employee (the title 'land agent' was used to denote this position on some other estates). Stephen Jay took an active part in the theatricals. His name is signed on several items in the music collection, principally violin music and guitar music. On the Burton Constable census return for 1851, he is listed as a 'visiter' and given the status 'gent'. On some pieces of music he appended 'R.A.M.' to his name, and he had indeed been a student at the Royal Academy of Music, studying the violin there between May 1840 and October 1843, and leaving when he would have been 20 years old. His musical skills may well have been a factor in his obtaining the position with the Constable family. He even published a composition for piano, *The Marian Polka*, dedicating it to Lady Clifford Constable.[16] Some of the music he owned found its way into the compilation volumes described above. For example, the first item in a volume marked on the spine 'Piano Forte, 1846' and on the front 'Lady Clifford Constable' is Charles d'Albert's *The Bridal Polka*, inscribed 'To Stephen Jay Esq with M. d'Albert's [?compliments]'; there are other such items in the same volume. (The ending of the last word has been cut off in the binding process.)

Stephen Jay must have been highly regarded; his picture was one of those drawn by Searle of the members of the theatrical and musical

---

[16] Stephen Jay, *The Marian Polka*, London, *c.* 1850.

house party set. In his will, Sir Thomas Aston Clifford Constable made provision for 'my friend and secretary Stephen Octavius Jay' ahead of any member of the family save his widow and his son. In a second codicil to the will, dated November 1870, Constable made an additional bequest to his wife of 'my two violins, my best piano, the harp, the tenor, and any music she may select'. He made a further bequest to Jay: an additional one year's salary and 'also my violin that is marked with the name of Sir Charles Wolseley'.

The Constable family was Roman Catholic and remained loyal to the faith. The name 'Clifford' is that of one of the most important Roman Catholic families in the country. The family network included Catholic households, widened through extensive travel on the Continent. A collection of visiting cards received during a trip to Rome and faithfully preserved in an album turned out on closer inspection to pertain to another member of the family, George Clifford, who travelled to Italy with his wife and daughter in November–December 1836 and March 1837.[17] As well as attending receptions, they visited St Peter's and the Vatican, and attended a concert consisting largely of excerpts from operas by Rossini, Bellini, Pacini and Donizetti. This is very much the sort of trip that the Clifford Constables made. So significant a part of their life was spent in continental travel that a separate set of account books was kept for this activity The imprints of the music sellers on the copies shows that music was purchased from abroad as well as from local music sellers and from London.

Following the Act of Parliament of 1789 which lifted some of the restrictions on Catholic places of worship, the family rebuilt and extended a chapel in the village of Marton within the estate grounds (there is known to have been a priest at Marton from 1700). There had always been a chapel within the main house; in 1840 the billiard room was converted into the private chapel that remains to this day. There is, however, very little sacred music within the collection. Into the bound manuscript books have been copied a few settings of texts such as 'Ave regina coelorum', some of them anonymous, others by Samuel Webbe. There is some Pergolesi, and a Benedictus and Agnus Dei labelled 'from a Mass by Mozart. Selected from the works of Latrobe'. There are excerpts from Graun's 'Passion', and favourite choruses from Handel oratorios. Somebody has arranged these for three voices, presumably to suit the available resources. Two items may reflect travel experiences: a 'Chant. Played at St. Peter's Rome' and the 'Litany of the virgin, sung by the Friars of St Salvador at Jerusalem'. There is a violin part for an as yet unidentified mass, and a group of chord sequences labelled 'Dixit

---

[17] EYCAS, DDCC 150/82.

Dominus. Seventh tone' and so on. (The haphazard nature of the hand-written music is well illustrated by the fact that these last two items are in the same volume as a Spanish 'Cancion Patriotica', 'Fra poco a me', from Donizetti's *Lucia di Lammermoor*, and a comic song 'The Dog's Meat Man' set to the tune 'The White Cockade', together with another 15 assorted items.) In the printed music there is *The Catholic Music-Book*,[18] three Latin motets by John Lodge Ellerton, and one or two instrumental items such as 'Six Sacred Airs' arranged for harp by Bochsa. On the strength of the music collection, it is difficult to know what part music played in family devotions.

The picture which emerges from a study of this collection of music and a few family and local archive sources shows in many ways a survival from what we think of as the typical picture of the nobility and gentry of the previous century, with much time being given to such indoor pursuits as music and amateur theatricals. In these respects, the Clifford Constables were living in what we might term the Jane Austen mode, with music after dinner and for dancing, as in *Pride and Prejudice*, and house-party amateur theatricals, as in *Mansfield Park*. Much attention has quite rightly been paid to the ways in which music in England in the nineteenth century opened up to a wider social sphere; hence studies of brass bands, choral societies, sol-fa and music education, and the music of the front parlour. Yet for all that some aspects of life at Burton Constable may seem a relic of a previous age, the family were not oblivious of the new order. The chief claim to musical fame of this rather out-of-the-way country house is as the location, according to Enderby Jackson, of the first formal brass band contest to be held in this country, in 1845, instigated on the model of similar competitions which the Chichester sisters had encountered abroad.[19] Though in the absence of such documents as minute books we do not know the full story of Sir Clifford's patronage of the local choral society, we may feel entitled to surmise from his active musical interests that he was more than a figurehead. The music collection at Burton Constable shows a family still pursuing the fashionable accomplishments of music with relish, while developing a relationship with musical worlds outside.

---

[18] This is lacking its title-page, but is presumably *The Catholic Music-Book: containing appropriate and easy Pieces for most of the services of the Church*, London, [1851].

[19] Jackson, E., 'The Origins and Promotion of Brass Band Contests', p. 101.

PART SIX

Repertoire, Genre and Concert Life

'Personifying the Saviour?': English Oratorio and the Representation of the Words of Christ

Barbara Mohn

In 1732 the creator of English oratorio, George Frederic Handel, launched the genre with success on the stage of the King's Theatre in London. He had planned to perform his sacred drama *Esther* with scenery and action but due to the intervention of Edmund Gibson, the Bishop of London, this did not occur during the 2 May performance of the work. Undoubtedly, the Bishop's reaction against the theatrical representation of biblical figures came as no surprise. Since Elizabethan times plays based on the Holy Scriptures had been banned from stage performances, and the official censor of English drama, the Lord Chamberlain's Office, ensured that the practice was strictly observed.[1]

Handelian oratorio itself was actually a compromise – and a successful compromise at that. It was largely dramatic in structure and, musically, it was closely related to opera and was performed in an opera-house. However, since it was played without stage action, the representation of its biblical figures was to some extent left to the imagination of the audience and thus there was little danger that such representations would descend to the ridiculous.

Until well into the nineteenth century English oratorio was largely conceived in Handelian terms as regards genre definition. Texts were constructed either in epic or dramatic form and the words were either paraphrased from the Bible, or taken directly from the Bible itself.[2] The two favourite oratorios of nineteenth-century English choral societies, Handel's *Messiah* and Mendelssohn's *Elijah* (1846), were like two pil-

---

[1] See Murray Roston, *Biblical Drama in England from the Middle Ages to the Present Day*, London, 1968. The ban was still in force in the nineteenth century. See e.g. John Russell Stephens, *The Censorship of English Drama 1824–1901*, Cambridge, 1980.

[2] In his dramatic oratorios Handel refrained from setting to music words taken *directly* from the Holy Scriptures. His two well-known epic oratorios, *Messiah* and *Israel in Egypt*, whose libretti are based entirely on texts from the Scriptures, were criticized for that reason and offended parts of the audience when played in the theatre. See e.g. Richard Luckett, *Handel's Messiah: A Celebration*, London, 1992, pp. 140–43.

lars which represented the two ideals and styles of oratorio: the one epic and contemplative, and the other primarily dramatic, in which an Old Testament figure was its protagonist. These two archetypes were based entirely on literal quotations from the Bible, which indeed was the basis for most libretti which were composed during the nineteenth century at a time when the performance of oratorios had moved from the sphere of the theatre into the domain of choral societies. The dramatic oratorios in the nineteenth century featured a wide range of biblical figures who were portrayed, including Adam and Eve, angels and Satan, kings and queens, judges and prophets, St Paul, St Peter and St John the Baptist. None the less, one character is missing from the lists of the dramatis personae, and this is Christ himself.

On 25 February 1814 George Smart gave the first English performance of Ludwig van Beethoven's oratorio *Christus am Oelberge* (*The Mount of Olives*) at the Lenten oratorios at Drury Lane Theatre. According to the theatre bill announcing its fourth performance within only a fortnight, it 'met with the most rapturous applause'.[3] *The Mount of Olives* was played ten times during Lent and it was repeated during the following concert seasons. It was also introduced at some of the provincial festivals (including festivals at Liverpool 1823, Edinburgh 1825, Birmingham 1840) and at the Handel Commemorations at Westminster Abbey in 1834. But its success story is also a tale of religious scruples and opposition.

From the outset *The Mount of Olives* met with disapproval and suffered cuts and adaptations due to the 'objectionable nature of the German libretto'.[4] Indeed, the cathedral authorities of the Three Choirs Festival and the burgeoning choral societies throughout England, such as the Sacred Harmonic Society of London with its strong Nonconformist leanings, were reluctant to include the oratorio within their repertoires. The *Worcester Journal* of 8 September 1842 considered *The Mount of Olives* as 'unthinkable except to an audience of sceptics and freethinkers'.[5]

The primary objection was that in *The Mount of Olives* Christ is introduced as a person with a singing role, as a character of the drama. The English public considered it an unpardonable impropriety that not

---

[3] Oratorio Bill, Drury Lane Theatre, of Wednesday, 9 March 1814.

[4] Henry Hudson, Preface to his edition of *Engedi or David in the Wilderness, ... composed by L. van Beethoven*, Novello [1842].

[5] Harold Watkins Shaw, *The Three Choirs Festival*, Worcester and London, 1954, p. 35.

only was the Saviour included among the dramatis personae but that Christ also expressed the agony of his death in extended monologues and that he even engaged in a duet with an angel.

In 1855 George Alexander Macfarren remarked in a programme for the Birmingham Musical Festival: 'The English idea of the sanctity of the scriptural characters is different from that of every continental nation, and the representation of the personality of the Saviour, which abroad is regarded with solemn reverence, would here be revolting to religious minds.'[6]

As a consequence of this attitude, *The Mount of Olives* underwent numerous adaptations to suit the prevailing notion of propriety. Beginning with Smart's performance in 1814, Christ was eliminated from the score and the words originally attributed to him were changed into indirect narrative. According to the preface of Smart's edition 'the author [of the words] has thought it proper to alter the Persons, in conformity to the national feelings of religious propriety, which would be justly outraged by introducing the Saviour of the World as a character of the Drama'.[7] For example, the opening scene is not a direct narrative in which Christ cries out to God in the agony of his pain, but rather a report sung by the tenor voice, in which the direct speech of Christ is turned into indirect speech. The part, which is originally denoted in the score as 'Jesus' is simply marked 'tenor voice'. Compare the original text of the German libretto and the literal translation made by J. Troutbeck in 1877 with the adaptation by Arnold in the Appendix. The aversion to having Christ portrayed in dramatic dimensions is clearly demonstrated in the printed versions of this first recitative (No. 2).

In later adaptations a disciple, usually John, was substituted for the role of Christ. In the translation by Thomas Oliphant prepared for Moscheles' edition for Cramer, Addison and Beale in 1840 John delivers the prayer to God, which was originally allotted to Jesus in the original libretto (see Appendix).

---

[6] *Birmingham Triennial Festival, Programmes and books of the words 1855*, Birmingham, 1855, The Mount of Olives, p. IV.

[7] The author of the text is almost certainly S. J. Arnold. However, he is neither mentioned in the score (Chapell and Co. [1815]) nor on the oratorio bills of the first performances nor in the printed textbooks supplied for those performances. The name of the author is first mentioned on the theatre bill of 1 March 1820 (Drury Lane) in the following manner: ' ... The Words in Part, translated and adapted from the German by S. J. Arnold, Esq. As performed for the First Time in this Country at this Theatre.' Arnold is also named as the author of the text in George Grove (ed.), *The Dictionary of Music and Musicians*, 1st edn, 1880, by Pamela J. Willetts in *Beethoven and England. An Account of sources in the British Museum*, London 1970, and by G. A. Macfarren in his paper mentioned in footnote 6.

Fifteen years later a new adaptation was made for the Birmingham
Musical Festival by William Bartholomew, who had demonstrated the
mastery of his craft by translating Mendelssohn's *Elijah* for its English
première in 1846 and by writing the librettos for Costa's *Eli* (1855),
Naaman (1865) and his wife's *The Nativity* (1855). In Bartholomew's
version the role of Jesus is again assumed by a disciple (John), but the
words of Jesus are no longer simply turned into indirect speech, but
rather the entire passage is transformed into a descriptive and reflective
commentary on Jesus in the agony of his grief (see Appendix).

In 1858, published by R. Cocks and Co., yet another version appeared which was written by Joseph Warren, who was the organist at St
Mary's Roman Catholic Chapel, Chelsea. In this version the words of
Christ are treated in a narrative context but in addition, Warren also
frequently makes liberal changes to the original libretto, for example, at
the conclusion of the oratorio he included Peter's denial of the Lord.
His ideas clearly are to avoid those passages in which Christ indulges
heavily in his pain, and to follow the account according to the Bible
with words taken directly from the Scriptures rather than follow the
original libretto.

In spite of such attempts to alter the libretto, the adaptations by
Arnold, Oliphant, Bartholomew and Warren did not go far enough to
suit all. In 1842 Henry Hudson of Dublin furnished Beethoven's music
with a completely new libretto, entitled *Engedi*. The story is no longer
about Christ in the agony of death and the arrival of the Roman
soldiers to take him captive, but rather its theme and protagonist was
now David, who according to 1 Samuel 13 hid from King Saul who had
set out to kill him in the wilderness at Engedi. Hudson – as he emphasized in his preface to *Engedi*[8] – had been induced to adapting the new
story for *The Mount of Olives* by the 'analogies of the sacred history'.
Indeed the events in these two stories are similar: In *Engedi* David cries
out to God in the agony of death (as does Jesus in *The Mount of
Olives*), a Prophetess comforts David (just as the Angel comforts Jesus),
Saul's soldiers approach David at Engedi (similar to the Romans approaching Jesus at the mount), Abishai tries to avenge David with his
sword (just as Peter draws his sword for Jesus), and like Jesus in *The
Mount of Olives*, David stops him from carrying out this act. In *Engedi*
David is saved from death, whereas Jesus is not. None the less, both
versions end triumphantly in praise of God.

Engedi proved astonishingly successful; after its first performance in
1842 the *Morning Herald* even welcomed the new story as more appropriate for the music, which was often regarded as too light and operatic

---

[8] Hudson, Preface to his edition of *Engedi*.

to be truly 'sublime': 'The change has been made judiciously, and rather with an advantage to the music, for it cannot be said to be accordant in expression with the awful subject of the Redeemer's passion.'[9]

Another oratorio on this 'awful subject', Louis Spohr's *Des Heilands letzte Stunden,* met with the similar fate of opposition and adaptation. When Edward Taylor translated the oratorio for its first English performance in 1837 (first under the title of *The Crucifixion,* then as *Calvary*), he also made changes to the libretto, in deference to an English public which considered the introduction of the Saviour among the personages as a violation of propriety. He therefore allotted Christ's words to the apostle John. The slight musical changes which became necessary were in fact made by Spohr himself, to whom Taylor had explained his difficulties with regard to the text.[10] However, despite Taylor's precautions, the subject of the oratorio was still considered by some as an 'improper exercise for the musician's art', to quote Taylor. For example, Vicar Storr of Otley in Suffolk, who preached the opening sermon at the Norwich Musical Festival in 1839, where *Calvary* was performed, announced that 'all people who should go on Thursday, the day of its performance in St Andrew's Hall, would be eternally damned'.[11]

English oratorio was to a large extent – and particularly after the great success of Mendelssohn's *Elijah* in 1846 – dramatic, and included a list of characters and a story which unfolded through dialogue. But the dramatic nature of English oratorio brought with it the risk that such works could easily fall victim to the verdict of being too operatic or irreverent. A small but active contingent of the public objected to oratorios in general. They were mainly of the evangelical belief, of that type of evangelicalism which flourished within the Anglican Church in the first half of the nineteenth century and is associated with such figures as the seventh Earl of Shaftesbury, Edward Irving, John Newton, James Stephen, William Wilberforce, Henry Thornton and other members of the 'Clapham Sect'. Evangelicals branded oratorios as 'cathedral operas' or pronounced an oratorio performance in church to be – I quote the evangelical pastor Legh Richmond (1772–1827):

> a solemn mockery of God and forbidden by the clear principles of
> the Gospel. The making of the most solemn subjects which heaven

---

[9] Quoted in the *Reports of the Sacred Harmonic Society,* London, 1843, p. 42, following a performance of *Engedi* on 25 January 1842.

[10] Preface dated 1 December 1836 in Louis Spohr's *The Crucifixion,* London, 1836.

[11] Robin H. Legge and W. E. Hansel, *Annals of the Norfolk and Norwich Triennial Musical Festivals,* London, 1896, p. 79.

ever revealed to man, even to the Passion of Christ himself on the cross, a matter for the gay, critical, undevout recreation of individuals, ... I do from my heart believe to be highly offensive to God. [...] Vice rides triumphantly in such proceedings. The spirit of the world, the pride of life, the lust of the eye, all enter into these public gaities; and their false pretensions to partial sacredness, only render them more objectionable.[12]

Evangelicals generally shied away from using the word of God irreverently. Before an oratorio performance it was often lamented in the ultra-evangelical magazine *The Record* that 'the sublime language of scripture is desecrated to purposes of pleasure'.[13] That opera singers, a class of reputedly immoral individuals, should sing biblical words in which they obviously did not believe, was tantamount to 'crucifying the Son of God afresh'.[14] Naturally, the dramatic representation of the Saviour as a person was considered blasphemy.

The reluctance to personify Christ and the resultant special treatment which his words called for left its mark on the English oratorio of the nineteenth century. For instance, before 1870 there was a marked preference for librettos based on Old Testament themes or on a reflective theme (such as Omnipotence, Thanksgiving), which does not require the figure of Jesus at all. Between 1830 and 1870, a period when religious opinions played a significant role in the history of the oratorio, there is not a single English oratorio on the Passion or on the life of Christ apart from John Rippon's *The Crucifixion*, which was published in 1837, but of which no performance is known and which is basically a series of short reflections on Christ's entry into Jerusalem and the crucifixion, in which Jesus as a personage plays no part. Setting the seven words of Christ at the cross to music – a strong tradition in France – would have been unthinkable in England. New Testament subjects played virtually no role in that period, while some Old Testament themes were repeatedly set to music. For example, during this period

---

[12] T. S. Grimshawe, *A Memoir of the Rev. Legh Richmond*, London, 1828, pp. 385–6. Also quoted in [Isaac Robson], *Music and its Influence or an Enquiry into the Practice of Music, in reference to its effects on the Moral and Religious Condition of Mankind*, London and Huddersfield, 1846. p. 13.

[13] Edward Hodges, *An Apology for Church Music and Musical Festivals, in answer to the animadversions of the Standard and the Record*, London, 1834, p. 11.

[14] John Newton, *Messiah. 50 Expository Discourses, on the Series of Scriptural Passages, which form the Subjects of the celebrated Oratorio of Handel, preached in the years 1784, 1785, in the Parish Church of St. Mary Woolnoth, Lombard Street*, London, 1786, vol. 2, p. 459.

there are at least eight oratorios on Daniel,[15] four on the Deluge,[16] and several on David, the patriarchs and the prophets. Throughout the nineteenth century composers and librettists scoured the Old Testament for suitable subjects: for prophets, kings and judges. There were eight oratorios on Hezekiah[17] and there are even such protagonists as Micajah, Azariah or Jehoshaphat,[18] who may well be known to diligent Bible students, but to no one else.

The very few oratorios before 1870, which in fact require the figure of Christ, demonstrably try to avoid dramatizing the words of the Lord. A good example is William Sterndale Bennett's *The Woman of Samaria* (1867), a story taken from St John 5, which is about how Jesus revealed himself as the Messiah to a Samarian woman drawing water from a well. The work requires three soloists: an alto as a narrator, a soprano as the woman of Samaria and the bass as Christ. To avoid any personi-fication of Christ, Bennett assigns the bass to sing not only the words of Jesus but also the narrative texts, which accompany his entrances, despite the fact that narrative passages in all other cases are given to the alto, who is the actual narrator. This leads to some peculiar inconsisten-cies in the libretto, as in the following excerpt, which is recitative no. 4:

> Contralto (narrator): 'There cometh a woman of Samaria to draw water.'
> Bass (Jesus): 'Jesus saith unto her, Give me to drink.'
> Alto (narrator): 'Then saith the woman of Samaria unto him.'
> Soprano (The woman of Samaria): 'How is it that thou, being a Jew, asketh drink of me which I am a woman of Samaria?'
> Bass (Jesus): 'Jesus answered and said unto her, "If thou knowest the gift of God ... "'

Out of respect to the public, when Novello issued a reprint of the first edition under their label in 1873, it included the following remark in the preface: 'The words attributed to Our Saviour are, with one exception,

---

[15] John Barnett, *Daniel in the Den of Lions* (1841); John Henry Griesbach, *Daniel* (1854); Charles Edward Horn, *Daniel's Prediction or The Vision of Belshazzar* (1845); Francis Howell, *The Captivity* (1852); William Jackson, *The Deliverance of Israel from Babylon* (1847); George Lake, *Daniel* (1852); Marmaduke Miller, *Israel in Babylon* (1839); George Perry, *Belshazzar's Feast* (1836).

[16] Robert Nicholas Charles Bochsa, *Déluge Universel/The Deluge* (1822); William Lisle Bowles, *The Ark* (one song edn. 1822); Ernest Harcourt, *The Deluge* (date un-known); Charles Donald Maclean, *Noah* (1865).

[17] Philip Armes, *Hezekiah* (1878); Tom William Dodds, *Hezekiah* (1887); Alfred Robert Gaul, *Hezekiah* (1861); John Liptrot Hatton, *Hezekiah* (1878); George Frederick Perry, *Hezekiah* (1847); Hans Hugh Pierson, *Hezekiah* (1869); Edward Synge, *Hezekiah* (1865); Edmund Hart Turpin, *Hezekiah* (date unknown).

[18] William Creser, *Micajah* (1880); Marcus Hast, *Azariah* (1884); Charles Edward Allum, *Jehosaphat* (date unknown).

assigned to the Bass voice, the greatest care being taken that the singer who recites this portion of the text shall appear only as a narrator, and in no degree attempt to personate a character.'[19]

Another oratorio in which the presence of Jesus is demanded by the story is Edward Stephen's *The Storm of Tiberias,* the first Welsh oratorio, edited in 1847 by S. S. Wesley. Christ is asleep on a boat on Lake Genezareth with his disciples, when a storm breaks out, which is calmed by Jesus. The libretto musters a whole set of characters, not mentioned expressly in the biblical story, including Matthew, John, Mary, Martha, the Captain of the boat and Sailors, but the main character – Jesus – is conspicuously absent. The story leads up to the climax, at which point Jesus himself should appear to quell the storm. The climax is prepared in a lively and dramatic fashion solely through the use of dialogue. Mary is aware of the upcoming storm and sings in a duet with Martha 'Sister this calm too sweet, fills me with strange alarm', the captain shouts 'Sailors, to the topmast quick ascending, Haul your sails in ... ' (Air), a double chorus describes the wrestling wind, both the sailors and disciples pray to God singing a chorale, but then, when the climax should occur, all dramatic tension is thwarted when Matthew simply reports the dramatic events in an air:

> 'Then like a mighty King He rose
> With gravest looks, yet loving,
> And gentle even in rebuke,
> Our want of faith reproving.'

John continues, also in an aria:
> '"O ye!" He said, "of little faith!"
> Why, why are ye not braver?
> When will ye put your trust in God,
> The Lord, when cease to waver?'

Mary, Martha, John then join in a trio:
> 'Lo! the roaring sea is hushed, at his saying,
> Lo! The winds have homewards rushed, him obeying! ... '

The portrayal of Christ as a person is also avoided in the few other English oratorios on New Testament themes. Jules Benedict's *St. Peter* (1870), which is about Peter's trials and tribulations as a disciple of the Lord, could hardly have been written without the personage of Jesus. None the less, the words of Christ are always assigned to the narrator

---

[19] William Sterndale Bennett, *The Woman of Samaria,* London (Novello), 1873. The first edition of 1868 (Lamborn Cock, Addison and Co.) contained no preface, and the preface in the reprint of this edition by Novello in 1873 was clearly written by someone other than the composer himself.

(contralto), whereas the part of Peter is personified by the baritone soloist, as in recitative no. 17, which illustrates the scene at Lake Gennesaret, when Jesus walks on the sea (Matthew 14:25–31):

> Contralto: 'And Peter said,'
> Baritone: 'Lord, if it be Thou, bid me come unto Thee on the water.'
> Contralto: 'And He said, come! And when Peter saw the wind boisterous, he was afraid; and beginning to sink, cried,'
> Baritone: 'Lord, save me!'
> Contralto: 'And Jesus stretched forth His hand and caught him, and said, "O thou of little faith, Wherefore didst thou doubt?"'

However, occasionally after 1870 and increasingly in the 1880 oratorios and sacred cantatas with Jesus included among the dramatis personae appear.[20] The first composer to break with the prevailing prejudice against portraying Jesus as a dramatic, human figure seems to have been Arthur Sullivan in *The Light of the World* (1873). Christ's part is assigned throughout to the baritone soloist and it is treated like all the other characters. The only exception to this treatment is perhaps a cosmetic concession to the prevailing attitudes of the time: in the vocal score the designation of the character 'Jesus' is indicated above the baritone part simply as 'solo' whereas all the other soloists are designated in the score by their correct character names, for example Mary, a

---

[20] E.g. Arthur Edwin Dyer, *Salvator Mundi* (1880), Henry John Edwards, *The Risen Lord* (1906), Edward Elgar's *The Light of Life* (1896), *The Apostles* (1903) and *The Kingdom* (1906). In John Abram's *The Widow of Nain* (1874) the part of Jesus is sung by the tenor and treated like all the other persons portrayed in the oratorio. In *The Raising of Lazarus* (1873) John Francis Barnett casts the four soloists as follows: Soprano=Martha, Alto=Mary, Tenor=Narrator, Jesus, Messenger, Bass=Lazarus. However, the oratorio is not strictly dramatic in character and the soloists normally sing not only their dialogue but also the narrative passages that introduce their texts, e.g. in no. 17 the tenor sings 'Jesus saith unto her, Thy brother shall rise again', and the soprano answers 'Martha saith unto Him, I know that he shall rise again in the resurrection at the last day'. Joseph Parry's *Emmanuel* (1880) makes little use of words of Christ, and when they are called for they are always assigned to the bass, although the part is never denoted as 'Jesus' in the score, whereas all the other characters are mentioned. However, even in the last decades of the century many composers still avoided the dramatization of Christ: for example, George A. Macfarren's *The Resurrection* (1876) differs from his famous first oratorio *St. John the Baptist* (1873) and also the later ones in being not dramatic in structure, but in being a didactic oratorio without dramatis personae, in which the story is told by the baritone in the form of a 'recitation'. In Frank Nicholson Abernethy's biblical scene *The Lake of Gennesaret* (1895) characters such as Simon Peter are allotted sung texts, but as in many other English oratorios, Jesus's words are only part of the narration, which is sung by the soprano. In Henry John Edwards's *The Ascension* (1885) Jesus's words are woven into the narrative, which is divided between the three soloists. In Alfred J. Caldicott's *The Widow of Nain* (1878) and William Spark's *Immanuel* (1887) Christ's words are also part of the narrative.

Pharisee, the disciples. However, any personification of Christ is avoided in the crucifixion and resurrection scenes in the latter part of the oratorio, i.e., in those scenes which would normally have been regarded as the most sacred scenes.

After 1880 there were also an increasing number of renderings of the Passion story, in some of which Christ was personified. The most well-known work, even today, is John Stainer's *The Crucifixion* (1888) – although it is not a full-fledged oratorio, but a typical example of a Victorian sacred cantata, a genre for which similar religious dramatic restrictions existed. In this work the part of Jesus is rendered by the bass soloist up to no. 11, where the seven last words of Christ at the cross begin. Here and in the following six words of Christ, the text is sung by the men of the chorus in three or four parts. Thus, although Christ is partly personified in *The Crucifixion,* in the most crucial scene at the cross Stainer reverts to a less personal treatment of the text.

What had induced the change? Were the long-standing objections concerning the representation of the Saviour overcome through a change in the religious climate? The acceptance of Jesus as a dramatic figure in English oratorio was certainly brought about, in part, through one important work, which found its way into oratorio programmes in the early 1870s: Johann Sebastian Bach's *St. Matthew Passion.* The Passion had been known on the Continent since its famous rediscovery by Felix Mendelssohn Bartholdy in Berlin in 1829. However, it was virtually unknown in England before 1870. Sterndale Bennett had given a private and one public performance of it in 1854 and 1856, but both had little impact on the general oratorio public. However, in 1871 John Barnby performed the Passion as part of a special service in Westminster Abbey, an event which aroused great interest among the public. John Stainer also produced the *St. Matthew Passion* two years later at St Paul's Cathedral. Those performances were not only repeated annually, the Passion was also given at concerts outside the church: by well-known oratorio societies like the Sacred Harmonic Society at Exeter Hall or Barnby's Choir at St James's Hall, and at the musical festivals.

It was through this contact with the Lutheran *Historien* tradition that the 'singing Jesus' became generally accepted in England. It may have helped that the Passion restricts Jesus to singing only strictly biblical words, which is clearly different from the free and very human portrayal of the saviour in Beethoven's *The Mount of Olives.* What may also have made the *St. Matthew Passion* more acceptable for the public than all the other works before it was the liturgical character of the first performances, in which it was integrated into a service and was sung by members of the cathedral choir who were dressed in surplices.

The widespread success of the *St. Matthew Passion* encouraged other composers and paved the way for Jesus to be included and portrayed as a dramatic figure in English oratorios. It also dealt a deathblow to Beethoven's *Engedi*. In 1877, for the first time, a translation of the original libretto version of *The Mount of Olives* was prepared and performed at the Leeds Festival, whose committee still felt obliged to explain their decision in the programme book:

> The attention which has lately been drawn to the representation of the 'Passion Play' at Ober-Ammergau, and the general recognition of the form of the Passion music of J.S. Bach as performed in the Church service have, however, tended to ... show that the impersonation of our Lord is not incompatible with a reverent rendering of the composer's ideas.[21]

None the less, despite these changes the prejudices of the past and outmoded attitudes were not immediately abandoned. In 1890 the Three Choirs Festival at Worcester still performed the *Engedi*-version of Beethoven, and the production of Gounod's *The Redemption* seven years earlier had led an anonymous correspondent ('An English Musician') to protest in *The Musical Opinion*:

> It is much to be regretted that from the very outset the Saviour is introduced as one of the *dramatis personae*, having many solo entrances assigned throughout. As a matter of notoriety, Beethoven's 'Mount of Olives' and Spohr's 'Calvary' were remodelled in this respect before a performance in England was permitted, and it is a curious aspect of the times to find responsible Anglican clergymen sanctioning a performance of the *Redemption* in well-known edifices without having this unseemly feature eliminated ...[22]

Although the portrayal of Christ in oratorios is just one aspect of the study of the English oratorio, it leads to a broader understanding of the genre in the nineteenth century. The legendary success of oratorio in England and the long-standing high esteem in which is was held as the 'cathedral' among art forms,[23] cannot be accounted for solely on artistic grounds. Indeed, it is necessary to consider the religious climate in which these works were born. Oratorio served as an entertainment

---

[21] Frederick Spark and Joseph Bennett, *History of the Leeds Musical Festivals 1858–1889*, London, 1892, S. 133. That the Passion Play at Oberammergau also raised doubts among British Christians can be seen from e.g. F. W. Farrar, *The Passion Play at Oberammergau 1890*, London, 1890.

[22] *The Musical Opinion*, 6, (69), June (1883), 382.

[23] W. S. Rockstro, Article on 'Oratorio', in George Grove (ed.), *A Dictionary of Music and Musicians*, 1st edn, 1880, vol. 2, p. 559.

but at the same time it was looked upon as providing edification. It appealed to a large public in a predominantly religious age where church reforms were enacted and at a time when two large religious movements (the Evangelical Revival and the Oxford Movement) were founded. To be sure, in this era the climate was such that the presentation of a musical festival in a cathedral was hotly debated in pamphlets, magazines and even in church congresses. A certain mistrust of theatrical entertainments, which was probably a heritage of seventeenth century Puritanism and which certainly characterized evangelical views on the arts in the nineteenth century, was widespread, and it came to the fore whenever oratorio, a genre still associated with the theatre, was performed in a cathedral. Dramatizing biblical stories in oratorios was accepted, since they were not acted, but the public drew a line at the portrayal of the Saviour himself. English composers chose to live with a compromise. They continued to write dramatic oratorios, but they either avoided the figure of Christ or put his words into the mouth of some other, less revered character. In this form oratorio found a wide acceptance. Towards the end of the century, however, it also came in for strong criticism. The most outspoken critic, George Bernard Shaw, never ceased to attack oratorios for their sanctimonious character and he criticized the Puritanic public, who would not attend the theatre but would accept drama in religious disguise as an oratorio: 'It is wrong to hear the Covent Garden orchestra play Le Sommeil de Juliette, but if Gounod writes just such another interlude, and calls it The Sleep of the Saints before the Last Judgment, then nothing can be more proper than to listen to it in the Albert Hall.'[24]

The fact that in the nineteenth century the figure of Christ was treated in English oratorios in this dramatically unconvincing way reveals something about the Victorian view of religion and art. An aesthetic evaluation of English oratorio in this era must take into account that the relationship between ethics and aesthetics was closely intertwined and only gradually severed towards the end of the Victorian age.

---

[24] Review of 25 June 1890, in *Music and London 1890–94*, Standard Edition of the Works of G. B. Shaw, vol. 29, pp. 21–2.

Appendix: Adaptation of Beethoven's *Christus am Oelberge*, no. 2 (recitativo)

Franz Xaver Huber/ Breikopf and Härtel (1803)	S. J. Arnold/Chapell and Co. (1814)	Thomas Oliphant/ Cramer, Addison and Beale (1840)
Jesus: Jehova, du mein Vater! O sende Trost und Kraft und Stärke mir. Sie nahet nun, die Stunde meiner Leiden, von mir erkoren schon, noch eh die Welt auf dein Geheiß dem Chaos sich entwand.	*Tenor voice:* 'Jehovah! Thou! O father' said the Lord our Saviour, when with His Disciples upon the Mount of Olives; 'Now 'tis the hour of suff'ring which approaches! Before the world was made at Thy behest, I offer'd up myself a willing Sacrifice.'	*John:* Jehovah! God of mercy! send help and comfort to thy only Son; Now when his hour of suff'ring fast approaches. That hour ordained by thee, before the world from Chaos dark arose at thy command.
Ich höre deines Seraphs Donnerstimme, sie fordert auf, wer statt der Menschen sich vor dein Gericht jetzt stellen will.	The Seraph's thundering voice He hears around him! It calls on Him, Him, who for guilty Man will cast Himself before Thy Throne:	In thunder an angel voice I hear, Our Master calling to offer up his life upon the cross for guilty man.
O Vater! Ich erschein auf diesen Ruf. Vermittler will ich sein, ich büße, ich allein, der Menschen Schuld. [...]	O Father! He obeys thy heaven'ly call the Mediator! He will suffer, He alone dies for Mankind; [...]	O Father! He obeys thy sov'reign will; the Mediator comes to suffer, He alone for all mankind! [...]
Ach sieh! Wie Bangigkeit, wie Todesangst mein Herz mit Macht ergreift! Ich leide sehr, mein Vater! O sieh! Ich leide sehr, erbarm' dich mein.	Ah see! how agony, how agony and pangs his soul invade! He suffers much, O Father, ah see! He suffers much, have mercy on Him!	Behold! with agony, with agony his inmost soul is torn! O soothe his anguish, sooth his anguish; in pity spare thine only Son!

Appendix: continued

William Bartholomew/ Novello, Ewer and Co. (1855)	Joseph Warren/Robert Cocks and Co. (1856)	J. Troutbeck/Novello, Ewer and Co. (1877)
A Disciple (John): The Saviour prayed His father would, in His mercy, aid and comfort him; Knowing his hour of sorrow was approaching (For ere the world was made, He knew that man would sin and die, and live again through Him).	*Tenor:* Jehovah! O my Father, thus saith the Lord our Saviour on the Mount, Father if thou be willing, remove this cup from me; nevertheless, not my will, but thine, be done.	*Jesus (Tenor):* My Father, o my Father, be Thou my comfort, give me strength to bear! Now is the hour approaching, when I suffer. I chose to meet this hour, before the world, at Thy command, in order newly stood.
Behold him in the fulness of His glory; Angelic hosts surround His radiant throne: His will on earth, – in heaven is done!	From heaven there appeared an angel, to strengthen him; he pray'd more earnestly, in more agony:	I hearken to the voices of Thy seraphs; they cry aloud, Who will, in place of man, before Thy judgment-seat appear?
Behold him prostrate upon the earth; In prayer imploring strength to suffer and atone for Adam's race! [...]	O! Father, if thou be willing, remove this cup from me; not my will, no, not mine, but thine be done.	O Father! I appear at this their call. A Saviour will I be, atoning, I alone for all mankind. [...]
Our sorrows, our agonies, our chastisement, our stripes, by Him were borne. For our transgressions He was wounded: He was bruised; He bled, and died for all mankind.	And when he rose up from prayer, he spoke to his disciples: Why sleep ye? rise and pray.	Behold, how fearfulness, how pain of death, upon my soul have seiz'd. My heart is faint, my Father! Behold, my heart is faint; O comfort me!

Appendix: continued

Henry Hudson:
Engedi/Novello,
Ewer and Co. (1842)

David:
Jehovah! hear, oh hear
me. Thou art my hope.
Oh Lord, deliver me;
stretch forth Thy hand
to help me in my
trouble. I bless Thy holy
name, Thou art my
refuge and my shield; in
Thee alone I trust.

How awful is Thy
wrath, oh God of Israel!
Arise, oh Lord! and let
thine enemies be
scatter'd and flee before
Thee.

Oh Father! hear and
grant Thy servant's
pray'r, Who bends
before Thy Throne in
sorrow, for my foes have
sought my life. [...]

Behold how fearfully the
pains of death oppress
and wound my soul. My
heart is faint, my
Father! Behold, my
heart is faint, have
mercy, Lord!

CHAPTER THIRTEEN

The Benefit Concert in Nineteenth-Century London: From 'tax on the nobility' to 'monstrous nuisance'

Simon McVeigh

The history of concert life in nineteenth-century London has to a large extent been mapped as the history of musical organizations.[1] This is partly because an essentially insecure economic system projected itself in these terms, validating artistic significance, professionalism and quality assurance through the trappings of longevity and continuity from one season to the next. The typical curve followed by these organizations – early evangelizing rewarded by rising enthusiasm, a more or less stable plateau followed by decline and demise – thus at the same time reflects the self-consciousness of an emerging system and provides a natural model for historians of musical life.

Yet these central organizations, important and influential as they were, represent only one segment of the capital's concert life, and concentration on them holds up a distorting mirror to a complex and diverse musical structure. In our search for the origins of modern concert life we can be too easily seduced by apparent prophecies of twentieth-century attitudes towards the business of concerts, their audiences and their repertoire. Certainly a more thorough and deeply rooted investigation will in many ways cut across our preconceptions about Victorian musical life, especially too close an identification of its structure with that of the twentieth century.[2] Even leaving aside other less well-known organizations of a similar nature, still awaiting modern

---

[1] Recent authoritative studies include Cyril Ehrlich, *First Philharmonic: A History of the Royal Philharmonic Society*, Oxford, 1995, and Michael Musgrave, *The Musical Life of the Crystal Palace*, Cambridge, 1995. Other studies currently underway include those by Musgrave on the Sacred Harmonic Society, Christina Bashford on the Musical Union and Basil Keen on the Bach Choir.

[2] A selective but systematic database study (*Concert Life in Nineteenth-Century London*) is currently being undertaken in collaboration with Christina Bashford, Rachel Cowgill and Cyril Ehrlich. For a provocative article on the writing of concert history, see Cyril Ehrlich and Dave Russell, 'Victorian Music: A Perspective', *Journal of Victorian Culture*, 3 (1998), 111–22.

investigation, a myriad of different kinds of concert activity contributed to London's musical life. Of these, some achieved a measure of institutionalization from tradition and circumstance, as with the Lenten oratorio series organized annually by individual entrepreneurs. Others – the early season chamber music series in the years before the Musical Union, or the benefit concert system itself – should be regarded only in the loosest sense as institutions that persisted from year to year without any such standardization.[3]

The study of London's concert life during the nineteenth century needs to address trends in its institutional structure at all levels. Two principal mechanisms of transformation can be identified. The first is the radical break: either the invention or import of a new concert-type (chamber music concerts in 1835, the promenade concert in 1838) or, conversely, the death of an old one (the Lenten oratorios, which came to an abrupt end in 1843;[4] the Concert of Ancient Music in 1848). The second mechanism involves modification and transformation, a gradual process of adaptation resulting in seemingly new types of concert promotion in response to both social and musical pressures. The reasons for the foundation of an institution and for its continuation may be entirely different, and plotting how an organization reacts to changing circumstances represents a considerable challenge to the historian; likewise the cause of its final demise may be by no means self-evident or straightforward. Indeed, the end of an institution is often as intriguing as the birth of one, often as complex or difficult to explain (take, for example, the varied circumstances that contributed to the failure of the Sacred Harmonic Society).

What then happened to the benefit concert? Did it simply die too, outliving its usefulness in the 1840s alongside those two other eighteenth-century inventions mentioned above? Certainly rumours of its death have been greatly exaggerated: one modern author has written that 'in the 1830s the popularity of benefits was reaching its peak',[5] yet a memoir published in the 1890s observed that benefit concerts 'still live, and seemingly flourish – for where, in the sixties, one concert of this sort was given, there are now a dozen or a score'.[6] In fact the benefit concert survived repeated obituaries and the derision of serious-

[3] See Christina Bashford, 'Public Chamber-Music Concerts in London, 1835–50: Aspects of History, Repertory and Reception', PhD, University of London, 1996.
[4] Joel Sachs, 'The End of the Oratorios', in E. Strainchamps and M. R. Maniates (eds), *Music and Civilization: Essays in Honor of Paul Henry Lang*, New York, 1984, pp. 168–82.
[5] Joel Sachs, 'London: The Professionalization of Music', in Alexander Ringer (ed.), *The Early Romantic Era: Between Revolutions, 1789 and 1848*, London, 1990, p. 219.
[6] Alice Mangold Diehl, *Musical Memories*, London, 1897, p. 123.

minded critics right up to the end of the century; and the lack of detailed research into this important area of nineteenth-century concert life in London must be regarded as a major lacuna. In an attempt to begin to fill this gap, the present study offers a preliminary survey of the main themes involved.

This chapter is not concerned with one-off fund-raising benefits for charities, nor with concerts for indigent musicians fallen on hard times, such as the ageing tenor Mario or the pianist Arabella Goddard, both of whom called on an indulgent public some years into their retirement. Rather the focus will be on the concert promoted by an individual for profit, traditionally a one-off annual benefit for the capital's leading instrumentalists and singers. The eighteenth-century concept was modelled on theatrical practice, whereby the end of every season was crowded with benefits for the leading players, the financial terms jealously guarded in contracts. For the most prestigious actors, the management would pay the expenses, and such a 'clear benefit' could easily bring in as much as the annual salary.[7] The system was not so formalized in the less ordered world of concert life, though occasionally benefits were specified in the contracts of leading singers at subscription series. Quite exceptionally, Haydn too negotiated such a deal with Salomon in 1791, and in such circumstances the benefit could be highly lucrative: the contract included a benefit guaranteed at £200, with all expenses paid by the impresario; in the event it raised as much as £350.[8] For those not so fortunate, the high expenses introduced a strong element of risk, and it was quite possible to make a heavy loss; but nevertheless a leading virtuoso would anticipate a profit well into three figures, especially if some of the soloists waived payment by some reciprocal arrangement.

The benefit concept was therefore one of the pillars of London's concert structure during the eighteenth century, standing alongside the regular subscription concerts, the ancient concerts and Lenten oratorios (series with which they were closely associated). In 1795, for example, 15 concert benefits were given during the late spring, almost all by

---

[7] St Vincent Trowbridge, *The Benefit System in the British Theatre*, London, 1967. At Covent Garden in 1798–99, for example, Joseph Munden's benefit brought him £510 net profit, considerably more than his annual salary of £380.

[8] Further on contracts for subscription series, see S. McVeigh, 'The Professional Concert and Rival Subscription Series in London, 1783–1793', *Royal Musical Association Research Chronicle*, 22 (1989), 1–135; and on eighteenth-century benefits, S. McVeigh, *Concert Life in London from Mozart to Haydn*, Cambridge, 1993, especially pp. 35–8, 176–81. Further details of concert programmes can be obtained from S. McVeigh, *Calendar of London Concerts 1750–1800, Advertised in the London Daily Press*, Goldsmiths College, University of London.

musicians associated with the top West End concert organizations. Such concerts were regarded as prestigious high-points of the season where important new works might even be introduced. At Haydn's final benefit, for example, Brigida Banti premièred his last great scena:

Part 1

Haydn	Symphony ('Military', Part 1)	
Ferrari	Song 'Or dell' avverse sorte'	Rovedino
Ferlendis	Oboe concerto	Ferlendis
Haydn	Duet 'Quel tuo visetto amabile'	Mme Morichelli, Morelli
	[*Orlando Paladino*]	
Haydn	Overture (new, in D ['London'])	

Part 2

Haydn	Symphony ('Military', Part 2)	
Paisiello	Song 'Crudele, or colei piangi'	Mme Morichelli
Viotti	Violin concerto	Viotti
Haydn	Scena 'Berenice, che fai?'	Mme Banti
	Finale	

Haydn's benefit (4 May 1795, King's Theatre Room)[9]
Source: H. C. Robbins Landon, *Haydn in London*, London, 1976, pp. 306–9.

Such programmes were directly modelled on those of modern orchestral subscription concerts, though they often blended ancient and English items for wider appeal across other established musical constituencies (the Concert of Ancient Music, the Vocal Concert). Occasionally virtuoso instrumentalists would introduce some crowd-pleasing novelty like the 'regulated double sounds' the flautist Andrew Ashe promised at his benefit in the same year; but nevertheless the link with the leading concert organizations was unambiguous.

The benefit in the eighteenth century was therefore regarded as a reward for the most prestigious performers for good service – most publicly at subscription concerts, but also (and more fundamentally) at private concerts and in teaching, for we should not forget that public concerts were but a small part of a virtuoso's activities. A large proportion of the audience at a benefit would be personally known to the promoter, essentially defining the *beau monde*, the closely knit urban élite whose identity was publicly defined by attendance at the Italian

---

[9] All programmes are presented in three columns: composer, work, performer. Names and titles have been editorially standardized without comment.

opera and at fashionable concerts.[10] While tickets could be bought anonymously from music sellers, at a high price of half a guinea, it was taken as a matter of course and subservience that promoters would visit their patrons with cards in the manner of tradesmen.[11] Thus commercial concerns remained inextricably linked with traditional concepts of patronage. Regular patrons undoubtedly felt a strong pressure to support benefits, and Burney relates how Mrs Fox Lane (Lady Bingley) personally added to this pressure by exhorting her guests to buy tickets for the benefits of Giardini and Mingotti.[12] As a result, benefit tickets were routinely referred to during the later eighteenth century as a 'tax on the nobility', an imposition the *haut ton* sometimes condescended to enhance with additional gifts of their own. Thus promoting a benefit was an assertion of status within the musical profession, and it was regarded as a well-guarded privilege: small wonder that less favoured musicians constantly complained that those in receipt of a benefit were least in need of one.

The benefit in the eighteenth century thus neatly reflected current attitudes towards patronage, the subtle balance between paid employment and social prestige – between the services of a paid entertainer and the gentility of a respected artist who might even sit at a noble patron's table, a central issue in social acceptance. Many top performers succeeded in reconciling the apparent contradictions, showing no qualms about accepting personal gifts that would seem to emphasize their servility and dependence. Indeed in the eighteenth-century benefit system mutual dependencies were characteristically mingled, the ambiguities tacitly accepted or ignored: a benefit was projected as an honourable reward that called on the willing loyalty of patrons and fellow musicians alike.

Thirty years later the essential structure remained unchanged. Leading performers still expected to take an end-of-season benefit as a matter of course, taking charge of the organization and even writing out their own advertisements, as we learn from Hummel's papers.[13] The continuing appeal to personal contact and professional loyalty is vividly illustrated by surviving accounts for Weber's benefit at the Argyll Rooms in

---

[10] This concept is explored further in William Weber, 'La culture musicale et la capitale: l'époque du beau monde à Londres, 1700–1870', *Revue d'histoire moderne et contemporaine*, forthcoming.

[11] A standard card from William Lee, referring to a previous letter concerning his benefit, survives in the Banks Collection, British Library, Department of Prints and Drawings (Admission Tickets, vol. 6, item 409).

[12] F. Mercer (ed.), *A General History of Music*, London, 1935, vol. ii, p. 1014.

[13] British Library, Add. 33,965, f. 318, discussed in Joel Sachs, *Kapellmeister Hummel in England and France*, Detroit, 1977, p. 45.

1826.[14] Aided on this occasion by the ubiquitous concert-director Sir George Smart, Weber sold 149 tickets to named persons, as against 111 bought at various music shops and 40 at the door. In the event the concert was not much of a success: the earnest cantata *The Festival of Peace* (arranged from the *Jubel-Cantate*) failed to please the devotees of *Freischütz*, while the second half proved too much of a pot-boiler for the connoisseurs, suggesting a rare miscalculation of programme and venue by the normally astute Smart. Furthermore Weber faced rival attractions in Pierre Begrez's benefit at the Duke of St Albans's house and the running of the Oaks at Epsom. A paying audience of 300 was disappointing for such a celebrity: many performers waived their fees to oblige the ailing composer, so that expenses were low at £99, but even with a donation from Sir George Warrender the profit only reached £96.

Yet if the basic framework had remained constant, much within it had altered dramatically since the late eighteenth century. The sheer number of events reflected a change of emphasis. In his annual reviews in the *Quarterly Musical Magazine and Review* (*QMMR*) R. M. Bacon bemoaned a regrettable dilution of standards during the 1820s, viewing the proliferation of concerts as intrinsically detrimental to the art of music and to the prospect of another permanent series, for him a touchstone of artistic progress.[15] Certainly numbers were increasing steadily, with 30 benefits in 1825 rising to as many as 42 in 1828.[16] Pressure on time during the short season was so acute that the afternoon was brought into service, for so-called matinées at around two o'clock: in 1830 most of the 37 benefits took place in May and June, and around half of these were matinées. (This timing is a significant social indicator in itself, for it naturally excluded almost the entire male population of London, restricting audiences to the leisured few and to women.)

The ever increasing number of concerts was a clear indication that minor hopefuls were beginning to infiltrate the traditional system, so

---

[14] Smart papers, British Library, Add. 41,778, ff. 15–18; John Warrack, *Carl Maria von Weber*, London, 1968, pp. 341–2.

[15] See especially *QMMR*, 5 (1823), 251; 8 (1826), 176–8; 9 (1827), 86–90; 10 (1828–30), 88–94, 303–4, 310.

[16] Figures derived from *QMMR*, 10 (1828–30), 88. See also the Lord Chamberlain's register of licences for public performances, 1820–34, Public Record Office LC 7/11, which gives an unusually full picture, although it should be noted that benefits at private houses did not require a licence even when tickets were on sale. Further on benefits in this period, see William Weber, *Music and the Middle Class*, London, 1975, pp. 42–4, 50–51; Deborah Rohr, 'A Profession of Artisans: The Careers and Social Status of British Musicians 1750–1850', PhD, University of Pennsylvania, 1983, ch. 7; A.V. Beedell, *The Decline of the English Musician 1788–1888*, Oxford, 1992, pp. 125–6.

that the benefit was less and less regarded as a reward or mark of recognition, and more as a purely commercial undertaking. Yet at the same time there was a commercial downside. Expenses attached to the traditional benefit had doubled since the eighteenth century (when expenses of £100 had been the norm) as a consequence of larger orchestras, escalating fees for operatic divas and other soloists, and a public expectation of ever more numerous and varied attractions. This escalation was only partly offset by the continuing practice of performers giving their services for professional colleagues (the violinist John Ella claimed in 1845 that he had played gratis at 280 concerts in the previous 20 years).[17] At the same time the proliferation of benefits acutely exacerbated London's perennial problem of over-supply. Only a dozen or so star performers could be assured of a fashionable crowd: thus in 1836 the well-connected violinist and leader Nicolas Mori was able to transfer his benefit from the King's Theatre concert room to the Opera House itself, resulting in a profit estimated at £800.[18] Yet in the face of stiff competition even such magnets might be confronted with half-empty halls or forced to 'paper' the house with dozens of free tickets: Hummel, doyen of travelling pianists, struggled to attract an audience into three figures while Paganini-mania was at its height in 1831. Indeed John Ella could recall 'only four eminent artists whose genius and talent alone commanded a remunerative audience': Catalani, Rossini, Paganini and Thalberg.[19]

The situation was far worse for those lower down the ladder, who might find themselves supplementing a handful of loyal students prepared to pay half a guinea with hundreds of friends and relatives paying nothing at all: in 1845 the *Musical World* estimated that of 500 people attending the benefit of a young unknown only 100 would have actually paid for a ticket. A note of realism was sounded in a sobering letter to the same journal, in which a young professional with high hopes describes the finances of a (real or hypothetical?) benefit. Encouraged by acquaintances to engage only the best opera singers, such as Malibran and Grisi, his expenses amount to some £240: with an audience of 600 paying half a guinea each, he looks forward to a return of around 60 guineas. But in the event fewer than 100 tickets are sold before the day, and 17 at the door, resulting in losses of over £100, which he says (a

---

[17] Musical expenses typically came to £100–140 (even with gratis appearances) plus half as much again for the hall, advertising, and so on, according to *QMMR*, 5 (1823), 251. Ella's comment is in *Record of The Musical Union*, 1 (1845), 23.

[18] *Musical World*, 1 (1836), 142.

[19] Sachs, *Kapellmeister Hummel*, pp. 67–73; Weber, *Music and the Middle Class*, pp. 42–3; *Record of the Musical Union*, 1 (1845), 23; cf. *Musical World*, 20 (1845), 293–4.

recurrent refrain) would have been double but for the generosity of the performers in returning their fees.[20] William Cutler even went so far as to issue a public statement about his loss of £150 at a Whitsun Eve speculation 12 years earlier.[21] It is in this context that benefits came eventually to be regarded as loss-leaders, their overwhelming purpose to secure connections – in other words a form of advertising for teaching and private engagements.

Meanwhile the declining reputation of the benefit concert was exacerbated by poor standards of quality control. Benefits had already become divorced from the established concert series where a small core of top performers habitually performed together on a regular basis. Critics pointed to the lack of rehearsal, the inevitably hackneyed repertoire, the frequent changes and reordering of programmes, as prima donnas exercised their right to cancel at short notice – or were genuinely exhausted as they raced from one concert to the next (it was not at all uncommon for a singer to perform at three venues on one night). All this gave, in the words of Bacon, an impression of caprice and disorder:

> Thus instead of regularly digested, regularly conducted, and regularly rehearsed schemes, the public is allured to scrambling performances, where the absence of principals, the changes of the pieces, and the want of any trial of the parts together, but too often are alike disgraceful to the musician, destructive of the art, and disgusting to the real amateur.[22]

In Salomon's day benefit concerts had been regarded as a legitimate contribution to the cultural life of the season: now there was a general sense of artistic prostitution that reflected ill on the frenetic musical activity of the capital. Certainly this was the view of foreign visitors in 1829 such as Fétis (however much piqued English critics might seek to defend what they had once attacked); and Mendelssohn, who had particularly harsh words for the grasping Londoners: 'Here they pursue music like a business, calculating, paying, bargaining, and truly a great deal is lacking ...'[23]

One consequence of the more commercial approach was an escalating trend towards mixed programming, in an attempt to appeal in one concert to devotees of Italian opera, of the symphonic music at the Philharmonic, of Handel oratorio and ancient music, of the English

---

[20] *Musical World*, 2 (1836), 52–4.

[21] *QMMR*, 6 (1824), 234.

[22] *QMMR*, 10 (1828–30), 90.

[23] Fétis's reviews of musical life in London were translated in the *Harmonicon*, 7 (1829); Mendelssohn, *A Life in Letters*, ed. R. Elvers, New York, 1986, p. 106.

vocal school. Programmes developed into a long succession of the most appealing soloistic items, quite different from the sober and classical programming of the high-minded Philharmonic Society. Those of the 1830 season are typically pot-pourris dominated by vocal music: flashy and tuneful Italian arias by Rossini and Pucitta, or their operatic ensembles, ballads by Bishop and Callcott, Scots songs, English glees. Concertos are supplanted by virtuosic variations, fantasies and 'recollections' of seemingly every country in Europe, or sometimes extemporizations by lions of the keyboard on melodies provided by the audience. Not that all this repertoire was in truth so trivial as it was made out by severe critics: a work like Moscheles's *Recollections of Ireland*, performed at his benefit on 1 June, is an impressively sophisticated concert work with orchestra, weaving three Irish melodies into intricate counterpoint at the end. But the arch criticism of the *Harmonicon* typifies the serious critical reaction: in selecting Hummel's A minor Concerto, Lucy Anderson appealed 'to the sense of the audience', but in a polonaise by Herz 'to the non-sense'.[24] And while benefit promoters still employed full orchestras, the repertoire was generally restricted to a few popular overtures like *Freischütz* or *Zauberflöte*:

Part 1

Weber	Overture	
Rossini	Duet (*Guillaume Tell*)	Donzelli, Santini
Vaccai	New grand aria	Mme Lalande
[Mazzinghi]	Comic English duet 'When a little farm we keep' [*The Free Knights*]	Mme Malibran, De Begnis
Belloli	Grand horn fantasia	Puzzi
Martini	New terzetto	Blasis, Curioni, De Begnis
	Aria	Donzelli
Handel	Song [?'Gentle airs' (*Athalia*)]	Begrez (Lindley, cello)
Vaccai	Duet	Mlle Blasis, De Begnis
	Grand concertante variations: voice, piano, harp, violin	Mme Stockhausen, Mrs Anderson, Stockhausen, Mori
[Mayr]	Grand scena and aria 'I violini tutti' (*Il fanatico per la musica*)	De Begnis (acts and sings)

[24] *Harmonicon*, 8 (1830), 305. Information in this paragraph is mainly derived from this journal, *Morning Chronicle*, *Morning Herald*, *Morning Post* and *John Bull*.

Part 2

	Flute fantasia	Nicholson
Fioravanti	New buffo duetto	Lablache, De Begnis
Hummel	New aria, composed for her [Variations on a Tyrolese air, Op. 118]	Mme Malibran
Bellini	Duet	Blasis, Curioni
	Swiss air	Mme Stockhausen (Stockhausen, harp)
Mozart	Terzetto	Curioni, E Seguin, De Begnis
Rossini	Duet 'Si tu m'ami' (*Aureliano in Palmira*)	Mme Malibran, Mme Stockhausen
[Mozart]	Finale (*Don Giovanni*)	Mme Lalande, Mme Stockhausen, Mme Blasis, Begrez, Santini, Seguin, De Begnis

De Begnis's Benefit (21 May 1830, King's Theatre Room)
Source: Morning Chronicle, 20 May; reviews in *Morning Post*, 22 May and *Morning Herald*, 24 May.
A bassoon solo by Preumayr is mentioned in reviews.

Part 1

Beethoven	Overture *Prometheus*	
E Taylor	Song 'The rover's farewell'	E Taylor
Knyvett	Glee 'The rose of the valley'	Mrs Knyvett, Knyvett, Bennett, Phillips
Smith	Ballad 'Softly sleep, my baby boy'	Miss Cramer
	Harp fantasia	Miss A Windsor
Pacini	Cavatina 'Lungi dal caro' (*La sposa fedele*)	Mlle Blasis
Mozart	Song 'Batti, batti' [*Don Giovanni*]	Mrs Knyvett (Lindley, cello)
Mayseder	Violin fantasia	Mori
Mayr	Duet 'Con pazienza' [*Il fanatico per la musica*]	Mlle Blasis, De Begnis
Pucitta	Song 'Crudo amor' [*La caccia di Enrico IV*]	Bennett
Hummel	New Variations on a Tyrolese air [Op. 118]	Mme Malibran
Rossini	Quintet 'Oh! guardate' [*Il turco in Italia*]	Mlle Blasis, Mrs Knyvett, Begrez, Lennox, De Begnis

Part 2

Lindley	Cello fantasia	Lindley
Mozart	Aria 'Qui sdegno' [='In diesen heil'gen Hallen', *Die Zauberflöte*]	Phillips
Mozart	Duet 'Sull' aria' (*Le nozze di Figaro*)	Mme Malibran, Miss Cramer
Hummel	Grand trio: piano, violin, cello	Hummel, Mori, Lindley
Rossini	Aria 'Sorgete' [*Maometto II*]	Lennox
Rossini	Duet 'Di capricci' [*Matilde di Shabran*]	Mme Malibran, De Begnis
Castelli	Rondeau 'J'ai de l'argent'	De Begnis
Handel	Recitative and air 'Gentle airs' (*Athalia*)	Begrez (Lindley, cello)
Mercadante	Grand duet 'Vanne' [*Andronico*]	Mme Malibran, Mme Stockhausen
Dr Carnaby	Song 'Wandering Willie'	Miss Carnaby (accompanying herself on the piano)
Haydn	Finale instrumentale	

Lindley's Benefit (24 May 1830, King's Theatre Room)
Source: *Morning Chronicle*, 24 May, reviews in *Morning Herald*, 25 May, *Morning Post*, 26 May.

Certainly symphonies are by this date a rarity. Whereas the Philharmonic included a Beethoven symphony in almost every programme, it was very much the exception to find the Fifth at Mori's benefit on 10 May (one of 23 pieces 'by almost every body of any note') and quite unprecedented when Charles Neate programmed the Ninth at his concert on 26 April, only the second public performance in England.[25] Yet a few promoters still retained a classical veneer, especially those with links to London's older concert tradition and with the Philharmonic. J. B. Cramer, for example, had been a soloist at the Professional Concert back in 1785; and his Mozartian predilection was reflected in the inclusion of the D minor piano concerto in his programme on 20 May, albeit with the *spagnuola* finale substituted from his own Concerto No. 8. His brother Franz went further in this direction, his programme on 7

---

[25] *Harmonicon*, 8 (1830), 305–6. See also David Benjamin Levy, *Beethoven: The Ninth Symphony*, New York, 1995, pp. 148–57. Neate was both an acquaintance of Beethoven and one of the founders of the Philharmonic Society.

May deliberately reflecting those of the Philharmonic Society by including both Mozart's Symphony No. 39 and Beethoven's Second, as well as a Haydn quartet.

The social structure of the audience at benefits in the 1830s was evidently much more fluid than at those of the previous century. William Weber has analysed benefits as essentially concerts of high social status (reflected in the continuance of half-guinea tickets), but with a low artistic prestige and a popular tone that contrasted with the classical aspirations of the Philharmonic Society.[26] In particular the integrity of the audience was compromised by the handing out of reduced price or gratis tickets, liberating in terms of social mix, but too impermanent to provide the basis for a realignment of the audience base. This analysis largely follows the agenda of middle-class journalists of the time, anxious to preserve the aspirations of the wealthy bourgeois to the cultural élite; and it may exaggerate the trivialization of the repertoire, for (as we have seen) musicians showed themselves immensely flexible in their appeal to a range of audience tastes. But it is clear that, however they came by their tickets, a widening musical public was able to attend such events, formerly the preserve of the *beau monde*, at the very same time as the latter's patronage and control of the Italian Opera were gradually fragmenting.[27] An interesting pointer in this direction, and one that links the two milieus, is provided by the ticketing arrangements for Rossini's two concert benefits at Almack's in 1824. Social exclusivity was unabashedly the object of the organizers: tickets were priced at a very high one guinea, and furthermore the old system of lady patronesses was recalled in order to vet the clientele. In the event, however, the system broke down completely on the second night, when in order to fill the hall many were allowed in 'whom "nobody knew"'.[28]

As early as 1828 Bacon identified such mixed company, often with free or reduced price tickets, as a disincentive for those of more refined social aspirations (including, presumably, his own readership).[29] It was concern about the rampaging popularization of public concerts that led to a resurgence of private salon concerts in the late 1820s;[30] and some prestigious musicians, anxious to reassert their continuing connections

---

[26] Weber, *Music and the Middle Class*, pp. 42–4.

[27] Jennifer Hall, 'The Re-fashioning of Fashionable Society: Opera-going and Sociability in Britain, 1821–1861', PhD, Yale University, 1996.

[28] *Harmonicon*, 2 (1824), 122–3, 145; *QMMR*, 6 (1824), 230 and 7 (1825), 298.

[29] *QMMR*, 10 (1828–30), 90; cf. also 310.

[30] This interaction between public and private music represents one of the most important, if elusive, areas for research in nineteenth-century studies. Some consideration of the issues involved is to be found in Rohr, 'A Profession of Artisans', especially ch. 3.

with high society, began to react by holding benefits at their patrons' houses, rather than reaching out to a larger but in some ways less promising market. Madame Sala, for example, held her morning concert on 25 June 1830 at the house of Mr Penn, under the immediate patronage of the Duchess of Clarence and the Duke of Sussex: yet tickets priced at half a guinea were on sale to the public, at her own address or from the usual music shops.[31] Malibran was inevitably the star attraction here, and she also sang at the Stockhausens' benefit a week earlier, held at Sir George Warrender's house in Albemarle Street: but the tickets for this evening concert were twice as expensive, presumably justified by the lure of Hummel, Cramer, Moscheles and Lucy Anderson performing together on two grand pianos.[32]

All this would seem to toll the death-knell for the public benefit concert. In economic terms its essential problem was its mixed bag, catch-all nature, which required the increasingly voracious expense of the top opera singers and instrumental virtuosi, but could not be sustained in any numbers by the available market for high-price tickets. Furthermore the two most important constituencies – the *beau monde* and the connoisseur – were both turning away from concerts that were rapidly becoming down-market commercial pot-pourris. Serious musicians were equally anxious to maintain their musical and social reputations: it is striking that artistes like Spohr and Mendelssohn neglected to take benefits during the 1830s, as Viotti and Haydn had not hesitated to do four decades earlier. Indeed the role of the benefit reflected acutely the central issue in the status of the professional musician: the changing relationship with patronage, which (as we have seen) in the eighteenth century contained intrinsic if unspoken ambiguities. These came under direct scrutiny in the post-Napoleonic years, as artists began gradually to assert their independence and self-respect as professionals unbeholden to ties of patronage. The relationship between servility and gentility was redefined: a musician might aspire to be regarded as a gentleman because of his professional standing rather than despite it. In such a climate he expected commensurate reward on a professional basis, rather than payment in kind or the condescension implied in generous gifts; and the benefit concert, intrinsically linked to the old ways despite its commercial trappings, inevitably came under challenge.

In the theatrical world, this issue was explicitly addressed during the 1820s as some actors refused to take benefits, disdaining in particular the demeaning practice of additional presents or 'guineas'. William

---

[31] *Morning Herald*, 23 June 1830.
[32] *Morning Herald*, 15 June 1830.

Macready, for example, declined such gifts, wishing to appear a gentleman of an honourable profession rather than a servile player and retainer;
and his professional pride was characteristically expressed in his concern not to be embarrassed at the dinner-table with his donor.[33] Such
accounts are somewhat disingenuous, yet it is clear that the commercial
aspect of the benefit was not the primary concern, but rather the
traditional dependence and servility that it embodied.

Despite these fundamental shifts in the relationship between performers and their patrons, however, the benefit concert simply refused to
fade away. Indeed it showed remarkable tenacity in the face of repeated
obituaries, and by adapting, chameleon-like, to changing social and
musical demands it managed to survive in various forms (and sometimes under different names) until the end of the century. One direction
was the heterogeneous orchestral extravaganza, which reached its apogee in Benedict's 'monster concerts' based on the Parisian model. The
first of these took place in 1841, a matinée with a massive programme
of over 20 items, including arias by all the leading Italian Opera singers
– Grisi, Viardot-Garcia, Mario – and solos by Liszt, Vieuxtemps and
Benedict himself. The concert was a sensational success, attracting such
a vast crowd to the Opera House concert room that a third of the
audience was either standing or out of sight of the performers.[34] Such
long and brilliant showpieces were naturally attacked by high-minded
critics, not only for degrading the art of music, but also for raising
audience expectations far beyond what could normally be satisfied.[35]
An ostentatiously serious musician like John Ella regarded them as
'monstrous nuisances', as well as commercially dubious, the very high
expenditure allowing scant chance of profit unless the artists waived
their fees – especially, presumably, when they were put on in normal
concert rooms seating no more than 800.[36] In later years Benedict
removed to the large Covent Garden Italian opera theatre, and his
grand morning concerts – ostentatiously lavish, expensively priced, pa-
tronized by royalty and high society – became an annual institution
lasting over 40 years. In 1855, for example, the concert began at 1.30
p.m. and ended around 6 p.m., with a programme of more than 30
items: on the instrumental side, overtures including Benedict's own *The
Tempest*, a Bottesini duet for clarinet and double-bass, piano and violin
solos, and another piece for four pianists; on the vocal side, operatic
arias and ensembles, ballads and part-songs. The performers were the

[33] Trowbridge, *The Benefit System*, pp. 87–8.
[34] *The Times*, 18 May 1841.
[35] *Musical World*, **17** (1842), 165.
[36] J. Ella, *Musical Sketches, Abroad, and at Home*, London, 1869, vol. 1, p. 139.

full orchestra, chorus and principal singers of the Royal Italian Opera – many of whom had appeared in 1841 – and other celebrities such as Clara Novello and the violinist Ernst. The house was 'densely crowded by company of the most fashionable order', yielding receipts around £1 100.[37]

But this kind of high-profile extravaganza, taking the trends of 1830 to their ultimate conclusion – and foreshadowing pot-pourris at the Royal Albert Hall from Patti onwards – was very much the exception. Indeed by 1855 the orchestral benefit was something of a rarity, and listed separately in the annual *Musical Directory*: only eight this season as against 61 benefits. It was largely with the aim of introducing his new C minor symphony that Ernst Pauer promoted a Grand Evening Concert on 1 June, placing it in a strongly Austro-German programme alongside Viennese classics, a Hummel concerto, and three choruses by Mendelssohn performed by the London Deutscher-Männer-Chor.[38] Most benefit promoters were turning in a quite different direction, omitting the orchestra altogether and suggesting the ambience of a salon concert by preserving just the succession of arias, songs and instrumental show-pieces.

Part 1

Bellini	[From] Introduzione 'La luna, il sol' (*I puritani*)	Mme Gassier, Marras, Bottura, Gassier
Oberthur	Grande fantaisie: harp	Mlle Louise Christine
Meyerbeer	Romance 'O jours heureux' (*L'Étoile du Nord*)	Belletti
Verdi	Canzone 'Stride la vampa' (*Il trovatore*)	Miss Birch
Mendelssohn	Rondo et Caprice: piano [?Rondo capriccioso, Op. 14]	Mlle Speyer
Lillo	Romanza 'La desolazione'	Marras
Donizetti	Barcarola 'Or che in cielo' [*Marino Faliero*]	Marras
Bellini	Aria 'Ah! non credea' (*La sonnambula*)	Mme Gassier
Marras	Tre pensieri: Bolero	Belletti
	Duettino	Miss Birch, Miss Katherine Smith
	Melodia	Marras
Yradier	Duetto 'Tota de los toreros'	Gassier, Mme Gassier

[37] *Musical World*, 33 (1855), 367, 399; *Morning Post*, 18 June 1855.
[38] *Musical World*, 33 (1855), 334, 363.

Beethoven	Melodia 'Delizia'	Miss Katherine Smith
[*recte* Schubert	Arrangement of waltz, Op. 9 No. 2]	
Verdi	Quartetto 'Bella figlia' (*Rigoletto*)	Mme Gassier, Mme Bassano, Marras, Gassier
Bottesini	Fantasia: double bass	Bottesini
Ricci	Terzetto 'La scena' (*Scaramuccia*)	Belletti, Gassier, Marras
Verdi	Cavatina 'Tacea la notte' (*Il trovatore*)	Mme Lucia Escott
Part 2		
G Regondi	Morceaux de concert 'Les Oiseaux': concertina	Giulio Regondi
Beethoven	Aria 'In questa tomba oscura' [WoO 133]	Mme Bassano
	Canzoncine napolitane	Marras
Mozart	Aria 'Non più andrai' (*Le nozze di Figaro*)	Bottura
Yradier	Chanson andalouse 'La Jaca'	Mme Gassier
Verdi	Duettino e terzetto 'Si la stanchezza' (*Il trovatore*)	Mme Lucia Escott, Mme de Luigi, Marras
Bellini	Finale 'Se mai più vederei in vita' (*Giulietta e Romeo* [?*I Capuleti e i Montecchi*, unidentified])	Tutti

Piano: Pilotti, Campana

Marras's Grande Matinée Musicale (25 June 1855, The Pavilion, Hans Place)
Source: *Musical World*, 33 (1855), 402.

Even concerto movements could be played with piano accompaniment, or perhaps in arrangement for a few stringed instruments. Ella attacked the scaled-down benefit too, accusing promoters of mean commercial exploitation: and this development significantly coincides with a first attempt to increase audiences and widen accessibility through lower ticket prices. The introduction of a two-tiered system in reflection of theatrical practice (usually 10s. 6d. reserved, 7s. unreserved) was a remarkably belated concession to commercial opportunism, which at the same time attempted to retain traditional exclusive patronage through a thin veneer of social differentiation. Not surprisingly, J. W. Davison in the *Musical World* repeated many of the arguments of Bacon, arguing that concerts should be even cheaper if 'a genuine musical treat' was intended; and that if charity and mere advertisement were their main aspiration then there were other more suitable means to that end.[39]

Some benefit promoters were in fact already responding to a change in artistic tone in London's concert life, reflecting the more general recognition of the status of musical classics throughout Europe during the 1840s. The most important single influence on London benefit programmes was the rise of chamber concert series, first instituted in 1835. This development encouraged a surge of recognition of the Viennese classical repertoire, especially the quartets of Beethoven, and of later chamber music in that tradition by Spohr, Mendelssohn and their British imitators. Chamber concerts promoted by individuals – their soirées and matinées musicales, their séances and conversazioni – became an explicit statement of artistic seriousness, and to some extent these chamber series replaced individual benefits. They could even be presented in salon surroundings in an agreeably informal way that yet enforced attention on the music itself; and, if presented in their own homes, such concerts formed an important assertion of a musician's right to be regarded as a member of the literary and artistic community.

The 1855 season will serve to illustrate the direct effect on the benefit concert. Established chamber music societies such as Ella's Musical Union were joined by several short classical series, such as Sterndale Bennett's soirées or Hallé's so-called piano recitals – both consisting of classical piano music and chamber works leavened with vocal music:

Part 1		
Hummel	Quintetto, Op. 87: piano, violin, viola, cello, double bass	Sterndale Bennett, Sainton, Dando, Piatti, Reynolds
Beethoven	Liederkreis [*An die ferne Geliebte*]	Mme Clara Novello
Scarlatti, Handel, Bach	Selection: piano	Sterndale Bennett
Beethoven	Duo [Sonata from] Op. 5: piano, cello	Sterndale Bennett, Piatti
Part 2		
Mozart	Sonata in Bb: piano, violin [?K.454]	Sterndale Bennett, Sainton

[39] *Musical World*, 33 (1855), 121–2.

| Sterndale Bennett | Songs (MS): 'Indian love', 'Winter's gone' | Mme Clara Novello |
| Sterndale Bennett | Capriccio, Suite, Tema con variazioni: piano | Sterndale Bennett |

Sterndale Bennett's First Classical Pianoforte Soirée (13 March 1855, Hanover Square Rooms)
Source: *Musical World*, 33 (1855), 172.

Benefits, of course, approached from a diametrically opposite tradition, stemming from the vocal music and popular virtuoso showpieces. But the addition of serious classical works led to something of a similar mix, a confluence emphasized by the shared salon ambience. Thus a pupil of Sterndale Bennett, R. Harold Thomas, was specifically credited with following his teacher by programming a Beethoven violin sonata and a Mendelssohn cello sonata at his benefit.[40] Several other reviews in the *Musical World* this season directly refer to the dichotomy: thus

> Although entertainments of this kind do not pretend to aim at exclusiveness, and are rather invitations to pupils and friends than direct appeals to public attention or public support, the concert on Wednesday, in some respects, was addressed to the connoisseur, and thereby removed from the category of common benefits.[41]

In this case, a benefit for the Ferraris, the connoisseur was served the 'caviare' of Beethoven's Piano Trio in D (the 'Ghost') and Mendelssohn's Cello Sonata in the same key – though the reviewer noted that as 'the majority of the audience were ladies', these received scant applause. Robert Goldbeck's benefit a few days later at Devonshire House clearly separated the two modes. The first half included another Beethoven trio and piano music by Chopin and Mendelssohn, while the second consisted of Goldbeck's own music 'of a character to suit drawing-room audiences, and certain of the aristocratic *dillettanti* who do not attend the Musical Union'.[42] In similar vein, Mrs John Macfarren was credited with attempting to 'conciliate' the classical and the popular, to reach both the connoisseur and the uninitiated. Her programme at the New Beethoven Rooms set Mozart's G minor Piano Quartet and a Beethoven violin sonata (Ernst 'the incomparable violinist') alongside Thalberg's fantasia on *L'Elisir d'amore*; Mozart arias and Schubert's 'Gretchen' against 'The village blacksmith' and 'Home, sweet home'.[43] Certainly

---

[40] *Musical World*, 33 (1855), 251.
[41] *Musical World*, 33 (1855), 311.
[42] *Musical World*, 33 (1855), 284.
[43] *Musical World*, 33 (1855), 400.

the very replacement of Italian arias with Lieder and vocal duets by Schubert or Mendelssohn was a significant statement, both artistically and socially. Even Giulio Regondi, the celebrated concertina virtuoso, succumbed to classical chamber music: 'The execution of the quartet in F, Op. 18, of Beethoven, by four concertinas, was very satisfactory, considering their difference from stringed instruments; the executants ... maintaining throughout the most perfect *ensemble*.'[44] He also essayed Spohr's Eighth Violin Concerto ('in modo di scena cantante') to show off the expressive vocal qualities he was capable of coaxing from the instrument.

Despite the admission of 'serious' repertoire onto the virtuoso platform – a trend that had transformed concert programmes across Europe by 1865 – the benefit concert remained under attack from earnest commentators, and its demise was constantly predicted, an *idée fixe* of Henry Lunn's contributions to the *Musical Times* during the 1870s. The theatre witnessed fundamental changes in the organization of the season around this time. The introduction of the 'long run' in the 1860s, with the possibility of 200 performances of a single play, heralded a change of attitude among impresarios and some financial stability for actors, swiftly demolishing the benefit as an essential ingredient of a reasonable living. The concert benefit was, however, propelled by somewhat different forces, less intimately tied to an established financial structure and increasingly divorced from the subscription concert series. The doomsayers were again dismayed by a seemingly inexorable proliferation of benefits year after year. Alice Diehl, as we have seen, thought the number of benefits in the 1860s insignificant compared to the 1890s: and her assertion is apparently borne out by the *Musical Directory*, which listed 244 individual concerts during the 1889–90 season in central London alone.

Diehl, like Lunn, dismissed them as harmless ephemeralities, 'private affairs got up by certain artists to sell the tickets among their pupils and friends, and to give away the remainder' (private in a purely facetious sense, of course, since tickets were publicly on sale).[45] Into this category must fall Mrs M. Bolingbroke's evening concert in 1889, at which the printed programme was annotated in manuscript by a sharp-pencilled critic, who was dissatisfied even by one of the leading pianists of the age:

---

[44] *Musical World*, 33 (1855), 395.
[45] Diehl, *Musical Memories*, p. 123.

		'Concert badly attended half empty' '(Friedheim too awful for words)'
Part 1		
Brahms	Violin sonata in G [Op. 78]	Nachez, Arthur Friedheim 'Good (Pianist bad)'
Handel	'Thus saith' – 'But who may abide' [*Messiah*]	Mrs M Bolingbroke 'Amateurish unmusical voice contralto'
Handel	'Oh, worse' – 'Angels, ever bright' (*Theodora*)	Mrs Mary Davies 'as usual *full* of false notes'
Rossini	Duet 'Quis est homo' (*Stabat Mater*)	Fräulein Olga Islar, Mrs M Bolingbroke 'Fearfully tame'
	Violin solos:	
Bach	Chaconne [from BWV 1004]	Nachez
Schumann	'Träumerei' [arr. from *Kinderszenen*, Op. 15]	'very good'
Joachim	Variations	
Gounod	Jewel Song (*Faust*)	Fräulein Olga Islar 'Thin quality of voice good method'
Schubert	Rondo brillant: violin, piano [D.895]	Nachez, Friedheim 'Good'
Part 2		
Charles Dickens [jr.] reads Dickens's 'Boots at the Holly-Tree Inn'		
	[*Martin Chuzzlewit* or *Great Expectations*?]	'well done'
FH Cowen	'Is my lover on the sea' 'Love me if I live'	Mrs M Bolingbroke 'Good'
[Gounod]	'Quando a te lieta' [*Faust*]	'for encore'
	Piano solos:	
Liszt	Rhapsodie	Friedheim
Chopin	Polonaise	('horrible Champion slogger')
	Ballads:	
(Old English)	'The knight's three questions'	Mrs Mary Davies

	'One morn the maiden sought the mill' Violin solos:	'very quaint + pretty'
Rubinstein–Auer	Melodie	Nachez
Moszkowski	'Italy' (*From Foreign Parts* [arr. from *Aus aller Herren Länder*, Op. 23])	'Good'
Schubert	'Du bist die Ruh'	Fräulein Olga Islar
Taubert	''S Lerchle' [Op. 198]	'Good'
Balfe	Duet 'Trust her not' [No. 7 of *Seven Poems by Longfellow*]	Mrs Mary Davies Mrs M Bolingbroke

Conducted by A Randegger and Ernest Ford, pianos by Broadwood and Steinway

Mrs M Bolingbroke's Evening Concert (3 July 1889, Prince's Hall)
Source: British Library, Music c.373. (5).

Nachez was a soloist again at Miss Edith Greenop's afternoon concert at the Steinway Hall on 28 April 1890, where the programme also included a recitation ('Tom's little star'), an air from *Messiah*, English songs and some Chopin; but this time the promoter, a pianist, was considerably more ambitious, taking on both Schumann's *Papillons* and Mendelssohn's Piano Trio in C minor. The programme was typically disparate, an apparently random scattering across the entire spectrum of audience taste; yet at the same time it was also clearly an assertion of serious aspiration by the young pianist, who played 'with highly commendable earnestness and care' in the cautious words of the *Musical World* critic.[46]

Clearly such concerts, whether an act of vanity or a coming-out of the serious *débutante*, come into Alice Diehl's 'harmless' category. But her glib oversimplification disguises the astonishing diversity of concert types during this transitional period, and as yet we lack the data or typologies to analyse this diversity with any accuracy – whether in relation to audiences, performers or repertoire. The *Musical Directory*'s listing is in fact headed 'Miscellaneous Concerts, Soirées, Matinées, Recitals, Etc.'. There is clearly a problem of terminology here, for the term benefit has been dropped altogether (it was last used in the 1879 edition), while at the same time a new concept has been introduced: the solo recital.

---

[46] *Musical World*, 70 (1890), 356.

The first virtuoso concerts in London were those given by Paganini in 1831, a long series of showpiece performances at the end of the season, promoted not as benefits but as unashamed vehicles for solo display and adulation. Initially he appeared at the Opera House in partnership with the manager Pierre Laporte, who took one third of receipts of the order of £1 000 per concert. Paganini followed his usual practice of giving as many concerts in succession as the market would sustain, later controversially moving to the London Tavern in the City, which as Moscheles commented rather acidly 'was thought unworthy of a great artist; but it was all one to him, for he makes money there'.[47] No other performer attempted to exploit the market in quite this way – not even Liszt, whose solo concerts at the Hanover Square Rooms in 1840 are celebrated as the first London piano recitals, the chairs laid out informally, the pianist conversing with the audience between the pieces in true salon manner once again.

Recitals for several decades thereafter, including those of Hallé, mix chamber music and songs into programmes of classical and contemporary piano music. It was not until the rise of an international circuit of travelling virtuosi, supported by agents with world-wide networks and promoted by independent impresarios, that the pure solo recital became established as a norm for pianists and violinists:

Liszt	Sonata in B minor	Stavenhagen
Haydn	Variations in F minor	Stavenhagen
Beethoven	Sonata in Ab, Op. 110	Stavenhagen
Chopin	Nocturne in F [Op. 15 No. 1], Prelude in Db [Op. 28 No. 15]	Stavenhagen
Chopin	Polonaise-Fantaisie, Op. 61	Stavenhagen
Paganini–Liszt	Etudes in C and G# minor	Stavenhagen
Wagner–Liszt	Isolde's Liebestod (*Tristan und Isolde*)	Stavenhagen
Liszt	[Hungarian] Rhapsodie No. 13	Stavenhagen

Stavenhagen's Piano Recital (16 May 1890, St James's Hall)
Source: *Daily Telegraph*, 15 May 1890.

Such recitals represent the final transformation of the benefit, the concentration on a single virtuoso representing the ultimate validation of his professional status, and the unified programme confirming the stability of a concert structure that no longer required the alluring delights of the multicoloured benefit programme.[48] In this new guise, the benefit

---

[47] *Life of Moscheles, by his Wife*, London, 1873, vol. 1, p. 257.
[48] Cf. Weber, *Music and the Middle Class*, pp. 50–51.

had regained its standing as a respected and central part of concert life, now organized on a quite different basis. Agents and promoters such as Vert and Mayer developed a commercial framework on a modern international scale, a world apart from eighteenth-century concepts of patronage built on personal service and obligation. At the same time, they cemented changes in musical taste, for recital programmes were essentially built around the central classical canon and the more serious end of the nineteenth-century virtuoso repertoire. As the *Musical Times* put it in 1888, showing breathtaking assurance in its generalizations:

> Some time ago we commented upon the improvement which has gradually taken place in the quality of the works submitted to the public since the decline of the so-called 'Benefit Concerts,' when showy pianoforte pieces and vocal scraps culled from the popular operas of the day filled a programme of such length as to weary all save those whose sole object was to hear a choice specimen of the powers of as many artists as could be gathered together in one morning; ... but as the taste advanced music of a higher class became necessary to attract cultivated audiences, and upon the ruins of these 'monster' performances arose what are termed 'Recitals,' both vocal and instrumental, where chiefly classical compositions are presented.[49]

Certainly international celebrities such as Paderewski, Albeniz or Sarasate, all of whom visited London in 1890, allied showy virtuosity with serious canonic repertoire as a matter of course, and for such performers the notion of benefit would have seemed a quaint anachronism.

Yet the format of their concerts might still take many shapes, ranging anywhere between the pure solo recital and the old-style medley. Felix Berber, a young violinist of distinction promoted by Daniel Mayer, gave a Grand Evening Concert at the Prince's Hall on 12 June. The virtuoso items were Joachim's 'Hungarian' Concerto (with piano accompaniment) and a Vieuxtemps solo, but Berber also gave the London première of Sinding's Piano Quintet and led a string quartet arrangement of Liszt's 'Angelus'; piano music by Liszt and Chaikovsky, and a group of Lieder, made up the rest of the programme.[50] Though billed as a violin recital, Willy Hess's concert on 3 June interleaved a surprising range of songs and duets by Cimarosa, Beethoven, Henschel and Arthur Hervey into his chronological survey of the violin repertoire (Bach, Rust, Paganini, Ernst, Saint-Saëns).[51] Conversely vocal recitals often incorporate piano, violin or cello solos, and indeed might be shared with other singers. At the same time, some of the biggest stars, such as Paderewski

---

[49] *Musical Times*, 29 (1888), 406.
[50] *Daily Telegraph*, 10 June 1890; *Musical World*, 70 (1890), 496.
[51] *Daily Telegraph*, 27 May 1890; *Musical World*, 70 (1890), 456.

and Sarasate, demanded the larger stage of an orchestral context, without any vocal distractions:

Grieg	Suite *Peer Gynt*	
Lalo	Symphonie Espagnole [Op. 21]: violin, orchestra	Sarasate
Raff	*Die Liebesfee* [Op. 67]: violin, orchestra	Sarasate
Liszt	*Angelus*: strings [arr. from *Années de pèlerinage*, vol.3]	
Saint-Saëns	Jota aragonese [Op. 64]	
Sarasate	*Zigeunerweiser* [Op. 20]: violin, orchestra	Sarasate
Chopin	Nocturne in Eb [?Op. 9 No. 2]: violin	Sarasate [encore]
Wagner	Overture *Tannhäuser*	

Conductor: WG Cusins

Sarasate's Second Concert (14 June 1890, St James's Hall)
Source: *Daily Telegraph*, 11 June 1890; review in *Musical World*, 70 (1890), 497.

Albeniz's First Grand Orchestral Concert on 7 November 1890 similarly alternated the orchestral music of contemporary Spanish composers with performances of Mozart's 'Coronation' Concerto, the Schumann concerto, one of Liszt's Hungarian Fantasies and a set of solo piano pieces of his own.[52]

It is therefore difficult to confirm the unambiguous trend from miscellaneous benefits to classical recitals claimed by the contributor to the *Musical Times*, as in practice mixed programmes positioned themselves in varying degrees between the two possible extremes. Nevertheless the broad notion of the piano recital, the violin recital, the song recital and the chamber recital had become established by the 1890s, and still more specialized concerts were familiar – the all-Beethoven piano recitals favoured by Hallé, concerts of music by Russian composers or featuring the music of women composers such as Maude Valérie White;[53] or Fanny Davies's programme of music by Schumann and her teacher Clara given on 11 June 1890:

---

[52] Programme in British Library, Music c.371. (3).

[53] See the programme of Madame A. Svetloffsky's concert in British Library, Music d.487. During the 1890s White promoted several concerts of her own music (for example at the Prince's Hall on 24 June 1892); cf. also *Musical Times*, 35 (1894), 514, on the development of the one-man or one-woman programme (information kindly provided by Sophie Fuller).

C Schumann	Piano trio in G minor, Op. 17	Miss Fanny Davies, L Straus, Piatti
R Schumann	Three Lieder	Miss Fillunger
R Schumann	Kreisleriana, Op. 16	Miss Fanny Davies
C Schumann	Three Lieder	Miss Fillunger
R Schumann	Sketch in F minor, Canon in A♭	Miss Fanny Davies
C Schumann	Scherzo in D minor [Op. 10]	Miss Fanny Davies

Miss Fanny Davies's Grand Morning Concert (11 June 1890, Princes' Hall)
Source: Programme in British Library, Music c.373. (5).

It was in this same year that Arnold Dolmetsch gave his first public recital of 'early music', introducing his daughter Hélène on the viola da gamba.

Clearly this period calls for much more comprehensive and detailed study, especially into the mechanisms of concert promotion, which may well prove of even more fundamental importance than programming. There had already been far-reaching changes in ticketing policy, with prices much further stretched to reach audiences familiar with classical master-works from the relatively cheap Crystal Palace and Chappell's Popular Concerts. In 1890 individual concert prices typically range down in steps from half a guinea to one shilling. Though there were still many 'annual grand concerts' in the old benefit tradition, the concept was quickly being supplanted by more modern patterns of concert organization and planning. Both a more elevated musical taste, based around the canonization of the classics, and a more clearly ordered and stratified concert structure eventually worked against the benefit concert. By 1910, the *Musical Directory* heading has changed again to 'Concerts, Recitals, Etc.', and the vast majority of individual concerts are solo or chamber recitals at London's premier venues, the Aeolian, Bechstein and Steinway Halls. The benefit in its old form did not survive the First World War, but it had lasted far longer through the nineteenth century than anyone would have predicted – or than most modern commentators have been able to credit.

PART SEVEN
Analysis and Criticism

CHAPTER FOURTEEN

Towards a Tradition of Music Analysis in Britain in the Nineteenth Century

Catherine Dale

Although the nineteenth century was a period of intense analytical activity in Europe characterized by the writings of A. B. Marx,[1] Reicha,[2] Momigny,[3] Riemann,[4] Sechter,[5] Czerny,[6] Vogler,[7] Gottfried Weber,[8] Lobe[9] and Cherubini[10] to name but some of the principal theorists, Britain was, by comparison, generally regarded on the Continent not only as 'the land without music'[11] but also as 'the land without music analysis'. It was a country in which, as Donald Francis Tovey protested in his *Essays and Lectures in Music*, 'a person of general culture is a person who knows nothing about music and cannot abide musical jargon'.[12] Indeed, Tovey (1875–1940) himself is widely considered to be the first significant 'pioneer' of music analysis in Britain, 'the grand

---

[1] A. B. Marx, *Die Lehre von der musikalischen Komposition, praktisch-theoretisch*, 4 vols, Leipzig, 1837–47; A.B. Marx, 'Die Form in der Musik', in J. A. Romberg (ed.), *Die Wissenschaft im neunzehnten Jahrhundert, ihr Standpunkt und die Resultate ihrer Forschurgen*, vol. 2, Leipzig, 1856.

[2] A. Reicha, *Traité de Mélodie*, Par s, 1814, 2nd edn, 1832; A. Reicha, *Cours de composition musicale ou Traité complet et raisonné d'harmonie pratique*, Paris, 1816–18; A. Reicha, *Traité de haute composition musicale*, Paris, 1824–26.

[3] J.-J. de Momigny, *Cours complet d'harmonie et de composition*, Paris, 1803–05.

[4] H. Riemann, *Grosse Kompositionslehre*, 3 vols, Berlin and Stuttgart, 1902–13; H. Riemann, *Handbuch der Harmonie*, 4th edn, Leipzig, 1906.

[5] S. Sechter, *Die Grundsätze der musikischon Komposition*, 3 vols, Leipzig, 1853–54.

[6] C. Czerny, *School of Practical Composition, or Complete Treatise on the Composition of All Kinds of Music ... Together with a Treatise on Instrumentation*, op. 600, 3 vols, London, 1848; repr. New York, 1979.

[7] G. J. Vogler, *Handbuch zur Harmonie und für den Generalbass, nachden Grundsätze der Mannheimer Tonschule*, Prague, 1802.

[8] G. Weber, *Versach einer geordneten Theorie der Tonsetzkunst*, Mainz, 1817–21.

[9] J. C. Lobe, *Lehrbuch der musikalischen Komposition*, 4 vols, Leipzig, 1850–67.

[10] L. Cherubini, *Cours de contre-point et de fugue*, Paris, 1835.

[11] W. I. Turner, *English Music*, London, 1941, p. 7.

[12] D. F. Tovey, *Essays and Lectures on Music*, with an introduction by H. J. Foss, London, 1949, p. 134.

old man of British analytical history'.[13] This is a comparatively recent history, however, since most of Tovey's principal texts – *A Companion to Beethoven's Pianoforte Sonatas* (1931), *A Companion to 'The Art of Fugue' (Die Kunst der Fuge) J. S. Bach* (1931), the *Essays in Musical Analysis* (1935–39; 1944), major essays on Gluck, Haydn, Beethoven, Schubert and Brahms, and the revisions of the *Encyclopaedia Britannica* articles for the 14th edition (1944) – date from the period after 1927; in this respect his inclusion in a volume devoted to nineteenth-century studies may seem anachronistic. It may be argued, however, that most of Tovey's ideas concerning music were in fact fully formed during the closing years of the previous century and his biographer Mary Grierson[14] describes a *magnum opus* on musical aesthetics which he planned during his undergraduate days at Oxford and worked on between 1898 and 1900, which contained the embryo of all Tovey's later writings, a hypothesis which is borne out by the fact that some of the *Essays* in *Musical Analysis* appeared as early as 1902 and his study of 'The Classical Concerto' in volume 3 dates from 1903. In these early works the style and ideas may already be described as fundamentally 'Toveyan' and reveal no significant difference to those of his later writings.

In a now famous article dating from 1950 in which Joseph Kerman undertook the unenviable task of defending Tovey against the rising tide of criticism of his innate conservatism, Kerman makes the point rather more directly: 'Tovey effectively died as a critic in 1905'.[15] Indeed, he maintains that 'every fragment of his opinion was hardened'[16] by this date, and all his subsequent writings were merely refinements of these initial ideas; he springs to his subject's defence, seeking to justify Tovey's conservatism with the observation that 'In 1900 Victorian dogma was not yet entirely disgraced; Tovey's mind was made up before the popularity of iconoclasm and the more sophisticated trends of modern criticism'.[17] The major influences and traditions on which this late Victorian man of letters drew thus lay entirely within the nineteenth century, and although this chapter will consider Tovey's views within the context of those of his European predecessors and contemporaries, it will argue that Britain, far from being the 'analytical wilderness' described above, already possessed a threefold tradition of technical,

---

[13] J. Dunsby and A. Whittall, *Music Analysis in Theory and Practice*, London, 1988, p. 73.

[14] M. Grierson, *Donald Frances Tovey: A Biography Based on Letters*, London, 1952.

[15] J. Kerman, 'Counsel for the Defense', *Hudson Review*, 3, (1950), 444.

[16] Ibid., p. 443.

[17] Ibid., p. 444.

pedagogical and 'programme-note' style analysis that contributed significantly to Tovey's own idiosyncratic style of music analysis.

Although 'technical' analysis had effectively been practised for more than two centuries, it was not until the beginning of the twentieth century that it began to detach itself from the eighteenth- and nineteenth-century study of compositional theory, and establish itself as a separate and systematic discipline. What issued from the pens of Tovey and the like under the name of technical analysis in Britain could hardly be equated with the more rigorous discipline known in Germany as *Musikwissenschaft*, however, and Allen Forte characterizes the period as one in which there was 'little new musical theory in the sense of systematic approaches to general problems of musical structure'. Indeed, he emphasizes the dependence of the discipline on nineteenth-century theoretical thought: 'Instead theory was generally only a classroom discipline, and theory textbooks were usually pastiches of nineteenth-century writings by A. B. Marx, Bellermann, Sechter, Reicha, Cherubini and others. The subjects included harmony stemming from Rameau, species counterpoint stemming from Fux, fugue, and eighteenth- and nineteenth-century forms.'[18]

The British readership relied principally upon the Riemann-inspired writings of Ebenezer Prout on instrumentation, harmony, counterpoint and double counterpoint, fugue and fugal analysis dating from 1878 to 1895.[19] The practical application of Prout's theories of fugue may be seen in his *Analysis of J. S. Bach's Forty-Eight Fugues (Das Wohltemperirte Clavier)*, published in 1910, which consists of an introductory list of definitions of the constituent parts and techniques of fugue, and a more general definition in which he describes fugue as a ternary form divided according to key structure or methods of treatment. The ensuing analyses consist of prose descriptions of each formal section of the fugue, in each case quoting the subject and examples of inversion and motivic fragmentation, and noting the key scheme and any departures from the definitions stated in the introduction. A representative passage of Prout's method is illustrated by his analysis of Fugue no. 2 in C minor from Bach's *Forty-Eight Preludes and Fugues*, shown in Figure 14.1.

---

[18] A. Forte, 'Theory', in J. Vinton (ed.), *Dictionary of Twentieth-Century Music*, London, 1974, p. 754.

[19] E. Prout, *Instrumentation*, London, 1878; E. Prout, *Harmony: Its Theory and Practice*, London, 1889, rev. 1903; E. Prout, *Counterpoint, Strict and Free*, London, 1890; E. Prout, *Fugue*, London, 1891; E. Prout, *Fugal Analysis*, London, 1892; E. Prout, *Double Counterpoint and Canon*, London, 1893; E. Prout, *Musical Form*, London, 1893; E. Prout, *Applied Forms: A Sequel to 'Musical Form'*, London, 1895; E. Prout, *Analysis of J. S. Bach's Forty-Eight Fugues (Das Wohltemperirte Clavier)*, L.B. Prout (ed.), London, 1910.

Analysis of J. S. Bach's

FUGUE 2
C MINOR (THREE VOICES).

Exposition.—This fugue is not only much simpler but much more regular in form than No. 1. Its subject is announced in the alto :—

The leap from tonic to dominant in the first bar requires a leap from dominant to tonic in the answer, which is therefore **tonal.** The answer is given to the treble, while the alto continues with a countersubject, which begins on B natural; the third semiquaver of bar 3, and ends on the first note of bar 5. This countersubject accompanies the subject or answer on every appearance throughout the fugue except the final one in the coda (bar 29).

Between the end of the answer and the next entry of the subject a codetta is introduced (bars 5 to 7). The upper part is founded on a sequential treatment of the first notes of the subject, a descending sixth being substituted for a fourth. The alto, also sequential, is formed from the commencement of the countersubject taken by contrary motion. At bar 7 the bass enters with the subject, the countersubject being now taken, according to rule, by the treble—the voice that had just before given the answer. The exposition is now complete.

Middle Section.—The first episode (bars 9, 10), with which the middle section of the fugue begins, consists of an imitation between the two upper parts of the opening notes (a) of the subject, accompanied by the descending scale passage with which the

Figure 14.1   Analysis of Bach, Fugue no. 2 in C minor from E. Prout, *Analysis of J. S. Bach's Forty-Eight Fugues, (Das Wohltemperierte Clavier),* Louis B. Prout (ed.), London, 1910, p. 14

An earlier example of fugal analysis in Britain may be seen in Samuel Wesley and C. F. Horn's *New and Correct Edition of the Preludes and Fugues of John Sebastian Bach*, published in London in 1810–13. Wesley and Horn's analyses, like those of Reicha and Cherubini, present the score with symbolic, structural annotations but no accompanying text. They state in their Introduction that the engraving includes 'Annotations, explanatory of the several ingenious and surprizing Contrivances in the Treatment of the Subject throughout all the Fugues'.[20] The symbols, shown in Figure 14.2, indicate whether the subjects are in normal form, inverted, in diminution or augmentation; combinations of techniques are indicated by means of compound symbols. Example 14.1 presents their analysis of the opening bars of Fugue no. 2 for comparison with Prout's.

Tovey's discussion of fugue in his Encyclopaedia Britannica article demonstrates his abhorrence of rigid formal schemes, examined more fully below. He writes, 'Fugue is a texture the rules of which do not suffice to determine the shape of the composition as a whole. Schemes such as that laid down in Cherubini's treatise, which legislate for the shape, are pedagogic fictions'.[21] and his own analyses combine aspects of both nineteenth-century British precedents discussed above. Like Wesley and Horn he presents the score in full with similar symbolic annotations: $\wedge$ = subject; CS = countersubject; $\square$ = diminution; V = inversion and $\overset{*}{\wedge}$ = variation. His symbols are less versatile than those of Wesley and Horn, however, and he is obliged to qualify these throughout with prose comments. Like Prout, he indicates the motivic constituents of the subject and countersubject by means of lower case letters, as shown in Example 14.2.

The principal representatives of the more rigorous technical study of music analysis in Britain were Edwin Evans senior and Charles F. Abdy Williams. The aims of Evans's *Handbook to the Chamber and Orchestral Music of Johannes Brahms. 2nd Series*, subtitled 'Historical and Descriptive Account of Each Work with Exhaustive Structural, Thematic and Rhythmical Analyses, and a Rhythmical Chart of Each Movement' are indeed exhaustive and contain numerous pedagogical 'asides' to the student, warning him against the current trend of impressionistic criticism. He asserts that in order to supply the student with an accurate knowledge of the work 'nothing can be effective but analysis reaching to the rhythmical significance of every bar;

---

[20] S. Wesley and C. F. Horn, *New and Correct Edition of the Preludes and Fugues of John Sebastian Bach*, London, 1810–13, p. iii.

[21] D. F. Tovey, *Musical Articles from Encyclopaedia Britannica*, with an editorial preface by H. J. Foss, London, 1944, p. 36.

The present Edition is characterized not only by Clearness, and Precision in the Text, and the Manner of engraving it, but also by Annotations, explanatory of the several ingenious and surprizing Contrivances in the Treatment of the Subject throughout all the Fugues.

The following Marks are employed for the aforesaid Purpose.

⟨⟩ points out the Subject in its direct Ratio, or in its natural Order in the Scale of Intervals chosen for it.

⟨⟩ denotes the contrary, and that the Subject is inverted at the Interval where this Mark is applied.

⟨⟩⟨2⟩⟨3⟩ these shew that either the first, second, or third Subject (if so many are employed) are repeated in direct Ratio.

⟨⟩⟨2⟩⟨3⟩ denote the contrary, as in the Explanation of the second Mark above.

▯ shews that the Subject is diminished in its Measure, by one Half, or repeated in Interval as quick again as at first.

⇨ means that the Subject is diminished and inverted at the same Time.

▭ shews that the Subject is augmented in double Ratio, or that it is repeated in Intervals just as slow again as before.

Figure 14.2 Symbolic annotations of fugue from S. Wesley and C. F. Horn, *New and Correct Edition of the Preludes and Fugues of John Sebastian Bach*, London, 1810–13, p. iii

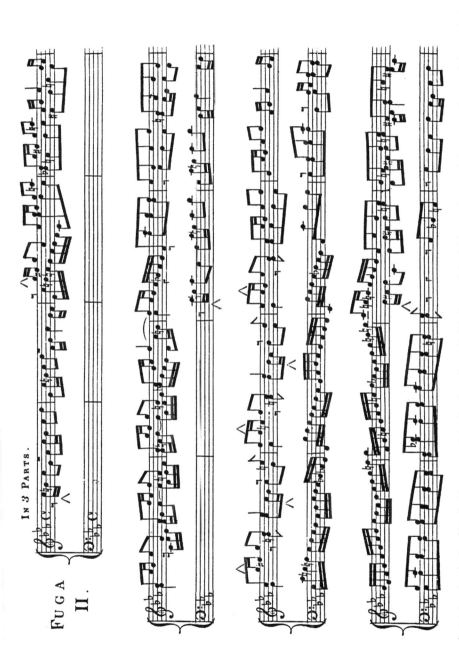

Example 14.1 Analysis of Bach, Fugue no. 2 in C minor from S. Wesley and C. F. Horn, *New and Correct Edition of the Preludes and Fugues of John Sebastian Bach*, London, 1810–13, p. 8

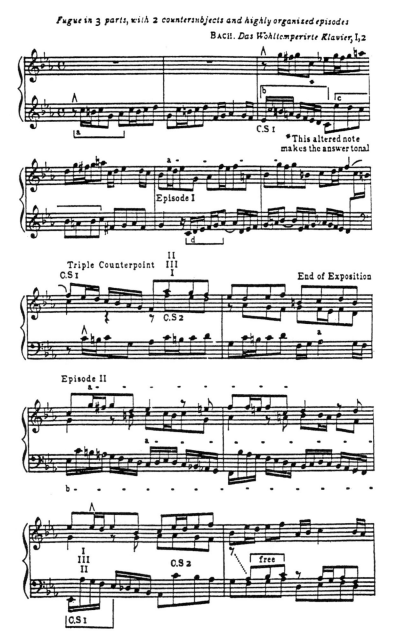

Example 14.2   Analysis of Bach, Fugue no. 2 in C minor from D. F. Tovey, 'Fugue', in his *Musical Articles from the Encyclopaedia Britannica*, with an editorial preface by H. J. Foss, London, 1944, p. 41

accounting for all material, whether subjects or intermediate motives; laying bare all formal proportions and developments; and fully describing all contrasts and characteristic features'.[22] The analyses of the works follow the same plan in each case and the quasi-scientific aspirations of these are expressed explicitly in Evans's inclusion of a 'Preliminary Note' to each work, the object of which is to outline details of a general or historical character in order to 'exclude from the articles under movement-headings everything which is not strictly technical comment'.[23]

The analyses begin with a complete rhythmical table of every movement, the purpose of which is to ascertain

1. The proportion of the entire extent which is assigned to statement of first, second or third subjects separately.
2. The relation between thematic material as stated in opening and at the return respectively.
3. The proportion allowed to Durchführung and Coda separately and the relation of these to one another.
4. The extent of purely episodial matter and that of theme development.
5. Particulars of all phrase-extensions.[24]

The rhythmical table reproduced as Table 14.1 illustrates the material and proportions of the first subject of the opening *allegro* of Brahms's First Piano Trio, Op. 8, and the internal divisions in the phrase structure (8 + 4, 8 + 4 + 3) in the manner of Tovey's 'technical' analyses in the *Companion to Beethoven's Pianoforte Sonatas*. The aim of the rhythmical table for a complete movement, Evans claims, is to bring 'one part of a movement to the elucidation of another',[25] that is, to reveal the relationships between sections. The analyses proceed with the discussion and musical quotation of the principal subjects, and conclude with what Evans terms an 'Epitome' of the movement in which he quotes any subjects which have not already appeared in the preceding discussion, summarizes the key structure, time signature, noting any changes, and length, concluding with a final table of the 'outline' of the entire movement. The 'outline' of the first movement of Brahms's Op. 8 is shown in Table 14.2. The degree of objectivity Evans sought in his

---

22 E. Evans snr, *Handbook to the Chamber and Orchestral Music of Johannes Brahms. 2nd Series*, London, 1935, p. 1.
23 Ibid., p. 2.
24 Ibid., p. 18.
25 Ibid., p. 3.

Table 14.1   The material and proportions of the first subject of the opening *allegro* of Brahms's First Piano Trio, Op. 8

Portion of movement	Description of material	No. of bars	Composed of	Extending to Bar
First Section (part of)	1st subject	12	8 + 4	12
		8	4 × 2	20
		15	8 + 4 + 3	35
		9	8 + 1	44
	Episodial principally	10*	8 + 2	54
		8*	8	62
		5	4 + 1	67
		8	4 × 2	75
	Introducing 2nd subject	8	4 × 2	83
Totals		83		83

Source: Evans, E. snr, *Handbook to the Chamber and Orchestral Music of Johannes Brahms. 2nd Series*, London, 1935, p. 18.

Table 14.2   The 'outline' of the first movement of Brahms's First Piano Trio, Op. 8

First section	Durchführung	Return	Coda
117	70	58	35

I	II	III			I	II	III	
83	26	8			26	26	6	

Source: Evans, E. snr, *Handbook to the Chamber and Orchestral Music of Johannes Brahms. 2nd Series*, London, 1935, p. 25.

purely technical brand of analysis is apparent in the concluding paragraph of his introduction in which he claims to have adopted

> a plan well calculated to restrain all play of personal feeling on our part. To subject a musical composition to minute analysis is to place it upon the scales of justice ... The results of this method of judgement are various, but that the general verdict to which they point admits of no doubt cannot at all events be imputed to any advocacy of partisan character.[26]

---

[26] Ibid., p. 3.

Williams's aims in *The Rhythm of Modern Music* (1909) are similarly objective since it is through rhythm, he maintains, that 'pleasant sounds' that appeal to the ear are regulated in such a way as to make them appeal to the intellect also: 'The satisfaction that is given us when musical sound is allied to Rhythm is intellectual.'[27] After a brief historical account of the development of rhythm from the sixteenth century to Williams's own time, the technical study proper begins with thorough definitions of his terms by analogy with poetic ones. The analyses take the form of annotations to the scores indicating periodic structure, measure numbers, anacruses, extensions, overlaps and masculine and feminine endings, and although the early examples are drawn almost exclusively from Beethoven and Brahms, the later ones do indeed extend to more 'modern music', including Tchaikovsky, D'Indy, Debussy, Stanford and Elgar. Example 14.3 shows the third movement (*Adagio*) of the latter's Symphony, No. 1 which demonstrates clearly Williams's method of annotating a piano reduction of the score. In more complex orchestral textures in which different rhythmic strata are overlaid he presents an abstract rhythmic model, as in Example 14.4 from the first movement of Tchaikovsky's *Symphonie Pathétique*.

It was not these scientifically rigorous volumes that set the standard for technical analysis in Britain, however. In a climate in which, it may be recalled, 'a person of general culture … cannot abide musical jargon', they were doomed to failure from the outset, and it was rather Tovey's own more 'populist critical dogma'[28] that made *him* 'the most widely read music critic in English-speaking countries'.[29] A contemporary review of Evans commented upon the current reaction against detailed analysis of music: 'It is called "dissection" (the word being used in a disparaging sense)',[30] and it was Tovey's own brand of 'technical' analysis, particularly that found in his *Companion to Beethoven's Pianoforte Sonatas*, that established the principal *modus operandi* for the discipline and seemed to offer the way forward for British music analysis.

On the surface, his 'bar-to-bar' method appears similar to that of Evans, but Tovey does not aspire to the scientific verifiability of Evans's work and constantly places the aesthetic effect of the music above objective rationality. His method is thus, as Ian Bent observes, 'a blend

---

27 C. F. A. Williams, *The Rhythm of Modern Music*, London, 1909, p. 4.

28 J. Kerman, 'Tovey's Beethoven', in A. Tyson (ed.), *Beethoven Studies*, vol. 2, London, 1977, p. 175.

29 Ibid., p. 172.

30 [Evans], Initialled review of Evans's 1935 *Handbook* … , in *Musical Times*, **112** (77), (1936), p. 803.

Example 14.3   Rhythmic analysis of Elgar, Symphony in A flat, Op. 55, movement III (*Adagio*) from C. F. A. Williams, *The Rhythm of Modern Music*, London, 1909, p. 300

Example 14.4   Rhythmic analysis of Tchaikovsky, *Symphonie Pathétique*, Op. 74, movement I from C. F. A. Williams, *The Rhythm of Modern Music*, London, 1909, p. 243

of the hermeneutic and the formalistic which implicitly stated that there are things in music beyond explanation',[31] and in the introduction to his method of harmonic analysis in the *Companion to Beethoven's Pianoforte Sonatas* Tovey maintains that 'it is better to know no "theory" at all than to drift into such a deafness to all dramatic expression in music. Harmonic analysis is useful only when it illustrates the composer's rhetorical power'.[32] His method of analysis follows the musical précis-writing style of Sir Hubert Parry. It proceeds from bar to bar

as the music pursues its course, and where several facts overlap they are stated in the order of their function in the design. Thus,

---

[31] I. D. Bent, 'Analysis', in S. Sodie (ed.), *The New Grove Dictionary of Music and Musicians*, vol. 1, London, p. 364.
[32] D. F. Tovey, *A Companion to Beethoven's Pianoforte Sonatas*, London, 1948, p. 5.

when a whole section is in a certain key, the key is mentioned at the
head of the paragraph; and, if it is not the tonic, its relation thereto
is mentioned ... Then the music is taken phrase by phrase. The first
point is the length of the phrase, and, together therewith the way in
which it is subdivided: – e.g., ... (6 + 4).
     ... In analysis the parts of themes that become detached and
recombined in various ways of development may be quoted and
identified by letters.[33]

The result of his synchronic method of analysis in which musical
events occur on the rhythmic surface is that many of Tovey's observations concern foreground temporal processes such as phraseology,
expectation and arrival and the pacing of events, and in this respect the
influence of his work may be readily perceived in that of a number of
later English-speaking analysts, notably Joseph Kerman,[34] James
Webster[35] and Charles Rosen,[36] particularly in the latter's assertion of
the primacy of tonal over thematic structure. In spite of this emphasis
on foreground structure, many of Tovey's analyses nevertheless encourage long-range linear hearing akin to the Schenkerian concept of
prolongation through the emphasis he placed on bass *Auskomponierung*
in preference to scale-steps and the identification of chordal roots prescribed by fundamental bass theory. One example to which Tovey referred
both in the introduction to his method of harmonic analysis in the
Companion to Beethoven's Pianoforte Sonatas and the article on 'Sonata Forms' in the *Encyclopaedia Britannica* was Beethoven's treatment
of the rising bass line in the second subject of the first movement of his
Piano Sonata, Op. 2, No. 2. In the first of these Tovey writes:

> Students ought to know that the second group in the first move-
> ment of Op. 2, No. 2 contains a series of remote enharmonic
> modulations; but the student who most rejoices in identifying the
> roots of the diminished sevenths concerned therein will be very
> likely to miss the enormously more important point that the bass is
> steadily rising. Indeed, students have been known to fail to recog-
> nize any change when roots have been substituted for that rising
> bass,[37]

---

[33] Ibid., p. 4.

[34] Kerman, 'Counsel for the Defense', pp. 438–46; Kerman, 'Tovey's Beethoven', pp.
172–91; J. Kerman, 'The Grove of Academe, reviews of selected articles on nineteenth-
century topics in *The New Grove Dictionary of Music and Musicians*, ed. Stanley Sadie
(Macmillan, 1980: 20 vols); Tovey, Sir Donald Francis, 'Michael Tilmouth', *19th Century
Music*, 5 (1981–82), pp. 168–9.

[35] J. Webster, 'Schubert, Sonata Form and Brahms's First Maturity', *19th Century
Music*, 2 (1978–79), pp. 18–35, and 3 (1979–80), pp. 52–71.

[36] C. Rosen, *The Classical Style: Haydn, Mozart, Beethoven*, London, 1972; C. Rosen,
Sonata Forms, New York, 1980.

[37] Tovey, *Musical Articles*, pp. 4–5.

whilst in the second he provides a skeleton reduction of the passage
which illustrates the rising bass, reproduced as Example 14.5. Moreover, his analysis of key relations in the first movement of Schubert's
String Quintet in the essay 'Tonality in Schubert'[38] demonstrates the use
of rhythmic notation in order to give hierarchical meaning to a tonal
reduction of the principal key areas, as shown in Example 14.6.

That these aspects of Tovey's analyses remain implicit in his method-
ology is in part a function of the readership to whom his writings were
directed. Like his Austrian contemporary Heinrich Schenker (1868–
1935), Tovey aimed to elucidate the mainstream of classical music
which, for him, extended from Alessandro Scarlatti to Brahms, and his
criterion for entry to this *élite corpus* of masterpieces – that of formal
perfection determined by the direction of the tonality – is clearly reminiscent of Schenker's own. Tovey's writings were addressed not to
Schenker's 'expert', however, but to a personage of his own invention,
the 'naïve listener', ostensibly unschooled in the language of music and
trusting only to his own naïve reactions and, of course, his steadfast
guide in all matters musical, Tovey himself.

The nature of Tovey's work suggests strongly that this was not in fact
the case, however, and his technical analyses presuppose a considerable
degree of musical literacy. He writes in *Essays and Lectures on Music*,
for example, that 'a conception so elementary and vital to the art of
Beethoven as classical tonality, is utterly unidentifiable by anybody
without some practice in actually reading music',[39] and this, together
with the fact that the 'not-so-naïve-listener' is expected to be conversant
with the concepts and terminology of musical forms, double counterpoint, stretto and the like, leaves one with the distinct impression that
Tovey's naïve listener has, as Kerman maintained, 'at least a pass degree
from Oxford University'.[40]

Tovey's acknowledgement of the overtly populist aims of his work led
him to place less emphasis on certain aspects, however, and this inevitably created flaws in his work. For there can be no doubt, as Hans Keller
claims, that 'Tovey was a great musician. His writings are a symptom of
a social tragedy, for they are both a function of the stupidity of his
audiences, the musical *nouveaux riches*, and too much of a mere reaction against the unmusicality of his academic forebears'.[41] Thus, Tovey
credits the naïve listener with only limited capacities for tonal memory

---

[38] Tovey, *Essays and Lectures*, p. 150.

[39] Ibid., p. 271.

[40] Kerman, 'Tovey's Beethoven', p. 175.

[41] H. Keller, 'K. 503: The Unity of Contrasting Themes and Movements – I', *Music Review*, 17 (1956), p. 49.

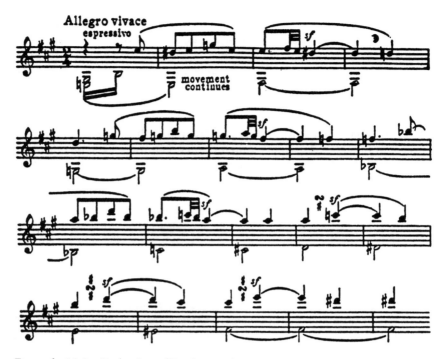

Example 14.5   Reduction of Beethoven, Piano Sonata, Op. 2, No. 2, movement
                I, bars 58–75 from D. F. Tovey, 'Sonata Forms', in his *Musical
                Articles from the Encyclopaedia Britannica*, with an editorial
                preface by H. J. Foss, London, 1944, p. 219

1st movement

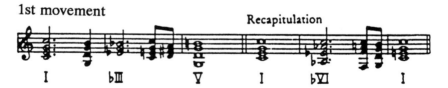

Example 14.6   Key relations in Schubert's String Quintet in C major, movement
                I from D. F. Tovey, 'Tonality in Schubert', in his *Essays and
                Lectures on Music*, with an introduction by H. J. Foss, London,
                1949, p. 150

and aural perception. In the *Companion to Beethoven's Pianoforte
Sonatas*, for example, he expresses the belief that 'after even one change
of key confirmed beyond the limits of a lyric melody, the original tonic
is recognized only by collateral evidence',[42] and he doubts whether the

---

[42] Tovey, *A Companion*, p. 26.

naïve listener is able to follow more than even two strands of a fugue concurrently. In this context, Tovey's most radical gesture was perhaps the introduction of even the most modest technical element into music criticism.

Yet he persisted with his notion of the naïve listener since he held firmly the typically Victorian conviction that art, like knowledge, should be democratically available to all. In his altruistic aim to educate his readers, Tovey aligned himself with such Victorian philanthropists as Henry Sidgwick, the Reverend H. R. Haweis, James Sully, Croom Robertson, F. W. Maitland and, particularly, in the field of music, Edmund Gurney (1847–88). Gurney's principal work on music, *The Power of Sound* (1880), represented a significant contribution to nineteenth-century musical aesthetics and theory, ranging from the physiology and psychology of musical perception to performance, criticism and formal structure, especially melodic structure. He considered music a national possession, and in an essay entitled 'A Permanent Band for the East End' he admits a sense of social responsibility towards 'those whose lives are struggling and forlorn'.[43] Indeed, he saw it as the social duty of the better-off to provide the masses with musical experience and strongly opposed the Wagnerian view that music should 'emanate from special performances for an *élite* few at some favoured centre'.[44]

The didactic aims of Tovey, expressed not least in his frequent asides to the student, and of the Victorian philanthropists were paralleled in more practical terms by the pedagogical wing of the mass education movement that gained increasing impetus in Britain in the nineteenth century following the awarding of government grants to education in 1833 and 1839. Although different in approach, it may be argued that the methods of these pedagogues proved equally relevant to the growth of music analysis in Britain since the application of a set of symbolical signs to the teaching of rhythm and pitch clearly presupposes an analytical act of interpretation; moreover, the adoption of a hierarchical classification of key relationships as a means of teaching modulation is reminiscent of Tovey's own 'Table of Key-Relationships' in the *Encyclopaedia Britannica* article on 'Harmony',[45] and other models proposed by nineteenth- and twentieth-century European theorists, notably, Arnold Schoenberg.

At a conference of Sunday school teachers held in Hull in 1841 the Reverend John Curwen was assigned the task of finding the most appropriate method of teaching singing. His aims were therefore as much

---

[43] E. Gurney, 'A Permanent Band for the East End', *Tertium Quid*, vol. 2, London, 1887, p. 99.

[44] E. Gurney, 'Wagner and Wagnerism', *Tertium Quid*, vol. 2, London, 1887, p. 92.

[45] Tovey, *Musical Articles*, pp. 62–3.

social and religious as purely musical. Curwen's early investigations led him to reject Pestalozzi's principles and the continental method currently taught in the 'singing schools' organized by John Hullah (1812–84), according to which pupils identified notes on the staff by sol-fa names which were permanently related to the key of C. Curwen observed the confusion that resulted when other keys were introduced, and adopted instead an indigenous system of sol-fa employed by Sarah Glover, a Norwich schoolmistress, in her *Scheme for Rendering Psalmody Congregational* (1835). Thus began the debate between the 'fixed' doh of the continental method and the 'movable' doh of Glover and Curwen.

Glover's method was a deductive one, proceeding from practice to theory, since she was concerned primarily with the aural effect of note relationships. She used the sol-fa initials, notated as capital letters, to represent the scale degrees, with the introduction of bah and ne for the sixth and seventh of the minor scale, whilst pulse and rhythm were indicated by equally spaced barlines with subsidiary beats separated by equidistant punctuation marks. The pitching of intervals was taught from her 'Norwich sol-fa ladder' (Plate 14.1) and it was this that formed the basis of Curwen's 'Modulator'; the most notable difference between the two was that Glover placed the symbol for the tonic midway in the octave, which she regarded as two conjunct tetrachords: sol-doh and doh-fah. The columns to the left and right of the central one show the related keys of the dominant and subdominant respectively.

Curwen's system of 'interpreting notation', designated 'Tonic Sol-fa' in order to emphasize its key-centred nature as opposed to the 'fixed' sol-fa advocated by Hullah, was essentially a refinement of Glover's method. It designated pitch by means of lower case sol-fa initials (Figure 14.3) and register by superscript and subscript commas (Figure 14.4). Chromatic notes, indicating transient modulation, were notated by changing the vowel of the sol-fa name, as shown in Example 14.7. In the case of extended modulation the new tonic is designated 'doh' and the transition is expressed by means of a 'bridge note' with a double name. In Example 14.8 the first name relates to the old key, the second to the new key, and the bridge note is sung as *s'doh*. Curwen's method does not employ key signatures but states the name of the key above the symbols at the beginning of a melody and at each point of modulation. Similarly, his notation of rhythm does not use time signatures but is based rather on two principal symbols: the barline and the colon. The barline functions as in staff notation whilst the colon precedes every weak beat within a bar. Subsidiary accents within bars are indicated by shortened barlines and equal beats are represented on the page by equal lateral spacing. Rhythmic figures are thus projected against a visible metrical background, as shown in Figure 14.5. Much of the pupil's early vocal experience

Plate 14.1   Sarah Glover and her Norwich sol-fa ladder. Engraving from J.
Curwen, *The Teacher's Manual of the Tonic Sol-Fa Method*, 5th
edn, London, *c.* 1880

d,   r,   m,   f,   s,   l,   t

Figure 14.3   Pitch designation

$d^1,$ s^1 $s_1,$ t_1

Figure 14.4   Register designation

Example 14.7   Notation of chromatic notes

Example 14.8   'Bridge note'

Figure 14.5   Notation of rhythm

involved the singing of melodies from Curwen's modulator (Figure 14.6), following the rise and fall of the teacher's pointer in order to realize a visual representation of intervals and the relationship between one key and another. As in the Norwich sol-fa ladder, the dominant is shown to

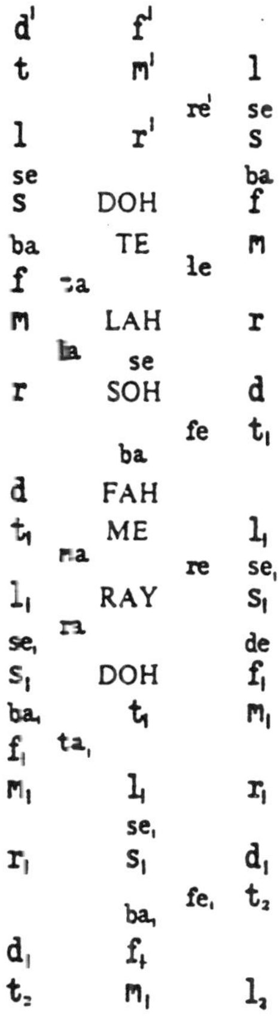

d^l f^l

t m^l l
                          re^l se
1   r^l s
se   ba
s   DOH   f
ba   TE   m
f   ta   le
m   LAH   r
     la
           se
r   SOH   d
                          fe t_1
           ba
d   FAH
t_1 ME l_1
     ra
                          re se_1
l_1 RAY s_1
se_1 ra
s_1 DOH   de
ba, t_1 f_1
f_1 ta_1
m_1 l_1 r_1
           se_1
r_1 s_1 d_1
           ba_1 fe_1 t_2
d_1 f_1
t_2 m_1 l_2

Figure 14.6   Curwen's modulator

the left of the tonic key and the Riemannian 'under-dominant', the sub-dominant, to the right. It was, then, these two models of hierarchically related keys that aligned the pedagogical methods of Curwen and Glover with the more systematic theories of tonality proposed by Riemann, Schoenberg and, to a certain extent, Tovey.

Tovey's classification appeared first in the *Encyclopaedia Britannica* article on 'Harmony' cited above and subsequently reappeared in slightly different formats in *Beethoven*, the *Companion to the Beethoven Piano-forte Sonatas* and the essay 'Tonality in Schubert'.[46] Tovey was less concerned to produce a systematic model of tonality, as Riemann or

---

[46] D. F. Tovey, *Beethoven*, with an editorial preface by H. J. Foss, London, 1944, pp. 12–13; Tovey, *A Companion*, p. 10; Tovey, *Essays and Lectures*, pp. 134–59.

TABLE OF KEY-RELATIONSHIPS
A. From Major Tonic.

	I	Direct Relationships	ii	iii	IV	V	vi
		Indirect through both I and the second key			iv	v	
Indirect through I IIIb VIb		Indirect through the second key		III			VI
Doubly indirect through the former indirect keys: iiib vib							
Neapolitan direct		IIb		VII and vii			
Neapolitan, indirect		iib					
Unconnected		IV♯ and iv♯ = Vb and vb and all enharmonic synonymns of other keys					
Ambiguous			II	VIIb and viib.			

Figure 14.7   Key-relationships from major tonic from D. F. Tovey, 'Harmony', in his *Musical Articles from the Encyclopaedia Britannica*, with an editorial preface by H. J. Foss, London, 1944, p. 62

Schoenberg had done, however, than to observe specific instances of it at work and to allow these to modify his overall conception. Tovey's model thus represents a historical, empirically derived observation of tonality from Alessandro Scarlatti to Brahms and Wagner. He follows the European tradition reaching back to C. P. E. Bach that received contemporary expression in Schoenberg's 'Charts of the Regions' in *Structural Functions of Harmony*[47] in which key relations are categorized according to the aesthetically determined degrees of nearness or remoteness. In Tovey's tables, reproduced as Figures 14.7 and 14.8, 'direct' relationships from the tonic are those formed on each degree of the scale, excluding the diminished triad on the seventh degree. 'Indirect' and 'doubly indirect' relationships are created by reversing the mode of each chord: thus the major triads IV and V become minor and the minor ones iii and vi become major. He comments in the *Companion* on the 'identity of major and minor keys on the same tonic' and

---

[47] A. Schoenberg, *Structural Functions of Harmony*, ed. L. Stein, London, 1983, pp. 20 and 30.

TABLE OF KEY-RELATIONSHIPS
B. From Minor Tonic.

	i	Direct Relationships	IIIb	iv	v	VIb VIIb
Indirect through i iii# vi#		Indirect through both I and the second key		IV	V	
		Indirect through the second key	iib			vib
Doubly indirect through the former indirect keys III#—VI#						
Neapolitan, direct		IIb				
Neapolitan, indirect		iib				VII# and vii#
Unconnected		IV# and iv# =	Vb and vb and all enharmonic synonyms of other keys			
Ambiguous	ii II vib					

Figure 14.8 Key-relationships from minor tonic from D. F. Tovey, 'Harmony', in his *Musical Articles from the Encyclopaedia Britannica*, with an editorial preface by H. J. Foss, London, 1944, p. 63

states that, as a result, Beethoven 'greatly extends the range of key-relations by changing the modes on either side, or even on both'.[48] Implicit in the tables is the importance of the fifth-relation in determining a hierarchy in which fifth-related keys arranged symmetrically above and below the tonic are paired, thus, dominant and subdominant, mediant and submediant. As a result of this fifth-related reciprocity, Tovey placed very little emphasis on the third-related relative minor and asserted in the *Companion* that 'the terms "relative major" and "relative minor" should be abandoned. The keys they represent are no more closely related than the other direct relations'.[49] The remaining chords on II and VIIb are described as 'ambiguous' since their categorization depends on context and may indeed differ according to this. Thus, II may appear as simply 'indirect' when it serves as the dominant of the dominant but elsewhere as 'very remote'. Similarly, the 'very remote' VIIb becomes merely 'indirect' when it functions as the dominant of IIIb.

---

[48] Tovey, *A Companion*, p. 6.
[49] Ibid., p. 9. Schenker also minimizes the significance of the relative minor.

Tovey's tables indicate that, like Schoenberg, he was firmly committed to the principle of monotonality and, in many respects, carried the notion one step further than Schoenberg in that he permitted relationships between two tonics only. Unlike Schoenberg, Tovey relates each new key back to the tonic and he maintains in the article 'Harmony' that 'a fundamental proposition in the aesthetics of tonality is that key-relationship subsists between two tonics only and has nothing to do with the intervention of a third tonic'.[50]

For Tovey, tonality was inseparable from form, which for him was equivalent to aesthetic content. Thus, the essential beauty of a form such as sonata lies in its sense of drama in absolute terms rather than in the illustrative nature of some extraneous programme or operatic plot, and this sense of drama is created by purely musical means, such as rhythmic structure, the placing of climaxes, the balance between sections and, above all, the tonal process.

Traditional formal analysis which considers a composition in terms of its degree of conformity to or deviation from the norm of an abstract model was anathema to Tovey since, in his view, form cannot exist *a priori* but grows from the necessities of the material. He strongly opposed this stereotyped approach to form in the *Companion to Beethoven's Pianoforte Sonatas*, attacking the conception of form as a 'jelly-mould instead of as a vital force',[51] and warning both pupil and teacher against the 'view of form as a mould into which matter can be shovelled'.[52] The criteria for determining the recognition of form differ widely, however, since for some analysts, identity or non-identity is determined by thematic character, for others, by key scheme, and still others, by length of units.

The divergence of views that existed in Britain alone at the end of the nineteenth century is apparent in the theories of Prout, Gurney and Tovey. For Prout key scheme is not really a consideration at all in recognizing binary form, for example, since he permitted ‖: tonic-tonic :‖: remote key-tonic :‖, and neither is thematic relationship, since he allowed AA'BA" as well as ABCB. The basic determinant for Prout is that the form should constitute 'two complete sentences': thus, ‖: A :‖: BA :‖. His theory is a highly determinate one and he writes in *Musical Form*:

> We cannot conceive of a painter going to his easel and beginning to work on his canvas without having decided what was to be the subject of his picture. Nobody but a lunatic would set to work before he made up his mind whether he was going to paint a bit of

---

[50] Tovey, *Musical Articles*, p. 57.
[51] Tovey, *A Companion*, p. 283.
[52] Ibid., p. iv.

'still life', a portrait, a landscape, or a piece of architecture. A composer goes to work on the same principle.[53]

Both Tovey and Gurney subscribed to a view that was far more akin to the romantic attitude held by A. B. Marx[54] in which form is self-determining, the specification of content from which it is inseparable. It is thus not an arbitrary convention following pre-established guidelines since there are ultimately no laws governing the form a composition should take; rather, it is a pattern abstracted from past practice and it is the 'patterns' of individual compositions that analysis seeks to reveal. Like Tovey, Gurney considered aesthetic beauty to be a function of form and perceived a work of art as an organism, not a mechanical construct. In contrast to Tovey, however, he believed that the most important aspects of musical form were not harmony or tonality but melody and rhythm since, he argues in *The Power of Sound*, it is the melody of each work that is new, the chords old; it is, therefore, the former that transfigures the latter.[55]

Although Tovey rebelled strongly against the 'jelly-mould' approach to form, he nevertheless felt obliged to accept its terminology; thus, the standard terms 'exposition', 'transition', 'development', 'recapitulation', 'coda', 'codetta' all appear in his analyses. He did reject the terms first and second 'subject', however, since 'there is no prescribed number of subjects in a movement in sonata form', and substituted the term 'group' for 'subject', which, he claimed, 'has the merit of not necessarily implying themes at all'.[56]

Thematic relationships did not enter into the equation in determining form for Tovey and he was notoriously sceptical about what Rudolph Réti was later to call the 'thematic process in music',[57] since he believed firmly that it was tonality and not thematic recurrence on which musical structure depended. Thus, in a recapitulation the thematic return merely serves to reinforce the tonal one and 'themes have no closer connexion with larger musical proportions than the colours of animals have with their skeletons'.[58] His emphasis on manifest contrast over and above latent unity frequently led him to designate as a 'new theme' a statement which is clearly derived from earlier material.

Given the pre-eminence of aesthetic effect, or what Tovey termed 'dramatic fitness',[59] and the overtly populist tenor of his writing, the

---

[53] Prout, *Musical Form*, p. 1.

[54] Marx, 'Die Form in der Musik', pp. 21–48; see in particular pp. 25 and 27.

[55] E. Gurney, *The Power of Sound*, London, 1880, p. 264.

[56] D. F. Tovey, *Essays in Musical Analysis*, vol. 1, *Symphonies*, London, 1935–39, p. 2.

[57] R. Réti, *The Thematic Process in Music*, New York, 1962.

[58] Tovey, *Essays and Lectures*, p. 275.

[59] Tovey, *Essays and Lectures*, p. 72.

question remains of how these priorities were to be expressed in terms of technical musical analysis, since 'dramatic fitness' may often be described only in the subjective, unverifiable language of metaphor. The very existence of this question for Tovey merely confirmed his belief in the equivalence of form and content, but he was not unaware of the difficulties it created. He stated in his Philip Maurice Deneke Lecture given at Lady Margaret Hall on 4 June 1934:

> The line between the technical and the aesthetic is by no means easy to draw, and is often, even by musicians themselves, drawn far too high, so as to exclude as merely technicalities many things which are of purely aesthetic importance ... The process miscalled by Horace the concealment of art is the sublimation of technique into aesthetic results.[60]

That Tovey drew this line so low is apparent in his conviction that everything in music should lie within the grasp of the naïve listener, and he perceived a sense of continuity between musical and everyday experience which enabled the listener to move easily between the two. This continuity permitted Tovey to accommodate his populist belief that art should be available to all, and he maintained that such extra-musical references were indeed necessary since musical analysis being 'more difficult than most analysis', an 'illustrative digression here and there ... is so much pure gain precisely because it breaks into the continuity of the argument'.[61] His 'analyses' are thus cast in a conversational style which almost matches that of Schumann's critical writings in its exuberant, florid prose style and abundance of literary allusions. Tovey's writings are littered with digressions, paradoxes, *non sequiturs* and metaphors in which the music 'floats', 'swims', 'sails', 'storms in', 'dies away', 'crashes out' and 'staggers as if under a falling sky'. And yet, this literary style coexists with more rigorous technical language in such a way as to suggest that neither a consistent nor a coherent aesthetic or technical theory is developed.

Rather, in Tovey's 'listener-oriented' world, a musical analysis is perceived as a story, a tracing of the same process through time that the 'naïve listener' experiences, and this is, of course, an ongoing, dynamic process rather than a retrospective, structural one. For, as Tovey asserted in his Introduction to the *Companion to Beethoven's Pianoforte Sonatas*:

> The first condition for a correct analysis of any piece of music is that the composition must be regarded as a process in time. There

---

[60] Ibid., pp. 164 and 165.
[61] D. F. Tovey, *The Goldberg Variations: An Essay in Musical Analysis*, London, no date, p. 4.

is no such thing as a simultaneous musical *coup d'oeil*; not even
though Mozart is believed to have said that he imagined his music
in that way. Some students begin their analysis of a sonata by
glancing through it to see 'where the Second Subject comes' and
other less unfortunately named sections begin. This is evidently not
the way to read a story ... [62]

Thus, Tovey tells his stories by means of a successive, bar-to-bar account of the work. His method is in part hermeneutic, achieved by his
'guided tour' style of analysis ('we find ourselves in the midst of the
recapitulation')[63] and by his characterization of the orchestra ('The
great clouds drift slowly away as the plaintive wailing of an oboe rises
and falls, losing itself among the other instruments'),[64] and of the work
itself

> (The dubious harmony ... now resolves with a chuckle, into one of
> the brightest keys that can be brought into relation with the tonic ...
> A cloud comes over it at its sixth bar; and it finishes its first sentence
> by explaining that it didn't mean to turn up in such a gaudy key, and
> will, if you will kindly overlook that indiscretion, continue in the
> orthodox dominant. It does so; blushes again ...).[65]

Tovey's essays thus serve as an introduction to the work that the
listener is about to hear, and it is this aspect that lends them the distinct
character of 'programme notes'. Tovey would have found ample prec-
edent for this style of writing in the third and final 'tradition' of music
analysis in nineteenth-century Britain: that of the analytical programme
note written by George Grove and August Manns for the Crystal Palace
concerts and by J. W. Davison, music critic of *The Times*, and subsequently by Joseph Bennett of the *Sunday Times* and later the *Daily
Telegraph*, for the Monday and Saturday Popular Concerts held in St
James's Hall, Piccadilly, between 1858 and 1898, for example, which
were in themselves further manifestation of the nineteenth-century aim
to bring music to the masses.

The most significant point with regard to these concert programmes
is the way in which their analytical content became increasingly detailed
as the century progressed. The early ones range in length from a mere
two paragraphs in the case of Mendelssohn's 'Scotch' Symphony, performed at the Crystal Palace on 21 September 1867, to some two pages.
In the Mendelssohn, reproduced in Figure 14.9, the movement headings
are listed and the text outlines the compositional history and dates of
completion and last performance of the work. The work itself is re-

---

[62] Tovey, *A Companion*, p. 1.
[63] Tovey, *Essays*, vol. 1, *Symphonies*, p. 114.
[64] Ibid., p. 86.
[65] Ibid., p. 63.

RESERVED SEATS

FOR THIS DAY'S CONCERT,

HALF-A-CROWN,

And Transferable Reserved Stalls for the double series of
Twenty-eight Concerts, Two Guineas,

May be had at the Ticket Stands in the Palace.

PROGRAMME.

Two o'clock.

DISPLAY OF THE TERRACE FOUNTAINS.

Three o'clock.

CONCERT.

SYMPHONY IN A MINOR *(Scotch)* . *Mendelssohn.*

1. **Andante con moto,** Allegro un poco.   3. Adagio.
2. **Scherzo :** Vivace non troppo.   4. Allegro un poco.

This is the chief record (the magnificent overture called the
"Hebrides" or "Fingal's Cave" being the other) of the impressions
made on Mendelssohn by his journey in Scotland in 1829. They
were both begun during his residence in Italy. The name, "Scotch
Symphony," is his own; though not attached to the Score it occurs
in his letters. It is the fourth and last of his Symphonies (counting
the Lobgesang as No. 3). It was not finally completed till 1842,
but that it occupied his thoughts more or less constantly during the
whole interval between that date and his visit to Scotland, is evident
from the frequent references to it even in the meagre selection of his
letters to which the executors have allowed the public access.

This noble work is so great and just a favourite, and overflows so
much with the beauties and characteristics of its author, as to need
no recommendation. It was last performed at the Saturday Concerts
on December 1, 1866.

Figure 14.9   Programme note for Mendelssohn, 'Scotch' Symphony, performed
at the Crystal Palace on 21 September 1867

ferred to only in the most general terms in a single sentence in the closing paragraph of the note ('This noble work is so great and just a favourite, and overflows so much with the beauties and characteristics of its author, as to need no recommendation'). The later notes range from 11 pages in 1886 to a colossal 18 in 1890 in the case of the note for Beethoven's *Les Adieux* Sonata, Op. 81, performed at the Popular Concert of 20 October 1890. The change in tone is evident from the statement at the outset of the Beethoven note that 'a brief analysis, strictly musical, will be the fittest aid to appreciation', and much of the discussion it contains is indeed of an explicitly technical nature:

> The 'free fantasia' sets out with an entirely new idea. This passing, by enharmonic transition to the dominant of B major, we have now the second subject in that key, together with a device by which the melody appears first in the bass, and then in the treble – a sort of free double counterpoint, which may be understood best if stripped of the harmony.

This final sentence clearly implies a reductive method of analysis; this technical commentary is coupled also with references to contemporary writers and theorists such as A. B. Marx and with the use of the standard terminology of musical form and tonal relations. The increase in length of the later programme notes is due in part to the increase in the number of musical examples (48 in the case of the Beethoven, Op. 81 notes), and this was symptomatic of a general trend in nineteenth-century theoretical texts, particularly those by Reicha and Czerny, to use a larger proportion of examples drawn from the musical repertoire rather than abstract illustrations composed by the theorist specifically for the purpose of analytical demonstration. Their use in the London concert programme notes implies a high degree of musical literacy among the audiences, and the analytical intentions of the author in citing them are evident from the annotations on the score. The illustration of the canonic passage in Mendelssohn's Quartet, Op. 44, No. 1, performed at the Monday Popular Concert of 15 November 1886, for example, bears the marking 'In octaves with Viola' and the subsequent return of the first theme is signalled also, as shown in Example 14.9.

It seems somewhat ironic that the language of programme notes written for 'popular' concerts should be more technical than that of Tovey's so-called *Essays in Musical Analysis*. For Tovey's title is indeed a misnomer; his 'analyses' are rather 'descriptions' of the technical means and aesthetic effect of the music which invite the reader to contemplate 'if not their logical or necessary connection, at all events their simultaneity and likely association'.[66] Hans Keller's attack on

---

[66] Kerman, 'Tovey's Beethoven', p. 177.

Example 14.9   Musical example from the programme note for Mendelssohn, Quartet, Op. 44, No. 1, performed at the Monday Popular Concert in St James's Hall, Piccadilly, on 15 November 1886

Tovey's method in general and on his partial 'analysis' of Mozart's Piano Concerto in C, K. 503 in 'The Classical Concerto' in particular, reinforces this point:

> Faultless descriptions are Tovey's speciality: his 'analyses' are misnomers, even though there are occasional flashes of profound analytical insight. Otherwise, there is much eminently professional tautology ... 'The pianoforte enters', reports Tovey, 'at first with scattered phrases. These quickly settle into a stream of florid melody ... '. But why are they scattered? How are they scattered? Why are they scattered in the way they are scattered? What, in short, is the

compositorial cause of these absolutely unprecedented, utterly 'new' triplets?[67]

Tovey is not concerned with a retrospective analysis of the work, however, but with looking forward to the effect it will create. Thus his 'analyses' rarely penetrate to the poietic level of compositional causality but remain rather on the esthesic, perceptual level of the naïve listener. His greatest omission may be seen to lie in his failure to expound a systematic theory behind his often perceptive observations that would have provided British music analysis with a firm theoretical foundation on which to build, and which would have paralleled the more rigorous systems of those European theorists referred to at the outset.

Bibliography

Bent, I. D., 'Analysis', in S. Sadie (ed.), *The New Grove Dictionary of Music and Musicians*, vol. 1, London, 1980.

————. 'Analytical Thinking in the First Half of the Nineteenth Century' in E. Olleson (ed.), *Modern Musical Scholarship*, Stocksfield, 1980, pp. 151–66.

————. 'The "Compositional Process" in Music Theory, 1713–1850', *Music Analysis*, 3 (1), (1984), 29–55.

————. *Analysis, The New Grove Handbooks in Music*, with a glossary by W. Drabkin, London, 1987.

Cherubini, L., *Cours de contre-point et de fugue*, Paris, 1835.

Curwen, J., *The Teacher's Manual*, 5th edn, London, *c.* 1880.

Czerny, C., *School of Practical Composition, or Complete Treatise on the Composition of All Kinds of Music ... Together with a Treatise on Instrumentation*, op. 600, 3 vols, London, 1848 Cocks; repr. New York, 1979.

Dunsby, J. and Whittall, A., *Music Analysis in Theory and Practice*, London, 1988.

Evans, E. snr, *Handbook to the Chamber and Orchestral Music of Johannes Brahms. 2nd Series*, London, 1935.

[Evans], Initialled review of Evans's 1935 Handbook ..., in *Musical Times*, 1123 (77), (1936), 803.

Forte, A., 'Theory', in J. Vinton (ed.), *Dictionary of Twentieth-Century Music*, London, 1974, pp. 753–61.

Glover, S. A., *Scheme for Rendering Psalmody Congregational; comprising a key to the sol-fa notation of music, and directions for instructing a school*, Norwich, 1835.

---

[67] Keller, 'K. 503', pp. 49 and 54.

Grierson, M., *Donald Francis Tovey: A Biography Based on Letters*, London, 1952.

Gurney, E., *The Power of Sound*, London, 1880.

――――. 'A Permanent Band for the East End', *Tertium Quid*, vol. 2, London, 1887.

――――. 'Wagner and Wagnerism', *Tertium Quid*, vol. 2, London, 1887.

Keller, H., 'K. 503: The Unity of Contrasting Themes and Movements – I', *Music Review*, 17 (1956), 48–58.

Kerman, J., 'Counsel for the Defense', *Hudson Review*, 3 (1950), 438–46.

――――. 'Tovey's Beethoven', in A. Tyson (ed.), *Beethoven Studies*, vol. 2, London, 1977, pp. 172–91.

――――. 'The Grove of Academe, reviews of selected articles on nineteenth-century topics in *The New Grove Dictionary of Music and Musicians*, ed. Stanley Sadie (Macmillan, 1980: 20 vols); Tovey, Sir Donald Francis, Michael Tilmouth', *19th Century Music*, 5 (2) (Fall 1981), 168–9.

Lobe, J. C., *Lehrbuch der musikalischen Komposition*, 4 vols, Leipzig, 1850–67.

――――. *Katechismus der Musik*, Leipzig, 1851.

Mackerness, E. D., 'Edmund Gurney and *The Power of Sound*', *Music and Letters*, 37 (1956), 356–67.

Marx, A. B., *Die Lehre von der musikalischen Komposition, praktisch-theoretisch*, 4 vols, Leipzig, 1837–47.

――――. 'Die Form in der Musik', in J. A. Romberg (ed.), *Die Wissenschaft im neunzehnten Jahrhundert, ihr Standpunkt und die Resultate ihrer Forschungen*, vol. 2, Leipzig, 1856.

Mickelsen, W. C. (trans.), *Hugo Riemann's Theory of Harmony, with a Translation of Riemann's 'History of Music Theory'*, Book 3, Lincoln, NB, 1962, 1977.

Momigny, J.-J. de, *Cours complet d'harmonie et de composition*, Paris, 1803–05.

Olleson, E. (ed.), *Modern Musical Scholarship*, Stocksfield, 1980.

Prout, E., *Instrumentation*, London, 1878.

――――. *Harmony: its Theory and Practice*, London, 1889; rev. 1903.

――――. *Counterpoint, Strict and Free*, London, 1890.

――――. *Fugue*, London, 1891.

――――. *Fugal Analysis*, London, 1892.

――――. *Double Counterpoint and Canon*, London, 1893.

――――. *Musical Form*, London, 1893.

――――. *Applied Forms: A Sequel to 'Musical Form'*, London, 1895.

――――. *Analysis of J. S. Bach's Forty-Eight Fugues (Das Wohltemperirte Clavier)*, L. B. Prout (ed.), London, 1910.

Rainbow, B., *The Land Without Music*, London, 1967.

Reicha, A., *Traité de mélodie*, Paris, 1814, 2nd edn, 1832.

———. *Cours de composition musicale ou Traité complet et raisonné d'harmonie pratique*, Paris, 1816–18.

———. *Traité de haute composition musicale*, Paris, 1824–26.

Réti, R., *The Thematic Process in Music*, New York, 1962.

Riemann, H., *Grosse Kompositionslehre*, 3 vols, Berlin and Stuttgart, 1902–13.

———. *Handbuch der Harmonie*, 4th edn, Leipzig, 1906.

Rosen, C., *The Classical Style: Haydn, Mozart, Beethoven*, London, 1972.

———. *Sonata Forms*, New York, 1980.

Schoenberg, A., *Structural Functions of Harmony*, ed. L. Stein, London, 1983.

Sechter, S., *Die Grundsätze der musikalischen Komposition*, 3 vols, Leipzig, 1853–54.

Tovey, D. F., *A Companion to 'The Art of Fugue' (Die Kunst der Fuge) J. S. Bach*, London, 1931.

———. *Essays in Musical Analysis*, vol. 1, Symphonies; vol. 2, Symphonies (II), Variations and Orchestral Polyphony; vol. 3, Concertos; vol. 4, Illustrative Music; vol. 5, Vocal Music; vol. 6, Supplementary Essays, Glossary and Index. London, 1935–39.

———. 'The Classical Concerto' (1903), in D. F. Tovey, *Essays in Musical Analysis*, vol. 3, Concertos, London, 1936.

———. *Beethoven*, with an editorial preface by H. J. Foss, London, 1944.

———. *Essays in Musical Analysis*, vol. 6, Chamber Music, London, 1944.

———. *Musical Articles from the Encyclopaedia Britannica*, with an editorial preface by H. J. Foss, London, 1944.

———. *A Companion to Beethoven's Pianoforte Sonatas*, London, 1948.

———. *Essays and Lectures on Music*, with an introduction by H. J. Foss, London, 1949.

———. *The Goldberg Variations: An Essay in Musical Analysis*, London, [no date].

Turner, W. J., *English Music*, London, 1941; rev 1947.

Tyson, A. (ed.), *Beethoven Studies*, vol. 2, London, 1977, pp. 172–91.

Vinton, J. (ed.), *Dictionary of Twentieth-Century Music*, London, 1974.

Vogler, G. J., *Handbuch zur Harmonielehre und für den Generalbass, nach den Grundsätze der Mannheimer Tonschule*, Prague, 1802.

Watkins S. H., 'The Musical Teaching of John Curwen', *Proceedings of the Royal Musical Association*, 77 (1950–51).

Weber, G., *Versuch einer geordneten Theorie der Tonsetzkunst*, Mainz, 1817–21.

Webster, J., 'Schubert's Sonata Form and Brahms's First Maturity', *19th Century Music*, 2 (1978–79), 3 (1979–80).

Wesley, S. and Horn, C. F., *New and Correct Edition of the Preludes and Fugues of John Sebastian Bach*, London, 1810–13.

Williams, C. F. A., *The Rhythm of Modern Music*, London, 1909.

Wintle, C., '"Humpty Dumpty's Complaint": Tovey Revalued', *Soundings*, 11, (1983–84), 14–45.

CHAPTER FIFTEEN

James William Davison, Critic, Crank and Chronicler: A Re-evaluation

Richard Kitson

James William Davison (1813–85) was in the forefront of British musical criticism for more than 40 years. Trained as a pianist under William Henry Holmes, and a student of composition with George Alexander Macfarren, Davison began his career as a performer and composer, but turned his complete attention to music journalism in the early 1840s.[1] At first he was an occasional contributor to sundry journals such as C. H. Purday's *The Musical Magazine* and the short-lived *Dramatic and Musical Review*. In 1843 Davison became editor of *The Musical Examiner* (1843–44), a sharp-edged weekly music magazine which thrived on controversial and often querulous opinions about many different matters concerning contemporary musical life. However, *The Musical World*, the pre-eminent London weekly journal of the period and, in 1843, edited by George Macfarren the elder, required the services of a new and less severe writer for reviews of new compositions owing to a readers' protest against the incumbent critic Alfred Day's disagreeable and harsh opinions. Davison received the appointment but, within a year, upon the sudden death of the elder Macfarren, Davison himself assumed the position of editor of *The Musical World*.[2] He continued to direct this enterprise until his final years. In addition, in 1848, upon the death of Alsager, city editor and writer of the 'slender' musical reports

---

[1] For a detailed account of Davison's career viewed from a family perspective see Henry Davison, *From Mendelssohn to Wagner, being the Memoirs of J. W. Davison Forty Years Music Critic of 'The Times'*, (London, 1912). See also William Barclay Squire, 'Davison, James William' in Leslie Stephen and Sidney Lee, (eds), *Dictionary of National Biography*, London, 1859–60, vol. 4, p. 627.

[2] Davison was assisted in the work at *The Musical World* by the dramatic and musical writer and sometime poet Michael Desmond Ryan (1816–68). It is difficult to distinguish Ryan's contributions from those of Davison since the majority of articles are unsigned, and strict anonymity was enforced throughout the periodical's run. The circumstances of the editorship of the journal are discussed in Richard Kitson, Introduction, *The Musical World 1836–1891*, Ann Arbor, MI, 1996, vol. 1, pp. xiii–xiv.

then current in *The Times*, Davison was appointed music critic of the newspaper.[3] A knowledgeable musician and an extremely fluent and prolific writer, Davison's criticism was also featured in numerous other publications including *The Graphic*, the *Saturday Review*, and the *Pall Mall Gazette*. The responsibilities of editor and critic of these two important publications, *The Musical World* and *The Times*, and the miscellaneous additional venues for musical reporting and discussion, placed Davison in an extremely powerful and visible position poised to become the leading voice in British music criticism during the Victorian period.

Davison's major enterprise was the almost single-handed weekly production of *The Musical World*. This journal was perhaps one of the most enduring of music publications of the nineteenth century. Approximately 1 827 music journals were created in Europe, North America and Australia during this period.[4] Some comprised a single issue; many were successful for a year or two and then surreptitiously disappeared; no more than a handful survived to rival the longevity of *The Musical World*.[5] Established by J. Alfred Novello in 1836, and still fairly vital up to the last issue in January 1891, *The Musical World* was unique in that it had an almost uninterrupted publication history of 2 861 weekly issues, each of eight to 16 pages, during its 55 years of existence. Only one issue was not published and this omission was rectified through an increase in the number of pages for two subsequent issues.

Along with Henry F. Chorley, Davison was considered by his contemporaries to be one of the most important music critics active in England during the Victorian period. However he, like Chorley, was not esteemed in every quarter, and a measure of criticism has dogged Davison's reputation into our own century. Fault was found on a number of levels, but three problems stand out as being somewhat detrimental to Davison's overall achievement as a critic and an editor. First, he held an extraordinarily conservative point of view which prevented him from accepting any new trends in composition or performance practice that appeared from the 1840s onward – in particular, the aesthetic and compositional ideas put forward by members of the new German school and those related to it, and the 'modern' performances techniques,

---

[3] See T. L. Southgate's obituary headed 'From the *Evening Standard*', reprinted in *The Musical World*, 63, (15), 11 April 1885, pp. 230–33.

[4] Statistics derived from Imogen Fellinger, 'Periodicals', *The New Grove Dictionary of Music and Musicians*, Stanley Sadie (ed.), 1980, vol. 14, pp. 433–535.

[5] The only analogous long-term music journals with unbroken records of publication during the nineteenth century are *Le Ménestrel* (1833–1914) and *La Gazette et Revue musicale de Paris* in France, and *Neue Zeitschrift für Musik* (1834–) in Germany.

styles and repertories of a new breed of instrumentalist which arose in
the second half of the century. The pianist-composer Anton Rubinstein
and pianist-conductor Hans von Bülow exemplify the category. Second,
Davison played partisan politics by means of republishing unending
notices about his musical heroes: for example, the English tenor Sims
Reeves, the contralto Charlotte Dolby and the pianist Arabella Goddard,
the latter, in fact, the editor's former piano pupil and from 1859 his
wife. This rather noble insistence on reporting the triumphs of native
artists was prompted, no doubt, as an antidote to the snobbish adulation of foreigners at that time current in Britain. But by emphasizing the
careers of his close associates, friends and family, Davison denied equally
talented British performers fair and equal representation, and thus left
himself open to criticism on this account.[6] Third, Davison had a peculiar and very personal sense of humour that erupted on to the very
pages of the journal during the first half of the 1860s, no doubt perplexing and intimidating confused readers unacquainted with the actual
meaning of the inhabitants of Davison's imagination. During this period
many published articles and letters to the editor from both real and
imaginary correspondents were signed by or addressed to members of
the so-called 'Muttonians', a group of 'puppet' personalities of Davison's
own peculiar invention. All the pseudonymous names printed in the
journal – typical examples are Thaddeus Egg, Caper O'Corby, Drinkwater
Hard, Rippington Pipe and Abraham Sadoke – were meant to represent
Davison himself or members of both his immediate circle or close
acquaintanceship.[7] One hundred and fifty years later readers of *The
Musical World* remain uninformed as to the actual meaning of these
names of addressees and signatories, and the relevance of the materials
they append. In the majority of such cases the content of the articles is
actually completely unintelligible without recourse to guidebooks.[8]

After Davison's death on 24 March 1885, many journals published
generally favourable obituaries and tributes to the memory of the critic.
Some, however, were touched with a modicum of doubt with respect to
the total achievement. Perusal of these obituaries allows us today to
gauge in part both the esteem and veiled derision afforded Davison's
memory by his contemporaries. These notices outline Davison's position

---

[6] For a discussion of the journalism dedicated to the career of Arabella Goddard see
chapters 14 to 16 of Charles Reid's *The Music Monster: A Biography of James William
Davison, Music Critic of the 'Times' of London, 1846–78*, New York, 1984.

[7] 'Thaddeus Egg' originally represented Davison but was transferred to Joseph Bennett.
See Joseph Bennett, Correspondence. 'Thaddeus Egg identified!' *The Musical Times*, 41
(683), 1 January 1900, 52.

[8] See Reid, *The Music Monster*, pp. 97–9 for a list of Davison's pseudonyms.

in musical society, his strengths and weaknesses as a writer on musical topics, and the particular nature of his personal preferences and dislikes. An assured and rather positive T. L. Southgate, writing in the *Musical Standard*, underlined the importance, in his opinion, of the deceased critic's role and place in Victorian music journalism: 'The influence which Davison extended on English music has been very considerable; it is hardly too much to say that he has shaped our musical press.'[9] Joseph Bennett, a writer of some significance, agreed with Southgate's opinion concerning the foundation of nineteenth-century British music criticism. In his notice 'In memoriam' published on 28 March 1885 in *The Musical World*, Bennett extolled Davison's prodigious memory for musical matters, his strong intellect, and the fluency of his written message.[10] Bennett underscored the fact that Davison was a bona fide member of the nineteenth-century musical élite, for he had been on close terms with many of the great artists and composers of the period. European musicians such as Mendelssohn, Berlioz, Stephen Heller, Moscheles and Joseph Joachim, and British musicians including William Sterndale Bennett, the organist E. T. Best and the baritone Charles Santley, to name only a very few, can be numbered among those with whom the editor-critic had close dealings. Davison's musical taste bespeaks a preference for compositions and performance styles of the first four decades of the century generally based on the model of the great classical heritage of Mozart, Haydn, Beethoven, Weber and Spohr, and the many other lesser composers who shared the manner and intent of the aforementioned well-known masters. Joseph Bennett explains the comfortable refuge afforded Davison in this musical tradition, but sounds a note of quiet alarm concerning Davison's partisan feelings:

> This was the musical world in which he lived, and into which a peculiar jealousy for his heroes forbade new-comers to intrude without the clearest credentials. As [he] advanced in years, he failed somewhat to keep in touch with the age. For him contemporary masters had but little interest; only the strange individuality of Richard Wagner now attracted, now repelled him. J. W. Davison lived with the great ones of a great age, and I can well understand that he saw none entitled to divide with them the allegiance of his intellect and his soul.

Not all writers were able, however, to brush aside Davison's neglect of the new music. The anonymous writer of the carefully worded but strangely brief obituary published in *The Musical Times* mixed praise

---

[9] Southgate, 'From the *Evening Standard*', p. 230.
[10] Joseph Bennett, 'In memoriam. James William Davison, Born, October 5th, 1813. Died, March 24th, 1885', *The Musical World*, 63 (13), 28 March (1885), pp. 200–201.

with criticism. The rather blunt concluding remarks read: 'Mr. Davison whose love of his art was sincere and passionate, exercised a powerful influence throughout his career. He was a strong conservative, and could see little good in the new men and methods of our own day.'[11]

A towering figure of French music journalism, however, appears to have maintained a very flattering opinion of Davison's value as a writer on music. A decade after Davison's death, Mrs Louis Diehl, the former Alice Mangold, a member of a well-known musical family, a piano student of Henselt in Paris during the 1860s, a performer in the London concert halls and the author of several novels, wrote positively and glowingly of Davison in both her fiction and her personal recollections. In the novel *Elsie's Art Life* (1894) Mrs Diehl introduces a character, the composer Berlioz, who hails Davison as 'the greatest critic in the world'.[12] This remark appears to have been based on one of Mrs Diehl's own experiences, for in her portrait of Berlioz given in *Musical Memories* of 1897 she recalls meeting the French composer and notes his comments revealed his 'intense feeling' and enthusiastic opinion of Davison. According to Mrs Diehl, Berlioz exclaimed 'you must know my great friend Davison. ... What a critic! what a man!' Mrs Diehl is very flattering in her opinion of Davison's critical abilities: 'He was a mind whose great forces acted with rapidity, and must have been hard to hold in check. As it was his articles in *The Times* were generally outbursts of eloquence.' *The Musical Times*'s anonymous reviewer of Mrs Diehl's reminiscences continues and expands the meaning of these thoughts to a greater degree:

> In her estimate of Davison strictly as a critic, Mrs. Diehl comes near the truth, but does not quite reach the whole of it. The real key to the criticism of Davison ... lies in the fact that his sympathies were often too strong for his judgment. In that I recognize his only weakness ... He would not hear of Schumann and Brahms, lest they should eclipse Mendelssohn of happy memory.[13]

Other nineteenth-century writers expressed puzzlement about certain of Davison's serious omissions and prejudices as expressed in the reviews of *The Musical World*. Two examples suffice to clarify the seriousness of this problem: first, the absence of comprehensive notices by the journal's own editor reviewing the commissioned London world première of Verdi's *I masnadieri* at Her Majesty's Theatre in 1847 (with a notable cast

---

[11] Obituary: James William Davison, *The Musical Times*, 26, 221.

[12] A discussion of and extracts from Mrs Diehl's *Musical Memories* is found in 'From my Study', *The Musical Times*, 38 (657), 1 October (1897), 737–9. See also the review in the same issue of *The Musical Times*, p. 690.

[13] Mrs Diehl, 'From my Study', pp. 737–9.

including Jenny Lind, Italo Gardoni and Luigi Lablache);[14] and, second, total indifference to the first London performance of Schubert's Symphony in C major at Crystal Palace in April 1856.[15] In this last case it is possible to surmise that Schubert's finest symphonic masterpiece embodied the feared eclipse of the symphonies of Davison's beloved Mendelssohn.

Two twentieth-century writers have been unkind to Davison's reputation as critic, and one appears to have condemned him (and his Victorian contemporaries) for singular attitudes at odds with the beliefs of the later age. Winton Dean, writing in the late 1970s, considers

> English music criticism during the 19th century [to have] drifted into a backwater ... For a generation music criticism in London was dominated by H. F. Chorley ... and J. W. Davison. Their gods among the moderns were Rossini in opera and Beethoven (except the last quartets) and Mendelssohn in instrumental music. They were narrow and conservative in their tastes ...

Dean goes on to state that, in his opinion, their greatest error lay in their denial of Verdi's talent for 'social rather than musical reasons. Verdi was attacked for the vulgarity of his tunes and his bad taste in bringing passionate emotions and contemporary subjects to the stage'.[16] This is, however, quite one-sided and greatly overstated, and appears to be a negative opinion based on a rather limited study of the full extent of Davison's writings and reporting in *The Musical World* and *The Times*. The early operas of Verdi were received contemptuously, coldly and even in a hostile manner. The hostility reaches a peak in Davison's denunciation of *Il trovatore*, which the critic claimed was 'written in contempt of all rules'.[17] Davison came to accept the composer's finer points, particularly in the middle operas. Reviews in the later years of the journal contain interesting observations on the singers who performed Verdi's demanding roles, and show insight concerning the powerful dramas that unfold in the musical settings. A notable series of

---

[14] For a list of articles and reviews about Verdi's *I masnadieri* in *The Musical World*, see Kitson, *The Musical World*, vol. 9, p. 3201. A rather lame explanation of Davison's inability to write a review of the Verdi opera is given in *The Musical World*, 22 (31), 31 July (1847), 491–2. Davison, in fact, was rather negative in his estimation of Jenny Lind's abilities. The sole review of the opera in *The Musical World* is found in 22 (33), 14 August (1847), 518. It comprises two extracts copied from *The Morning Post*.

[15] See F. E. G., 'Schubert's Music in England', *The Musical Times*, 38 (648), 1 February (1897), 81–4 where Davison's omission is discussed.

[16] Winton Dean, 'Criticism', *The New Grove Dictionary of Music and Musicians*, Stanley Sadie (ed.), 1980, vol. 5, p. 40.

[17] See *The Musical World*, 33 (20), 19 May (1855), 313–15 for Davison's caustic essay and a review of the first British production at Covent Garden by the Royal Italian Opera.

examples is found in Davison's reviews about different interpretations of the heroine of Verdi's *La traviata* by sopranos Maria Piccolomini, Angiolina Bosio and Christine Nilsson.[18] The critic's aural and visual memory for three dissimilar approaches by these three admired and respected interpreters is significant and shows considerable understanding of the demands of Verdi's treatment of this subject found so 'difficult' by Victorians. If the later operas written between *Il trovatore* and *Aida* were rejected by Davison for complimentary and extensive review, he was not alone in his attitude. Most of Verdi's operas written after 1852 failed to achieve an initial warm reception and soon disappeared from the repertoires of opera houses throughout Europe, not to re-emerge until the second and third decades of the twentieth century.[19] Dean it must be noted gives no comment on Davison's detailed criticism of and support for the works of British composers.

A rather severe denunciation of the critic and the man is contained in Charles Reid's *The Music Monster: A Biography of James William Davison, Music Critic of the 'Times' of London, 1846–78* published in 1984. This is a mean-spirited study as its primary aim is to discredit Davison and to diminish the importance of *The Musical World*. To accomplish this Reid compiled a 200-page volume mainly containing a negative commentary and reprints of what Reid believed to be Davison's errors of judgement concerning composition and performance – articles and reviews about Chopin, Verdi, Schubert, etc. – the details of petty squabbles that erupted in the course of the business of nineteenth-century musical life. This study also contains uncalled for remarks concerning the particulars of Davison's personal life since such gossip does little to enhance our knowledge and understanding of matters at hand. Unlike Dean, Reid calls Davison to task on account of his dogged support of British music and musicians.

All journalists and editors made and continue to make serious errors of judgement, and Dean and Reid fall readily into this category. Their opinions, in many cases, reflect the tastes of their own milieu or personal vindictiveness. But to criticize the overall accomplishments of a major figure from a bygone era on a very small sampling of so-called mistaken opinions, without reference to the positive aspects of that work (and thus to detract from the historical importance of such writings to later generations) is a serious mistake.

Davison's journal is outstanding when viewed as an uninterrupted historical record of music in Britain for a 50-year period. It comprises in

---

[18] For Davison's pertinent reviews of the *Traviata* prima donnas see *The Musical World*, **34** (22), 31 May (1856), 346–7 [Piccolomini]; **35** (21), 23 May (1857) [Bosio]; **45** (25), 15 June (1867), 388–9; **50** (23), 8 June (1872), 363 [Nilsson].

[19] See Julian Budden, *Verdi* London, 1985, p. v.

excess of 40 000 tightly printed double- and triple-column pages filled with a vast array of articles and reviews on an enormous range of topics. Analysis of the thousands of articles, reports, reviews, letters to the editor, biographical and historical sketches, and sundry miscellaneous columns contained in *The Musical World* shows Davison's accomplishments as the foremost chronicler of the musical life of the period. In fact, the information and opinions given in *The Musical World* constitute a history of music in nineteenth-century Britain unavailable in other sources. Moreover, it is an indispensable compendium of opinion and information concerning music and musicians not only in Britain and Europe, but also in North America and Australia. Thus it stands as a monument to nineteenth-century musical life on both a local and a world-wide scale. When studied as a chronological 'map of musical events', *The Musical World* represents a history of music-making and relative opinion in nineteenth-century Britain.

Index